Lecture Notes of the Institute for Computer Sciences, Social Informatics and Telecommunications Engineering 65

Cristian Borcea   Paolo Bellavista
Carlo Giannelli   Thomas Magedanz
Florian Schreiner (Eds.)

Mobile Wireless Middleware, Operating Systems, and Applications

5th International Conference, Mobilware 2012
Berlin, Germany, November 13-14, 2012
Revised Selected Papers

 Springer

Volume Editors

Cristian Borcea
New Jersey Institute of Technology, Computer Science Department
Newark, NJ 07102, USA
E-mail: borcea@cs.njit.edu

Paolo Bellavista
University of Bologna, Computer Science and Engineering Department
40126 Bologna, Italy
E-mail: paolo.bellavista@unibo.it

Carlo Giannelli
University of Bologna, Computer Science and Engineering Department
40126 Bologna, Italy
E-mail: carlo.giannelli@unibo.it

Thomas Magedanz
TU Berlin, Faculty IV, 10587 Berlin, Germany
E-mail: thomas.magedanz@tu-berlin.de

Florian Schreiner
FOKUS - Fraunhofer Institute for Open Communication Systems
10589 Berlin, Germany
E-mail: florian.schreiner@fokus.fraunhofer.de

ISSN 1867-8211   e-ISSN 1867-822X
ISBN 978-3-642-36659-8   e-ISBN 978-3-642-36660-4
DOI 10.1007/978-3-642-36660-4
Springer Heidelberg Dordrecht London New York

Library of Congress Control Number: 2013931555

CR Subject Classification (1998): C.2.0-6, C.5.3, H.5.3, H.3.4-5, H.4.1-3, D.2.11

Typesetting: Camera-ready by author, data conversion by Scientific Publishing Services, Chennai, India

Printed on acid-free paper

Springer is part of Springer Science+Business Media (www.springer.com)

Preface

This volume contains papers presented at the 5th International Conference on Mobile Wireless Middleware, Operating Systems, and Applications (MOBILWARE), held during November 13–14, 2012, in Berlin, Germany. The advances in wireless communication technologies and the proliferation of mobile devices have enabled the realization of intelligent environments for people and machines to communicate with each other, interact with information processing devices, and receive a wide range of mobile wireless services through various types of networks and systems everywhere, anytime. A key enabler of these pervasive and ubiquitous connectivity environments is the advancement of software technology in various communication sectors, ranging from communication middleware and operating systems to networking protocols and applications. MOBILWARE is dedicated to addressing emerging topics and challenges in various mobile wireless software-related areas. The scope of the conference includes the design, implementation, deployment, and evaluation of middleware, operating systems, and applications for computing and communications in mobile wireless systems.

MOBILWARE 2012 was the fifth edition of this conference, and it was made possible thanks to the organization/endorsement of the European Alliance of Innovation (EAI), the sponsorship of Create-Net, and most importantly the hard work of the TPC members. The theme of this year's Mobilware conference was: "Mobile Middleware for M2M Interaction and Smart City Applications."

Similar to the last successful editions, we received high-quality submissions (32 this year), reflecting the international interest for the conference topics. After a thorough review process, we finalized an excellent technical program including 18 regular papers from 11 countries and four continents. These papers have been grouped into five technical sessions on:

- Internet of Things and Mobile Sensing
- Mobile Middleware Platforms
- Mobile Networks
- System Support for Mobile Applications
- Context Awareness

We want to express our sincere gratitude to all the authors who submitted their papers to this conference and to all the TPC members whose diligent work was crucial for the finalization of this high-quality final technical program.

Additionally, the technical program had two excellent keynote speeches: "Experimentation for the Internet of Things," and "Universities for Future Internet (UNIFI)." The first was given by Mesut Günes, Freie Universität Berlin. The second, covering insights into academic mobile/NGN testbed deployments in Chile, Thailand, and Vietnam, was given by three speakers: Alfonso Ehijo, Universidad de Chile; Nguyen Huu Thanh, Hanoi University of Science and Technology;

and Prasit Prapinmongkolkarn, Department of Electrical Engineering, Chulalongkorn University.

The technical program also includes a "Panel on Mobile Apps and IT for Energy Efficiency," organized by Klaus David, University of Kassel, Germany.

We thank the keynote speakers and the panelists for contributing to the quality and the success of this event.

Finally, we would like to thank Paolo Bellavista and Thomas Magedanz, the General Co-chairs, for their constant motivation and support, as well as Carlo Giannelli, the Publication and Web Chair, for helping in all the organizational matters. In addition, we would like to thank the whole EAI team for their constant support this event happen.

We hope you enjoy the proceedings and gain a snapshot of the state of the art in mobile wireless middleware, operating systems, and applications.

November 2012   Cristian Borcea
                                                   Florian Schreiner

Organization

Steering Committee Chairs

Paolo Bellavista	University of Bologna (Italy)
Carl Chang	Iowa State University (USA)
Imrich Chlamtac	Create-Net (Italy)
Thomas Magedanz	FOKUS Fraunhofer Institute (Germany)

Organizing Committee

General Chairs

Paolo Bellavista	University of Bologna (Italy)
Thomas Magedanz	FOKUS Fraunhofer Institute (Germany)

Program Chairs

Cristian Borcea	NJIT (USA)
Florian Schreiner	FOKUS Fraunhofer Institute (Germany)

Tutorial Chair

Iulian Sandu Popa	University of Versailles Saint-Quentin (France)

Publication and Web Chair

Carlo Giannelli	University of Bologna (Italy)

Publicty Chair

Carlos Becker Westphall	Federal University of Santa Catarina (Brazil)

Technical Program Committee

Juan José Alcaraz Espín	Universidad Politecnica de Cartagena, Spain
Adel Al-Hezmi	Qatar wireless innovation center, Qatar
Paolo Bellavista	University of Bologna, Italy
Emmanuel Bertin	France Telecom, France
Cristian Borcea	NJIT, USA
Matthieu Boussard	Alcatel Lucent Bell Labs France, France
Jiannong Cao	Hong Kong Polytechnic University, Hong Kong

Table of Contents

Internet of Things and Mobile Sensing

Mobile Middleware Platforms

Mobile Networks

System Support for Mobile Applications

Context Awareness

AIRS: A Mobile Sensing Platform for Lifestyle Management Research and Applications

Dirk Trossen[1] and Dana Pavel[2]

[1] Cambridge University Cambridge, UK
dirk.trossen@cl.cam.ac.uk
[2] University of Essex Colchester, UK
dmpave@essex.ac.uk

Abstract. Utilizing mobile devices for gaining a better understanding of one's surrounding, physiological state and overall behavior has been argued for in many previous works. Despite the increasing usage of mobile devices for research in this space, few platforms developed are readily available for supporting the wider research community. This paper presents a mobile sensing platform that allows for exploiting the latest and ever-increasing capabilities residing in mobile devices. While we highlight the main design and implementation characteristics of this solution, we also outline our experiences with this platform for typical usage scenarios in lifestyle management.

Keywords: mobile sensing, gateway, platform, lifestyle management, context awareness.

1 Introduction

The importance of mobile devices and their capabilities has long been recognized within research projects such as [1-4, 23] as well as commercial solutions such as [5,6]. This is due to mobile devices becoming increasingly more powerful in recent years. Processor speeds have exceeded 1GHz with storage capacities in the tens of GBs. Connectivity options now span from short-range Bluetooth over WLAN to high-speed cellular, while capabilities to locate mobile devices are almost ubiquitous nowadays. Furthermore, the penetration of smartphones has surpassed 50% in some markets such as the US or the UK throughout 2011.

Beyond hardware improvements, the mobile software space has exploded as well, with applications created for any possible usages. Such dramatic growth in mobile applications is driven by easier to use development tools as well as the support of an ecosystem provided by companies such as Apple or Google. Using such tools, it is possible to create applications capable of harvesting a growing pool of information that originates from or can be collected through such devices.

There is no need to justify here the advantages of a platform-based approach. Platforms are found now at various levels within computing architectures and works such as [7] discuss the advantages of this approach within embedded systems. What

C. Borcea et al. (Eds.): MobilWare 2012, LNICST 65, pp. 1–15, 2013.

we argue for is the need for an open-source, **widely available** mobile sensing platform that is flexible enough to be used for various purposes, allows for both automatic and manual input and not only enables new applications but also provides valuable support for user research. While other mobile-based sensing platforms have been developed during the years (e.g., [1][3][4]), we think there is value in presenting our platform, which can be immediately downloaded and used by the research community, therefore minimizing the time it takes to deal with sensing-specific issues and, instead, focusing on developing advanced algorithms that make use of such collected information. Our initial motivation behind creating a mobile-based sensing platform and gateway started a long time ago, with a Symbian-based platform [2], when it became clear to us that mobiles will become the more pervasive computing devices, with ever-increasing capabilities for collecting, processing and interacting with end users. However, the more recent developments of mobile devices, software development environments and even user attitudes towards sensing, allowed us to greatly improve the platform by making it easier to add new sensors, functionalities and user interaction means.

Based on our work and experiments within the area of lifestyle management applications[1], we have continuously improved the platform to address requirements of such application area, including allowing end users to get more involved in collecting and interpreting information through their mobiles.

In this paper, we discuss challenges, design solutions and implementation issues as well as the scenarios and experiments we have conducted to test our platform. For this, we organize the remainder of the paper as follows. We start by describing the setting in which we have been using our platform; present the challenges we encountered and the derived requirements while also including references to related work. Such challenges and requirements are important as they drive the design of our platform, which we describe before presenting our current implementation. We further include details about our experiments with the platform. We finally conclude our paper and discuss future work.

2   Scenarios and Challenges

Our recent platform development has been driven by our activities within lifestyle management systems. For that, we have used and further developed the mobile-based platform as one main information provider within a larger system capable of collecting various user context information that covers various dimensions, such as physiological, spatial, social, environmental, or emotional [18]. The main goal of our system was to provide its user with support for better understanding what happened and why it happened by allowing information correlation within a complex space.

The area of lifestyle monitoring is very well represented both in research [1-4] as well as in the commercial space [5][6][10-15], with mobile phones providing means

---

[1] Some of the work described in this paper has been funded by EPSRC and TSB through the PAL project [17] (grant number TP/AN072C), a research project investigating future healthcare services in the context of self-monitoring and lifestyle management.

for data collection, processing and remote access. Utilizing mobile devices for such scenarios, however, comes with challenges, in particular since the devices are not dedicated sensor platforms but they are primarily meant for personal or professional use [3]. Many of these challenges have been identified and partially addressed within related work, with [21] providing a particularly good overview.

The biggest challenge we have encountered is **battery life**. While advances in processor speeds or storage capabilities have largely been following Moore's Law, battery capacity has developed at a slower pace. Hence, any solution for mobile sensing must be sensitive to battery consumption. As mobile phones are still primarily used for other purposes, any sensing platform must cater to the need of an end user to sustain a certain level of battery that can be used beyond the desired mobile sensing task. One solution is the **configurability** of the platform, allowing for setting larger intervals for polling sensors, such as location and wireless connectivity (wifi, signal strength, etc.). Such options allow the end users to tradeoff the requirements of the experiments with their own needs, e.g., regarding battery life or storage.

Within self-monitoring scenarios, even when end users do not permanently record, there is still a considerable amount of data being generated. Therefore, **storing** and **synchronizing** recorded data has to be taken into account. Here we encountered various models, such as remote provisioning of such data [12][15] or utilizing the local storage of the mobile device [10][13][16]. We found that a platform created for self-monitoring has to provide solutions for storing information both locally and remotely. While local storage capacities have increased, there is still the issue of **safety of data** when considering how likely mobile devices are to be misplaced, stolen or destroyed. Hence, any solution needs an easy way to sync stored data, both within end user's own data space and with other trusted parties. This brings in the issue of **connectivity**. While data connectivity has improved in recent years, simply relying on always-on wireless connectivity can limit the applicability of the sensing platform. Instead, any solution should support a wide range of syncing (and sharing) options, from real-time (if the scenario demands it) to periodic.

Given the continuous addition of sensors on mobile devices as well as external ones (which can use the mobile device as a sensing gateway), a mobile sensing platform has to be designed with **extensibility** in mind, as also pointed out in [8]. Another challenge that comes from the continuous development of mobile devices, and their increased complexity is the impossibility of anticipating all malfunctioning scenarios. Therefore, for scenarios that require long-running experiments it is important to create platforms that ensure persistence of the measurement itself as well as for its recordings, e.g., through automatic restarting in the case of failures and emergency data saving.

Beyond technical challenges involved in building such platforms, using such mobile sensing platforms for recording user information poses major challenges with regard to user needs and concerns. A major challenge relates to **privacy**, as most of the user information collected is of a personal nature, as also discussed in [4]. Another important issue that arises from a sensing solution running on a device with a different main purpose as well as a (still) reduced screen capability is related to **user interactions**. Any solution should blend into the (device) platform-specific interaction model to avoid overburdening the end user. However, within scenarios such as the ones we have considered, purely relying on automated data collection is not enough. For instance, people like to add their own annotations, which help them identify interesting moments during the day. Therefore, we provide means for such interactions allowing for exploiting user's knowledge and enriching automatic recognition algorithms such as [16].

Social communication is an essential part of our lives and the current trend we can observe is that people are willing to share more and more information. Therefore, such platforms have to provide means for **sharing** either individual or aggregated information with various circles. However, such sharing has to happen under the control of the end user.

A specific challenge arises from our ambition to serve the wider research community. While open sourcing is a means to ensure platform extension, it is not enough. Traditionally, many projects in this area have built their own platforms, which survived for a number of years and were then discontinued. We provide here an actively growing Android-based mobile sensing solution that allows for extensive sensing and is already available in the application store, ready to be installed, configured and used according to any research needs.

3   The AIRS Platform

In this section, we describe the AIRS platform from design to implementation. The design takes into account the various challenges we encountered when building lifestyle management applications.

We chose Android for a number of reasons, the main ones being: (1) its flexibility in terms of customizing user interfaces and interactions, as it allows for controlling font and icon sizes (important in healthcare scenarios), as well as easier interactions and increased awareness through widgets and the notification bar; (2) allowing access to a large number of sensors as well as system information without requiring special root rights; (3) the potential for integrating with future healthcare products through the Bluetooth Health Device Profile (HDP), supported by the most recent Android platform release Ice Cream Sandwich (4.0.4).

The AIRS platform offers the following functionalities:

- Supporting and integrating a wide range of current and future sensors
- Sensor configuration interface, allowing for customizing certain platform settings and behaviors, polling intervals and accuracy levels for certain sensors as well as adding or removing certain sensors
- Quick start mode from the main application launcher screen, using the last selected sensors (if they are still available)
- Inspecting and visualizing current recordings through the notification bar
- Provide two widgets, one used for free-text user annotations and one used for mood-related annotations
- Local recording, where sensors values are stored in a phone-local database
- Remote recording, where data is sent to a remote server for storage.

For simplicity, we describe in this paper only the local recording mode.

3.1   Main Abstractions

Let us refer to Figure 1 for the various classes being realized in our platform and outline how this particular design addresses the aforementioned challenges.

The sensors that can be recorded by the platform are represented by *Sensor* objects and their values can be provided by various resources, being physical (e.g., phone microphone, light sensor) or virtual (e.g., calendar, user annotations). A sensor can be either simple (i.e., when using a single resource) or complex (i.e., when using data from multiple resources). The actual recording is realized through a *Handler* class, which implements Discover() and Acquire() methods that are specific to the set of sensors included within that abstraction. The class also provides interfaces for resource management (destroyHandler()) as well as sharing of data (Share()). The extensibility requirement is addressed by integrating the various Handlers into a *HandlerManager* class, which instantiates the implementations at platform start.

The configurability challenge is addressed by providing a *HandlerUI* implementation for certain handlers. These implementations are made available through the *HandlerUIManager.*

When starting the local recording, each Handler implementation is instructed to discover the available sensors it implements, creating a *Sensor* instance for each available sensor. Each *Sensor* instance is inserted into the *SensorRepository,* which allows for retrieving a value instance at any time.

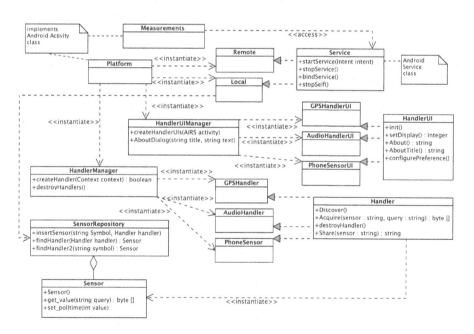

Fig. 1. AIRS implementation diagram

Since we directly base our platform on the Android design and implementation guidelines, as outlined in the SDK [20], any interaction with the end user is implemented as a so-called *Activity* [20]. The *Platform* class in Figure 1 is the main activity, which is started through the icon in the application launcher of Android. This activity provides access to the configuration for the overall platform as well as the handlers that expose a *HandlerUI* implementation. The main activity also allows for launching the local recording. For this, a long-running *Local* service is started, directly realizing the Android concept of a *Service* [20]. Before the service is started, a user dialogue allows for selecting the particular sensors to be recorded or perform a quick start. The current recording can be controlled by the *Measurements* activity, launched when clicking on the appropriate icon in the Android notification bar. The activity displays the latest value for each recorded sensor and also allows for pausing/resuming or exiting a recording.

3.2   Supported Sensors

The number and type of sensors supported by our platform have been increasing, driven by our applications scenarios, any new needs found through user experiments and through the growing ability of the Android system to access information.

As a consequence, our platform currently supports a wide range of information to be recorded. Apart from physical sensors that include location (of various kind such as based on GPS or cell information), gyroscope, accelerometer, pressure, temperature as well as magnetometer, the platform integrates a large variety of platform information such as tasks running, RAM size (used memory), headset status, battery status, cell information, and many more[2]. Given the inherent challenges of getting an accurate ambient temperature through the phone sensor as well as our increased usage of data connectivity, we also utilize web services for gathering information such as the local weather, humidity, wind speed and so on. Furthermore, we also support sensors that can be attached via Bluetooth technology, such as the Alive heart and activity monitor [9]. Figure 2 shows the various information types (left side) currently supported by our platform, in relation to processed information derived from these sensors along several user context dimensions, as implemented in work described in [18]. Based on these types, the current platform implementation exposes in excess of 60 sensor values.

As described above, all sensors are accessed through Handler implementations. Usually, certain groups of sensors are realized by a single Handler providing a common way of accessing this group. For instance, a dedicated Handler implementation realizes the access to the Alive monitor by implementing the particular BT-level protocol. This Handler actually provides values from 6 different sensors provided by the monitor.

Furthermore, the design of the platform allows for directly integrating information processing into the platform through creating a hierarchy of Handler implementations,

---

[2] We do not utilize the camera as a sensor since Android requires the camera preview to be visible, which contradicts our requirement of being able to use the device as usual.

if so desired. Such decision is driven by factors such as disconnected operation, limiting the amount of data to be sent off for processing purposes, on-the-phone visualizations, "abstract and discard" operations, and so on.

Any addition or change to the supported sensor pool requires re-compiling and re-installing the platform. In order to address the extensibility as well as the battery life requirements, we recommend two important best practice guidelines. Firstly, Handler implementations should access information through callbacks instead of polling, making use of the various OS-level mechanisms that allow for minimizing overall battery consumption. Secondly, any Handler should verify the existence of any necessary resource before using it, avoiding runtime exceptions when the resources are not available. This is particularly important when integrating a new sensor that might not be widely available in most handsets.

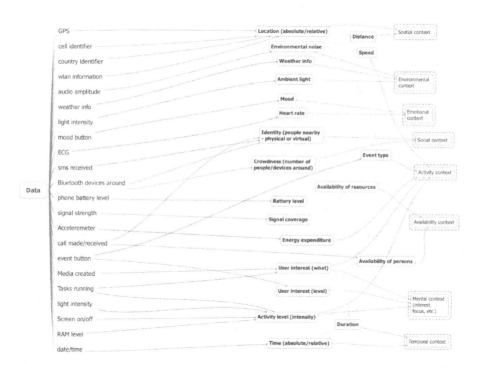

Fig. 2. Sensors supported by AIRS and types of processed information

3.3 Storing and Sharing

Local recordings are stored in an Android database within the local file system. This database approach provides additional security since the underlying file is only accessible to our platform, i.e., it cannot be read by other applications. At any time, the recordings can be synchronized via Android sharing options, such as Bluetooth (transferring the files to a laptop), email (sending the files over the Internet) or through any other installed means (e.g., Facebook, etc.). For this, the platform generates on-the-fly text-based files that can be parsed at the receiving end. These temporary files start with a timestamp that indicate the start of the recording. Following this, every line carries three different entries. The first one represents the time relative to the initial timestamp, followed by the sensor ID as given in the discovery of each sensor. Finally, the value of the current reading is written in text-encoded format. If a sensor produces a multi-line string, each line is separated with a carriage return. Byte array recordings are written in separate files with the file name being recorded in the Value field.

Once transferred, there are many possibilities to save and work on the data. For instance, we provide a Java program that parses the recordings and saves the data into a MySQL database. Once in the database, the data can be accessed and processed in any way desired. For example, in the mentioned PAL project, data collected through the AIRS platform is combined with data collected from other sources, such as physiological sensors and desktop, further interpreted and visualized through PHP-based scripts, utilizing a story-based approach for depicting interesting moments during a day [18].

Another way to share individual sensor values is provided in the *Measurements* activity (started through the notification bar). Here, individual readings can be seen and shared through any system-internal content provider, after long-pressing the particular sensor in the list of values. While such provider could be Bluetooth or email, it also allows for sharing the value through social networks like Facebook or Google+. To enable such sharing, every Handler implements a human-readable text for each individual sensor.

3.4   Addressing the Battery Consumption Issue

Let us now return to one of the most important issues within the usage of platform, namely the battery consumption.

Within our platform, we rely on three approaches to cater to the need for conserving battery. For that, all handlers attempt to utilize callback functions wherever provided by the Android operation system. For this, we register a so-called broadcast receiver [20] to a particular event (e.g., the cellular signal level). An acquisition thread for this particular sensor then simply sleeps until the OS provides the most recent value through the registered callback function. This significantly reduces overall battery consumption compared to polling mechanisms. In the current realization of the platform, only five groups of information are realized through polling, namely Bluetooth (for discovering surrounding devices), audio (for surround noise measurements), WLAN (for detecting SSID and signal strength of surrounding access points) as well as the RAM size and running tasks of the system. We consider the last two as being less relevant for battery consumption since retrieving this information consumes little power (assuming polling intervals of several seconds and beyond). WLAN and BT are power-expensive resources (although the latest BT version 4.0 significantly reduces consumption, according to specifications). The same holds for the noise level measurements, for which frequent recordings through the local microphone are required.

For all polling mechanisms, the intervals for polling can be configured by the end users, giving them control over the overall consumption. In addition, WLAN scanning can be aligned with the overall device policy, if desired by the end user (i.e., on many devices, WLAN is set to sleep once the screen is switched off).

The end user can also configure to only record values when there is user activity, i.e., when the screen is turned on. This gives a significant control over the power usage of these particular sensors, while still leaving the ability to set a critical level for stopping the recording altogether. Although not implemented through polling, GPS is considered another heavy battery consumer, when used in recordings, especially when its availability varies and frequent signal re-scanning is required. However, the configuration settings allow for determining minimal intervals as well as timings for recording new location values. This allows for using efficient Android callback functions instead of frequent polling. This results in no platform activity in cases where the end user remains stationary.

The platform also provides a setting that exits the recording when a defined battery level is reached (e.g., 30%). With that, users can define their desired amount of battery that should be preserved. The user is notified through the Android notification bar once such killing setting has been executed.

3.5   User Interactions in AIRS

We have mentioned before that one crucial aspect in our experiments was to be able to allow for user interactions in order to (1) configure recording parameters according to various needs and constraints; (2) interact with the running recording for visualizing what is being recorded; (3) allow end users to input their own annotations. We describe here how the platform addresses all these aspects.

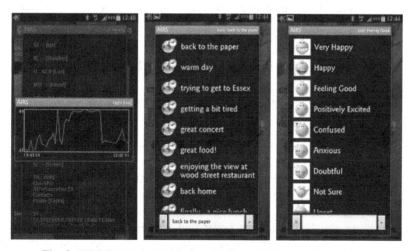

Fig. 3. AIRS Screenshots: (a) visualization; (b)(c) annotation widgets

The configuration mode for setting up the various recording parameters is enabled by the various *HandlerUI* implementations that expose settings for certain sensors (accessed through a *Handler*). Furthermore, the platform itself provides settings that allow for adjusting its overall operation. Each *HandlerUI* implementation makes use of the Android concept of a *PreferenceActivity* [20], which minimizes any necessary code for the particular configurations.

The user can also interact with the platform while the recording is running through the notification bar. The *Measurements* activity allows for inspecting recent recorded values as well as accessing certain visualizations for certain sensors (by pressing on the corresponding item), as seen in Figure 3(a).

As part of our experiments with designing and building lifestyle management systems, it was essential that we better understand what people consider most interesting to be captured within their daily stories. As the mobile phone is one of the most likely devices to be used every day and in multiple situations, we realized that the AIRS platform would be best suited to collect such information, especially in relation to the other recorded information provided by sensors. For this, we utilize the concept of an Android Widget [20] by directly placing a user interface element on the user's home screen. This interaction is one the closest abstraction to pressing a button to annotate while also allowing for adding a meaning to such operation. Figure 3(b) shows the interface for the user annotation, which allows for any text to be inserted and even remembered (by configuring the list size). The user can select a previous annotation or add a completely new one. While emotion recognition is making progress even on mobile phones [16], humans are still better suited to recognize and describe their own emotions. For this reason, we also created a widget that allows for fast mood-related annotations. The user can select from a set of 12 pre-defined mood icons or use an own mood description.

These two widgets connect to two specific Handler implementations of the platform. The value selected or defined through these two widgets is treated the same as any other platform sensor.

4   Usage-Based Experiments and Their Challenges

While the previous sections focused on highlighting certain aspects we consider essential in understanding our platform, we describe next the experiments and experience we have had with using this platform within the lifestyle management setting. What is special about such scenarios is that they usually require recording a multitude of sensors (in order to create a diverse user context picture) and for longer periods of time (in order to cover more aspects of user's daily activities and life).

However, with large amount of data comes the challenge of making sense of it as well as identifying what is really of interest to the end user. As mentioned before, our experiments were mainly focused on better understanding what people consider of importance during the day. For this, we conducted recording experiments with six end users over several days, followed by semi-structured interviews.

We started our experiments by using available physical annotation means provided by the Alive monitor (a binary button). Based on the received feedback from experiments and user interviews, we realized that there is a lot of value in allowing end users to self-annotate their data with their own words, as it makes it much easier to remember what was going on at a certain moment as well as reflect on what has happened before, after, who was there, why she put that annotation and so on. This insight led us to introduce the widget-based annotation means presented in Section 3.5. While coming out of a need to identify interesting moments in time, the interaction means provided by our platform became an interesting study on what goes on in the process of annotating, as users became more aware of what was really the most meaningful description of the situation at hand. Even more, it became obvious that given such tool, end users will try not to replicate information recorded through the AIRS sensors, such as location, focusing instead of descriptions hard to capture through automatic means.

Apart from this specific input regarding annotation, our experiments generally showed the value of having an extendable, controllable and interactive mobile-based sensing platform, as it allowed us to collect and correlate user meaningful lifestyle information both automatically (objective) and human-driven (subjective) instead of using commonly available methods, such as periodic polling or questionnaires.

However, within such recording scenarios, battery consumption becomes a real challenge as it affects the length of the recording as well as the likelihood of users performing such recordings with their own mobile phones. An obvious route to obtaining an insight into battery consumption is through experiments but measuring battery consumption within real-life scenarios is riddled with challenges. Firstly, the used devices are of personal nature (in contrast to purpose-built sensing devices) and each user has different, often parallel usages. Also, each user's environment and movement patterns differ, making statements about using features such as GPS, WLAN or BT futile since the exact environment of the experiment (defined by effort it takes to obtain a GPS fix, the number of access points or BT devices as well as the frequency of scanning) cannot be kept identical between users or even the same user within different situations. Hence, battery statistics are bound to vary significantly.

Furthermore, the variety of available handsets makes any study regarding battery consumption difficult since consumption will inevitably vary according to processor generation, radio chipset and radio environment (such as positioning of the antenna in the case of WLAN or BT) and even OS configurations. Hence, battery statistics can at best be given for certain (reference) devices.

Also, the general consumption caused by the various callback sensors is very difficult to normalize since their consumption will heavily depend on the particular rate of triggering the callbacks. Given the nature of the information (such as battery charging, handset plugged in/out, change in radio signal), this rate inevitably depends on the particular usage scenario and any artificially defined usage scenario is therefore of little value to understanding the overall consumption expectation. In all this, the configurability of the platform adds additional variance to any statement of battery consumption.

For these reasons, we present here results from experiments within a lifestyle recording scenario, where the mobile phone is used by a single person within a realistic setting over a month, in comparison with a more controlled recording scenario that only focused on recording 3 of the most battery consuming sensors: GPS, WiFi and Bluetooth in relation to location (a 'wardriving' scenario [19]).

The lifestyle scenario involved one of the authors using the platform during one month of usual usage of his personal mobile phone. Information recorded included GPS, BT, noise level as well cellular information (signal strength, location area, cell identifier), activity information (headset status, mood and event widget input, call as well as SMS information) and system information (RAM, battery, tasks running, music played, files created). GPS and Bluetooth were configured for 30 seconds updates while surrounding noise was determined every three seconds (recording for one second to determine the noise level). With this, we generated a moderate to heavy load created by our platform. The end user made use of his handset within the typical range of activities, including synchronizing content frequently during office hours (from 9am to 7pm). The data is averaged over a month and includes activities from office work over home working to international travel. Recording was conducted from about 9am to 8pm, on occasions longer when there were late evening activities.

Our diary experiment was conducted with a Galaxy Nexus on Android 4.0.2, while two Samsung Galaxy S with Android 2.3.6 were used for the 'wardriving' scenario, carried at the same time to encounter similar environmental conditions. In the latter case, the handsets differed in their configuration of the polling interval (15 seconds for the 'heavy' and 30 seconds for the 'light' case). In order to emulate a dedicated wardriving usage, the handsets were not used throughout the measurements for anything else, eliminating any variance through user usage.

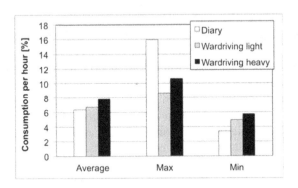

Fig. 4. Battery consumption in various scenarios

Figure 4 shows the battery consumption for these usage-based experiments. The diary use case results in a larger variance since the handset was normally used (the maximum value, for instance, is caused by a prolonged browsing session during a domestic travel). On average, the platform consumed about 6.3% battery per hour for the activity recording, with an average battery consumption of the phone without recording at around 2.5%. With that, such recording is possible throughout a normal working day (of, say, about 12 hours) without recharging. Although less callback sensors are used in our second scenario, the usage of WLAN (in exchange for the noise recording) leads to an increase in consumption. We explain this with the necessary wakelock [20] on the WLAN radio in order to perform the frequent scanning. Hence, WLAN never switches off. We can see that increasing the polling interval for WLAN only leads to a small increase from 6.7 to 7.7%.

The takeaway from our experiments is that the battery consumption of our platform is moderate even in experiments that record a significant number of sensors. Using wireless radio resources increases the overall battery consumption, which is expected. This is even more the case when using, e.g., BT-attached sensors like the ones in [9]. Their individual consumption, however, heavily depends on the used radio protocol as well as the rate of communication. Newer technologies, such as BT 4.0, are expected to reduce power consumption for these scenarios.

5   Conclusions and Future Work

Given the almost ubiquitous availability of mobile handsets as well as their ever-increasing capabilities, utilizing their power is desirable for many mobile sensing scenarios. This is especially the case within the lifestyle management area that is concerned with increasing self-awareness through self-monitoring, information processing and visualizations. In order to focus research and development on what matters, namely the intelligence to make use of the increasing pool of information that could be gathered, a platform approach is essential as it can accommodate individual or group requirements. Although we see the area of self-monitoring through mobile phones taking off (both in research and the mobile application area), mainly fragmented, short-lived or purpose-oriented solutions are created.

There are currently few generic and widely available mobile device based sensing platforms that provide the wide range of features we have described, combining both automatic as well as user-based information gathering, perfectly suited for self-monitoring scenarios where not everything of value to users can be sensed or recognized automatically. In this paper we provided the main challenges we have encountered in our work together with several design and implementation choices we made in order to address them. We specifically addressed one of the essential challenges of any mobile-based sensing platform, which is battery consumption. Our experiments show that the platform allows for sustaining daily recording activities over a wide range of information without significantly degrading the overall device performance.

In order to establish the platform as a possible basis for research and development activities alike, we released the work to the open source community as well as to the general software market [22] as free software. At the time of writing, more than 4000 users have downloaded the application with more than 400 active installations.

Apart from general application developers, we see the research community at large as a beneficiary of our work as the platform can be immediately downloaded and used, allowing researchers to focus on processing recorded information. We also see our support for interaction as being useful in various user research studies or even for aiding automatic recognition of certain situations.

For our future work, we intend to focus on the information processing and visualization aspects involved when gathering such a multitude of information. Story-based approaches [18] to presenting information have so far yielded promising feedback from end users with many ideas for extensions. These ideas include correlating existing sensors with any type of media created during recording (e.g., pictures and videos taken). We also plan on extending the support for the wider community by enabling the addition of Handlers without the need to re-compile and re-install the platform. This will allow for establishing code repositories, which can be enriched over time by the wider community. These extensions are planned in collaboration with the wider research community, initiated through our software market and open source release. To foster this engagement with the community, we have set up a dedicated blog platform as well as an online manual that is directly accessible through the mobile application. We also provide increasing insight into example handlers with the attempt to encourage the development of novel extensions to the core platform. We also plan on making available code repositories for the wider community where handlers can be downloaded for free in order to optimize the AIRS platform for any experiment that is planned by community members. The most important community engagement, however, is the usage of the platform as well as the reporting of its usefulness, potential bugs and errors as well as suggestions for extensions. Our current online blog platform provides the means for this interaction through feature requests, blogging about new features, and often encountered Q&As.

References

1. Raento, M., Oulasvirta, A., Petit, R., Toivonen, H.: ContextPhone: A Prototyping Platform for Context-Aware Mobile Applications. IEEE Pervasive Computing 04(2), 51–59 (2005)
2. Trossen, D., Pavel, D.: NORS: An Open Source Platform to Facilitate Participatory Sensing with Mobile Phones. In: Conference on Mobile and Ubiquitous Systems: Networking and Services (2007)
3. Siewiorek, D., Smailagic, A., Furukawa, J., Krause, A., Moraveji, N., Reiger, K., Shaffer, J., Wong, F.L.: SenSay: A Context-Aware Mobile Phone. In: Seventh IEEE International Symposium on Wearable Computers (2003)
4. Sung, M., Pentland, A.: LiveNet: Health and Lifestyle Networking Through Distributed Mobile Devices. In: Workshop on Applications of Mobile Embedded Systems, MobiSys (2004)
5. Sportstracker (2010), http://www.sports-tracker.com/#/home
6. Endomondo (2012), http://www.endomondo.com
7. Carloni, L.P., De Bernardinis, F., Pinello, C., Sangiovanni-Vincentelli, A.L., Sgroi, M.: Platform-Based Design for Embedded Systems. The Embedded Systems Handbook (2005)
8. Trossen, D., Pavel, D., Singh, J., Bacon, J., Guild, K.M.: Information-centric Pervasive Healthcare Platforms. In: Pervasive Health Conference (2010)
9. Alive Technologies, "Alive Heart and Activity Monitor" (2010), http://www.alivetec.com/products.htm

10. WristCare, `http://www.istsec.fi/eng/Emikakoti.htm`
11. SenseWear BMS (2010),
    `http://www.sensewear.com/BMS/solutions_bms.php`
12. Philips Lifeline solutions (2010),
    `http://www.lifelinesys.com/content/home`
13. iFall (2010),
    `http://www.imedicalapps.com/2010/04/`
    `ifall-android-medical-app/`
14. OBS (2010), `http://www.obsmedical.com/products`
15. CardioNet patient solutions (2010),
    `http://www.cardionet.com/patients_01.htm`
16. Rachuri, K.K., Rentfrow, P.J., Musolesi, M., Longworth, C., Mascolo, C., Aucinas, A.: EmotionSense: A Mobile Phones based Adaptive Platform for Experimental Social Psychology Research. In: ACM Ubicomp (2010)
17. PAL project (2012), `http://www.palproject.org.uk`
18. Pavel, D., Callaghan, V., Dey, A.K.: Supporting Wellbeing Through Improving Interactions and Understanding in Self-Monitoring Systems. In: Handbook of Ambient Assisted Living – Technology for Healthcare, Rehabilitation and Well-Being, vol. 11. IOS Press (2012)
19. Wikipedia, "Wardriving" (2012),
    `http://en.wikipedia.org/wiki/Wardriving`
20. Android Developer online resources (2012),
    `http://developer.android.com/index.html`
21. Lane, N.D., Miluzzo, E., Lu, H., Peebles, D., Choudhury, T., Campbell, A.T.: A Survey of Mobile Phone Sensing. Comm. Mag. 48, 140–150 (2010)
22. AIRS: Android Remote Sensing platform (2012),
    `https://play.google.com/store/apps/details?id=com.airs`
23. SENSEI FP7 project (2012), `http://www.sensei-project.eu/`

Crowd-Based Smart Parking: A Case Study for Mobile Crowdsourcing

Xiao Chen[2,1], Elizeu Santos-Neto[1], and Matei Ripeanu[1]

[1] Department of Electrical and Computer Engineering,
University of British Columbia
[2] Department of Computer Science and Technology,
Shanghai Lixin University of Commerce
{xiaoc,elizeus,matei}@ece.ubc.ca

Abstract. An increasing number of mobile applications aim to enable "smart cities" by harnessing contributions from citizens armed with mobile devices that have sensing ability. However, there are few generally recognized guidelines for developing and deploying crowdsourcing-based solutions in mobile environments. This paper considers the design of a crowdsourcing-based smart parking system as a specific case study in an attempt to explore the basic design principles applicable to an array of similar applications. Through simulations, we show that the strategies behind crowdsourcing can heavily influence the utility of such applications. Equally importantly, we show that tolerating a certain level of freeriding increases the social benefits while maintaining quality of service level offered. Our findings provide designers with a better understanding of mobile crowdsourcing features and help guide successful designs.

Keywords: mobile crowdsourcing, smart parking, collaborative sensing.

1   Introduction

The definition of crowdsourcing has evolved to cover a variety of online activities that exploit collective contribution/intelligence to solve complex problems. Since the value of the related product or service is usually far beyond the cost of incentivizing individual participants to contribute, crowdsourcing has become an economical, effective, and justified mechanism to carry out initiatives that offer social benefits but cost too much to be deployed by any single entity. Notable examples include Wikipedia and Salt Lake City's use of crowdsourcing for transit planning [1]. A remarkable trend in crowdsourcing is the use of mobile devices: these break the time and space barriers between people and enable them to share information and knowledge. For example, mobile applications like *txteagle* are emerging alternatives to traditional platforms like AMT (Amazon Mechanical Turk) [2]. With the popularity of mobile social networking,and the emergence of ideas like participatory sensing, mobile crowdsourcing has the potential to help tackle an array of new problems that involve real-time data collection from and coordination among a large

C. Borcea et al. (Eds.): MobilWare 2012, LNICST 65, pp. 16–30, 2013.
© Institute for Computer Sciences, Social Informatics and Telecommunications Engineering 2013

number of participants. In particular, mobile crowdsourcing can be harnessed to design smart parking solutions.

The parking problem has existed in big cities for decades. Studies show that an average of 30% of the traffic in busy areas is caused by vehicles cruising for vacant parking spots [3]. The situation is getting worse in developing countries like China, where the number of private cars has soared recently, while the investment in parking facilities has lagged. The additional traffic causes significant problems from traffic congestion, to air pollution, to energy waste. Some local governments try to mitigate these issues by deploying *smart parking* systems: systems that employ information and communication technologies to collect and distribute the real-time data about parking availability and may guide drivers so that they find parking spots quicker.

For example, the city of San Francisco installed thousands of sensors at on-street parking spaces in busy areas to make parking availability information public. Although the benefits of such a centralized approach are immediate, its huge initial investment and maintenance cost inhibits a widespread adoption in most other cities: the average maintenance cost for each sensor monitoring a single parking space is beyond $20 per month [4]. Even in San Francisco, the majority of parking spaces are not covered by the system likely due to its cost.

This paper studies the properties of crowdsourcing in the context of smart parking. More specifically, this work investigates the use of information collected through crowdsourcing for parking guidance, which is integrated into a road navigation system (as a design alternative to lower the cost to install and maintain a dedicated infrastructure). It is important to note, for example, that *Waze* [6] has already demonstrated that crowdsourcing using road navigation devices is feasible and has accumulated millions of users in over 45 countries. *Waze* collects most of the data we also employ for parking guidance; and, our system can be easily implemented as an extension to it.

This work, however, improves over existing approaches in a number of ways. First, by integrating crowdsourcing and a road navigation system, we eliminate unnecessary drivers' manual operations during the parking search process. This complies with the current safety regulation in most countries. Unlike applications such as *Open Spot* [8], which require drivers to launch them separately to search parking spots, we only ask drivers for their manual input at the beginning and the end of their trips. By simplifying operations, we are more likely to recruit a larger number of contributors, a key factor to crowdsourcing success.

Second, since drivers who contribute also benefit from the system, our approach heavily depends on a pattern of mutual assistance, which excludes the complexities caused by monetary rewards [5]. On the one hand, we demonstrated that the system is resilient to the existence of free riders (Section 5). On the other hand, as we assume a centralized control the distribution of collected date, the system can create incentives by providing users with different quality of service (e.g., better parking suggestions, request prioritization) based on their contribution records.

Finally, we guide/coordinate the crowdsourcing behavior among participants to improve data collection efficiency and system utilization. In contrast to existing approaches that only share information about parking vacancies, our system also tries to identify occupied areas through user's sensor data (or explicit input) so as to help drivers avoid unnecessary cruising. Also, we assign parking spaces to users dynamically, according to the reported capacity of parking spots to eliminate races between participants. Furthermore, we take a proactive strategy to crowdsource when the knowledge is limited: more specifically, the system might direct drivers to unexplored areas so that it can expand its knowledge about parking availability in these areas.

Our contributions in this paper fall in two categories: On the one hand, we demonstrate, through simulations, that mobile crowdsourcing is a feasible and cost effective approach to deploy a smart parking system. On the other hand, we regard this application as a case study to demystify some rumors that have influenced the design of mobile crowdsourcing-based applications for a long time. We find that recruiting more participants may not necessarily lead to a better performance if the crowdsourcer fails to coordinate people's behavior in the context of these applications. We show that people can provide valuable data even through the simplest manual operation in a dynamic mobile environment if they are coordinated. We also discover that a proper policy to deal with free-riders will improve social benefits without sacrificing the quality of the crowdsourcing-based service. These findings can serve as a catalyst to facilitate the development of similar mobile applications and help double the number of success stories.

The rest of the paper is organized as follows: Section 2 positions this work among the related literature; Section 3 describes the parking guidance system and its different strategies to harness crowdsourcing; Sections 4 and 5 present the simulation design and the evaluation results; Section 6 concludes the paper with final remarks and discusses directions for future work.

2   Related Work

The huge demand for transportation-related services to simplify daily life is the driver for mobile crowdsourcing applications. Thanks to data crowdsourced through thousands of mobile devices, drivers are able to pick a better route to avoid a road segment that was detected as congested in the previous five minutes by Waze, to refill at a gas station with a lower price by GasBuddy [7], or find a parking place using applications like Open Spot [8]. Similarly, taxi drivers might improve their routes by knowing colleagues' trajectory [9] and commuters can get the real-time transit information from Roadify [10]. One feature shared by these mobile crowdsourcing scenarios is that they rely on data contributed by the consumers of these services. Therefore, these crowdsourcing-based services become sustainable if they can attract a sufficient amount of users.

Although the aforementioned applications have attracted great attention in the market (e.g., as estimated by their download count), they are orthogonal to the research interests of the academic community. As Kanhere discusses [11], current studies in mobile crowdsourcing or participatory sensing generally focus more on new applications (e.g., personal health monitoring [12], environmental surveillance [13], or enhanced social media [14]) than on the impact of participating rates and crowdsourcing strategies. Issues like privacy preservation, incentive design, or evaluating the trustworthiness of data remain major concerns when deploying these applications into practice.

As far as smart parking is concerned, the majority of existing studies either assume the availability of gadgets installed at the parking lots or require *all* drivers to comply with the same protocol when reporting parking availability. Systems like [15] and SPARK [16] employ wireless sensors and, respectively, VANET (Vehicular Ad-hoc Network) devices to collect and disseminate information about parking availability to help drivers find vacant parking spaces. CrowdPark [5] assumes a seller-buyer relationship between drivers, who are going to leave or parking at the lots, to deal with the parking reservation problem. A relevant study [17] tries to realize smart parking by solving an optimal resource allocation problem according to drivers' various parking requirements. However, the reservation-based solutions might complicate drivers' operation and can collapse if only a few drivers follow their rules.

One remarkable initiative that realizes smart-parking by the infrastructure-based approach is the SFPark [18] project in San Francisco. Although the benefit is obvious, few cities worldwide can afford the high initial investment and the maintenance cost. Alternatively, some pure crowdsourcing-based solutions like Open Spot [8] are emerging but, to date, failed to solve the problem effectively. We believe there is a viable approach between these two extremes. More specifically, our approach is to introduce a central entity to coordinate participants' behavior in order to make mobile crowdsourcing not only a cheap but also an effective solution to the smart parking problem.

3   System Design

The **basic idea behind our design is to build** a system that acquires, possibly approximate or aggregate, parking availability information through crowdsourcing: each participating **driver** helps with data acquisition. **In return, the system provides** either the aggregate parking availability map and users make uncoordinated decisions or the system provides customized **recommendations of parking locations and navigation to the participants** and thus attempts to coordinate their behavior.

3.1   Assumptions

The goal of smart parking is to inform drivers of a parking vacancy as soon and as close to their destination as possible. The desired effect is to save the time and the fuel spent in cruising, reduce unnecessary walking, and reduce the traffic congestion and fuel waste. To this end, the crowd-based smart parking system collects relevant data from participating drivers, and then uses this data to navigate them to the right parking slots. For convenience, we refer to the drivers who participate in the system as *smart parkers (SP)* in contrast to those who do not participate as *ordinary drivers (OD)*.

The system consists of three components: central servers, client devices, and smart parkers. Figure 1 shows the relationships and the data flows between them. We make the following assumptions about their responsibility or functionality.

Central Servers: The servers collect data from drivers, who report their current location and destination, car speed, and parking availability on a certain street through client devices. Using the information collected in real time, the servers maintain a dynamically annotated parking availability map. When a smart parker arrives close to his destination, the servers search the dynamic map for potential parking vacancies according to the parker's current location and destination. Then they inform the client device of the search result, which might be either the specific location of the parking spot or the direction of the next turn to the parking spot.

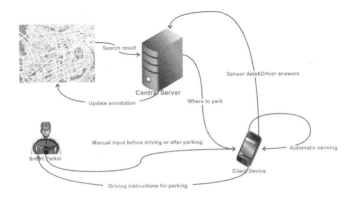

Fig. 1. Data flow among the central server, the client device, and the smart parker

In addition to this dynamic data, we also assume the servers have access to static data, which are relevant to parking guidance, such as the parking price, legal periods, and areas to park, and statistics about the arrival rate of vehicles and parking rate around a certain region during a certain period. In fact, an increasing number of cities provide these kinds of data online [20].

Client Devices: Drivers have on-board devices that can communicate with the server. They upload geo-tagged data and can download the result of queries regarding parking slots availability. It is reasonable to assume that such devices have GPS capability and Internet connection. A variety of off-the-shelf consumer electronics like smart phones, tablet PCs, and versatile GPS navigators can play this role. The client devices have a simple user interface that allows smart parkers to input relevant data manually when they are not driving. The devices can also collect geo-tagged sensor data automatically without drivers' intervention when the car is moving. We draw a self-loop on client devices in Figure 1 because the device might process the collected sensor data before sending them to the server.

Smart Parkers: Smart parkers are the drivers who have access to the service through their client devices. Like ordinary users of GPS navigators, a smart parker will input her destination before she starts driving. Then she will receive recommendations from the system about potential free parking slot when she approaches her destination. The smart parker can choose whether or not to follow such recommendations, but the client device will report her cruising trail to the server. At the beginning and the end of a trip, with the car stopped, the smart parker is expected to answer a question about parking availability in the area by manually handling the client device.

3.2   Problem, Key Questions, and Required Data

Three key questions guide the design of any crowdsourcing system: *What is the required data? How can this data be obtained through crowdsourcing? How can the acquired data be used in the specific application scenario?*

In our parking scenario, we model each road segment as a parking lot with several parking spots along it. To realize on-street smart parking, we need to navigate smart parkers to streets that are not fully occupied. In other words, we need to acquire the status of the parking availability along each road segment.

From the server's perspective, each road segment could have one of the three statuses for its parking availability: *available, occupied,* or *unknown*. Initially, the status of all streets is marked as *unknown*. Once information is received the status can switch to *available* or *occupied*.

Unlike smart parkers, ordinary drivers do not provide data thus when they arrive at or leave from a parking space, the change in status is not observed by the central server. Thus, for all parking spots, we automatically change the status to *unknown* when a timer expires. The timer length can be derived from statistic data or occupancy prediction [19] and can be adjusted through the observation of the crowdsourced data. In addition to the occupancy status, the system also needs to know the capacity of each on-street parking lot to determine if it can navigate two cars to the same street at the same time.

3.3   Crowdsourcing Data Acquisition

Crowdsourcing data acquisition in a mobile environment poses some challenges. An obvious problem is that a limited user interface and drivers' tight schedule require the device operation to be as simple as possible. In the case of a smart parking scenario, we might want smart parkers to observe the streets carefully and report a specific number for the parking capacity. However, most smart parkers will likely prefer to answer a much simpler Yes/No question by just pressing a button on their devices. Experiences from similar applications like Waze show that user-friendly interface and simple operation are key factors to recruit contributors.

We explore the impact of the varying accuracy of crowdsourcing based information (Table 1). *Our study (Section 5) shows that the answer to a simple Yes/No question is sufficient even with a low participation rate in the crowdsourcing system.*

Table 1. Different kinds of questions smart parkers could be asked

#	Question	Answers	Capacity
Q1	How many parking spots on the street?	0,1,2,3...	As the answer
Q2	Any more parking spots on the street?	Yes/No	1(Yes)/0(No)
Q3	No question	No answer	Always 1

In addition to the above requirement for a simplified operation, the limited view of the participants could restrict their ability to provide accurate data. For example, by answering, smart parkers only inform the server of the situation of the street where they parked but tell nothing about the occupied streets they cruised through. However, we can infer such information from crowdsourced sensor data. More specifically, we assume a car to be cruising if it follows the server's instructions to reach a certain road segment but still keeps moving at low speed. Then we consider the road segment where the car starts cruising as *occupied*. Furthermore, all streets the car cruises without parking can also be regarded as *occupied*. In addition, we can mark a street as *available* if a car leaves from there. Since a car's cruising speed is only 20% of its normal driving speed, we can infer the above by just observing the sensor data like speed and location. We enumerate all three kinds of inference in Table 2.

Table 2. Different types of inference through sensor data

#	Observed behavior	Inference	Capacity
I1	Reach the assigned street and continue at low speed	The assigned street is occupied	0
I2	Move at low speed after I1	The past street is occupied	0
I3	Launch the application and drive away	New vacancy in the street	+1

3.4   Parking Guidance Alternatives: Coordinated vs. Uncoordinated

Once the server annotates each street on the map with its parking availability status, the simplest way to do parking guidance is to display the locations of available parking slots on a map directly to all drivers without attempting to coordinate them. However, this uncoordinated approach (also adopted by Open Spot) can lead to several problems.

First, it is usually difficult for drivers to integrate all information on the annotated map to make a good decision when driving. They could always focus on the same parking slots reported by other drivers, which might not always be their best choice. Furthermore, when drivers cruise along occupied streets, they cannot help others to avoid such areas which in turn contribute to longer cruising time. Due to the uncoordinated nature, smart parkers are less likely to explore unknown areas, where there could be more available parking slots closer to the destination.

To mitigate the problems, we propose to coordinate the drivers (instead of letting them choose where to park by themselves). To eliminate the race between two smart parkers for the same parking spot, we keep track of the capacity of each road segment and navigate smart parkers according to the streets' current available capacity. To find out the parking status around the *unknown* areas, we assume each *unknown* street has a capacity of one. Once a street is assigned to a smart parker, its capacity is reduced by one and we only navigate cars to streets with a non-zero capacity. If the assigned street is already fully occupied when the smart parker arrives there, we navigate the car to cruise toward streets with non-zero capacity. This way, we not only help the smart parker avoid unnecessary cruising but also increase the server's knowledge about *unknown* streets. The difference between our approach and uncoordinated crowdsourcing is shown in Figure 2. In simulation experiments we explore the sensitivity of the solution to the number of smart parkers that follow the coordination suggestions of the server.

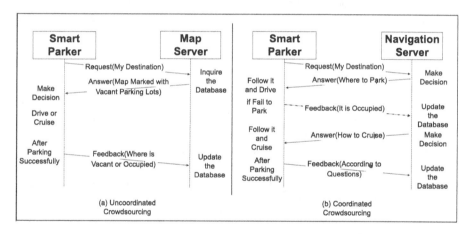

Fig. 2. Illustration between uncoordinated and coordinated parking guidance

4   Simulation Methodology

We explore the design space delimited by the design choices highlighted in the previous section through simulations. This section presents the situation settings.

4.1   Simulation Environment

To simulate the crowdsourcing-based system in the context of smart parking scenario, we need to take care of two aspects. On one hand, the simulations should reflect features in realistic road traffic environment like road layout, car following patterns, and individual driving behaviors. On the other hand, the simulation environment should be configurable to take into account the system design factors discussed in

Section 3. Since no existing simulation environments can satisfy all requirements, we modified an open source road traffic simulator, SUMO [21], to meet our needs.

SUMO is a microscopic road traffic simulator, which allows simulating thousands of vehicles moving through a road network. The simulator is capable of capturing the geospatial properties of each vehicle in motion like location and speed at any moment. This corresponds to our assumption about smart parkers: they should be able to report such information to the server. However, the existing environment heavily depends on predefined configuration files to determine the departure time and the route of each vehicle.

To simulate the dynamic scenario, in which vehicles arrive according to a Poisson process and cruise around for an open spot to park, we integrate the logic of vehicle generation and routing into the simulator. In addition, the adapted simulator adds the parking capacity as a new property of each street in the road network so that smart parkers will keep cruising in search of open parking slots until they enter a street with a non-zero parking capacity. Furthermore, we have implemented the data collection process and parking navigation inside SUMO to reflect the different crowdsourcing strategies mentioned in Section 3.

4.2   Simulated Scenario and Parameter Setting

Scenario: The simulation aims to evaluate the feasibility of the aforementioned crowdsourcing system in a simple but realistic scenario, where hundreds of vehicles are heading for the same destination during a short period of time and few cars leave the parking lots at that time. This often happens around office buildings and park-and-ride facilities [22] during rush hours or at a stadium before a game kicks off. This scenario helps us focus on the impact of different design choices for the crowdsourcing system rather than on the statistics related to parking lot usage around a certain area.

Parameter Setting: The road network in our simulations is modeled as a 1 km^2 region divided into a 9*9 grid by four-lane bidirectional streets. Each road segment has a parking capacity of 5 for either side of the street. In the simulator, the block in the center is assumed as a common destination and everyone tries to park close to it in order to reduce the walking distance. In each round of simulation, a sequence of about 1,000 vehicles enters the map according to a Poisson process. The arrival rate is set to one car every 15 seconds.

The simulator determines whether a new coming driver is a smart parker by a certain probability so that it is possible to control the approximate ratio between the two groups of drivers. If an ordinary driver cannot find an open spot on the destination street, he will have to cruise around randomly until he can find one somewhere else. The speed limit for normal driving is 50km/h while the cruising speed is below 10km/h.

When a smart parker moves close to the desired destination, the server will show her suggestions about the available parking place. If she follows the server's suggestion but reaches a fully occupied on-street lot, she also needs to cruise.

However, the parking guidance will help during the cruising if we adopt a coordinated guidance strategy. We run each simulation from 5 to 35 times and plot the average value.

5   Evaluation Results

We explore the impact of three key design decisions: the impact of global coordination; the impact of collecting approximate data that leads to increased usability of the client devices; and the social impact of freeriding.

There are two success criteria for our system: the walking distance from the parking spot found to the actual destination (measured in 'blocks' – i.e., the distance between two crossroads) and the average cruising time to find a parking spot. Our results highlight that coordinated crowdsourcing is not only effective but also practical in the real world.

5.1   Uncoordinated VS Coordinated Crowdsourcing

The first question we focus on is: *Do smart parkers outperform ordinary drivers regardless of the type of crowdsroucing strategy used by the system?* We first assume that the system adopts a pure uncoordinated crowdsourcing strategy so that each smart parker just follows a predecessor who managed to park the closest to its destination and signals that parking spaces are still available in the area.

Figure 3(a) compares two groups of drivers with regard to the average walking distance. We collect the data as the participation rate (i.e., the ratio of smart parkers in the system) increases from 10% to 50% of the driver population. As Figure 3(a) shows, uncoordinated crowdsourcing leads to longer walking distance for smart parkers than for ordinary drivers. Since the system does not provide smart parkers with a global view around the region, they miss potential vacancies closer to their destination.

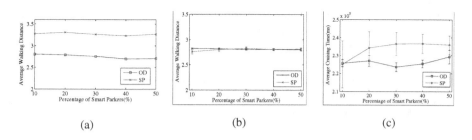

(a)   (b)   (c)

Fig. 3. Performance comparison between ordinary drivers and smart parkers adopting an uncoordinated crowdsourcing approach. The walking distance in (a) and (b) is measured in number of blocks away from the central destination. Error bars here indicate the 95% confidence interval.

Smart parkers might not always follow directions to the recommended spots, which are far away from the destination. Thus we next assume that they choose to cruise by themselves and ignore the system's recommendation if the recommended spots are more than three blocks away from the destination, which is the median value for the walking distance. The resulting walking distance and average cruising time are shown in figure 3(b) and 3(c) respectively. Although smart parkers don't lose to ordinary drivers in terms of average walking distance this time, about 40% of them spend more average search time than ordinary drivers.

The previous figures show that the uncoordinated crowdsourcing approach, also used by Google's Open Spot, fails to help users do a better job than ordinary drivers in the search of parking spots regardless of how many drivers participate.

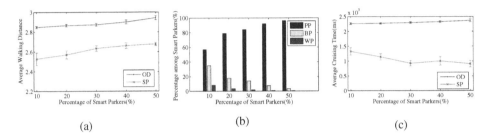

Fig. 4. Performance of smart parkers when their behavior is coordinated in the crowdsourcing system. Error bars here indicate the 95% confidence interval.

We assume now a coordinated approach where the system collects information by applying option Q1 in table 1 and I2 in table 2. In addition, it assigns smart parkers to explore unknown areas and helps them cruise more efficiently by avoiding occupied streets. As the figure 4(a) shows, such an approach achieves a lower average walking distance for smart parkers.

To report results, we divide the smart parkers into three groups: the majority of them can find an open spot immediately according to the system's navigation and we call them perfect parkers (PP). Those who still need to cruise but spend less time than the average cruising time of ordinary drivers are referred to as better parkers (BP). The rest are called worse parkers (WP) as they spend more time cruising. Figure 4(b) shows the change of the composition of smart parkers as more drivers participate. More than 90% of the smart parkers do not need to cruise when the membership covers about 40% of all drivers. For BP and WP, we calculate their average cruising time and plot the result in figure 4(c). *All these figures show that the coordinated crowdsourcing is more effective in the smart parking scenario.*

5.2   Impact of Various Design Options Leading to Increased Usability

The second question we try to study concerns both developers and users: *Could the data collection process be simpler (user friendly) while still achieving the application objectives?* To make it clear, we let smart parkers answer simpler questions (as in

Table 1) to report relevant information to the server and then estimate their impact on system efficiency (for which we use the number of perfect parkers as a proxy). We plot the results in figure 5(a) with each line for a specific question. The figure reflects that the answers to a Yes-No parking availability question provide sufficient information for the server to implement a useful navigation service. Next, we repeat the experiments without inferring the occupancy through cruising vehicles. By comparing figure 5(a) and 5(b), we find that the information inferred through cruising cars is helpful when only a few smart parkers participate but its importance diminishes as more drivers join the system.

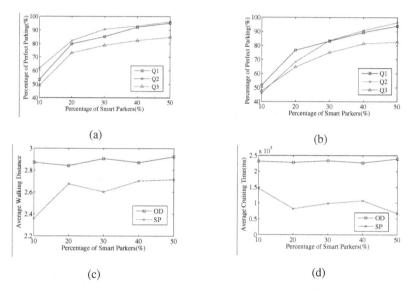

Fig. 5. Influence of various crowdsourcing options to the performance of smart parking system. In (a) and (b), we ask different questions after smart parkers find their spots. We first turn on in (a) and then turn off in (b) the option to infer occupancy through cruising cars. In (c) and (d), we only ask drivers if or not there are additional spots on the street where they parked the cars.

To increase confidence in the preliminary conclusion we can derive (i.e., answers to simpler questions can still provide sufficient information to navigate smart parkers properly) we assume that smart parkers only answer question Q2 and no information is inferred when they are cruising. In other words, the server only asks the Yes-No question this time and makes no inference about *occupied* streets when smart parkers are cruising. We compare smart parkers with ordinary drivers again with regard to the average walking distance and cruising time in figure 5(c) and 5(d) respectively. Since the majority of smart parkers (at least 50% of them) do not cruise at all, we only plot in figure 5(d) the average cruising time for those smart parkers who need to cruise, namely the better parkers(BP) and the worse parkers(WP). *The figures show that the crowdsourcing system is still effective even when participants only answer simple questions.*

5.3   The Impact of Free Riders

The last set of simulations deals with another realistic question: *How should the system handle free riders?* In the context of our system, free riders are those participants who only want to take advantage of the service but refuse to answer any question. As part of the feasibility evaluation, we need to evaluate how tolerant the crowdsourcing system is to freeriding and decide how to handle them: tolerate or attempt to exclude them.

The average walking distance among all drivers and the average cruising time of ordinary drivers do not change much across all experiments. Therefore we use them as a reference to test if smart parkers can still find the open spot quickly and park closer to their destination even in the presence of free riders. In the following simulations, we only ask Yes-No question without data inference during drivers' cruising. We assume that 30% to 40% of all drivers are smart parkers. Among the smart parkers, the percentage of free riders grows from 10% to 90%. We plot the normalized walking distance for smart parkers in figure 6(a), namely the average walking distance of the smart parkers divided by the average walking distance among all drivers. Similarly, we plot the normalized cruising time for smart parkers in figure 6(b). The figure shows that the navigation system works well until the percentage of free riders exceeds 60%. In other words, we can infer that the quality of the service is still acceptable as long as at least 12% of all drivers are willing to contribute.

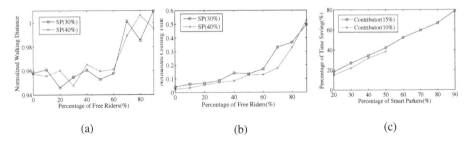

(a)   (b)   (c)

Fig. 6. Tolerance for free riders in the crowdsourcing-based smart parking system. In (a) and (b), we assume two fixed percentages of smart parkers among all drivers and record their performance as more smart parkers become free riders. In (c), we assume two fixed percentages of contributors among all drivers and record how much cruising time can be saved as more people become free riders.

As mentioned, the average cruising time of ordinary drivers does not change much as the share of smart parkers grows. This means that the overall cruising time of all drivers will remain a constant if the smart parking system is not available. If we use this cruising time as a measure of social welfare, allowing freeriding could boost social welfare, which means the overall time and fuel consumption will be reduced, as long as the service is still usable. In the following simulations, we assume the contributors account for 10% or 15% among all drivers while the percentage of smart parkers (including both contributors and free-riders) grows from 20% to 90% of the population. Then we calculate the percentage of the time saving as long as the system is able to keep smart parkers closer to their destination. As figure 6(c) shows, when contributors and free riders account for 15% and 35% of the population respectively, above 40% of the overall cruising time can be saved. As we mentioned before, it is difficult to maintain the quality of the service if the number of free-riders keeps growing while only 10% of all drivers contributing to the system. However, if the amount of contributors reaches 15%, the system can accommodate much more free-riders and reduce the overall cruising time significantly. *These results show that we should allow free riders to exist if there are enough contributors in the crowdsourcing system.*

6   Conclusion

Mobile crowdsourcing is an increasingly popular mechanism to realize applications that harness a large volume of real-time data to improve daily life. Crowdsourcing, however, brings several new issues that arise only in the context of participatory, peer-to-peer systems. In this paper, we take smart parking as a usecase and explore the possible design options to deal with these issues. At the same time, we summarize design guidelines to build mobile crowdsourcing applications.

In particular, our study leads to the following findings:

First, a naïve crowdsourcing implementation in a mobile environment can lead to 'herd' behavior rather than collective intelligence since each participant only has a limited view of his surroundings and a global picture of the physical world is not realizable. To deal with this issue, we propose 'coordinated crowdsourcing', in which a server integrates all information from participants and encourages them to explore unknown area. Our simulations show that the coordinated crowdsourcing is an effective approach in a mobile environment.

Second, the participation rate is more important than the volume of information each individual contributes. Our simulations show that, when the membership rate of a crowdsourcing system passes a certain threshold, the outcomes remain stable regardless of how much information each individual contributes and its accuracy. However, if the participation rate is low, a sophisticated data collection mechanism becomes necessary to compensate the lack of data sources.

Finally, the crowdsourcing-based application might continue to increase social welfare by tolerating free riders, as long as it can maintain a moderate level of contribution among participants. In the context of mobile crowdsourcing, free riders could reduce the quality of the crowdsourcing-based service as they might benefit from the system, and change the status of the physical environment without reporting new information. However, the aggregated social benefit for all participants could still rise significantly (at the cost of a slightly degraded service quality) as long as a certain percentage of the members keep contributing their data.

References

1. Brabham, D.C., et al.: Crowdsourcing Public Participation in Transit Planning: Preliminary Results from Next Stop Design Case. In: TRB 89th Annual Meeting Compendium (2010)
2. Sorokin, A., Forsyth, D.: Utility data annotation with Amazon Mechanical Turk. In: Computer Vision and Pattern Recognition Workshops (2008)
3. White, P.: No Vacancy: Park Slopes Parking Problem And How to Fix It, http://www.Transalt.org/newsroom/releases/126
4. Kessler, S.: How Smarter Parking Technology Will Reduce Traffic Congestion (2011), http://mashable.com/2011/04/13/smart-Parking-Tech/
5. Yan, T., et al.: CrowdPark: A Crowdsourcing-based Parking Reservation System for Mobile Phones. UMASS Technical Report, Tech. Rep. UM-CS-2011-001 (2011)
6. Waze, http://www.Waze.Com/
7. GasBuddy, Find Low Gas Prices in the USA and Canada, http://gasbuddy.Com
8. Kincaid, J.: Googles Open Spot Makes Parking A Breeze, Assuming Everyone Turns Into A Good Samaritan, http://techcrunch.com/2010/07/09/google-Parking-Open-Spot/
9. Li, B., et al.: Hunting or waiting? Discovering passenger-finding strategies from a large-scale real-world taxi dataset. In: Pervasive Computing and Communications Workshops (2011)
10. Lamba, N.: Social Media Trackles Traffic (2010), http://www.Wired.com/autopia/2010/12/ibm-Thoughts-on-a-Smarter-Planet-8/
11. Kanhere, S.S.: Participatory Sensing: Crowdsourcing Data from Mobile Smartphones in Urban Spaces. In: Mobile Data Management, MDM (2011)
12. Reddy, S., et al.: Image Browsing, Processing and Clustering for Participatory Sensing: Lessons from a DietSense Prototype. In: Workshop on Embedded Networked Sensors (2007)
13. Mun, M., et al.: PEIR, the Personal Environmental Impact Report, as a Platform for Participatory Sensing Systems Research. In: MobiSys 2009 (2009)
14. Miluzzo, E., et al.: Sensing Meets Mobile Social Networks: The Design, Implementation and Evaluation of the CenceMe Application. In: ACM SenSys, USA (November 2008)
15. Chinrungrueng, J., et al.: Smart Parking: An Application of Optical Wireless Sensor Network. In: Applications and the Internet Workshops (2007)
16. Lu, R., et al.: SPARK: A New VANET-Based Smart Parking Scheme for Large Parking Lots. In: INFOCOM 2009, pp. 1413–1421. IEEE (2009)
17. Geng, Y., Cassandras, C.G.: A new "smart parking" system based on optimal resource allocation and reservations. In: Intelligent Transportation Systems, ITSC (2011)
18. SFMTA, SFPark- About the Project, http://sfpark.org/about-the-Project/
19. Caliskan, M., et al.: Predicting Parking Lot Occupancy in Vehicular Ad Hoc Networks. In: IEEE 65th Vehicular Technology Conference, VTC 2007, pp. 277–281 (Spring 2007)
20. Anonymous "Parking Meter Rates and Time Limits", http://vancouver.ca/vanmap/p/parkingMeter.html
21. Behrisch, M., et al.: SUMO - Simulation of Urban MObility: An Overview. In: The Third International Conference on Advances in System Simulation, SIMUL 2011 (2011)
22. Tsang, F.W.K., et al.: Improved modeling of park-and-ride transfer time: Capturing the within-day dynamics. Journal of Advanced Transportation 39 (2005)

Making P-Space Smart: Integrating IoT Technologies in a Multi-office Environment

Orestis Akribopoulos, Dimitrios Amaxilatis, Vasileios Georgitzikis,
Marios Logaras, Vasileios Keramidas, Konstantinos Kontodimas,
Evangelos Lagoudianakis, Nikolaos Nikoloutsakos, Vasileios Papoutsakis,
Ioannis Prevezanos, Georgios Pyrgeris, Stylianos Tsampas,
Vasileios Voutsas, and Ioannis Chatzigiannakis

Computer Technology Institute & Press, and
Computer Engineering and Informatics Department, University of Patras
{akribopo,amaxilatis,tzikis,logaras,ichatz}@cti.gr,
{keramidas,kontodimas,lagoudiana,nikoloutsa,papoutsaki,prevezan,
pyrgeris,tsampas,voutsas}@ceid.upatras.gr

Abstract. Internet of Things technologies are considered the next big
step in Smart Building installations. Although such technologies have
been widely studied in simulation and experimental scenarios it is not so
obvious how problems of real world installations should be dealt with. In
this work we deploy IoT devices for sensing and control in a multi-office
space and employ technologies such as CoAP, RESTful interfaces and
Semantic Descriptions to integrate them with the Web. We report our
research goals, the challenges we faced, the decisions we made and the
experience gained from the design, deployment and operation of all the
hardware and software components that compose our system.

Keywords: Internet of Things, Wireless Sensor Networks, Smart Buildings, Building Automation, CoAP.

1 Introduction

Internet of Things (IoT) refers to the integration of uniquely identifiable Smart
Objects and web-based semantic entities and services via the Internet. Ultimately, IoT will offer abstractions for the sensor and actuator hardware and
wireless networking technologies that will allow application developers to operate freely without worries for low level restrictions or limitations. Although a lot
of research has been devoted towards this direction such abstractions for deploying and annotating sensor devices as smart objects is neither straightforward nor
fully standardized. Thus application development for the IoT is still tied up to
some negative characteristics of WSNs. Therefore it is still important to address
fundamental problems, as described in [5], like:

- hardware, software and networking heterogeneity,
- intermittent connectivity,

C. Borcea et al. (Eds.): MobilWare 2012, LNICST 65, pp. 31–44, 2013.

- application scaling issues,
- simplification of the development and deployment cycle,
- absence of standardized service and capability descriptions,
- big data management

Research dedicated to solving the issues and facilitate large scale installations resulted in the design and development of some important software systems like *SenseWeb* [1], *GSN* [2], *sMAP* [6] and *Cosm*[1]. These systems focus on some of the problems mentioned above and provide scalable solutions for management of big data. Yet, further research and engineering work is required.

One major challenge that has not been addressed at adequate level is to provide bidirectional communication between IoT applications and smart objects in an abstract way. In IoT applications issues like monitoring and controlling devices and workplaces require the interaction of smart objects with data and services residing on the web. The ability to trigger actions in response to special events or situations is critical to achieve goals like minimizing energy requirements or adapting environmental conditions to user preferences.

In this work, we present how we employed IoT technologies and research results to address common everyday issues in a prototype system installed in a multi-office space located in Patras, Greece called P-Space. We deal with all the levels of the system: (a) design and installation of low level hardware devices, (b) wireless networking issues for interconnecting smart objects to the Web, (c) storage of the data generated to provide historical comparisons, and (d) high level interfaces to facilitate user interaction.

The smart objects deployed in P-Space are of our own design based on the Arduino open-source electronics prototyping platform[2]. Wireless networking is achieved by attaching XBee 802.15.4 modules[3] to the arduino boards. In particular we used the ATmega328 enabled Arduino Pro Mini to drive our control and sensing boards on objects like desks, lamps, doors and faucets. The resulting smart objects are wirelessly connected, have low cost and are compatible with a broad range of sensor and actuator components.

Communication for querying smart objects for sensor data and sending commands to actuate attached devices we used the CoAP protocol [12]. We incorporate in CoAP high level descriptions of the sensor and actuator devices and utilize CoAP extensions for providing notifications for events or sensor readings on the sensor devices.

We combine CoAP with Überdust[4][3], a brokerage web service for connecting smart objects to the Internet of Things, providing storage, sharing and discovery of real-time and historical data from smart objects, devices & building installations around the world via the Web. Überdust provides high-level language-independent APIs so IoT application developers may choose their favorite programming or scripting languages. Communication with Überdust is

---

[1] https://cosm.com/
[2] http://arduino.cc/
[3] http://www.digi.com/xbee/
[4] https://github.com/Uberdust/webapp/wiki

achieved using the Überdust RESTfull and Websocket APIs, offering an easy-to-use, resource-oriented model to expose services. Publishing and consuming functionalities are implemented using both the HTTP and CoAP Get and Put methods to represent data exchange. Überdust acts as our entry point to the smart objects network, providing important IoT functionalities for the interaction of end users with the smart objects mentioned above, like CoAP [12] , RESTful interfaces and Semantic descriptions.

Finally, we also implemented a number of IoT applications to provide control and browsing capabilities over the deployed platforms. The characteristics of our system allowed us to experiment with multiple programming and scripting languages based on the requirements of each application. We experimented and developed applications with Python, Java, JavaScript, PHP and even Bash Shell scripts to perform various tasks with the sensor and actuator capabilities of the whole installation.

In order to organize the smart objects and provide interfaces and methods for querying and controlling the devices in a natural way, we propose the abstraction of Virtual Node. The idea is to group real devices that match specific semantic description as unified semantic entities. Then the application developer as well as the user can used them as a single entity. Our experience indicates that this abstraction is very useful for improving the overall ability to maintain the system and develop applications.

The next Section presents a high level architecture of the system we designed, the targets set and the design choices we made. Section 3 presents the smart objects we designed, the requirements for each device, the issues we faced and the experience we gained. Section 4 presents the CoAP protocol we used for communication in all levels of our system. Next, in Sections 5&6 we present the user interfaces we implemented to facilitate interaction with users and finally in Section 7 we explain the experience we gained from this work, the major issues still to be solved and our future targets.

2   High Level System Architecture

We designed our system in 3 separate layers that communicate with each other by exchanging messages of commands or sensor readings. Figure 1 shows the 3 independent layers and their communication via RESTful and Websocket APIs offered by Überdust.

The bottom layer comprises of the hardware sensor boards we designed and attached to objects inside P-Space. This layer provides sensor readings over wireless communication to a central controller device that acts a translator between 802.11 frames and 802.15.4 packets.

Überdust is the nerve center of our system as it is responsible for connecting the low level hardware devices with the IoT applications and interfaces enabling the rapid development of IoT applications. Überdust is designed as a Machine-to-Machine system and its functionality is provided through a semantic-based approach to facilitate IoT application development. The most innovative feature

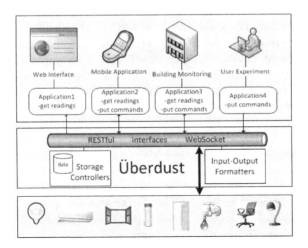

Fig. 1. High level architecture

of Überdust, is that it focuses not only on collecting data but also on allowing bidirectional communication between IoT applications and smart objects. Überdust offers a centralized control mechanism for all devices together with the storage of historical data that due to space limitations cannot be stored on the devices themselves. All messages to and from the devices pass through Überdust, which in general terms provides the functionality of an entry point so that any application can communicate with IoT devices and vice-versa.

On top of Überdust, the highest level of our system is the IoT application layer for monitoring sensor readings and controlling actuators. Most users do not actually need or have to interact directly with the sensor devices but with the abstraction provided at this level. This abstraction is one of the most interesting features of Überdust, as smart object devices can be grouped based on their semantic descriptions. We call this abstraction a Virtual Node, that is, a grouping of real devices as a common semantic entity. Usually in Multi-office or Smart building scenarios such semantic entities cover small areas like workspaces and offices, rooms, building floors or equipment groups like the heating or plumbing. We believe that Semantic entities (i.e., Virtual Nodes) are more suitable for user interfaces than the smart objects themselves as they represent in a more natural way the functions they support. Finally, this layer also includes a number of applications that are not designed for direct user interaction, like the applications that control lights based on the occupancy of the rooms or workplaces.

2.1 Integration of Applications

Überdust offers RESTful (HTTP and CoAP) and Websocket APIs for applications and smart objects. The RESTful API, based on the REpresentational State Transfer web service model, offers an easy-to-use, resource-oriented model to expose services. Publishing and consuming functionalities are implemented using both the HTTP and CoAP, Get and Put methods to represent data exchange. CoAP support is based on Californium [10], a library for parsing and generating CoAP messages, allowing direct top to bottom communication.

The WebSocket API offers the same functionalities using the IETF standardized WebSocket protocol [7]. WebSocket is a web technology providing bidirectional, full-duplex communications channels over a single TCP connection which can be used by any client or server application. Using a Websocket connection applications can receive new and historical readings or issue commands to actuators. Also, controller devices can use a Websocket connection to continuously stream new readings to the storage web service and receive actuator requests to forward to the sensors. All data messages exchanged using the WebSocket API are serialized using Google's Protocol buffers[5] a language and platform independent, extensible mechanism for encoding structured data in an efficient and extensible format.

2.2   User Interfaces

Überdust itself offers a very basic interface with no user authentication mechanism for publishing, accessing and sending information to the system as it is designed solely as a M2M system. So to provide all the above we designed applications on top of Überdust. A Drupal Website was designed to provide web based access to the system with specific drupal modules for operations, like switching lights on, controlling the HVAC units and accessing information in using time series diagrams, heat maps or pie charts. Also, as smartphones are always present in our everyday life, we designed two mobile applications for the Android and the Windows Phone platforms. The mobile phone applications offer the same operations as the Web interface, adapted to the special characteristics of each platform, focusing on the benefits of mobile devices. Both Drupal and Mobile applications use an authentication mechanism to address issues like privacy and security which are prerequisites in a Multi-office environment.

2.3   High Level Description of Available IoT Technologies

CoAP is another basic component of our architecture. All of the application and the smart objects we designed are CoAP enabled. This means that they exchange information in an standardized format, that all layers of our system can understand. The CoAP messages exchanged also contain semantic descriptions for observed events. Semantic descriptions offer access to some other IoT technologies like RDF [9] descriptions and SPARQL [13] queries. RDF is a standard model for data interchange on the Web that supports the evolution of schemas over time without requiring any changes to data consumers. RDF describes properties of devices with structured triples that can be exchanged between applications. SPARQL is a query language used to express queries over RDF structured data.

---

[5] http://code.google.com/p/protobuf/

SPARQL contains capabilities for querying required and optional graph patterns along with their conjunctions and disjunctions. As a result all IoT applications can eventually be described in a completely abstract model as a number of SPARQL queries over the RDF data provided by the smart object network.

2.4   Automatic Configuration

All the applications and hardware platforms we designed to operate with minimal human intervention. Smart objects are automatically registered on the web application when they are turned on within the communication range of controller, while updates on their metadata (e.g., location) are available only by the administrator of the system. All interfaces or applications are configured based on the information of the Überdust web application. Users or administrators simply need to provide the url of the Überdust endpoint and then menus and information or control pages are generated based on the metadata and the semantic descriptions available. As a result installation of a similar system in a different environment or building is simplified.

2.5   Use Case

The major problems we target with our work are energy conservation and intelligent building configuration. Individual rooms, offices, or even entire buildings should go into energy saving mode when unoccupied disabling any communication networks, light, climate control, warm water or standby appliances to significantly reduce their power requirements. Implementing such behaviors in low level, independent systems with no access to information about the general situation in the building is extremely difficult and not at all adaptive to changes. IoT technologies on the other side provide all the necessary tools, described above, to deal with such problems with more adaptive and targeted solutions. Also by using external information about user preferences and requirements we can create a more personalized and pleasant experience.

3   Hardware

In order to integrate the main electric and electronic appliances with the Web we developed a series of hardware boards. Our main design goals is to support wireless communication, remote programming, be inexpensive, and well supported by the open source community to get feedback. We used an Arduino Pro Mini, combined with a IEEE 802.15.4 XBee® RF module.

3.1   Smart Lamps

The Arduino boards we designed are attached to ceiling and desk lamps in every room of P-Space. To control the $230V$ AC Lamps from the $5V$ I/O pins of the Arduino we use relays. Each board is able to control up to two different lamps so that we can provide users with multiple levels of lighting, e.g., low during a sunny day or high during the night. This allows us to reduce the power requirements as people tend to turn all the lights during the whole day. Furthermore we decided to introduce a manual override in case of hardware failure.

On top of the above, boards are also equipped with sensors for measuring luminosity, temperature and motion via Pyroelectric infrared sensors (Figure 2).

Fig. 2. Sensor Board for Smart Lamps

The Smart Lamps are operated by an application running at the top layer of our architecture. The sensed values for luminosity are periodically reported to Überdust and motion events generated by the PIR sensor are reported on a per-event basis. The application combines these values to decide when to turned on and off the lamps to provide better working conditions. To achieve the requirement of an energy-saving application when no people are present in the room or building (based on the readings provide by the PIR sensors), an energy saving scheme is initialized. At this point only lamps are turned off to conserve energy, but in the future the target is to extend the installation to control devices like printers or monitors that operate in stand-by modes while not in use but still conserve even small amounts on power.

3.2   Smart HVAC

The HVAC controller is a developed in order to substitute the 38 KHz IR controllers used (Toyotomi brand) by an Arduino. For this purpose we developed a software library which allows us to autonomously control a wide range of HVAC devies, that are compatible with a specific IR protocol used widely in this particular area. The library, provides an API which substitutes all functions supported by a `R51L1/BGE` remote controller used principally by Toyotomi. Additionally, the API provides us an extra function in order to send a raw input signal, modulated in 38 KHz carrier frequency.

Our library is structured so that it supports scalability by adding new, more complex functions, or functions compatible with a wider range of HVAC models even modulated in different carrier frequencies. As an overview of the IR protocol, we see the following general characteristics in the majority of the supported functions:

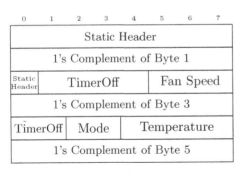

0	1	2	3	4	5	6	7
Static Header							
1's Complement of Byte 1							
Static Header	TimerOff			Fan Speed			
1's Complement of Byte 3							
TimerOff	Mode		Temperature				
1's Complement of Byte 5							

(a) Toyotomi Control payload   (b) HVAC control board

Fig. 3. HVAC controller Payload and Arduino Board

1. The useful information consists of 6 bytes which are complementary in pairs at the level of bits.
2. In most functions, the three non-inverted bytes (1st, 3rd and 5th) contain coded the whole new state, represented in absolute values.
3. Every single bit of the above 48 ones, is encoded as follows: $1 \rightarrow 1000$ and $0 \rightarrow 10$.
4. A static head and tail piece of information is added to the above signal.
5. In the final input signal, every single bit take 21 cycles of 38 KHz frequency, i.e. about 553 μs.
6. The input signal is modulated with a 38 KHz carrier signal and the final one drives an IR LED in order to be transmitted to the HVAC unit.

Figure 3(a) shows how data are structured inside a control message and in Figure 3(b) depicts the final version of the control board in its casing.

3.3   Security Sensors

Another important part of the system is the sensors that report the state of the windows and doors (open/closed). Although the operation of these sensors is pretty simple and straightforward their operation is important in many other sub systems. To understand whether windows are open we used the very simple and widely tested Hall effect sensors used in home alarm systems. This obvious benefit from this installation is that the infrastructure can be used as a highly advanced low-cost alarm system, that can facilitate sophisticated notification systems. The list of supported notification targets include mobile phones via SMS, email, prerecorded telephone calls even using technologies like Skype, desktop notification systems in addition to the common but always effective sound and visual alarms. A second very important contribution of this application is that based on the state of the windows we can disable the operation of the HVAC units as it is completely environmentally unfriendly, e.g., to use Air conditioning while windows are open.

3.4 Smart Faucet

This board provides control of a water valve in an integrated method to the general system designed. It allows controlling the water supply to avoid flooding or detect possible leakages that may result is loss of water. The board designed operates in 3 levels. Locally it can control a vale in order to provide water by a faucet in the bathroom. Also the initial target was to use two valves in order to provide water in a predefined acceptable temperature but this proved to be unrealistic due the operation restrictions of the valves, as it was not possible to control the flow of the water accurately. A second part of the board detects flooding with a simple circuit that short-circuits submerged in water. If this is detected then the water supply is stopped to prevent problems with electrical equipment and possible damage to furniture or the building.

A `Sharp` `GP2Y0A02` infrared distance sensor was used to detect hands placed under the faucet. The sensor measures the distance of any obstacle within a range of 5-120cm. Distance is measured via the voltage change on the two ends of the sensor as a resistor using the analog inputs of the Arduino. Voltage level is polled using a time interval of some milliseconds and the measurements are translated to distance values measured in cm.

Calculating the exact distance was not as important as detecting the any obstructions (e.g., hands) under the faucet is the only case we examine, thus the sensor's precision was inadequate. When the distance measured by the sensor, drops below 35cm, which is the distance between the sensor and the washbasin, the water valve is activated, letting the user use the faucet.

4 CoAP

The Constrained Application Protocol (CoAP), is a draft by IETF CoRE working group which deals with Constrained Restful Environments. It provides exactly the subset of HTTP methods (`GET, PUT, POST, DELETE`) which is necessary to offer RESTfull web services in WSNs. We work with the implementation of the 8th version [12] of CoAP presented in [4]. Messages follow a specific message format, which is simple enough to be processed and used by both IoT desktop applications and smart objects.

4.1 Quality of Service

CoAP communication between endpoints is based on a lightweight request/response model. Message exchange is asynchronous and based on UDP as reliable and unreliable CoAP. With the unreliable model, endpoints transmit their messages and there is no way to confirm delivery of each individual message. On the reliable model, acknowledgement messages are sent upon delivery, something similar to TCP, acknowledging the other endpoint for the receipt of the message. Messages that are not acknowledged, either because of communication or hardware failure are retransmitted up to 4 times in exponentially increased time intervals. Responses are by default piggybacked on the acknowledgement messages so that the actual response is part of the acknowledgement. Piggybacking is also enabled by default to reduce the messages exchanges in half and thus reduce the traffic inside the network and the total power requirements. Separate response messages if the applications request it explicitly.

4.2 Notification Mechanism

A common problem when dealing with active sensors is how often we need to request an updated value for the sensor. We always want to know the latest value available, but working on WSNs with many constrained devices, would be catastrophic for the network's efficiency and the power consumption to request new values about multiple resources every a few seconds. To solve this problem CoAP introduces the **Observe** [8] CoAP extension which defines a mechanism for clients to register as observers and for servers to push updated resource representations to interested clients, while still keeping the properties of the RESTful interface. New values are automatically pushed to the registered clients while clients can define threshold values in order to be notified only when the updated values fit their interests. In order to get a fresh value even if it's below the threshold, CoAP Observe, periodically pushes the latest values to clients, like a notification that the device is still functional.

4.3 Discovery of Resources

The discovery of resources offered by a CoAP endpoint is extremely important in machine-to-machine applications where no humans intervene in the loop and static interfaces result in fragility. Our CoAP endpoints support the CoRE Link Format [11] and offer the .well-known/core resource which responds with all the available resources on the server. This defines how a CoAP endpoint can inform a Client of its resources, in a format that is recognized from both ends. Together with the resource URIs several attributes can be included (like Semantic descriptions), offering information about the resource type, the interface description, the expected size or even a text description. Explicit request of available resources from one CoAP endpoint is avoided and mainly done during the auto configuration phase. Client requests for available resources and nodes, are directly answered by the gateway where all nodes register themselves.

4.4 Sensing and Actuation with CoAP

As mentioned before, we use CoAP to facilitate communication between IoT applications and smart objects. CoAP offers this functionality through the RESTful api available on the Endpoints. Like in the HTTP protocol, CoAP offers

GET,PUT,POST & DELETE methods for interaction with the resources of the end-point. In our system we use only GET and PUT. GET resources describe sensing capabilities. Applications can register on them to receive notification for all the new values that become available. PUT resources, on the other hand are used to describe the actuator of our system. When actuators receive a put request for one of their resources the equivalent action is performed.

5   Drupal Web Interface

User interfaces are a key factor for every system. In order to make the automations of P-Space accessible to end users, we needed a friendly, easy-to-use environment accessible from everyone everywhere. We developed a web site using the open source Drupal CMS, because of it's flexibility, reliability and security.

Using Drupal's API combined with our technologies, we developed a package of modules to view the status and control the actuators of P-Space. The communication with Überdust is done using the RESTful interface and JSON formatted data. Sending commands is limited to certain authorized users only, utilizing the easily configurable permission system of Drupal. The modules developed are :

Monitor Module: Users and guests can view the location and status of every node in P-Space, over a bird's eye view of the building. To print the image, we used the Scalable Vector Graphics (SVG) format, which can be produced dynamically from our code and create areas for each node which can then be easily handled with JavaScript to produce effects on specific events or to change styles based on the state reported by the sensors.

Control Interface: Users can view the status and control lights in each room by clicking on switches. On click, via Javascript an HTTP request is sent to Überdust using the RESTful interface in order to trigger the suitable action on the smart lights hardware. Instead of continuously polling the status of all the lights in the building we use WebSockets to receive notifications of the changes in the state of the smart lights in real time. Polling is a feature that has adverse effects on both the utilization of the available bandwidth as well as on the operation of the core web service.

HVAC Control: A user interface created on top of the actual image of the remote control of the HVAC units is used to control it via the website. Settings for the two fully controlled units in the two rooms change using Drupal's Form API and then the commands are sent once again to Überdust using the RESTful interface.

Finally, each smart object is available on its own page, where we can retrieve all the associated information. This interface supports a special operation used mainly for debugging in the first stages of the installation of the system where users can send explicit binary messages to the smart object.

All modules can be easily configured and extended to include specific support for any new devices added to Überdust. All information for the devices like the position and the capabilities is actually stored using Überdust and configuration done via request to the RESTful interface resulting to a completely adaptable system to all changes that may happen like device failures, repositioning of devices or extension of the underlying network.

6 Mobile Phone Applications

We develop an alternative approach to monitoring and controling P-Space that is available for Android®and Windows Phone®. Both implementations act as clients for Überdust web services and offer browsing of sensor readings and actuator status based on the privileges of each user. Some of the features offered by the Überdust mobile applications are:

- the authentication mechanism where, after launching the application, users needs to enter their credentials to get access to the functionality provided by their role.
- Important information about a specific workplace or room, like temperature, humidity, luminosity, the status of a lights, or the current consumption of electrical devices (computers, a/c units), etc.
- A notification mechanism for special aspects like security security through the notifications from motion sensors or sensors on windows and doors.
- Also we can simplify our life by having remote access to control electrical devices such as boilers or a/c units without the need to search for the remotes, or switches.

The Android application was developed for Android 2.2, API Level 8. Connection with the web server is accomplished through a RESTful interface by using JSON formatted data. The application needs a minimal bandwidth to operate on permanent basis as data for sensors are cached and not retrieved every time the user launches the application. Also, the user interface uses the external android library ViewPagerIndicator which allows us to have smooth transitions by sliding through different views. The GraphView library also added support for graph of the historical data available on Überdust to have better view of how sensor readings change over time in order to identify special events (e.g., power spikes or sudden temperature changes).

The Windows Phone application was developed for Windows Phone 7.1 using "Microsoft®Visual Studio Express for Windows Phone" SDK. Its functionality is similar to the Android application and operates using Überdust RESTful interface to retrieve data in JSON format.

Both applications offer support for multiple profiles where users can setup different Überdust servers to use (e.g., their home and office buildings). Retrieved information is sorted based on the location of the devices. Users can also go through a different list based on the functionality each device or room offers. Especially for actuators authenticated users can send commands to nodes that are controlling devices like setting the temperature of the a/c unit or switch on lights or the boiler.

P-Space Overview Page

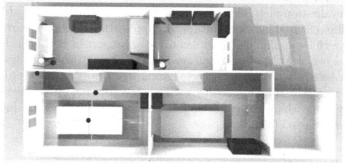

7   Conclusion

The Internet of Things is a technological revolution that represents the future of computing and communications while its development depends on dynamic technical innovation in a number of important fields, and especially in wireless sensor networks. Connecting sensory networks to the Internet creates endless opportunities for applications and services, new emerging models of operation.

Currently many researchers are working on designing, developing and evaluating new protocols, embedded IP stacks and operating systems for WSNs. Many ongoing projects are aiming at interconnecting WSNs with the Internet and establishing programming environments for developing applications.

In this work we presented our efforts in designing smart services for a multi-office building, developing and deploying hardware extensions for electric and electronic appliances and integrating their operation with the Web. Our work shows how IoT devices can be applied to real world scenarios and installations by using very recent technologies and open standards.

Indeed some methodologies and technologies such as CoAP, RESTful interfaces, WebSockets, JSON format are very usuful fo the integration of the software systems across the IP-stack with the hardware devices. Furthermore the Virtual Nodes abstraction offered by Überdust was very helpful in reducing the complexity of controlling multiple devices as a single logical device and aggregating readings from multiple sensors and across different time windows. We reported newly-developed Drupal modules that simply implement application logic and provide human-computer-interaction using Web technologies. Similarly the smartphone applications exploit the same RESTful interfaces and WebSocket APIs in order to access the current state of the devices in JSON format. Both environments offer all the necessary tools to establish communication and manipulate the data received with minimum programming effort.

However, we believe that our approach was complex and required a big team for the development of applications exploiting the merged infrastructure. The current methodologies & technologies available are not enough to have a tremendous impact on the development of Future Internet applications. This is due to the fact that despite the IP-based integration of the embedded world, application-level protocols, software and development environments, but also design and evaluation methodologies in the Internet and in the embedded world are vastly different and lack integration. An application developer currently still has to bridge this gap manually; he has to be an expert in both worlds.

There is a lot of future work that needs to be done in this direction so that devices can be self-configured using semantic descriptions and by minimizing human intervention. It is important to work towards infrastructures that can adapt to dynamic changes in the environment as new devices are introduced, rellocated or removed from the space.

Acknowledgements. This work is partially supported by the European Union under contract numbers ICT-258885 SPITFIRE.

References

1. Kansal, J.L.A., Nath, S., Zhao, F.: Senseweb: An infrastructure for shared sensing. In: IEEE MultiMedia, pp. 8–13 (2007)
2. Aberer, K., Hauswirth, M., Salehi, A.: The Global Sensor Networks middleware for efficient and flexible deployment and interconnection of sensor networks. In: 7th Int. Middleware Conference (2006)
3. Akribopoulos, O., Amaxilatis, D., Chatzigiannakis, I.: Towards integrating iot devices with the web. In: 7th IEEE Conference on Emerging Technologies & Factory Automation, ETFA 2012 (2012)
4. Amaxilatis, D., Georgitzikis, V., Giannakopoulos, D., Chatzigiannakis, I.: Employing internet of things technologies for building automation. In: Conf. on Emerging Technologies & Factory Automation, ETFA 2012 (2012)
5. Corcho, O., García-Castro, R.: Five challenges for the semantic sensor web. Semantic Web 1(1,2), 121–125 (2010)
6. Dawson-Haggerty, S., Jiang, X., Tolle, G., Ortiz, J., Culler, D.: Smap: a simple measurement and actuation profile for physical information. In: 8th ACM Conf. on Embedded Networked Sensor Systems, SenSys 2010, pp. 197–210 (2010)
7. Fette, I., Melnikov, A.: The websocket protocol. Proposed statndard, IETF (2011)
8. Hartke, K.: Observing Resources in CoAP. Internet-Draft, IETF (2012) (work in progress)
9. Hayes, P. (ed.): RDF Semantics. W3C Recommendation. World Wide Web Consortium (2004)
10. Kovatsch, M., Mayer, S., Ostermaier, B.: Moving application logic from the firmware to the cloud: Towards the thin server architecture for the internet of things. In: 6th Int. Conf. on Innovative Mobile and Internet Services in Ubiquitous Computing, IMIS 2012 (2012)
11. Shelby, Z.: CoRE Link Format. Internet-Draft, IETF (2011) (work in progress)
12. Shelby, Z., Hartke, K., Bormann, C., Frank, B.: Constrained Application Protocol (CoAP). Internet-Draft, IETF (2011) (work in progress)
13. SPARQL query language for RDF. Technical report, World Wide Web Consortium (2008)

Middleware for Semantic Multicast
in Spontaneous Multi-hop Networks

Paolo Bellavista and Carlo Giannelli

DISI – Università di Bologna
Viale Risorgimento 2, 40136 Bologna, Italy
{paolo.bellavista,carlo.giannelli}@unibo.it

Abstract. Spontaneous Multi-hop Networks (SMNs) are emerging as a novel networking and communication paradigm, strongly pushed by the widespread availability of smartphones equipped with heterogeneous wireless connectivity and powerful computing capabilities. SMN nodes can opportunistically exploit peer-to-peer contacts to seamlessly share resources/content in an impromptu and transient way. The paper presents a novel 3-layer modeling abstraction for multicast in SMNs, in order to characterize the different kinds of possible inter-node interaction based on different degrees of expressiveness and social-aware collaboration. In addition, we originally present the design and implementation of some novel semantic-based multicast mechanisms that efficiently target SMN nodes based on user interests and that are integrated into our SMN middleware solution. First preliminary results show the feasibility of the approach and its limited overhead.

Keywords: Spontaneous Multi-hop Networking, Multicast, Resource/Content Sharing, Smartphones, Middleware.

1 Introduction

Spontaneous networking is receiving growing attention for its promising aspects of better exploitation of available wireless connectivity, resource connectivity sharing, and immediate connectivity in regions with difficult coverage [1, 2]. The most relevant and specific property of Spontaneous Multi-hop Networks (SMNs) is that they are enabled by the willingness of social interaction and resource sharing via impromptu interconnection of people and their carried mobile personal devices, e.g., smartphones and tablets [3, 4]. In SMNs mobile devices should seamlessly discover and interact one another opportunistically and without any prior mutual knowledge, by exploiting any wireless opportunity available, e.g., Bluetooth ad-hoc links and Wi-Fi infrastructure-based ones. In particular, group-related behaviors and the ever increasing willingness to share rich user-generated contents, also pertaining to the personal sphere, call for a user-centric communication paradigm shift, where the ad-hoc interconnection of mobile devices in direct visibility plays a central role.

Sharing user-generated content (and, more in general, under-utilized resources) over SMNs requires new forms of node collaboration and communication, also

C. Borcea et al. (Eds.): MobilWare 2012, LNICST 65, pp. 45–61, 2013.
© Institute for Computer Sciences, Social Informatics and Telecommunications Engineering 2013

responding to new and/or extended paradigms, possibly always based on the standard substrate of universally available IP protocols for immediate deployability, but substantially enhancing their expressive power and effectiveness when applied to the novel SMN scenarios. In particular, we claim the primary importance of supporting a multiplicity of different multicast communication paradigms (e.g., based on a variety of mechanisms, from simple-to-manage and efficient syntax-based packet dispatching to more powerful and complex semantic-based discovery) at different layers of abstraction and at the same time, suitable for different application requirements.

To clarify the envisioned scenario by starting with some practical usage scenarios, let us consider the following examples of SMN collaboration, at different abstraction layers, aiming to discover and invoke a collaborative file sharing service (Figure 1):

1) in a simple and traditional deployment scenario, nodes are located in the same private IP subnet and can exchange data in a "direct" way, e.g., by exploiting UPnP to discover/advertise available services or SAMBA to expose local directories as if they were network drives;

2) in the second case, SMN nodes residing in two or more non-coordinated IP subnets (with possibly overlapping and conflicting IP addresses) are willing to collaborate by working together on dispatching packets from senders to receivers at a higher level of abstraction. For instance, node A may send discovery packets via local flooding in order to retrieve the nodes in its locality that host the file sharing service; neighbor nodes may cooperate by dispatching the request to remote nodes residing in other IP subnets; finally nodes offering the file sharing service may reply to node A, possibly by exploiting the chain of dispatchers used for service discovery. Note that in this case nodes can participate to many-to-many communications even if they are located in different private IP subnets with clashing addresses by performing packet dispatching at the application layer and by solving addressing/routing issues at this higher layer. However, if nodes have limited knowledge of their surrounding environment, discovery packets should be sent via flooding, with all the potentially connected limitations in terms of overhead and scalability;

3) in the third and most challenging/innovative scenario, we would like to have nodes (typically smartphones carried by users) enabled to maintain and share content related to their users. As a practical example, let us consider a semantically-enhanced and opportunistic file sharing service. Alice specifies that she is interested in music and skiing contents, Bob in skiing and gardening, and Cate in tennis. When discovering a file sharing service, Alice specifies that she is interested only in nodes whose users have common content interests, e.g., thus preventing from connecting to Cate's node and its offered contents. Of course, this requires mechanisms to proactively acquire additional knowledge about some SMN nodes, with the possibly associated costs in terms of overhead and scalability.

The paper presents a novel 3-layer multicast model for service discovery and content sharing in SMNs that clearly categorizes and describes the different mechanisms and opportunities available in the three scenarios rapidly described above. The three layers of the model are supported by an original middleware solution for SMNs that we have designed and implemented. In particular, in this paper we originally focus on our solution for novel semantic-based multicast mechanisms (third layer), which represent the most novel and challenging case of multicast communication based on users' contextual metadata. The proposed solution exploits Semantic Web mechanisms to describe user characteristics and appropriately dispatch packets to most interested users. Thus, it performs packet delivery while completely decoupling senders and receivers, by focusing on users' characteristics rather than locations/addresses of their associated nodes.

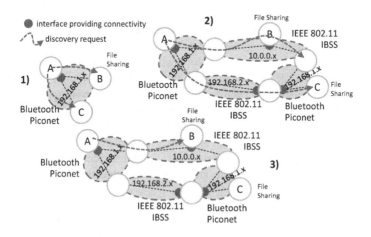

Fig. 1. Service discovery in SMNs at different layers of abstraction

The remainder of the paper is organized as follows: Section 2 details our novel and layered multicast model. Section 3 presents our original multicast mechanisms for SMNs based on semantic data, by describing the primary design/implementation choices we made in the realization of their prototype. Some preliminary performance results, followed by related work and conclusive remarks, end the paper.

2   A 3-Layer Multicast Model for SMNs

We identify three different layers of abstraction for multicast in SMNs, corresponding to three different possible communication overlays, each one characterized by a different degree of node collaboration and different definition of communication endpoints, in relation to both endpoint identifiers (how to specify the identity of a participating node) and endpoint addresses (how participating nodes can be reached by multicast communications). In particular:

1) **The Traditional IP** layer is based on IP addressing (both for endpoint identity and addressing) in private subnets where nodes interact one another directly. On the one hand, networking and local broadcasting issues are automatically solved by traditional IP-based solutions at layer3 and layer4 of the classical OSI stack.

On the other hand, there is the strong limitation that only nodes in the same private IP subnet can cooperate directly, e.g., in order to avoid address clashing between possibly overlapping IP namespaces;

2) **The Spontaneous Multi-hop** layer stems from the need of a multi-hop routing overlay in order to allow SMN nodes to dispatch packets from senders to receivers that do not reside in the same private IP subnet, by solving the associated identification and addressing issues. In this case, SMN nodes should be willing to collaborate more actively, not only in the case they are service endpoints: intermediary nodes have to offer a portion of their computing/communication resources to receive, manage, store, and forward traversing packets. Let us point out that SMNs based on users' cooperation usually originate from the opportunistic interconnection of private IP subnets in proximity [3]: users create layer2 links via multiple and possibly heterogeneous wireless interfaces; this usually leads to the configuration of IP parameters in an uncoordinated way, e.g., IP addresses are assigned autonomously by each node to its clients. As a consequence, multi-hop paths in SMNs have to exploit different single-hop IP networks, without a homogeneous address space (making unsuitable the exploitation of traditional IP-based identification and packet routing). As better detailed in the following section, the proposed spontaneous multi-hop layer solves endpoint identity and addressing issues by exploiting absolute node identifiers and subjective DSR-like multi-hop paths, respectively [5];

3) **The Semantic Dispatching** layer enables the delivery of multicast packets in a completely distributed way among loosely coupled endpoints. It does not require the sender to know its destination endpoints (neither identifiers nor addressing) when generating communication packets, because the dynamic determination of suitable endpoints is based on semantic data associated with the multicast packet and SMN nodes relationships. In other words, senders specify the characteristics of the endpoints that should receive the multicast communication rather than their identities or addresses. On the one hand, to enable this higher expressive power, node cooperation should be higher because nodes have to collaborate not only to dispatch packets, but also to agree on formats to describe users' interests and contents (and to disclose these data to participating nodes). On the other hand, this overlay potentially enables better exploitation of shared resources because it allows to multicast packets only to dynamically determined and really interested receivers. Let us notice that this layer has the notable positive side-effect of greatly facilitating the automatically filtered management of the ever increasing amount of reachable nodes (and their offered discoverable resources/services). For instance, users interested in retrieving only jazz music in a SMN could feel uncomfortable if they are forced to discover and access a large number of apparently similar instances of the same file sharing service, check all the corresponding lists of shared content, and manually identify the only jazz-related files; on the contrary, once users' contextual data are available, it is possible to prioritize the available file sharing instances, e.g., by first inquiring only the SMN nodes that belong to users who are fond of jazz music.

3   The Design of a Middleware Solution Implementing Our 3-Layer Multicast Model

We claim that content sharing in SMNs calls for the availability of middleware support with mechanisms at all the layers of our previously presented model: mechanisms at the three different layers should not be mutually exclusive but coexist, also in the same deployment environment; endpoints should dynamically adopt the layer best fitting their application requirements, by possibly benefitting from different layers even in different phases of the same interaction. For instance, the semantic dispatching layer can be exploited to discover the set of remote users sharing at least k topics of interest with the sender while, once identified a specific content, its delivery can use the traditional IP or the spontaneous multi-hop layers, e.g., depending on whether endpoints are in the same IP subnet or not.

Table 1. Concise summary of the properties of the introduced multicast layers

Layer	Scenario	Cooperation	Endpoint
Traditional IP	Basic layer, suitable by itself for static/administered/small networks	Service provisioning	IP address as both identifier and address
Spontaneous Multi-hop	Packet delivering in heterogeneous, contiguous, dynamic, and uncoordinated networks	Packet dispatching	nodeId as identifier (absolute), DSR-like IP sequence as address (relative)
Semantic Dispatching	Efficient service discovery in large spontaneous networks	Information sharing	Semantic-based: either direct (relative) or blind (absolute)

In the following, we recall very concisely the main characteristics and properties of the traditional IP layer and of the spontaneous multi-hop one (already described in the literature); on the contrary, we will go into the needed architecture and design detail about our novel middleware support for semantic dispatching multicast.

3.1   Traditional IP Layer

As well-known, the traditional IP layer identifies remote hosts via IP addresses and receiving processes via port numbers. Nodes residing in the same IP subnet easily communicate in a direct way, possibly exploiting native broadcast mechanisms. However, let us recall that for inter-subnet communications there is the need of managing routing tables, by updating them whenever nodes join, leave, or move. For this reason, the traditional IP layer is generally considered unsuitable by itself for the interconnection of SMN islands [1]. In fact, the self-organized, not explicitly administered, and volatile nature of SMNs pushes for novel solutions, not based on proactive configuration of network topology, but taking advantage of mission-oriented connectivity created among nodes that opportunistically collaborate to support their socially interacting users, e.g., to share personal pictures or transmit multimedia streams.

3.2   Spontaneous Multi-Hop Layer

One possible solution to support multicast communications at the spontaneous multi-hop layer is given by our Real Ad-hoc Multi-hop Peer-to-peer (RAMP) middleware, in particular by its RAMP Dispatcher component [6]. RAMP supports spontaneous multi-hop communication independently from how underlying (possibly heterogeneous) links/IP sub-networks have been autonomously and independently created. RAMP nodes cooperate at the middleware layer to dispatch packets, with no need to modify routing tables at the operating-system level, thus achieving the degree of dynamicity needed in SMNs [7].

On the one hand, our RAMP middleware supports a notion of endpoint different from traditional IP, by identifying remote nodes in terms of globally unique *nodeIds*. On the other hand, RAMP performs addressing in a DSR-like fashion, i.e., based on traditional IP addresses of intermediary nodes composing the path between senders and receivers. In this way RAMP distinguishes between identifiers (used to refer nodes) and addresses (used to reach nodes). In addition, while traditional IP addressing is absolute and shared among every node, RAMP addressing is relative to the sender, since different nodes may exploit different intermediaries to reach the same destination through different paths (composed by different and heterogeneous links).

3.3   Semantic Dispatching Layer

The semantic dispatching layer has the goal of completely decoupling senders and receivers, effectively supporting the abstraction of content-based multicast. In fact, it allows specifying endpoints based on shared contents and semantic similarity, i.e., by detailing receiver characteristics rather than its identifier or the path to reach it.

As a consequence, the communication semantic is inherently multicast, as relates to both destination nodes (multiple nodes may receive the same packet) and destination processes (multiple processes on the same node may receive the same packet). The idea is that the semantic dispatching middleware should be able to transparently manage packet exchange and to check whether a node should receive a packet or not, while application-level senders know neither the identities nor the addresses of their receivers. To this purpose, we propose a middleware solution that stores local user's data together with (a subset of) information about previously contacted remote users (partial local knowledge of SMN participants, opportunistically built at runtime based on launched queries). As better detailed in Section 4, to shorten the bootstrap phase and leverage the semantic-based discovery of remote users, collaborative nodes distribute partial knowledge about their spontaneous network by periodically broadcasting subsets of local user's data. In addition, it is worth noting from the beginning that the semantic dispatching layer should exploit the potential advantages of a cross-layer approach between user information and routing layers.

The rest of the section introduces our mechanisms to support semantic-based content delivery, namely, semantic multicast and semantic forward. The former is based on two novel communication primitives aiming at completely decoupling sender and receiver endpoints; the latter allows efficiently widening the scope of packet delivery based on distributed awareness of the established SMNs. The main objective is to achieve a proper trade-off among delivery correctness (packets delivered only to interested nodes) and efficiency (in terms of both communication and processing overhead), by also considering specific requirements expressed at the sender side.

3.3.1 Semantic Multicast

Multicast senders define their sets of interested receivers, possibly with the fine granularity of the single packet, based on their criteria specification (see the following). The set of semantic multicast receivers may depend on the location where and the time when delivery criteria are checked. In fact, different SMN nodes may have very different runtime knowledge of other SMN participants, e.g., since a node may have joined the network before/after other nodes or may have interacted less/more frequently with neighbors. Also based on this observation, we have identified (and decided to support) two types of semantic multicast primitives, namely Direct Multicast and Blind Multicast, with different characteristics in terms of delivery correctness and communication overhead.

Direct Multicast is based on the concept of applying delivery criteria on senders. Very concisely, depending on node-related data collected by a sender, our middleware identifies the set of nodes the packet should be delivered to; then, packets are sent directly to destination nodes via unicast communication; finally, receiving nodes propagate the packet upward to the application layer, without performing any additional check/filtering operation.

Let us note that our Direct Multicast implements the above delivery semantics lazily, with no strict consistency. In fact, senders usually have incomplete and not up-to-date knowledge of remote nodes' data (e.g., about their preferences), it is not possible to ensure that only and all the nodes actually verifying the specified criteria will receive an associated packet. For instance, the sender could not be aware of the fact that a remote user has just added/removed "skiing" in her interest list. For this reason, Direct Multicast is unsuitable for scenarios with highly varying preferences or stringent correctness requirements. However, the associated computing/communication overhead is limited because criteria are checked only once on the sender-side and packets are directly delivered to locally-selected destination nodes.

Figure 2 depicts a simple and practical example of Direct Multicast. Only some nodes are semantically-enabled, i.e., manage and dispatch local and remote preference data (dashed circles). Node S sends a packet via Direct Multicast to nodes interested in "gardening" ("g" tag). The packet is delivered only to a subset of potential receivers, i.e., node X and node W; node Z does not receive the packet since it has just joined the network and not yet exchanged preference data with node S.

Blind Multicast is based on the idea of applying delivery criteria only on the receiver side. Criteria are attached to packets and delivered exploiting the RAMP Dispatcher broadcast mechanism, by flooding packets to SMN participants in a TTL-bound fashion. Nodes receiving these packets dispatch their content to local applications registered to receive multicast packets only if the specified criteria are locally verified.

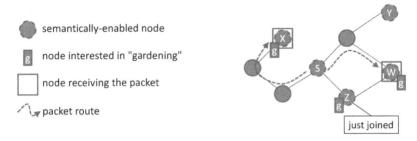

Fig. 2. Direct Multicast

Let us stress that, if compared with Direct Multicast, Blind Multicast can ensure a larger coverage of the multicast destination group. In fact, since each node has full and up-to-date knowledge of its own context (e.g., updated preference data), only and all applications running on top of nodes actually verifying the specified criteria at packet reception time will receive the packet. In addition, since packets are delivered by exploiting the RAMP Dispatcher broadcast mechanism [6], also nodes unknown by senders at packet sending time will receive the packet. However, the disadvantage is in i) packet delivery also to not interested SMN participants and ii) criteria checking needed at any node.

Figure 3 shows that Blind Multicast, if compared with Direct Multicast, also allows packet delivery to nodes the sender has not previously interacted with, e.g., node Z. Node S sends the packet to every nearby node, even if only a subset of them is actually interested in receiving it; of course, nodes outside the TTL boundaries are not interested by the blind multicast, e.g., node X.

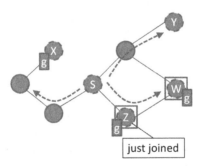

Fig. 3. Blind Multicast (with TTL=2)

3.3.2 Semantic Forward

Based on Direct and Blind Multicast primitives, our middleware also supports the capability of forwarding multicast packets in such a way to maximize the coverage of interested SMN nodes while minimizing communication overhead. The basic idea is that a subset of SMN nodes, which are particularly willing to collaborate, after receiving a multicast packet (either via Direct or Blind Multicast), not only propagate the payload to the local application layer but also re-transmit the packet to remote nodes.

Nodes receiving forwarded packets perceive them as if they were sent by original senders. Note that a node could forward a packet even if it is not interested in it, e.g., in the case of a Blind Multicast packet whose criteria are not locally verified.

To achieve a good tradeoff between coverage and limited overhead, we exploit the principle of locality: the primary assumption is that the closer a receiver node, the greater the interest of the sender that the node receives the packet. Based on this consideration, our solution forwards packets by exploiting Blind Multicast when close to senders, Direct Multicast when far from senders. As much as the distance from original senders increases, our solution adopts the following equation to decrease the probability to re-transmit packets via Blind Multicast:

$$BP = SBP \cdot ED^{\#FW} \qquad\qquad\qquad \text{if } \#FW \leq MF \qquad (1)$$

where **Blind Probability (BP)** in the [0,1] range is the probability forwarding nodes exploit the Blind Multicast mechanism to re-send packets, **Starting Blind Probability (SBP)** in the [0, 1] range is the BP value at the first forward, and **Exponential Decaying (ED)** in the]0, 1] range tunes how packets should be forwarded in the successive forwarding steps. At each forward, the middleware computes the BP value and exploits Blind Multicast if a randomly generated value in the [0, 1] range is lower than or equal to BP, Direct Multicast otherwise. Moreover, retransmissions are inhibited if the amount of forwards has reached the **Max Forwards (MF)** value.

Based on (1) and as a general consideration, our solution adopts Blind Multicast more probably in initial forwards and Direct Multicast in the following ones. Thus, it achieves the notable effect of disseminating information with a decreasing overhead and correctness gradient, i.e., the greater the distance from the original sender, the lower the imposed overhead and the lower the probability that interested nodes receive the packet. Application developers can tune the behavior of the forwarding mechanism by appropriately setting MF, SBP, and ED values, in a fine-grained and per packet way. In particular,

- the greater the SBP value, the greater the communication overhead; on the contrary, the lower the SBP value, the lower the probability to reach far nodes interested in the packet. For instance, if SBP is equal to 1, the first forward is always performed in a Blind way, while if SBP is equal to 0, forwards are always performed according to the Direct way;
- the greater the ED value, the slower our middleware switches from Blind to Direct mechanisms. ED equal to 1 means that BP is always equal to SBP, ED equal to 0.5 means that at each forward the BP value halves, ED value equal to 0.1 means that at each forward the BP value is 1/10 of the previous forward step.

Packet forwarding is performed either if packets are sent via Direct Multicast and the local nodes are receivers or if packets are sent via Blind Multicast and TTL is equal to 0. In other words, in case of Direct Multicast only actual receivers can forward packets, while in case of Blind Multicast only last receivers can forward them.

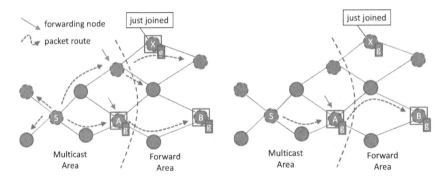

Fig. 4. Packet Forward based on Blind (left) and Direct (right) Multicast

Figure 4 provides two examples at the two extremes in the range of possible cases. On the left, node S performs a Blind Multicast with TTL = 2 and SBP = 1; on the right, node S performs a Direct Multicast with SBP = 0 (nodes dispatch local interests to neighbors at 2-hop distance); MF and ED are ignored in the depicted scenario for the sake of clarity. In the former case, the packet is correctly delivered to every node with interest in it, but at the cost of transmitting the packet also to additional nodes; in the latter case, traffic overhead is lower, but node X does not receive the packet.

3.3.3 Semantic Dispatching Information Management

To support our solution for interest/content matching, senders and receivers must adopt a common vocabulary. To this purpose, we adopt simple and reasonably lightweight Semantic Web mechanisms to store and manage data: user preference data are stored as Resource Description Framework (RDF) graphs, while packet delivery criteria are implemented as SPARQL Protocol and RDF Query Language (SPARQL) queries. We have implemented query and application examples based on the Friend Of A Friend (FOAF) vocabulary. By adopting a specific ontology, on the one hand, we demonstrate the feasibility of our approach and provide final users with ready-to-use examples (see below); on the other hand, we encourage middleware extension and refinement by providing developers with a template on how to, for instance, include a wider set of queries and adopt additional ontologies. Let us note that anyway the proposed multicast and forward mechanisms are independent from the selected Semantic Web solutions for preference management and query representation.

For the sake of clearness, consider the FOAF document below about Alice, identified by her email (`foaf:maker`), specifying that she is interested in skiing&music (`foaf:topic_interest`) and knows Bob (`foaf:knows`).

```
<?xml version = "1.0"?>
<rdf:RDF xmlns:rdf = "http://www.w3.org/1999/02/22-rdf-syntax-ns#" [...]
    <foaf:PersonalProfileDocument rdf:about = "" >
        <foaf:maker rdf:resource = "mailto:alice@example.org" />
        <foaf:primaryTopic rdf:resource = "mailto:alice@example.org" />
        <foaf:name>Profile of Alice</foaf:name>
```

```
    </foaf:PersonalProfileDocument>
    <foaf:Person rdf:about = "mailto:alice@example.org" >
        <foaf:name>Alice</foaf:name>
        <foaf:topic_interest>Skiing</foaf:topic_interest>
        <foaf:topic_interest>Music</foaf:topic_interest>
        <foaf:knows>
            <foaf:Person rdf:about= "mailto:bob@example.org" >
                <foaf:name>Bob</foaf:name>
            </foaf:Person>
        </foaf:knows>
        ...
    </foaf:Person>
</rdf:RDF>
```

Each SMN node can store multiple graphs, one graph for the FOAF document of each local user (typically one only graph and user, especially for smartphones), other graphs for FOAF documents of remote users (one different graph for each user). As better detailed in Section 4, when nodes opportunistically interact one another, they exchange a subset of their graphs based on relationships among users. Note that graphs related to remote users provide only a partial (and possibly not up-to-date) view of the remote user information, since they contain only RDF triples exchanged depending on previous node interactions. Triples of the local graph are tagged in order to specify different visibility rules; we currently support three sets:

1) *known people (KP)*, available to the set of users directly known by the local users;
2) *known people plus people known by known people (KP+)*, available to the previous set plus the social contacts of people known by the local user;
3) *public*, available to everyone.

Each node contains specific rules to define KP and KP+ sets in relation to the local user. For instance, considering the previous FOAF document, possible rules are:

```
[ knownPersonRule: ( mailto:alice@example.org foaf:knows ?p ),
        notEqual( mailto:alice@example.org, ?p )
        -> ( ?p rdf:type ramp:KnownPerson )]
[ knownByKnownPersonRule: ( mailto:alice@example.org foaf:knows ?p ),
        notEqual( mailto:alice@example.org, ?p ),
        ( ?y foaf:knows ?z ), notEqual( ?y, ?z ),
        notEqual( mailto:alice@example.org, ?z )
        -> ( ?z rdf:type ramp:KnownByKnownPerson ) ]
```

where `KnownPerson` and `KnownByKnownPerson` are additional Ontology Web Language (OWL) classes defined to create the `KnownPersonAndKnownByKnownPerson` as union of type collection of `KnownPerson` and `KnownByKnownPerson` classes.

SPARQL queries of Construct type (providing sub-graphs as results) are exploited to create a view of the local graph that fits the visibility rules that are dynamically considered suitable for a given remote user. For instance, the SPARQL query "Privacy Filter" below creates a graph including Alice's data by considering Bob's visibility rules.

```
CONSTRUCT {
    mailto:alice@example.org ?prop ?obj.
    WHERE {
        <mailto:alice@example.org> ?prop ?obj.
        ?privacyRule ramp:onPerson <mailto:alice@example.org>.
        ?privacyRule ramp:onProperty ?prop.
        ?privacyRule ramp:permittedRole ?class.
        <mailto:bob@example.org> a ?class.
    }
}
```

Finally, Blind and Direct Multicast are performed by exploiting SPARQL queries of Ask type (providing true/false values as results), the former on senders, the latter on receivers. For instance, the query below is attached to a Blind Multicast packet to specify that the payload should be propagated at the application layer only if the local user is interested in Music.

```
ASK {
    ?ppd a foaf:PersonalProfileDocument.
    ?ppd foaf:primaryTopic ?user.
    ?ppd foaf:maker ?user.
    ?user foaf:topic_interest Music.
}
```

4   Design/Implementation Insights and Preliminary Experimental Evaluation

Based on our multicast model and the design guidelines presented in the previous section, we have implemented a middleware prototype based on two primary layers: the Communication layer and the Semantic layer (see Figure 5). The **Communication layer** exploits the "traditional" RAMP solution to send/receive unicast and broadcast packets in SMNs and to advertise/discover the set of locally/remotely available services [7]. The **Semantic layer** includes novel middleware components to support the dynamic management and dispatching of user preferences and to provide application developers with API i) to receive semantically-enabled packets, ii) to perform Direct/Blind Multicast, and iii) to enable/disable our Semantic Forward mechanism.

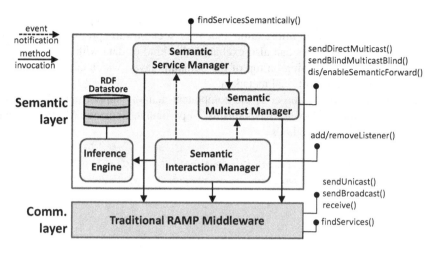

Fig. 5. The component architecture of our semantic multicast prototype

RDF Datastore and **Inference Engine** exploit the Jena framework to store and manage RDF triples [8]. The RDF datastore manages multiple named graphs, each one related to a remote user, and a default graph, related to the local user. The Inference Engine is in charge of applying rules to infer KP and KP+ sets based on local information, creating sub-graphs via Construct SPARQL queries and verifying Ask SPARQL queries.

Semantic Interaction Manager is in charge of interacting with remote users to spread preference data related to the local user and gather analogous data by remote users. In particular, each node periodically sends a so-called *social beam* message as a RAMP broadcast packet (default TTL and period values of 3 hops and 30s respectively), containing the local node unique identifier; for instance, in the case of FOAF vocabulary, it is possible to send the `foaf:maker` value. Then, nodes receiving the social beam message reply via unicast providing the portion of the graph of the local node, based on the original sender node visibility and by exploiting the Privacy Filter SPARQL query. Moreover, Semantic Interaction Manager provides the capability of receiving packets in an event-based way, via the registration of packet listeners implementing the `ISemanticListener` interface below.

```
void addListener(ISemanticListener listener) ;
void removeListener(ISemanticListener listener) ;

interface ISemanticListener {
  onEvent(LocalProfileUpdateEvent evt);
  onEvent(RemoteProfileUpdateEvent evt);
  onEvent(RemoteProfileRemoveEvent evt);
  onEvent(MulticastMessageReceivedEvent evt);
  onEvent(UnicastMessageReceivedEvent evt);
}
```

Finally, it is worth noting that Semantic Interaction Manager represents the basic mechanism to share social information (such as social-aware preferences) among nodes; however, SMN nodes can also exchange this kind of data with other mechanisms, e.g., applications running on top of the Semantic layer, which can populate and enrich RDF stores with additional metadata.

Semantic Multicast Manager is the component actually supporting Direct/Blind Multicast and Semantic Forward mechanisms. In particular, Semantic Multicast Manager offers the following methods

```
sendDirectMulticast(pattern, forwardParameters, payload);
sendBlindMulticast(ttl, pattern, forwardParameters, payload);
enableSemanticForward();
disableSemanticForward();
```

to support Direct/Blind Multicast and enable/disable Semantic Forward mechanisms respectively. Both Direct and Blind Multicast methods require a SPARQL query of Ask type, a byte array payload, and (optionally) Semantic Forward parameters, i.e., SBP, ED, and MF. In the case of Direct Multicast, the SPARQL query is run locally and then the payload sent via multiple unicast packets, one for each locally stored named graph verifying the query. In the Blind case, the SPARQL query is sent within the packet payload, via RAMP broadcast at `ttl` maximum distance.

Semantic Service Manager exploits Semantic Multicast Manager to support the discovery of services hosted on remote nodes. Similarly to Semantic Multicast Manager, Semantic Service Manager provides two different methods for service discovery exploiting either Direct or Blind Multicast. In the former case, the middleware sends discovery requests via unicast to nodes only if their locally stored named graph verifies the SPARQL query. In the latter case, the SPARQL query is sent via broadcast together with the service name and receivers check if the required service is available; only in the positive case, they reply to the sender.

```
findServicesDirect(pattern, forwardPar, serviceAmount, serviceName);
findServicesBlind(ttl, pattern, forwardPar, serviceAmount, serviceName);
```

We have performed some first tests over real testbeds and measured first quantitative performance results of our middleware implementation, with the main aim of validating our Semantic layer and of comparing the performance of "traditional" RAMP communications with semantically-enabled ones. For the sake of briefness, here we focus on the results that show how the adoption of semantic multicast can improve the quality of the discovery process perceived by final users, while imposing very little overhead. First of all, our semantic multicast reduces the set of nodes involved in packet exchange because it allows the dynamic retrieval of only the data that final users are interested in. To provide a quantitative example, consider the case of a user who is fond of jazz music and is looking for a related File Sharing service. The target SMN consists of N nodes (plus the sender), FS (< N) nodes providing a generic File Sharing service, J (< N) users interested in jazz; JFS is the intersection of J and FS nodes. In case of no semantic multicast, in RAMP we would be forced to have:

- 1 flooding-based service discovery to retrieve FS nodes, involving N nodes;
- FS responses sent by nodes hosting the service;
- FS requests from the client to service replicas to gather the list of shared files;
- FS responses with file list to the client.

Instead, in case of Direct/Blind Multicast there are (for simplicity, suppose that the client's local list of nodes interested in jazz music is complete):

- J unicast/1 flooding-based service discovery, involving J/N nodes;
- JFS responses;
- JFS requests of shared file list;
- JFS responses with the file list.

In short, our semantic-based solution can take advantage of (partial) knowledge of interest heterogeneity of socially interacting users to filter out useless discovery traffic and to limit the associated overhead in a probabilistic way.

Secondly, we have collected results to quantitatively show that the usage of carefully selected and lightweight Semantic Web techniques does not affect too much the multicast overhead and the time required to retrieve data, at least in SMNs. Table 2 reports about the time required to discover a remote service in case of "traditional" RAMP-based service discovery and our novel semantic-enabled discovery based on Blind Multicast. The reported results are obtained while varying path length and RDF dataset size; the employed small/medium/large datasets contain 10/250/750 `foaf:knows` and 10/50/200 `foaf:topic_interest` relationships respectively. The table shows that our semantic-enabled discovery increases latency but only linearly in relation to both path length (IEEE 802.11b ad-hoc links) and RDF dataset size (the greater the dataset, the more time required to run SPARQL queries). It is important to note that, even in the challenging case of three wireless hops and large RDF datasets composed of hundreds of entries, our implementation of the semantic-based discovery gets a response in less than 0.3s, thus demonstrating the practical applicability of the approach in all the application domains of interest for SMNs and the good efficiency of our prototype implementation.

Table 2. Latency of our semantic-enabled multicast discovery

		Path length (#hops)		
Service Discovery		1	2	3
Traditional		0.03 s	0.06 s	0.07 s
Semantically enabled	small dataset	0.06 s	0.13 s	0.18 s
	medium dataset	0.06 s	0.14 s	0.21 s
	large dataset	0.07 s	0.15 s	0.28 s

5   Related Work

Consolidated literature about context-aware middleware include some interesting and relevant solutions to support interest-based group communication primitives [9].

More recently, the use of semantic information to improve final user satisfaction has gained growing attention, also pushed by increased availability of shared user generated content associated with semantic tags. For instance, [10] combines ontology-based solutions with information gathered by tagging mechanisms typical of social networks, in order to provide a semantically enabled recommendation system. Instead, [11] supports a distributed social network based on recommendation structures implemented as RDF graphs. In particular, it supports the spread of data and resources based on semantically rich information stored in FOAF documents. Even the exploitation of semantic information in mobile environments is receiving growing attention. For instance, the Yarta middleware considers the heterogeneity of mobile nodes and data adopting RDF triples to store and spread semantic information [12]. In this manner application developers can easily share information and create/delete semantic-based inter-user social relationships.

Focusing on semantic multicast, OntoNet supports flexible and scalable packet delivery in emergency scenarios on top of mobile ad-hoc networks [13]. To efficiently propagate messages, OntoNet adopts tree-shaped topologies and perform multi-query aggregation. OntSum aims at discovering desirable resources based on semantically rich information, exploiting heterogeneous ontologies [14]. To maximize scalability, inter-node topology is dynamically reconfigured to make nodes with similar ontologies close one another, thus creating different ontology-based clusters. In this manner OntSum provides a concise index to efficiently route queries towards the right location, i.e., close to nodes satisfying query constraints. Instead, MobiSN adopts ontologies to spread information along participants of mobile social networks [15]. In particular, the proposed solution forwards discovery packets based on semantic information among one-hop distant nodes: the main goal is to select the best node towards the packet should be forwarded to.

Finally, it is worth noting that our definition of multicast is similar to multi-hop content-based pub-sub communication [16], but without a sharp distinction among subscribers, brokers and broker network. In fact, the Semantic Dispatching layer efficiently supports advanced forms of service discovery specifically designed for innovative and challenging SMN environments.

6   Conclusions

The originally proposed 3-layer multicast model points out the opportunities opened by different forms of node collaboration, at different levels of abstraction, in SMN environments in order to enhance advanced forms of communications, e.g., by completely decoupling packet senders and receivers. Designing and implementing middleware solutions that follow the proposed multicast model can also permit to improve the quality of experience and satisfaction of mass-market final users, e.g., by focusing user attention only on discoverable resources that provide content of most probable interest. First performance considerations and achieved results confirm that the proposed solution can decrease the number of SMN participants uselessly involved in discovery thanks to semantic-based filtering, thus increasing overall scalability, at the same time while imposing very limited overhead.

The encouraging results achieved up to now are stimulating our further research activities, on the one hand, on the integration with widespread social networking applications via emerging standard APIs, on the other hand, on building trust estimations based on past interactions (stability of collaborations, previous mobility patterns, willingness to offer local resources, etc.).

References

1. Ferreira, L.S., De Amorim, M.D., Iannone, L., Berlemann, L., Correia, L.M.: Opportunistic Management of Spontaneous and Heterogeneous Wireless Mesh Networks. IEEE Wireless Comm. 17(2), 41–46 (2010)
2. de Amorim, M.D., Ziviani, A., Viniotis, Y., Tassiulas, L.: Special Issue on Practical Aspects of Mobility in Wireless Self-organizing Networks. IEEE Wireless Comm. 15(6) (2008)
3. Feeney, L.M., Ahlgren, B., Westerlund, A.: Spontaneous Networking: an Application Oriented Approach to Ad Hoc Networking. IEEE Comm. Mag. 39(6), 176–181 (2001)
4. Latvakoski, J., Pakkala, D., Paakkonen, P.: A Communication Architecture for Spontaneous Systems. IEEE Wireless Comm. 11(3), 36–42 (2004)
5. Johnson, D.B., Maltz, D.A., Broch, J.: DSR: The Dynamic Source Routing protocol for multi-hop wireless ad hoc networks. In: Perkins, C.E. (ed.) Ad Hoc Networking, ch. 5, pp. 139–172. Addison-Wesley (2001)
6. Bellavista, P., Corradi, A., Giannelli, C.: The Real Ad-hoc Multi-hop Peer-to-peer (RAMP) Middleware: an Easy-to-use Support for Spontaneous Networking. In: 15th IEEE Symp. on Computers and Communications (ISCC 2010), Rimini, Italy (2010)
7. Bellavista, P., Corradi, A., Giannelli, C.: Application-Driven Management Middleware for Differentiated Service Provisioning in Spontaneous Networks. IEEE Pervasive Computing (in press), doi:10.1109/MPRV.2011.59
8. McBride, B.: Jena: a Semantic Web toolkit. IEEE Internet Computing 6(6), 55–59 (2002)
9. Yau, S.S., Karim, F., Wang, Y., Wang, B., Gupta, S.K.S.: Reconfigurable Context-sensitive Middleware for Pervasive Computing. IEEE Pervasive Computing 1(3), 33–40 (2002)
10. Passant, R., Raimond, Y.: Combining Social Music and Semantic Web for music-related recommender systems. Social Data on the Web (2008)
11. Ghita, S., Nejdl, W., Paiu, R.: Semantically Rich Recommendations in Social Networks for Sharing, Exchanging and Ranking Semantic Context. In: Proc. of the 4th International Conference on The Semantic Web Pages, pp. 293–307 (2005)
12. Toninelli, A., Pathak, A., Issarny, V.: Yarta: A Middleware for Managing Mobile Social Ecosystems. In: Riekki, J., Ylianttila, M., Guo, M. (eds.) GPC 2011. LNCS, vol. 6646, pp. 209–220. Springer, Heidelberg (2011)
13. Kopena, J.B.: Boon Thau Loo: OntoNet: Scalable Knowledge-based Networking. In: IEEE 24th Int. Conf. on Data Engineering Workshop, pp. 170–175 (2008)
14. Li, J., Vuong, S.: OntSum: A Semantic Query Routing Scheme in P2P Networks Based on Concise Ontology Indexing. In: 21st Int. Conf. on Advanced Information Networking and Applications, pp. 94–101 (2007)
15. Li, J., Khan, S.U.: MobiSN: Semantics-Based Mobile Ad Hoc Social Network Framework. In: IEEE Global Telecommunications Conference, pp. 1–6 (2009)
16. Martins, J.L., Duarte, S.: Routing Algorithms for Content-based Publish/Subscribe Systems. IEEE Communications Surveys & Tutorials 12(1), 39–58 (2010)

Automotive Proxy-Based Security Architecture for CE Device Integration

Alexandre Bouard[1], Johannes Schanda[2], Daniel Herrscher[1], and Claudia Eckert[3]

[1] BMW Forschung und Technik GmbH, D-80788 Munich, Germany
alexandre.bouard,daniel.herrscher@bmw.de
[2] itestra GmbH, D-80796 Munich, Germany
schanda@itestra.de
[3] Technische Universität München, D-85748 Garching, Germany
claudia.eckert@in.tum.de

Abstract. Increasing adoption of Consumer Electronic (CE) devices in the automotive world encourages car makers to propose new CE-related features each year. However, car complexity and security concerns slow down this process. The ubiquitous and personal nature of such devices represents a real threat for car IT systems. We believe that the arrival of IP standards in car should solve most of these issues. In this paper, we describe a proxy-based security architecture for an on-board IP-based network allowing deep and total integration of external mobile wireless services. The proposed architecture has been integrated in an automotive IP-based communication middleware and supports security mechanisms complying with the highly demanding automotive requirements.

Keywords: Security, Access Control, Middleware, Data Labelling, CE Device, Mobile Device, Automotive Application, Car-to-X Communication.

1 Introduction

Consumer electronics (CE) devices like smartphones or tablets have become more and more powerful and ubiquitous. New use cases, unimaginable a decade ago, appear everyday. A few years ago automotive manufacturers started to propose numerous on-board services directly accessible from the CE device. Music, navigation, phone calls, car status... the applications are various and connected through a plethora of interfaces such as USB, Bluetooth or GSM. But albeit numerous, the applications stayed similar and are only developed by the automotive manufacturers themselves or partner companies; security concerns and high system complexity slow down the release of new CE device accessible functions.

Originally conceived to develop IP-based solutions for automotive on-board communications, the SEIS project [1] aims at reducing the complexity of the network infrastructure and at designing a suitable security layer for both middleware and applications. We believe that the introduction of IP standards in

C. Borcea et al. (Eds.): MobilWare 2012, LNICST 65, pp. 62–76, 2013.

cars will considerably simplify the integration of mobile CE devices and provide the security level needed to make on-board functions available from any external communication partner.

In this paper, we describe an automotive architecture for holistic CE device security while addressing shortcomings of traditional automotive security. We propose on-board distributed mechanisms for cooperative security evaluation and enforcement complying with the highly demanding automotive requirements. In addition, a first in-car implementation of the proposed security concepts is available for ETCH [2], an open-source middleware that we are currently extending for automotive and mobile platform use.

The remainder of this paper is organized as follows. Section 2 provides some background information on traditional and next generation automotive security and threats related to the integration of CE devices. Afterwards, we present our proxy-based security architecture in Section 3 and 4. In Section 5 we describe our prototype implementation. Section 6 discusses the advantages and disadvantages of this architecture and future work. Finally Section 7 provides a conclusion.

2   Scope and Related Work

In this section we provide background information on automotive networks and security. We explain the threats related to the introduction of CE device applications in cars. Then, we present the security requirements and attacker model considered by this work.

2.1   Automotive Network and Security

During the last decade, the car has become a very complex distributed system; a premium vehicle can include up to 70 electronic control units (ECUs) interlinked by at least 5 networking technologies using complex application gateways. We believe that future use cases will involve more resources, more inter-ECU communication and more external communication partners. As mentioned in the introduction, the SEIS project proposes to alleviate the forthcoming functional issues with the development of IP solutions for automotive middleware. But the use of IP standards is not without risk. The underlying protocols and systems are well-known standards and attacks could be potentially directly applicable to the car.

Recently, work has highlighted numerous security issues of automotive infrastructure, such as the lack of encryption and authentication of controller area network (CAN) protocols [3,4] or weaknesses at the ECU level [5]. Aware of these problems, some projects aimed at providing long-term security solutions and proposed security architecture [6,7], but didn't consider the security requirements of integrating external services. The SEIS project proposes security solutions for application and IP-based communication. In Section 4 we outline their approach and use it as basis for our CE device adapted security architecture.

Today, automotive CE integration is provided via three different technologies:

- Bluetooth: Standard methods allow communication encryption and PIN-based authentication, but the features used in-car are generally limited and not security critical, e.g. phone book, phone call functions, audio system, etc.
- GSM/3G: Communications from the CE device are routed through a back-end server acting like a firewall and delivering to the car only authorized and valid function calls. Access to some critical functions is possible (e.g door locking).
- Wired (USB) interface: authorized applications establish a secure communication channel and are equipped with a certificate from the car manufacturer defining rights for a pre-defined set of infotainment and car status functions.

Industry projects about Car-to-X (C2X) security [8] already propose security solutions for on-board C2X communication platforms and protocol standardisation. Academic works [9,10] have designed car-to-car security and privacy communication protocols, but in each case the focus was on communication and authentication at the edge of the on-board network. Few consider risk analysis and authorization management. They generally propose access control list (ACL) and firewall based systems at the network entry points, but these solutions don't provide the scalability and flexibility in a reliable and efficient way that is required for new services from untrustworthy CE devices or developed by a third-party.

2.2   CE Device Related Threats

The short life cycle of CE devices [11] and their increasing power might soon allow automotive manufacturers to consider these mobile devices as virtual automotive software/hardware upgrades [12] for new applications running on the CE device and potentially communicating with any internal automotive service.

User-installable applications allow customization of CE devices. This can generate substantial risks. Malicious applications can corrupt a valid automotive application running on the CE device, directly send exploits, worms or viruses to the car and leak sensitive information provided by the car. Weak security configurations (e.g. weak password, no or misconfigured security software) can increase the risk of corruption of a CE device. Attackers can take advantage of this and, for example, steal secret authentication credentials directly from the device (password, keys). Additionally, CE devices communicate over untrusted wired or wireless channels, where messages can be listened to, intercepted, altered, injected and replayed, facilitating attacks aimed at impersonating an authorized CE device or at invoking a function with an illegal input.

In other terms, integrating CE devices is challenging; the car has to enforce appropriate security mechanisms that are both adapted to the capabilities of the CE device and its operating system (OS) and additionally provide safe and secure access to in-car functions and data.

To circumvent some of these problems, mobile OSes provide libraries implementing secure communication protocols, strong authorization and isolation mechanisms, which are reliable as long as the device is well-configured and not rooted or jailbroken. For Android, academic work proposes additional solutions such as taint tracking[13], virtualization [14], behavioral analysis[15], enforcement of mandatory access control[16] or analysis of remote duplicates[17]. These approaches mostly concern internal CE device security and are not applicable to our automotive use cases. Promising work about remote attestation for mobile devices has been published [18,19], but is based on trusted hardware which is still far from reaching mass production.

Interesting approaches may reside in secure integration of mobile devices for corporate networks [20,21]. But such solutions mostly include heavy security protocols like IPSec, not suitable for mobile device purposes [22], and rely on integrity measurements provided by hardware based security mechanisms. Additionally these approaches only regulate network access and usually lack specifications for internal function calls and data handling.

2.3   Attacker Model

As attack surface we define every communication channel present in current and future vehicles that is potentially usable by CE devices for short (USB, Wi-Fi, Bluetooth) and long range communication (GSM, UMTS, LTE) able to carry IP packets. We consider as out of scope the systems for key-entry, radio-channels and other addressable channels (emergency calls, remote diagnostics).

As attacker, we define a person having physical access to the car or being able to contact any remote interface of the car and wanting to use an in-car function in an unauthorized way. Regarding her technical capabilities, we consider that she has good knowledge of the system (standard protocols, open-source technologies) but that her computation capacities are limited (no possible brute force attack of a large encryption key). However, she can compromise or steal an authorized CE device. She has no time limit for her attack, but we assume that she has no physical contact with the on-board network or ECUs (no addition or extraction of in car components).

2.4   Automotive Security Requirements for CE Integration

With regard to the security risks and challenges described above, we define the following security requirements for CE integration.

Functional Requirements: The system should provide scalability and performance, essential goals when dealing with safety-relevant use cases. Additionally, it should provide good usability and limit the system complexity both for system development and for the end-user.

Communication Requirements: Considering the untrustworthiness of external communication networks, the protocols used should enforce mutual authentication to provide proof of origin for both car and CE device, data confidentiality due to encryption methods to not disclose sensitive information, and finally data integrity to avoid unauthorized tampering with the messages during their travel.

Car Requirements: The introduction of external services should not disturb or compromise the car runtime and its integrity, therefore strong isolation techniques should be used. The car should be able to judge the health of the CE device and enforce strong access control based on authentication mechanisms and reliable authorization management based on available context information. Finally, the car should assure the continuous operation of its internal services, even while using strong security mechanisms or under attack.

3   SEIS and Car-to-CE (C2CE) Communication

As mentioned in the introduction, one of the goals of the SEIS project is to develop an automotive middleware for IP-based communication in the car. The middleware, by definition, provides abstracted interfaces and hides the network complexity. In addition, it can automate the security management with an appropriate security configuration.

3.1   SEIS Security Middleware for On-board Network

Figure 1 presents the modularization adopted by SEIS for a three-layer security framework [23]. Such an architecture offers enough adaptivity to comply with highly demanding requirements. The first layer provides security decisions by means of static policies governing authorized on-board communications and application access controls (Policy Management) and by monitoring the reaction of the system both at the ECU and network level (Intrusion detection). The two remaining layers are in charge of security enforcement (e.g. protocol implementation and filtering). The bottom layer, Key management and Cryptographic service Management, may be included in the ECU hardware. Such a configuration allows an additional hardware-based protection for cryptographic keys and platform integrity.

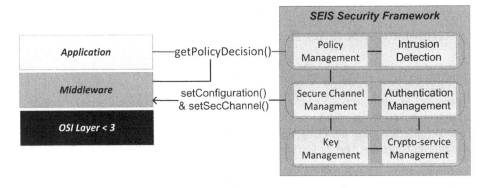

Fig. 1. SEIS Security Framework for internal IP-based communication

The automotive system is subject to drastic safety and performance requirements and generally can't afford the latency and the risk of errors induced by complex security mechanisms. Most of the configuration of the framework is therefore set up statically during vehicle assembly or during periodic system updates. This encompasses security policies and setup of security associations for on-board IPSec communication channels between ECUs.

3.2   Towards Secure Automotive Proxy-Middleware

The static automotive configuration requires a new communication infrastructure when dealing with external partners. CE devices are heterogeneous and their capabilities depend on several factors, e.g. their OS and hardware. Car manufacturers cannot restrict the C2CE connectivity to a certain class of device; therefore the architecture needs to be adaptive, as does the underlying security. The car has to be able to integrate external CE-based services communicating over a wide range of media and communication protocols (e.g. automotive middleware- or web services-based). At the same time the car has to limit its system complexity. We propose the use of a communication proxy, an entity in charge of managing access between on-board and external networks. The proxy will realize a protocol decoupling, allowing flexibility for outside communication and optimal security solutions on the inside. This approach is contrary to most corporate network solutions, where mobile devices need to provide a strict security configuration in order to be considered as an internal entity and directly access internal resources.

Security for the proxy is essential and requires a new dynamic policy engine, authentication schemes and an intrusion detection system. The protocol decoupling makes internal ECUs context-unaware and forces the proxy to enforce security for both inbound and outbound messages at the edge of the internal network. On the other hand, the introduction of IP over Ethernet as internal communication standard allowing bigger bandwidth than today's networks will raise the complexity of the software components and of the exchanged objects, e.g. processing of object models for radar environment perception or download of high resolution maps for micro navigation from different external sources. The verification of both security requirements and packet validity for every message of each external communication partner will be impossible at the proxy level alone. We propose to share the security enforcement between proxy and ECU: the proxy provides external security protocols and supports the ECU in enforcing security for applications and resources. More details about our proposed architecture are given in the next section.

4   Security for CE Adaptive Communication Proxy

In this section, we explain the concept of "Proxy-ECU Cooperation" previously motivated and present our CE adaptive security architecture for Proxy and ECU.

4.1   Proxy-ECU Cooperation for C2CE Security

Security for CE device integration aims to prevent malicious disturbance of the automotive systems and to control the release and propagation of data related to CE devices. The "Cooperation" concept is about enforcing information flow labeling between proxy and ECU in order to avoid system corruption. We define "Security Level" (SL) as a formal security description of an information flow coming from and to a CE device. It may include information about the CE device, communication link and other security requirements that car and CE device fulfill or have to fulfill. The SL is included like a tag in every CE device related on-board message.

Information flow control is essential. ECUs internally exchange genuine messages and therefore only necessitate secure channels and simple access control mechanisms. External messages can not be dealt with in the same manner, inbound and outbound messages need to be tracked because they can harm the system and disclose private or secret information. A good SL definition should provide appropriate expressiveness of the CE device communication situation and be efficiently transmittable and interpretable. Figure 2 shows the life cycle of SL tags. We differentiate two types of SL: the SL_{CE} generated by the proxy and the SL_{ECU} provided by applications on the ECU.

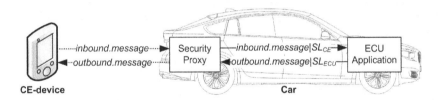

Fig. 2. Cooperative data tagging between proxy and ECU

The SL_{CE} describes the contamination risk presented by the data and the CE device security exposure, it includes information about the device, its state of health and about the security present on the communication link. Derived from a continuous reevaluation of the CE device security context, this tag is transmitted from the proxy to the ECU middleware, which adapts the message treatment and policy decision in consequence. The security mechanisms induced after interpretation of the SL allow reducing the security risk to an acceptable level in order to be passed to the application.

On the other hand, the SL_{ECU} or secrecy tag characterizes the risk of privacy infringement or industrial secret disclosure and concerns outbound messages only. Supplied by the ECU, this tag includes the user or class of user allowed to receive this data, as well as the security requirements that the user and the communication link have to fulfill. To release the message, the proxy verifies if the tag matches the concerned CE device.

The *SL* metric defines qualitative levels obtained from quantitative security parameters. The metric maps abstract security concepts and requirements to concrete protocols and mechanisms (cf. Section 5.2). The quantitative part of the metric is easily updated, because it is located only in the proxy and follows the evolution of the security techniques during the car's lifetime. Our system follows strict mandatory access control. The CE device adaption is supported by use case adapted security engines providing the testing and non-harmfulness verification of inbound and outbound messages.

4.2   CE Adaptive Security Architecture

Figure 3 presents a more concrete view of the proxy and ECU infrastructure. They both rely on a secure middleware like the one mentioned in Section 3 to establish secure communication channels. For more flexibility and independence, the proxy has its own C2CE Authentication Manager, adapted to store and verify security credentials of CE devices (password or certificates). Policy decisions from the C2CE Policy Manager and protocol decoupling are enforced in the Secure network access (SNA) module. Inbound messages are authorized based on the accessed domain (e.g. for infotainment, driving assistance...) grouping several ECUs, whereas outbound messages are released after verification of the SL_{ECU}. Secure Proxy Middleware and C2CE SL Evaluator are in charge of the tag management.

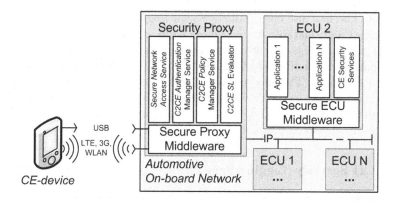

Fig. 3. CE adaptive security architecture

After reception of an SL_{CE} tagged message, the ECU middleware extracts the tag and decides whether the security information contained by the tag is sufficient to allow an appropriate access control or whether, based on the tag, the incoming data requires specific security treatment in order to be processed. In case of a complex function receiving a critical object as argument, like executable code, from a CE device which does not qualify for complete trust, the middleware can invoke specific CE Security Services for data "decontamination". Like a quarantine zone, the decontamination services perform some tests in an isolated part of the system and allow avoiding or detecting potential application corruption by verifying the data's non-harmfulness (e.g. syntax check, execution in a virtualized environment). These tests are adapted for each use case depending on its requirements. Additionally, the tag can help to prevent the waste of ECU resources, for example by verifying before processing the data if the CE device is authorized to get a response potentially containing sensitive information.

The SL_{ECU} are managed by the middleware, they are first statically defined at compilation time and can later evolve according to authorization and intrusion detection based policies. We previously said that the SL_{CE} can help to enforce a control on the ECU output. However in certain cases where the ECU isn't aware of a "fresh" SL_{CE}, the addition of a new tag, the SL_{ECU} may be necessary, either because the ECU instantiates the communication or because the packet might get forwarded outside without its knowledge e.g. in case of publish/subscribe services where the ECU is a publisher. Additionally, like the inbound message case, security engines adapted for outbound messages are supported by CE Security Services. They enforce data anonymization when possible and may even exclude critical message sections in order to prevent unauthorized disclosure of sensitive information.

5   Prototype Implementation

In order to evaluate our concepts, we set up two realistic scenarios for CE devices integration. The first use case, called "Social Flight Mode", provides a way to release private information. An on-board application provides the CE device with a video stream of the front camera and a real-time instrument cluster. The second use case, called "Remote Window Control", concerns controlling internal automotive functions. The user opens and closes the four windows directly from her CE device. Access to the driver windows is subject to credential verification at the application level. Based on these use cases, we developed two applications running on an Android 3.2 tablet.

5.1   ETCH Security Tagging Service

As prototype basis for an automotive IP-based middleware we use the remote procedure call framework ETCH [2]. ETCH is an open-source software developed as an Apache Incubator project under the Apache 2.0 licence. It benefits from a modular architecture, offering efficient message serialization and flexibility to develop new security features. The prototype is implemented in Java. The proxy runs on a Windows PC and the ECU application/middleware on another Windows PC connected to the car CAN bus.

Figure 4 shows the architecture of the ETCH middleware. We included in the Transport Handler the capability to serialize and deserialize the SL tags from the ETCH packet. Additionally we customized this layer with some other features of the SEIS security framework presented in Section 3 for authorization

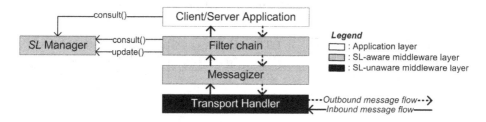

Fig. 4. ETCH architecture and SL tag management

and establishment of secure communication channels. The SL Manager stores SL_{ECU} and SL_{CE} in a hash table and provides support to enforce policies both at the application- and middleware-level, in the Filter Chain, a native module of ETCH that we adapted for our tag management. The Messagizer is in charge of dispatching the packet received from the Transport Handler to the right application and vice versa.

The security interface "consult()" for SL support of both application and middleware is motivated by complex applications willing to enforce a more granular access control. For example, the application controlling the four windows verifies specific CE device accreditation included in the tag for the driver window.

Regarding the definition of the SL_{CE}, we added the possibility to directly declare a vector representing the minimum SL in the declaration of the interface description language (IDL) before compilation of the service. This feature allows the application developer to potentially remain security-unaware.

5.2   Mirroring Proxy Middleware

We developed a mirroring service for communication protocol decoupling in the proxy. The Management Service in the proxy informs the CE device about which interface of the Mirror Service to contact. The Mirror Service provides sockets accessible from the CE device and a naming similar to the actual internal service. The CE device application has the impression of directly communicating with the internal service. For simplicity, the CE device supports the ETCH middleware and communicates over the ETCH protocol. The mirror service adds or extracts SL tags and enforces access control rules as mentioned in Section 4.1. The rules for SL_{CE} evaluation are defined within the mirror service. The tag consists of functional parameters describing the CE user (e.g. driver-, owner-status, ID...) and three security parameters, each of them evaluated with a four-level scale, describing the strength of the protocol encryption, its integrity and its authentication scheme.

5.3   Performance Overhead

In this section, we present an experimental evaluation of the performance impact of our proxy for communications between CE device and automotive application.

Table 1. Performance overhead of the ETCH-proxy

Configuration			1)Throughput		2) Channel Establishment
Decoupling - *SL* Tag - TLS			([Call+Response]/s)	Penalty	Latency (ms)
no	no	no	351	-	n/a
yes	no	no	336	4,3%	10
yes	yes	no	195	44,4%	15
yes	yes	yes	190	45,9%	45

We measure 1) the throughput of message processing for a simple service and 2) the latency resulting from the communication establishment between CE device and proxy in order to generate the mirroring services. For these experiments we deploy a simple case: an application on a CE device sends a function call message to an ECU service behind our ETCH proxy and receives a boolean as an answer. Our experiments are conducted on an Intel Core i7 2Ghz machine with 6GB RAM running Linux for the proxy and an Intel Core 2 Duo 2,4GHz with 4GB RAM running Windows XP for the ECU. The CE device is a Motorola Xoom with a Nvidia Tegra 2 chip. The CE device and the proxy are communicating over a 54 Mbit WLAN network, proxy and automotive application over a Gigabit Ethernet link. Function call and response messages are IP packets with a payload of 30 and 50 bytes respectively. In order to compare the middleware throughput and the communication establishment latency, we vary the following parameters:

– Communication Decoupling, the decoupling is enforced by the proxy, for the case "no decoupling" the proxy is replaced by a simple packet forwarder.
– *SL* Tag Evaluation, on top of decoupling the communication the proxy evaluates the *SL* tag and enforces adapted filter rules.
– External network security, the link between CE device and proxy is secured using the Transport Layer Security (TLS) protocol providing mutual authentication and data encryption.

Table 1 shows the average throughput for message processing (1) and the latency resulting from the communication establishment (2). This experiment does not produce much application processing; it mostly stresses the middleware and network mechanisms. In our set up the ETCH middleware and the communication decoupling decrease the throughput by 4,3%, with the evaluation of the security tag by 44,4%. The lower performance of the system is a consequence of the user and kernel context switching due to the network inputs/outputs. The process of encryption and decryption of the TLS protocol does not cause a visible performance loss when added to the decoupling and *SL* evaluation. The channel establishment latency results from the service discovery process and the generation of the mirroring services. Without any security feature enabled this process lasts 10 ms, with the *SL* tag evaluation 15 ms and with the TLS feature 45 ms. The first latency increase is caused by the context evaluation and the tag generation, the second one by the TLS authentication handshake. We believe that the overhead of our system becomes less significant for realistic and more complex automotive applications requiring more application processing.

6   Discussion and Future Work

In this section, we offer a brief evaluation of the security architecture, based on the requirements and threats defined in Section 2.

Functional requirements: Protocol decoupling offers several advantages. First the CE device application developer can chose the communication protocol. As long as the proxy provides an adapted translation plug-in, the car adapts its security levels in consequence. Second, internal communications can be run over a car-wide strong security solution like IPSec. However, due to potential heavy traffic (still insignificant in comparison to the volume of exchanged messages between ECUs) caused by numerous external communication partners, the proxy might become a bottleneck. Our prototype presents a throughput penalty of 44% with the security enabled, a value still allowing time demanding use cases and the possibility to have several simultaneous communication partners while maintaining quality of service. Though further investigations and tests need to be done, for example concerning external communications over different application or middleware protocols, e.g. HTTP, even if it would require a translation layer and induce more delay. Additionally, our implementation and benchmark were done in Java on powerful computers, more realistic scenarios would involve smaller ECU with an implementation in C code, but should not suffer from a considerable performance degradation [24].

Communication requirements: The difference in computing power between ECUs and their inability to dynamically adapt their security configuration motivated our choice of decoupling external communications. By trusting the security proxy's integrity and its CE device security evaluation, the ECU is able to make an adapted security decision. Further investigation needs to be done to precisely define the SL metric in order to provide a holistic security understanding of CE devices. Several use cases, such as software download and firmware update require end-to-end security solutions. For such cases, the proxy has to provide a secure tunnel; external entity and capable ECUs (e.g. Head Unit) negotiate the secure channel through this intermediary.

Car requirements: The ECUs rely on the proxy's integrity for delivery of a valid and accurate SL_{CE}. A potential attack would be to corrupt the proxy and tamper the tagging process. The malicious message would be handled with a lower security treatment and would have access to more functions. Our proxy is a single point of failure, therefore a security resistant architecture is necessary. Weyl et al. [6] propose a secure hardware architecture, which offers several advantages such as physical protection of encryption keys and secure boot. The second advantage, assuring proxy integrity, relies on hardware-based integrity measurements that can be performed only during the ECU boot, e.g. when the car starts. This solution couldn't therefore detect a corruption happening after boot. More promising approaches reside in isolation and monitoring techniques.

Technologies like hypervisor and microkernel allow a separation of the message treatment and the tagging process: Each CE device communication is treated by one isolation cell and can not interfere with its neighbor. Further investigations need to be done in order to determine the suitability of these concepts.

7   Conclusion

The customizable and non-regulated nature of CE devices raises several automotive security concerns. In this paper, we have presented a flexible security architecture aimed at mitigating this risk. We have proposed a design for an automotive security proxy enforcing the communication decoupling between internal and external networks. It allows the car to communicate over a wide range of protocols with the outside while internally keeping an optimal security protocol and limiting the increase of complexity of the inside. Our approach proposes CE adaptive security mechanisms relying on cooperation between a Security Proxy and ECUs, enabled by an in-band signaling protocol managed by the middleware. This architecture integrates various technologies to secure external communication and evaluate trust between CE device and car. The prototype of our architecture has been implemented and integrated in car and offers the performance required for automotive use cases. We are not aware of other research projects designing and implementing CE secure adaptive architecture for distributed systems with high functional requirements like cars.

Acknowledgments. The authors would like to thank Benjamin Weyl for valuable discussions about future on-board automotive security and the anonymous reviewers for their constructive comments.

Some of the research presented here, took place within the project SEIS - Security in Embedded IP-based Systems. The research project explores the usage of the Internet Protocol as a common and secure communication basis for electronic control units in vehicles. The project is partially funded by the German Federal Ministry of Education and Research (support codes 01BV0900 - 01BV0917). We would like to thank all SEIS partners directly or indirectly involved in our research.

References

1. Glass, M., Herrscher, D., Meier, H., Piastowski, M., Shoo, P.: SEIS - security in embedded ip-based systems. ATZelektronik worldwide, 2010-01, 36–40 (2010)
2. Apache ETCH homepage, http://incubator.apache.org/etch/
3. Hoppe, T., Kiltz, S., Dittmann, J.: Security Threats to Automotive CAN Networks – Practical Examples and Selected Short-Term Countermeasures. In: Harrison, M.D., Sujan, M.-A. (eds.) SAFECOMP 2008. LNCS, vol. 5219, pp. 235–248. Springer, Heidelberg (2008)

4. Koscher, K., Czeskis, A., Roesner, F., Patel, S., Kohno, T., Checkoway, S., McCoy, D., Kantor, B., Anderson, D., Shacham, H., Savage, S.: Experimental Security Analysis of a Modern Automobile. In: 31st IEEE Symposium on Security and Privacy, pp. 447–462. IEEE Computer Society, Washington, DC (2010)

5. Checkoway, S., McCoy, D., Kantor, B., Anderson, D., Shacham, H., Savage, S., Koscher, K., Czeskis, A., Roesner, F., Kohno, T.: Comprehensive Experimental Analyses of Automotive Attack Surfaces. In: 20th USENIX Security Symposium, p. 6. USENIX Association, Berkeley (2011)

6. Weyl, B., et al.: EVITA Project, D3.2 - Secure On-board Architecture Specification. Technical Report (2010), http://evity-project.org/

7. Wolf, M., Weimerskirch, A., Paar, C.: Security in Automotive Bus Systems. In: 2nd Workshop on Embedded Security in Cars (ESCAR 2004) (2004)

8. Bißmeyer, N., et al.: simTD Security Architecture: Deployment of a Security and Privacy Architecture in Field Operational Tests. In: 7th Workshop on Embedded Security in Cars (ESCAR 2009) (2009)

9. Raya, M., Hubaux, J.-P.: Securing Vehicular Ad hoc Networks. J. Comput. Secur. 15, 39–68 (2007)

10. Plöíl, K., Federrath, H.: A Privacy aware and Efficient Security Infrastructure for Vehicular Ad hoc Networks. J. Comput. Stand. Interfaces 30, 390–397 (2008)

11. Ferreira, A.: Android OS changes smartphone life cycle (2011), http://www.theusdvista.com/mobile/business/android-os-changes-smartphone-life-cycle-1.2000033

12. Endt, H., Weckemann, K.: Remote Utilization of OpenCL for Flexible Computation Offloading Using Embedded ECUs, CE Devices and Cloud Servers. In: International Conference on Parallel Computing. IOS Press, Amsterdam (2011)

13. Enck, W., Gilbert, P., Chun, B., Cox, L., Jung, J., McDaniel, P., Sheth, A.: TaintDroid: an Information-Flow Tracking System for Realtime Privacy Monitoring on Smartphones. In: 9th USENIX Conference on Operating Systems Design and Implementation, pp. 1–6. USENIX Association, Berkeley (2010)

14. Lange, M., Liebergeld, S., Lackorzynski, A., Warg, A., Peter, M.: L4Android: A Generic Operating System Framework for Secure Smartphones. In: 1st ACM Workshop on Security and Privacy in Smartphones and Mobile Devices (SPSM 2011), pp. 39–50. ACM, New York (2011)

15. Xie, L., Zhang, X., Seifert, J.-P., Zhu, S.: pBMDS: a Behavior-based Malware Detection System for Cellphone Devices. In: 3rd ACM Conference on Wireless Network Security (WiSec 2010), pp. 37–48. ACM, New York (2010)

16. Muthukumaran, D., Sawani, A., Schiffman, J., Jung, B.M., Jaeger, T.: Measuring Integrity on Mobile Phone Systems. In: 13th ACM Symposium on Access Control Models and Technologies (SACMAT 2008), pp. 155–164. ACM, New York (2008)

17. Portokalidis, G., et al.: Paranoid Android: Versatile Protection for Smartphones. In: 26th Annual Computer Security Applications Conference (ACSAC 2010), pp. 347–356. ACM, New York (2010)

18. Nauman, M., Khan, S., Zhang, X., Seifert, J.-P.: Beyond Kernel-Level Integrity Measurement: Enabling Remote Attestation for the Android Platform. In: Acquisti, A., Smith, S.W., Sadeghi, A.-R. (eds.) TRUST 2010. LNCS, vol. 6101, pp. 1–15. Springer, Heidelberg (2010)

19. Bente, I., Dreo, G., Hellmann, B., Heuser, S., Vieweg, J., von Helden, J., Westhuis, J.: Towards Permission-Based Attestation for the Android Platform. In: McCune, J.M., Balacheff, B., Perrig, A., Sadeghi, A.-R., Sasse, A., Beres, Y. (eds.) Trust 2011. LNCS, vol. 6740, pp. 108–115. Springer, Heidelberg (2011)

20. VOGUE Project homepage, `http://www.vogue-project.de/`
21. Cisco NAC appliance - Clean Access Manager Installation and Configuration Guide, Release 4.9, `http://www.cisco.com`
22. Arjona, R.: An Introduction to IPsec VPNs on Mobile Phones (2009), `http://msdn.microsoft.com/en-us/magazine/ee412260.aspx`
23. Bouard, A.: SEIS Projekt, AP4.3, Security der Middleware für IP-basierte Bordnetzarchitekturen (2011), `http://www.strategiekreis-elektromobilitaet.de/public/projekte/seis/das-sichere-ip-basierte-fahrzeugbordnetz/pdfs/TP4_Vortrag2.pdf`
24. Weckemann, K., Satzger, F., Stolz, L., Herrscher, D., Linnhoff-Popien, C.: Lessons from a Minimal Middleware for IP-based In-Car Communication. In: Proceedings of the Intelligent Vehicles Symposium (IV), pp. 686–691. IEEE (2012)

Formalization of a Fully-Decoupled Reactive Tuple Space Model for Mobile Middleware

Suddhasil De, Diganta Goswami, Sukumar Nandi, and Suchetana Chakraborty

Department of Computer Science and Engineering,
Indian Institute of Technology Guwahati, Assam – 781039, India
{suddhasil,dgoswami,sukumar,suchetana}@iitg.ernet.in

Abstract. This paper suggests an approach for formalizing Tuple Space based Mobile Middleware (TSMM) that contains a fully-decoupled reactive tuple space model as coordination medium. Formalization of TSMM is carried out using Mobile UNITY.

Keywords: mobile middleware, coordination, tuple space, Mobile UNITY.

1 Introduction

Mobile middleware [1], an emergent area of middleware research, originates to support execution of a variety of distributed applications in presence of mobility and dynamics in underlying infrastructure. Like other existing middleware, mobile middleware incorporates a suitable *coordination medium* for managing asynchronous interactions between different active components of an application, called *agents*, whose execution is supported by computing environments called *hosts*. Tuple space model [2], a popular coordination model, supports multiple inherent decoupling qualities [3], and as such is a potential coordination medium for mobile middleware [4], called Tuple Space based Mobile Middleware (TSMM). In TSMM, *tuple* is considered as basic unit of information exchanged during interaction of agents via a shared repository (called *tuple space*), while *antituple* is considered as basic unit of search key to identify some specific tuples residing in tuple space. Tuple space model subsequently includes reactivity, a powerful programming construct, to accomplish *synchronization decoupling*, another decoupling quality for agent interaction [3]. Recently, further decoupling ability is added to reactivity itself to achieve complete coordination decoupling in agent interaction [5]. TSMM, with this fully-decoupled tuple space model, facilitates application designers in developing robust and flexible applications.

Like other software/hardware design, formalization of TSMM is essential for performing an appropriate analysis of robustness and flexibility in its design. This paper suggests an approach for formally specifying and developing a TSMM, which incorporates a fully-decoupled reactive tuple space model, to define its precise semantics and lay the foundation for its implementation. A general-purpose formal reasoning tool, Mobile UNITY [6], which is an extension of well-known UNITY model [7], is used for formalizing this TSMM. After specifying and stepwise refining behaviors of TSMM in terms of Mobile UNITY, if the specifications

C. Borcea et al. (Eds.): MobilWare 2012, LNICST 65, pp. 77–91, 2013.
© Institute for Computer Sciences, Social Informatics and Telecommunications Engineering 2013

satisfy desired safety and progress properties, that TSMM is considered suitable for supporting robust and flexible applications. Authors believe that exhaustive formalization of any TSMM has not yet presented, though preliminary specifications of some functionalities exist in literature [8,9]. In both these works, basic tuple space operations and agent mobility are respectively formalized using Mobile UNITY, with reference to LIME. Moreover, in [9], formalization of agent mobility of other coordination models are also depicted. These works differ from this paper in several ways. First, this paper focuses on formalizing different aspects of a particular TSMM exclusively. Second, this TSMM has achieved full decoupling while coordinating agent interactions, which is widely dissimilar from LIME. Third, all functionalities of this TSMM, including fully-decoupled coordination, reactivity as well as associated communication and discovery mechanisms, are formalized in this paper. Agent mobility is only abstracted in this formalization as one macro to simplify its representation. Fourth, this paper also shows the construction of formal representation of an entire TSMM by combining individual specifications of its different functionalities using notations of a standard formal tool. Rest of the paper is organized as follows. Section 2 gives a brief overview of TSMM having a fully-decoupled reactive tuple space model, which is next formalized using Mobile UNITY in Section 3. Finally, Section 4 concludes the paper.

2   Overview of TSMM Having Fully-Decoupled Reactive Tuple Space Model

TSMM is the coordination tool to support agent interaction in mobile distributed applications, and it intends to provide ubiquity to the wide variety of activities a user performs. It assumes that connectivity of underlying network infrastructure can be *dynamic* and *unreliable*, whereas coordination between its two interacting agents is *asymmetric*. Former assumptions are essential to deal with host mobility and wireless connectivity of underlying infrastructure, while latter assumption brings more control on interacting agent, as it can accept/deny interactions with other available agents based on context, like users' choice, link capacity etc.

Architecture. TSMM comprise of several components, each of which are specific to agent or host. Each agent contains a local tuple space, called *agent tuple space* (ATS), and interfaces of ATS. Besides these two components, another component handles invoke of local primitives, while a pair of components handle invoke of remote primitives. Also, asymmetric interaction in each agent is enforced by acquaintance list. Each instance of host, running in each device, supports execution of multiple agents. In each host, different components manage functionalities of communication, discovery, host's core functionalities, a common tuple space called *host tuple space* (HTS), interfaces of HTS, agent management and mobility etc. Architecture of TSMM with all its components is shown in figure 1.

Tuple Space Model. In TSMM, tuples and antituples are considered as *unordered* sequence of heterogeneously typed fields, as presented in [10]. During

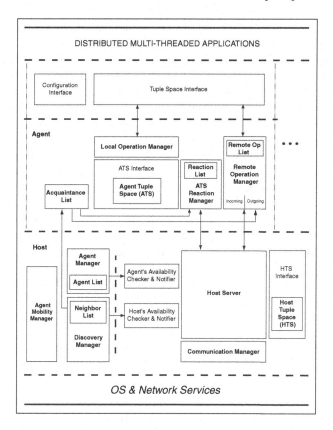

Fig. 1. Architecture of TSMM showing its significant components

interaction between any pair of agents (initiator of interaction is *reference agent* and destination becomes *target agent*), reference agent is interested in some tuples of tuple space, termed *sought tuples* [11], which are related to its interaction. It uses *antituple* to identify these sought tuples. While searching for sought tuples, antituple fields are compared with tuple fields following 'type-value', 'exact value' and 'polymorphic' matching conditions. Only fields of sought tuples match positively with fields of given antituple. Before reading/withdrawing sought tuples, they are first identified from tuple space by following tuple-antituple matching using given antituple. Different primitives are defined to carry out writing, reading and withdrawing tuples from tuple space. Tuple space is partitioned into *preamble* and *tuple store* for identifying *apposite* tuples. Apposite tuples refer to those tuples present in tuple space, whose fields are suitable for matching with all constituent fields of an antituple according to matching conditions. In other words, sought tuples are selected from the set of apposite tuples. Preamble of tuple space holds all index tables corresponding to different constituent fields of all tuples present in tuple space, while tuple store is the actual storehouse of those tuples. Each index table is a list holding a set of indices of tuples in tuple store, which contains at least one constituent field having name or type identical or polymorphically-related to table name. Any tuple-reading or -consuming primitive first identifies index table, whose content indicates locations of different apposite tuples in tuple store for given antituple. Moreover, tuple-consuming primitives, after withdrawing one/more sought tuples, update all relevant index tables in preamble. On the other hand, tuple-producing primitives first write given tuple(s) in tuple store, and update indices of written tuple(s) in all required index tables. Both ATS and HTS follow this structure of tuple space.

Both local and remote tuple-producing, tuple-reading and tuple-consuming primitives are present for handling tuple space operations in ATS. Tuple-producing primitives cover out and outg, while tuple-reading primitives include rd, rdp, rdg and rdgp, and tuple-consuming primitives are in, inp, ing and ingp. Remote primitives are both blocking as well as nonblocking, whereas local primitives are solely nonblocking. Each agent carries out invoked local primitives in its ATS. Local primitives include out, outg, rdp, rdgp, inp and ingp, whereas, remote primitives supported are out, outg, rd, rdp, rdg, rdgp, in, inp, ing and ingp, details of which are given in [5]. For executing remote operations, parameters of invoked primitives are shipped by reference agent to specified target agent(s), executed in ATS of each target agent and results of execution, if any, are sent back to reference agent. On the other hand, only two special primitives, viz. inject and eject, which are tuple-producing and -consuming respectively in nature, are provided for managing operations locally on HTS. However, only primitives corresponding to ATS are provided as application programming interfaces (APIs) for application programmers.

Reactivity Model. For achieving synchronization decoupling (i.e. decoupling reference agent from its invoked remote primitives), TSMM incorporates *reactivity* in ATS, which is the ability of ATS to monitor and respond to different circumstances (called *events*) during execution [12]. Reactivity is implemented by generating and registering *reaction* in ATS for monitoring and responding to events (like, presence of a particular sought tuple in tuple space etc.). For recognizing relevant event, reaction expects some condition to be specified by means of antituple. If condition gets satisfied, desired event is said to happen and corresponding registered reaction fires. Firing of reaction signifies that some application-defined actions (called reactive codes) will be executed subsequently, like notifying presence of tuples, withdrawing tuples from ATS etc, and responses are sent back to reference agent. Mode of a reaction indicates its active period, and is of two types in TSMM, viz. ONCE and ONCE/TUPLE. With ONCE modality, reactions fire once irrespective of the number of matching tuples and immediately get deregistered, while reactions with ONCE/TUPLE mode continue firing for each positively-matched tuple of ATS. Typically, a reaction comprises of antituple, name of invoked primitive, reactive code, identity of ATS, mode, user identity etc., of which antituple, invoked primitive name, reactive code and ATS identity are mandatory components.

Fully-Decoupled Coordination Model. In TSMM, interactions among different agents are completely decoupled by using decoupled reactivity model [5].

In this reactivity model, HTS is the additional layer of decoupling medium that accomplishes complete decoupling of agent interaction. HTS is used for storing two special tuples (viz. reaction tuple and response tuple). Reaction tuples are created from different parameters of invoked remote primitives, while response tuples are created from the result of execution of different remote primitives as well as while maintaining consistency in agent interaction. Reaction tuples and response tuples are both unordered tuples [10], and so their arity and nature of constituent fields vary with nature of invoked remote primitives. Reaction tuple is first inserted into HTS of reference host using inject primitive. On availability of target host (different from reference host), it is withdrawn from reference host's HTS using eject, passed over communication links to reach target host, and subsequently inserted into its HTS. Eventually, reaction tuple is withdrawn from target host's HTS, once desired target agent becomes available. It is processed next to extract parameters of invoked primitive, and execution of invoked remote primitive starts at ATS of target agent. In case of remote tuple-reading and -consuming primitives, target agent packs results of execution (viz. sought tuple(s) from ATS of target agent) and other necessary parameters into response tuple. Following previous approach, that response tuple eventually reaches reference agent, and sought tuple(s) are extracted from it. For achieving consistency in this asynchronous form of coordination, reference agent responds back with ACK tuple and NACK tuple when it has invoked any tuple-consuming primitives. ACK tuple positively acknowledges target agent about selection of its responded tuple as sought tuple, whereas NACK tuple returns non-selected responded tuple back to target agent. These special tuples are converted into response tuples before dispatch to target agents.

Additional Supporting Concepts. For execution over unreliable and dynamic underlying infrastructure, TSMM includes its own communication and discovery mechanisms that interfaces with transport service of corresponding device to achieve data transmission. Among the underlying infrastructure, this paper considers that Infrastructure Basic Service Set (iBSS) is deployed under TSMM. When deployed over iBSS, three categories of hosts are earmarked for TSMM, viz. *stationary host, mobile host* and *access point*. Stationary hosts are provided with only wired network connectivity, whereas mobile hosts are only having wireless network connectivity. Access point acts as a "mediator" either between a pair of mobile hosts, or between a mobile host and a stationary host, as it contains both wired and wireless network interfaces. Discovery mechanism furnishes an updated knowledge of available agents (along with their hosts) that are reachable from (i.e. neighbors of) reference host. This knowledge, utilized by other components of TSMM, is attained by sending and receiving beacons and is preserved in NeighborList. However, communication mechanism emphasizes on reliably transferring reaction/response tuples from one host to another. It uses additional acknowledgement mechanism to achieve this reliability. However, acknowledgement mechanism is only required when mobile hosts and their associated access point are communicating via wireless network interfaces.

System *TSMM*

  Program $host(i)$ **at** λ

     ⋮   ⋮   {Program description of $host(i)$, given separately}

  Program $agent(k)$ **at** λ

     ⋮   ⋮   {Program description of $agent(k)$, given separately}

Components
  $\langle [\![\, i :: host(i)\, \rangle\ [\![\ \langle [\![\ k :: agent(k)\, \rangle$

Interactions
  {Attach $\mathcal{T}_w$ of all hosts with wired network interfaces as transiently-shared variable}
  $shared_w ::$
  $\langle [\![\, i,j :: host(i).\mathcal{T}_w \approx host(j).\mathcal{T}_w$
      when $\big(\texttt{isSH}(host(i)) \vee \texttt{isAP}(host(i))\big) \wedge \big(\texttt{isSH}(host(j)) \vee \texttt{isAP}(host(j))\big)$
      engage $host(i).\mathcal{T}_w$ **disengage** current $\|\bot$
  $\rangle$

    {Attach $\mathcal{T}_{wL}$ of mobile host and access point as transiently-shared variable, only when colocated}
  $[\![\ shared_{wL} ::$
  $\langle [\![\, i,j :: host(i).\mathcal{T}_{wL} \approx host(j).\mathcal{T}_{wL}$
      when $\big((\texttt{isMH}(host(i)) \wedge \texttt{isAP}(host(j))) \vee (\texttt{isAP}(host(i)) \wedge \texttt{isMH}(host(j)))\big)$
          $\wedge\ (host(i)\Gamma' host(j))$
      engage $host(i).\mathcal{T}_{wL}$ **disengage** current $\|\bot$
  $\rangle$

    {Prepare to register active agents in respective hosts}
  $[\![\ regAgent :: \langle [\![\, i,k :: host(i).\mathcal{Q}_{in} := host(i).\mathcal{Q}_{in} \bullet agent(k).aid$ **when** $(host(i).\lambda = agent(k).\lambda)\ \rangle$

    {Prepare to deregister terminated/migrated agents from respective hosts}
  $[\![\ deregAgent :: \langle [\![\, i,k :: host(i).\mathcal{Q}_{out} := host(i).\mathcal{Q}_{out} \bullet agent(k).aid$ **when** $\neg(host(i).\lambda = agent(k).\lambda)\ \rangle$

end

Fig. 2. Mobile UNITY system of TSMM

3   Proposed Approach of Formalization of TSMM

This section proposes an approach of formalization of TSMM as a Mobile UNITY system, comprising of a set of formal programs representing different agents and hosts. Favoring Mobile UNITY over other formal tools is due to its suitability for formalizing inherently non-terminating programs (like mobile middleware), reasoning about agents temporal behavior using its proof rules, and following stepwise specification and refining. In **System** *TSMM*, as shown in Figure 2, several instances of two Mobile UNITY programs are components of whole system, and their interaction are specified in **Interactions** section. i-th host is specified by **Program** $host(i)$, whereas k-th agent is represented by **Program** $agent(k)$, where i and k are assumed to be quantified over appropriate ranges. Different conditions for two hosts or a host and an agent to interact in **Interactions** section are enforced through **when** clauses. **engage** and **disengage** clauses, and **current** construct are used for effecting transient sharing between different hosts. Also, first two statements in **Interactions** section, labeled as $shared_w$ and $shared_{wL}$, are reactive statements as they have used "$\approx$" notation [13].

Program $agent(k)$ **at** λ

declare

$\quad type\ :\ \in\{stationary, mobile\}\ [\!]\ aid, taid, a\ :\ \text{agentid}\ [\!]\ taids\ :\ \text{sequence of agentid}$

$\quad [\!]\ \mathbf{T}\ :\ \text{tuple space}\ [\!]\ t, tuple\ :\ \text{tuple}\ [\!]\ \mathbf{t}, tuples\ :\ \text{set of tuple}\ [\!]\ \mathbf{a}, atuple\ :\ \text{antituple}$

$\quad [\!]\ \mathbb{T}\ :\ \text{set of }\{agentid, \text{set of tuple}\}\ [\!]\ r\ :\ \text{RT}_{\text{tuple}}\ [\!]\ \mathcal{Q}_{T^S_{a_k}}, \mathcal{Q}_{T^R_{a_k}}\ :\ \text{queue of RT}_{\text{tuple}}\ [\!]\ prid\ :\ \text{primitiveid}$

$\quad [\!]\ ROL\ :\ \text{sequence of (primitiveid, primitivename, set of agentid of target agents)}$

$\quad [\!]\ RL\ :\ \text{sequence of (reactionid, primitiveid)}$

$\quad [\!]\ prType\ :\ \in\{local, remote\}\ [\!]\ prName\ :\ \in\{\textsf{OUT, OUTG, RD, RDG, RDP, RDGP, IN, ING, INP, INGP}\}$

$\quad [\!]\ mode\ :\ \in\{\textsf{ONCE, ONCE/TUPLE}\}\ [\!]\ TAs, rform\ :\ \text{natural}\ [\!]\ prBulk, prRdIn, UsrRdy4Evt\ :\ \text{boolean}$

always

$\quad aid := \texttt{getMyAgentID}(k)\ [\!]\ type := \texttt{getAgentType}(stationary, mobile)$

$\quad [\!]\ \texttt{isPresent}_{\text{in}ROL}(prid, taid) \equiv \langle\ \exists e :: (e \in ROL) \wedge (e \uparrow 1 = prid) \wedge (aid \in e \uparrow 3)\ \rangle$

$\quad [\!]\ \texttt{isEmpty}_{\text{in}ROL}(prid) \equiv \langle\ \exists e :: (e \in ROL) \wedge (e \uparrow 1 = prid) \wedge (e \uparrow 3 = \emptyset)\ \rangle$

initially

$\quad \lambda = \texttt{Location}(k)\ [\!]\ TAs = 0\ [\!]\ rform = 0\ [\!]\ \mathbf{T} = \perp\ [\!]\ ROL = \perp\ [\!]\ RL = \perp\ [\!]\ \mathbb{T} = \emptyset$

$\quad [\!]\ t = \varepsilon\ [\!]\ tuple = \varepsilon\ [\!]\ \mathbf{t} = \emptyset\ [\!]\ tuples = \emptyset\ [\!]\ \mathbf{a} = \varepsilon\ [\!]\ atuple = \varepsilon\ [\!]\ \mathcal{Q}_{T^S_{a_k}} = \perp\ [\!]\ \mathcal{Q}_{T^R_{a_k}} = \perp$

$\quad [\!]\ UsrRdy4Evt = false$

assign

$\quad\quad \{\text{Migrate to different location}\}$

$\quad [\!]\ \lambda := \texttt{Location}(\texttt{Move}())$

$\quad\quad \{\text{Capture different parameters when user application is ready}\}$

$\quad [\!]\ \langle\ prType, prName, UsrRdy4Evt := \texttt{getPrimType}(), \texttt{getPrimName}(), false$

$\quad\quad \|\ prRdIn, prBulk := \texttt{getPrimRDorIN}(), \texttt{getPrimBulk}()$

$\quad\quad \|\ tuple := \texttt{getTuple}()\quad \text{if}\ \big((prRdIn = false) \wedge (prBulk = false)\big)$

$\quad\quad \|\ tuples := \texttt{getTuples}()\quad \text{if}\ \big((prRdIn = false) \wedge (prBulk = true)\big)$

$\quad\quad \|\ atuple := \texttt{getAntiTuple}()\quad \text{if}\ (prRdIn = true)$

$\quad\quad \|\ TAs := \texttt{getTargetAgentCount}()\quad \text{if}\ (prType = remote)$

$\quad\quad \|\ \langle\| a : 1 \le a \le TAs :: taids[a] := \texttt{getTargetAgentID}(a)\rangle\quad \text{if}\ (prType = remote)$

$\quad\quad \|\ mode := \texttt{getMode}(\textsf{ONCE, ONCE/TUPLE})\quad \text{if}\ \big((prType = remote) \wedge (prRdIn = true)\big)$

$\quad\ \rangle\quad \text{if}\ (UsrRdy4Evt = true)$

$\{\text{- - - - - - - - - - Start of } \textsf{Local Operation Manager} \text{ - - - - - - - - -}\}$

$\quad\quad \{\text{Perform different local tuple space primitives}\}$

$\quad [\!]\ \langle\ t, tuple, prType := tuple, \varepsilon, \varepsilon\ \rangle\quad \text{if}\ \big((prType = local) \wedge (prName = \textsf{OUT}) \wedge \neg(tuple = \varepsilon)\big)$

$\quad [\!]\ \langle\ \mathbf{t}, tuples, prType := tuples, \emptyset, \varepsilon\ \|\ \texttt{outg}(\mathbf{t}, \mathbf{T})$

$\quad\ \rangle\quad \text{if}\ \big((prType = local) \wedge (prName = \textsf{OUTG}) \wedge \neg(tuples = \emptyset)\big)$

$\quad [\!]\ \langle\ \mathbf{a}, atuple, prType := atuple, \varepsilon, \varepsilon$

$\quad\quad \|\ \langle\ t := \texttt{rdp}(\mathbf{a}, \mathbf{T})\ \|\ \texttt{retTuple2Usr}(t)\ \rangle\quad \text{if}\ (prName = \textsf{RDP})$

$\quad\quad \|\ \langle\ \mathbf{t} := \texttt{rdgp}(\mathbf{a}, \mathbf{T})\ \|\ \texttt{retTuples2Usr}(\mathbf{t})\ \rangle\quad \text{if}\ (prName = \textsf{RDGP})$

$\quad\quad \|\ \langle\ t := \texttt{inp}(\mathbf{a}, \mathbf{T})\ \|\ \texttt{retTuple2Usr}(t)\ \rangle\quad \text{if}\ (prName = \textsf{INP})$

$\quad\quad \|\ \langle\ \mathbf{t} := \texttt{ingp}(\mathbf{a}, \mathbf{T})\ \|\ \texttt{retTuples2Usr}(\mathbf{t})\ \rangle\quad \text{if}\ (prName = \textsf{INGP})$

$\quad\ \rangle\quad \text{if}\ \big((prType = local) \wedge \neg(atuple = \varepsilon)\big)$

$\{\text{- - - - - - - - - - End of } \textsf{Local Operation Manager} \text{ - - - - - - - - -}\}$

Fig. 3. Mobile UNITY **Program** $agent(k)$: part 1

{- - - - - - - - - - Start of Remote Operation Manager - - - - - - - - - -}

{Initiate (as reference agent) execution of different remote tuple space operations}

$[\!]\ \langle\ \ t, tuple, prType := tuple, \varepsilon, \varepsilon \parallel prid := \texttt{getPrID}(prName) \parallel rform := 1$
$\parallel \langle \parallel a : 1 \leq a \leq TAs :: \mathcal{Q}_{T^S_{a_k}} := \mathcal{Q}_{T^S_{a_k}} \bullet \texttt{createRTuple}_r(rform, prid, prName, t, mode, aid, taids[a]) \rangle$
$\rangle\ \ \text{if } \big((prType = remote) \wedge (prName = \textsf{OUT}) \wedge \neg(tuple = \varepsilon)\big)$

$[\!]\ \langle\ \ t, tuples, prType := tuples, \emptyset, \varepsilon \parallel prid := \texttt{getPrID}(prName) \parallel rform := 1$
$\parallel \langle \parallel a : 1 \leq a \leq TAs :: \mathcal{Q}_{T^S_{a_k}} := \mathcal{Q}_{T^S_{a_k}} \bullet \texttt{createRTuple}_r(rform, prid, prName, \mathbf{t}, mode, aid, taids[a]) \rangle$
$\rangle\ \ \text{if } \big((prType = remote) \wedge (prName = \textsf{OUTG}) \wedge \neg(tuples = \emptyset)\big)$

$[\!]\ \langle\ \ a, atuple, prType := atuple, \varepsilon, \varepsilon \parallel prid := \texttt{getPrID}(prName) \parallel rform := 1$
$\parallel ROL := ROL \cup \{prid, prName, taids\}$
$\parallel \langle \parallel a : 1 \leq a \leq TAs :: \mathcal{Q}_{T^S_{a_k}} := \mathcal{Q}_{T^S_{a_k}} \bullet \texttt{createRTuple}_r(rform, prid, prName, \mathbf{a}, mode, aid, taids[a]) \rangle$
$\rangle\ \ \text{if } \big((prType = remote) \wedge (prRdIn = true) \wedge \neg(atuple = \varepsilon)\big)$

$[\!]\ \langle\ \ r, \mathcal{Q}_{T^R_{a_k}} := \texttt{head}(\mathcal{Q}_{T^R_{a_k}}), \texttt{tail}(\mathcal{Q}_{T^R_{a_k}}) \parallel prid := r \uparrow prid$
$\parallel \langle\ \mathbb{T}_{prid} := \mathbb{T}_{prid} \cup \{r \uparrow \text{tAid}, r \uparrow data\} \parallel \langle\ \exists e : (e \in ROL) \wedge (e \uparrow 1 = prid) :: e \uparrow 3 := e \uparrow 3 \setminus r \uparrow \text{tAid}\ \rangle$
$\rangle\ \ \text{if } \big((r \uparrow \text{rAid} = aid) \wedge \texttt{isPresent}_{\text{inROL}}(prid, r \uparrow \text{tAid})\big)$ {Handling Response tuple}
$\rangle\ \ \text{if } \big(\neg(\mathcal{Q}_{T^R_{a_k}} =\perp) \wedge (\texttt{head}(\mathcal{Q}_{T^R_{a_k}}) \uparrow rform = 2)\big)$

{Return result of execution of remote tuple-reading or -consuming operation to user}

$[\!]\ \langle \parallel e : (e \in ROL) \wedge (e \uparrow 3 = \emptyset)$
$:: \ \ prid, prName := e \uparrow 1, e \uparrow 2 \parallel ROL := ROL \setminus e$
$\parallel \langle\ \langle \parallel e : e \in \mathbb{T}_{prid} :: \mathbf{t} := \mathbf{t} \cup e \uparrow tuples\ \rangle \parallel \texttt{retTuples2Usr}(\mathbf{t})$
$\parallel \langle \parallel e : e \in \mathbb{T}_{prid} \wedge ((prName = \textsf{ING}) \vee (prName = \textsf{INGP}))$
$:: \mathcal{Q}_{T^S_{a_k}} := \mathcal{Q}_{T^S_{a_k}} \bullet \texttt{createRTuple}_{r'}(3, prid, prName, aid, e \uparrow \text{tAid})\ \rangle$
$\rangle\ \ \text{if } \big((prName = \textsf{RDG}) \vee (prName = \textsf{RDGP}) \vee (prName = \textsf{ING}) \vee (prName = \textsf{INGP})\big)$
$\parallel \langle\ \langle \parallel e : e = e'.(e' \in \mathbb{T}_{prid}) :: t, taid := e \uparrow tuple, e \uparrow \text{tAid}\ \rangle \parallel \texttt{retTuple2Usr}(t)$
$\parallel \mathcal{Q}_{T^S_{a_k}} := \mathcal{Q}_{T^S_{a_k}} \bullet \texttt{createRTuple}_{r'}(3, prid, prName, aid, taid)$
$\hspace{6cm} \text{if } \big((prName = \textsf{IN}) \vee (prName = \textsf{INP})\big)$
$\parallel \langle \parallel e : e \in \mathbb{T}_{prid} \wedge \neg(e \uparrow \text{tAid} = taid) \wedge ((prName = \textsf{IN}) \vee (prName = \textsf{INP}))$
$:: \mathcal{Q}_{T^S_{a_k}} := \mathcal{Q}_{T^S_{a_k}} \bullet \texttt{createRTuple}_{r'}(4, prid, prName, e \uparrow tuple, aid, e \uparrow \text{tAid})\ \rangle$
$\rangle\ \ \text{if } \big((prName = \textsf{RD}) \vee (prName = \textsf{RDP}) \vee (prName = \textsf{IN}) \vee (prName = \textsf{INP})\big)$
$\rangle$

{- - - - - - - - - - End of Remote Operation Manager - - - - - - - - - -}

Fig. 4. Mobile UNITY **Program** $agent(k)$: part 2

Different agent behavior, including functionalities of ATS, Local Operation Manager, Remote Operation Manager, ATS Reaction Manager etc. are contained in $agent(k)$ as shown in Figure 3, Figure 4, and Figure 5. Similarly, functionalities of different components of host, including Transport Interface, Discovery Manager, Communication Manager, Host Server, Agent Manager etc., are contained in $host(i)$ as shown in Figure 6, Figure 7, Figure 8, Figure 9, and Figure 10. However, in above formal system, many aspects of TSMM are not directly formalized, to keep this formal system simple. Among these aspects, formalizing the mechanism to handle agent mobility (i.e. migration of agents from one host to another) is already shown in literature [14,9]. Also, correctness of above formal system (i.e. proving its safety/progress properties, and safety/progress properties of its individual components and of statements specified in **Interactions** section) is omitted here.

{- - - - - - - - - - Start of ATS Reaction Manager - - - - - - - - -}

{Complete execution of different remote tuple space operations}

$[\![$ $\langle$ $r, \mathcal{Q}_{T^R_{a_k}} := \text{head}(\mathcal{Q}_{T^R_{a_k}}), \text{tail}(\mathcal{Q}_{T^R_{a_k}})$ $\|$ $prid := r \uparrow \text{prid}$ $\|$ $prName := r \uparrow \text{pName}$

$\|$ $prBulk := true$

    if $\big((prName = \text{RDG}) \vee (prName = \text{RDGP}) \vee (prName = \text{ING}) \vee (prName = \text{INGP})\big)$

  $\sim$ $false$

    if $\big((prName = \text{RD}) \vee (prName = \text{RDP}) \vee (prName = \text{IN}) \vee (prName = \text{INP})\big)$

$\|$ $\langle$ $\langle$ $t := r \uparrow \text{data}$ $\|$ $\text{out}(t, \mathbf{T})$ $\rangle$ if $(prName = \text{OUT})$

 $\|$ $\langle$ $\mathbf{t} := r \uparrow \text{data}$ $\|$ $\text{outg}(\mathbf{t}, \mathbf{T})$ $\rangle$ if $(prName = \text{OUTG})$

 $\|$ $\langle$ $a := r \uparrow \text{data}$ $\|$ $t := \text{rd}(a, \mathbf{T})$ $\rangle$ if $(prName = \text{RD})$

 $\|$ $\langle$ $a := r \uparrow \text{data}$ $\|$ $\mathbf{t} := \text{rdg}(a, \mathbf{T})$ $\rangle$ if $(prName = \text{RDG})$

 $\|$ $\langle$ $a := r \uparrow \text{data}$ $\|$ $t := \text{rdp}(a, \mathbf{T})$ $\rangle$ if $(prName = \text{RDP})$

 $\|$ $\langle$ $a := r \uparrow \text{data}$ $\|$ $\mathbf{t} := \text{rdgp}(a, \mathbf{T})$ $\rangle$ if $(prName = \text{RDGP})$

 $\|$ $\langle$ $a := r \uparrow \text{data}$ $\|$ $t := \text{in}(a, \mathbf{T})$ $\rangle$ if $(prName = \text{IN})$

 $\|$ $\langle$ $a := r \uparrow \text{data}$ $\|$ $\mathbf{t} := \text{ing}(a, \mathbf{T})$ $\rangle$ if $(prName = \text{ING})$

 $\|$ $\langle$ $a := r \uparrow \text{data}$ $\|$ $t := \text{inp}(a, \mathbf{T})$ $\rangle$ if $(prName = \text{INP})$

 $\|$ $\langle$ $a := r \uparrow \text{data}$ $\|$ $\mathbf{t} := \text{ingp}(a, \mathbf{T})$ $\rangle$ if $(prName = \text{INGP})$

 $\|$ $rform := 2$

 $\|$ $\mathcal{Q}_{T^S_{a_k}} := \mathcal{Q}_{T^S_{a_k}} \bullet \text{createRTuple}_{r'}(rform, prid, prName, t, aid, r \uparrow \text{rAid})$ if $(prBulk = false)$

 $\|$ $\mathcal{Q}_{T^S_{a_k}} := \mathcal{Q}_{T^S_{a_k}} \bullet \text{createRTuple}_{r'}(rform, prid, prName, \mathbf{t}, aid, r \uparrow \text{rAid})$ if $(prBulk = true)$

 $\rangle$ if $\big((r \uparrow \text{tAid} = aid) \wedge (r \uparrow \text{rform} = 1)\big)$ {Handling Reaction tuple}

$\|$ $\langle$ $t := r \uparrow \text{data}$ $\|$ $\text{out}(t, \mathbf{T})$

 $\rangle$ if $\big((r \uparrow \text{tAid} = aid) \wedge (r \uparrow \text{rform} = 4)\big)$ {Handling NACK tuple}

$\rangle$ if $\big(\neg(\mathcal{Q}_{T^R_{a_k}} = \perp) \wedge$

      $\big((\text{head}(\mathcal{Q}_{T^R_{a_k}}) \uparrow \text{rform} = 1) \vee (\text{head}(\mathcal{Q}_{T^R_{a_k}}) \uparrow \text{rform} = 3) \vee (\text{head}(\mathcal{Q}_{T^R_{a_k}}) \uparrow \text{rform} = 4)\big)\big)$

{- - - - - - - - - - End of ATS Reaction Manager - - - - - - - - - -}

{Discard messages destined for other agents}

$[\![$ $\mathcal{Q}_{T^R_{a_k}} := \text{tail}(\mathcal{Q}_{T^R_{a_k}})$ if $\big(\neg(\mathcal{Q}_{T^R_{a_k}} = \perp) \wedge \neg(\text{head}(\mathcal{Q}_{T^R_{a_k}}) \uparrow \text{dstAg} = aid)\big)$

end

Fig. 5. Mobile UNITY **Program** $agent(k)$: part 3

Different variables pertaining to behavior of hosts and agents in TSMM are used in this formal system. For instance, $\mathcal{Q}$ is used to express any queue used to define different activities of TSMM; its subscripts represent purpose of using it. In this specification, $\text{head}(\mathcal{Q})$ returns front element of $\mathcal{Q}$, while $\text{tail}(\mathcal{Q})$ returns all elements of $\mathcal{Q}$ except front element. Also, $\mathcal{Q} \bullet M$ inserts M in the rear end of $\mathcal{Q}$ and returns updated $\mathcal{Q}$. Each message M comprises of message identity mid, source host's identity src, destination host's identity $dest$, type of message $kind$, data encapsulated within the message $data$, and network interface, ni, through which the message will be transmitted. M is generated by calling $\text{newMsg}(src, dest, kind, data, ni)$, which inserts its mid to return the complete message. Possible types of messages included in the specification are BCON, RT, ACK, Locate, and Found messages.

Program $host(i)$ **at** λ

declare

      $type$: $\in \{stationary, mobile, accesspoint\}$

⫿ hid : hostid

⫿ $nwdeploy$: $\in \{iBSS, IBSS\}$

⫿ $status$: $\in \{standalone, associated\}$

⫿ T' : tuple space

⫿ $\mathcal{Q}_{T_{a_k}^S}, \mathcal{Q}_{T_{a_k}^R}$: queue of RT$_{\text{tuple}}$

⫿ a : agentid

⫿ $\mathcal{A}$: set of agentid

⫿ $\mathcal{Q}_{in}, \mathcal{Q}_{out}$: queue of agentid

⫿ $assoc$: set of hostid

⫿ $\mathcal{H}$: set of (MH$_{\text{hostid}}$, AP$_{\text{hostid}}$, timestamp)

⫿ $\mathcal{L}$: set of (MH$_{\text{hostid}}$, RT$_{\text{tuple}}$, timestamp)

⫿ $\mathcal{CS}$: message

⫿ $\mathcal{LRT}$: set of (AP$_{\text{hostid}}$/MH$_{\text{hostid}}$, RT$_{\text{msgid}}$)

⫿ $\mathcal{N}$: set of (Host$_{\text{hostid}}$, set of agentid, timestamp, extant)

⫿ $\mathcal{Q}_{S_B}, \mathcal{Q}_{R_B}$: queue of message

⫿ $\mathcal{Q}_{S_{RT}}, \mathcal{Q}_{R_{RT}}$: queue of message

⫿ $\mathcal{Q}_{RT_S}, \mathcal{Q}_{RT_R}$: queue of RT$_{\text{tuple}}$

⫿ r : RT$_{\text{tuple}}$

⫿ $\mathcal{T}_\mathsf{W}, \mathcal{T}_{\mathsf{WL}}$: message

⫿ $\mathcal{Q}_{S_\mathsf{W}}, \mathcal{Q}_{S_{\mathsf{WL}}}$: queue of message

⫿ $\mathcal{Q}_S, \mathcal{Q}_R$: queue of message

⫿ M, m : message

⫿ $clock, lastHTSchk, lastRTsent, lastBsent, newRTGap, rtAtmpt$: natural

Fig. 6. Mobile UNITY **Program** $host(i)$: part 1

3.1 Formalization of *agent(k)*

Each agent is represented by program $agent(k)$, which comprises of **declare**, **always**, **initially** and **assign** sections. Agent behavior is specified by different variables that are declared in **declare** section. In particular, aid and $type$ are declared as agent identity and nature (viz. stationary agent/mobile agent) of any $agent(k)$. T is declared as ATS of $agent(k)$. Also, $prid$ is declared as identity of invoked primitive of $agent(k)$. ROL is declared as remote operation list of $agent(k)$, and RL is declared as reactive list of $agent(k)$. $\mathcal{Q}_{T_{a_k}^S}$ and $\mathcal{Q}_{T_{a_k}^R}$ are declared as queues to interface between agents and their supported hosts. These queues are defined to transfer request/response tuples from agents to hosts and vice versa. When user application is generating an event for any tuple space operation, corresponding agent must capture different parameters required to complete that operation. In the specification, readiness of user application is abstracted by $UsrRdy4Evt$, a boolean variable. Once user application is ready, capturing values of different parameters are specified by using different functions.

always

$B_{iBSS_W} = $ IBSSBROADCASTADDRESS$_{DS}$ [] $B_{iBSS_{WL}} = $ IBSSBROADCASTADDRESS$_{BSA}$

[] $B_{IBSS_{WL}} = $ IBSSBROADCASTADDRESS

[] $\lambda := $ Location(i)

[] $hid := $ getMyHostID(i)

[] $type := $ getHostType$(stationary, mobile, accesspoint)$

[] $nwdeploy := $ getUnderlyingInfra$(iBSS, IBSS)$

[] $mhGap = $ SYSTEMMHVALIDITYINTERVAL [] $HTSaccessGap = $ SYSTEMHTSACCESSINTERVAL

[] $locateGap = $ SYSTEMLOCATEMSGINTERVAL [] $bconGap = $ SYSTEMBEACONINTERVAL

[] $mhGap = $ SYSTEMMHVALIDITYINTERVAL [] $bLife = $ SYSTEMBEACONLIFETIME

[] isPresent$_{\mathcal{H}}(mhid) \equiv \langle \exists e : (e \in \mathcal{H}) \wedge (e \uparrow 1 = mhid) \rangle$

[] isPresent$_{\mathcal{L}}(mhid) \equiv \langle \exists e : (e \in \mathcal{L}) \wedge (e \uparrow 1 = mhid) \rangle$

[] isPresent$_{\mathcal{N}}(hostid) \equiv \langle \exists e : (e \in \mathcal{N}) \wedge (e \uparrow 1 = hostid) \rangle$

[] isPresent$_{\mathcal{L}RT}(hostid) \equiv \langle \exists e : (e \in \mathcal{L}RT) \wedge (e \uparrow 1 = hostid) \rangle$

[] isRepeat$_{\mathcal{L}RT}(hostid, msgid) \equiv \langle \exists e : (e \in \mathcal{L}RT) \wedge (e \uparrow 1 = hostid) \wedge (e \uparrow 2 = msgid) \rangle$

[] isValid$_{\mathcal{H}}(e, now) \equiv ((e \in \mathcal{H}) \wedge ((now - e \uparrow 3) \leq mhGap))$

[] isValid$_{\mathcal{L}}(e, now) \equiv ((e \in \mathcal{L}) \wedge ((now - e \uparrow 3) \leq locateGap))$

[] isValid$_{\mathcal{N}}(e, now) \equiv ((e \in \mathcal{N}) \wedge ((now - e \uparrow 3) \leq e \uparrow 4))$

[] isMsgBcon$(msg) \equiv (msg \cdot kind = Beacon)$

[] isMsgRT$(msg) \equiv (msg \cdot kind = RT)$

[] isMsgACK$(msg) \equiv (msg \cdot kind = ACK)$

[] isMsgLocate$(msg) \equiv (msg \cdot kind = Locate)$

[] isMsgFound$(msg) \equiv (msg \cdot kind = Found)$

[] isNotOwnMsg$(msg) \equiv \neg(msg \cdot src = hid)$

[] isSH$(host) \equiv (host \cdot type = stationary)$

[] isMH$(host) \equiv (host \cdot type = mobile)$

[] isAP$(host) \equiv (host \cdot type = accesspoint)$

initially

$clock = 0$ [] $lastHTSchk = 0$ [] $lastRTsent = 0$ [] $lastBsent = 0$

[] $status = standalone$ [] $assoc = \emptyset$ [] $\mathcal{H} = \emptyset$ [] $\mathcal{L} = \emptyset$ [] $\mathcal{L}RT = \emptyset$ [] $\mathcal{A} = \emptyset$ [] $\mathcal{N} = \emptyset$

[] $\mathbf{T}' = \perp$ [] $\mathcal{T}_W = \perp$ [] $\mathcal{T}_{WL} = \perp$ [] $\mathcal{C}S = \perp$

[] $\mathcal{Q}_{T^S_{a_k}} = \perp$ [] $\mathcal{Q}_{T^R_{a_k}} = \perp$ [] $\mathcal{Q}_{in} = \perp$ [] $\mathcal{Q}_{out} = \perp$ [] $\mathcal{Q}_{RT_S} = \perp$ [] $\mathcal{Q}_{RT_R} = \perp$

[] $\mathcal{Q}_{S_B} = \perp$ [] $\mathcal{Q}_{R_B} = \perp$ [] $\mathcal{Q}_{S_{RT}} = \perp$ [] $\mathcal{Q}_{R_{RT}} = \perp$ [] $\mathcal{Q}_{S_W} = \perp$ [] $\mathcal{Q}_{S_{WL}} = \perp$ [] $\mathcal{Q}_S = \perp$ [] $\mathcal{Q}_R = \perp$

Fig. 7. Mobile UNITY **Program** $host(i)$: part 2

3.2   Formalization of $host(i)$

Like $agent(k)$, $host(i)$ is also composed of **declare**, **always**, **initially** and **assign** sections. Different variables related to host behavior is declared in **declare** section. In particular, hid is declared as host identity of any $host(i)$, whereas $type$ specifies nature of $host(i)$ (viz. stationary host/mobile host/access point). $\mathbf{T}'$ is declared as its HTS. $\mathcal{H}$ and $\mathcal{L}$ are declared for History (that records path of successful data transfer to different mobile hosts) and location list (that keeps mobile hosts with ongoing location search) respectively for $host(i)$ of stationary hosts and access points. Moreover, $\mathcal{L}RT$ and $\mathcal{C}S$ are declared for LastRT (that records message identity of last data messages received from different hosts) and CommStash (that buffers data messages) respectively of $host(i)$ of mobile hosts

assign

      {Increment the clock}
      [] $clock := clock + 1$

{- - - - - - - - - - Start of Transport Interface - - - - - - - - - -}

      {Organize a message for onward transmission}
      [] ⟨ $M, \mathcal{Q}_S := \mathrm{head}(\mathcal{Q}_S), \mathrm{tail}(\mathcal{Q}_S)$
          ‖ ⟨ $\mathcal{Q}_{S_\mathrm{W}} := \mathcal{Q}_{S_\mathrm{W}} \bullet M$ if $(M \cdot ni = \mathrm{W})$ ‖ $\mathcal{Q}_{S_\mathrm{WL}} := \mathcal{Q}_{S_\mathrm{WL}} \bullet M$ if $(M \cdot ni = \mathrm{WL})$ ⟩
      ⟩ if $\neg(\mathcal{Q}_S = \perp)$

      {Transfer a message from $\mathcal{Q}_{S_\mathrm{W}}$ to $\mathcal{T}_\mathrm{W}$; make $\mathcal{T}_\mathrm{W}$ empty after some time}
      [] $transmit\&reset_\mathrm{W}$ :: ⟨ $\mathcal{T}_\mathrm{W}, \mathcal{Q}_{S_\mathrm{W}} := \mathrm{head}(\mathcal{Q}_{S_\mathrm{W}}), \mathrm{tail}(\mathcal{Q}_{S_\mathrm{W}})$ if $\neg(\mathcal{Q}_{S_\mathrm{W}} = \perp) \wedge (\mathcal{T}_\mathrm{W} = \perp)$;
                        $\mathcal{T}_\mathrm{W} := \perp$ ⟩

      {Transfer a message from $\mathcal{Q}_{S_\mathrm{WL}}$ to $\mathcal{T}_\mathrm{WL}$; make $\mathcal{T}_\mathrm{WL}$ empty after some time}
      [] $transmit\&reset_\mathrm{WL}$ :: ⟨ $\mathcal{T}_\mathrm{WL}, \mathcal{Q}_{S_\mathrm{WL}} := \mathrm{head}(\mathcal{Q}_{S_\mathrm{WL}}), \mathrm{tail}(\mathcal{Q}_{S_\mathrm{WL}})$ if $\neg(\mathcal{Q}_{S_\mathrm{WL}} = \perp) \wedge (\mathcal{T}_\mathrm{WL} = \perp)$;
                        $\mathcal{T}_\mathrm{WL} := \perp$ ⟩

      {Transfer a message from $\mathcal{T}_\mathrm{W}$ to $\mathcal{Q}_R$}
      [] ⟨ $\mathcal{Q}_R := \mathcal{Q}_R \bullet \mathcal{T}_\mathrm{W}$ if $\mathrm{isNotOwnMsg}(\mathcal{T}_\mathrm{W})$ ⟩ reacts-to $\neg(\mathcal{T}_\mathrm{W} = \perp)$

      {Transfer a message from $\mathcal{T}_\mathrm{WL}$ to $\mathcal{Q}_R$}
      [] ⟨ $\mathcal{Q}_R := \mathcal{Q}_R \bullet \mathcal{T}_\mathrm{WL}$ if $\mathrm{isNotOwnMsg}(\mathcal{T}_\mathrm{WL})$ ⟩ reacts-to $\neg(\mathcal{T}_\mathrm{WL} = \perp)$

{- - - - - - - - - - End of Transport Interface - - - - - - - - - -}

      {Organize a received Beacon/RT/ACK/Locate/Found message for further processing}
      [] ⟨ $M, \mathcal{Q}_R := \mathrm{head}(\mathcal{Q}_R), \mathrm{tail}(\mathcal{Q}_R)$
         ‖⟨ $\mathcal{Q}_{R_B} := \mathcal{Q}_{R_B} \bullet M$ if $\mathrm{isMsgBcon}(M)$
           ‖ $\mathcal{Q}_{R_{RT}} := \mathcal{Q}_{R_{RT}} \bullet M$ if $\mathrm{isMsgRT}(M) \vee \mathrm{isMsgACK}(M) \vee \mathrm{isMsgLocate}(M) \vee \mathrm{isMsgFound}(M)$
         ⟩
      ⟩ if $\neg(\mathcal{Q}_R = \perp)$

Fig. 8. Mobile UNITY **Program** $host(i)$: part 3

and access points. Also, $\mathcal{N}$ and $\mathcal{A}$ are declared to represent NeighborList and AgentList respectively of any host. Different macros related to various aspects of discovery and communication mechanisms, used in this specification, are skipped in this paper for space limitations.

At the lowest level, TSMM interacts with transport service of supporting device, which is formalized as Transport Interface by a set of assignment statements. Discovery Manager and Communication Manager interchange messages with Transport Interface through two different queues, viz. $\mathcal{Q}_S$ and $\mathcal{Q}_R$. Behavior of Discovery Manager and Communication Manager are abstracted according to the nature of host, which is subscripted in corresponding macro. These macros are, in turn, used in different assignment statements to complete various functionalities of Discovery Manager and Communication Manager. Host Server interchanges request/response tuples (represented as $\mathrm{RT}_\mathrm{tuple}$) with Communication Manager through $\mathcal{Q}_{RT_S}$ and $\mathcal{Q}_{RT_R}$, which is formalized via a set of assignment statements. Similarly, in this specification, a pair of assignment statements formalizes registration/deregistration functionalities of Agent Manager.

{- - - - - - - - - - Start of **Discovery Manager** - - - - - - - - - -}

{Prepare to send **Beacon** message to destination}

⟦ ⟨ $\mathcal{Q}_{S_B}, lastBsent := \mathcal{Q}_{S_B} \bullet \texttt{discSend}_{\text{W}_{iBSS}}(), clock$ if $(\texttt{isSH}(hid) \wedge (nwdeploy = iBSS))$

∥ $\mathcal{Q}_{S_B}, lastBsent := \mathcal{Q}_{S_B} \bullet \texttt{discSend}_{\text{WL}_{iBSS}}(), clock$ if $(\texttt{isMH}(hid) \wedge (nwdeploy = iBSS))$

∥ $\mathcal{Q}_{S_B}, lastBsent := (\mathcal{Q}_{S_B} \bullet \texttt{discSend}_{\text{W}_{iBSS}}()) \bullet \texttt{discSend}_{\text{WL}_{iBSS}}(), clock$

if $(\texttt{isAP}(hid) \wedge (nwdeploy = iBSS))$

⟩ if $((clock - lastBsent) > bconGap)$

{Process received **Beacon** message}

⟦ ⟨ $\texttt{discRcv}_{\text{SH}_{iBSS}}(\mathcal{Q}_{R_B})$ if $(\texttt{isSH}(hid) \wedge (nwdeploy = iBSS))$

∥ $\texttt{discRcv}_{\text{MH}_{iBSS}}(\mathcal{Q}_{R_B})$ if $(\texttt{isMH}(hid) \wedge (nwdeploy = iBSS))$

∥ $\texttt{discRcv}_{\text{AP}_{iBSS}}(\mathcal{Q}_{R_B})$ if $(\texttt{isAP}(hid) \wedge (nwdeploy = iBSS))$

⟩ if $\neg(\mathcal{Q}_{R_B} = \bot)$

{Remove expired entries from $\mathcal{N}$}

⟦ $\texttt{discValid}_{\mathcal{N}_{iBSS}}()$ if $((\texttt{isSH}(hid) \vee \texttt{isMH}(hid) \vee \texttt{isAP}(hid)) \wedge (nwdeploy = iBSS))$

{Update $assoc$ on account of change in associated AP of MH}

⟦ ⟨ $\texttt{discUpdt}_{\text{MH}_{iBSS}}()$ if $(\texttt{isMH}(hid) \wedge (nwdeploy = iBSS))$ ⟩

⟩ if $(\neg \texttt{isPresent}_{\mathcal{N}}(assoc[0]) \vee \neg \texttt{isValid}_{\mathcal{N}}((\exists e : e \uparrow 1 = assoc[0] :: e), clock))$

{- - - - - - - - - - End of **Discovery Manager** - - - - - - - - - -}

{Organize a **Beacon** message for onward transmission}

⟦ ⟨ $\mathcal{Q}_S, \mathcal{Q}_{S_B} := \mathcal{Q}_S \bullet \texttt{head}(\mathcal{Q}_{S_B}), \texttt{tail}(\mathcal{Q}_{S_B})$ ⟩   if $\neg(\mathcal{Q}_{S_B} = \bot)$

{- - - - - - - - - - Start of **Host Server** - - - - - - - - - -}

{Process received RT from different agents}

⟦ ⟨⟦ $k :: \langle r, \mathcal{Q}_{T_{a_k}^S} := \texttt{head}(\mathcal{Q}_{T_{a_k}^S}), \texttt{tail}(\mathcal{Q}_{T_{a_k}^S}) \parallel \texttt{inject}(r, \mathbf{T}') \rangle$ if $\neg(\mathcal{Q}_{T_{a_k}^S} = \bot)$ ⟩

{Process received RT from COMMUNICATION module}

⟦ ⟨ $r, \mathcal{Q}_{RT_R} := \texttt{head}(\mathcal{Q}_{RT_R}), \texttt{tail}(\mathcal{Q}_{RT_S}) \parallel \texttt{inject}(r, \mathbf{T}') \rangle$ if $\neg(\mathcal{Q}_{RT_R} = \bot)$

{Periodically extract RT from HTS for onward transfer to target agents in same/different hosts}

⟦ ⟨ ⟨∥ $a : a \in \mathcal{A} :: r := \texttt{eject}(a, \mathbf{T}') \parallel \langle \mathcal{Q}_{T_a^R} := \mathcal{Q}_{T_a^R} \bullet r$ if $\neg(r = \varepsilon) \rangle$ ⟩

∥ ⟨∥ $e : (e \in \mathcal{N}) \wedge (\mathbf{A} = e \uparrow 2) :: \langle ∥ a : a \in \mathbf{A} :: r := \texttt{eject}(a, \mathbf{T}') \parallel \langle \mathcal{Q}_{RT_S} := \mathcal{Q}_{RT_S} \bullet r$ if $\neg(r = \varepsilon) \rangle \rangle$ ⟩

∥ $lastHTSchk := clock$

⟩ if $(clock - lastHTSchk > HTSaccessGap)$

{- - - - - - - - - - End of **Host Server** - - - - - - - - - -}

Fig. 9. Mobile UNITY **Program** $host(i)$: part 4

{- - - - - - - - - Start of Communication Manager - - - - - - - - - -}

{Prepare to send RT/Locate message to destination}

⟦ ⟨   commSend$_{SH_{iBSS}}$($\mathcal{Q}_{RT_S}$)   if (isSH(hid) ∧ ($nwdeploy = iBSS$))

‖ commSend$_{MH_{iBSS}}$($\mathcal{Q}_{RT_S}$)   if (isMH(hid) ∧ ($nwdeploy = iBSS$))

‖ commSend$_{AP_{iBSS}}$($\mathcal{Q}_{RT_S}$)   if (isAP(hid) ∧ ($nwdeploy = iBSS$))

⟩ if ¬($\mathcal{Q}_{RT_S} = \perp$)

{Process received RT/Locate/Found message, and prepare to send RT/ACK/Found message}

⟦ ⟨   commRcv$_{SH_{iBSS}}$($\mathcal{Q}_{R_{RT}}$)   if (isSH(hid) ∧ ($nwdeploy = iBSS$))

‖ commRcv$_{MH_{iBSS}}$($\mathcal{Q}_{R_{RT}}$)   if (isMH(hid) ∧ ($nwdeploy = iBSS$))

‖ commRcv$_{AP_{iBSS}}$($\mathcal{Q}_{R_{RT}}$)   if (isAP(hid) ∧ ($nwdeploy = iBSS$))

⟩ if ¬($\mathcal{Q}_{R_{RT}} = \perp$)

{Resend RT message whose ACK fails to reach before timeout}

⟦ ⟨ $\mathcal{Q}_{S_{RT}} := \mathcal{Q}_{S_{RT}}$ • commReSend$_{RT_{iBSS}}$()   if ((isMH(hid) ∨ isAP(hid)) ∧ ($nwdeploy = iBSS$))

⟩ if (($clock - lastRTsent$) > $newRTGap$)

{Process RT message whose destination is presently not available}

⟦ ⟨   ⟨ $\mathcal{Q}_{RT_R} := \mathcal{Q}_{RT_R}$ • CS· $data$ ‖ $CS := \perp$ ⟩   if (isMH(hid) ∧ ($nwdeploy = iBSS$))

‖ ⟨ $\mathcal{Q}_{S_{RT}} := \mathcal{Q}_{S_{RT}}$ • newMsg($hid, B_{iBSS_W}, Locate, CS$· $dest$, W)

‖ $\mathcal{L} := \mathcal{L} \cup \{(CS$· $dest, CS$· $data, clock)\}$ ⟩   if (isAP(hid) ∧ ($nwdeploy = iBSS$))

⟩ if (¬($CS = \perp$) ∧ ($rtAtmpt > 3$))

{Remove expired entries from $\mathcal{H}$ and $\mathcal{L}$, and preserve unsent RT}

⟦ commValid$_{\mathcal{HL}_{iBSS}}$()   if ((isSH(hid) ∨ isAP(hid)) ∧ ($nwdeploy = iBSS$))

{- - - - - - - - - End of Communication Manager - - - - - - - - - -}

{Organize RT/ACK/Locate/Found message for onward transmission}

⟦ ⟨ $\mathcal{Q}_S, \mathcal{Q}_{S_{RT}} := \mathcal{Q}_S$ • head($\mathcal{Q}_{S_{RT}}$), tail($\mathcal{Q}_{S_{RT}}$) ⟩   if ¬($\mathcal{Q}_{S_{RT}} = \perp$)

{- - - - - - - - - Start of Agent Manager - - - - - - - - - -}

{Register active agents in $\mathcal{A}$}

⟦ $\mathcal{A}, \mathcal{Q}_{in} := \mathcal{A} \cup$ head($\mathcal{Q}_{in}$), tail($\mathcal{Q}_{in}$)   if ¬($\mathcal{Q}_{in} = \perp$)

{Deregister terminated/migrated agents from $\mathcal{A}$}

⟦ $\mathcal{A}, \mathcal{Q}_{out} := \mathcal{A} \setminus$ head($\mathcal{Q}_{out}$), tail($\mathcal{Q}_{out}$)   if (¬($\mathcal{Q}_{out} = \perp$) ∧ (head($\mathcal{Q}_{out}$) ∈ $\mathcal{A}$))

{- - - - - - - - - End of Agent Manager - - - - - - - - - -}

end

Fig. 10. Mobile UNITY **Program** $host(i)$: part 5

4   Conclusion

This paper has proposed an approach of formalization of a TSMM, which incorporates a fully-decoupled reactive tuple space model, using Mobile UNITY. It has been formally specified as a Mobile UNITY system, which is comprised of components representing different behaviors of agents and hosts of TSMM.

References

1. Bruneo, D., Puliafito, A., Scarpa, M.: Mobile Middleware: Definition and Motivations. In: Bellavista, P., Corradi, A. (eds.) The Handbook of Mobile Middleware, pp. 145–167. Auerbach Pub. (2007)
2. Gelernter, D.: Generative Communication in Linda. Transactions on Programming Languages and Systems 7(1), 80–112 (1985)

3. Eugster, P.T., Felber, P.A., Guerraoui, R., Kermarrec, A.M.: The many faces of Publish/Subscribe. Computing Surveys 35(2), 114–131 (2003)
4. Cabri, G., Ferrari, L., Leonardi, L., Mamei, M., Zambonelli, F.: Uncoupling Coordination: Tuple-Based Models for Mobility. In: Bellavista, P., Corradi, A. (eds.) The Handbook of Mobile Middleware, pp. 229–255. Auerbach Pub. (2007)
5. De, S., Nandi, S., Goswami, D.: Modeling an Enhanced Tuple Space based Mobile Middleware in UNITY. In: Proc. 11th IEEE International Conference on Ubiquitous Computing and Communications, IUCC 2012 (June 2012)
6. Roman, G.C., McCann, P.J., Plun, J.Y.: Mobile UNITY: Reasoning and Specification in Mobile Computing. Transactions on Software Engineering and Methodology 6(3), 250–282 (1997)
7. Chandy, K.M., Misra, J.: Parallel Program Design: A Foundation. Addison-Wesley, Reading (1988)
8. Murphy, A.L., Picco, G.P., Roman, G.C.: Lime: A Coordination Model and Middleware supporting Mobility of Hosts and Agents. Transactions on Software Engineering and Methodology 15(3), 279–328 (2006)
9. Roman, G.-C., Payton, J.: Mobile UNITY Schemas for Agent Coordination. In: Börger, E., Gargantini, A., Riccobene, E. (eds.) ASM 2003. LNCS, vol. 2589, pp. 126–150. Springer, Heidelberg (2003)
10. De, S., Nandi, S., Goswami, D.: On Performance Improvement Issues in Unordered Tuple Space based Mobile Middleware. In: Proc. 2010 Annual IEEE India Conference, INDICON 2010 (December 2010)
11. Gelernter, D., Bernstein, A.J.: Distributed Communication via Global Buffer. In: Proc. 1st Symp. on Principles of Distributed Computing (PODC 1982), pp. 10–18 (August 1982)
12. Denti, E., Natali, A., Omicini, A.: On the Expressive Power of Language for Programming Coordination Media. In: Proc. Symposium on Applied Computing (SAC 1998), pp. 169–177 (August 1998)
13. McCann, P.J., Roman, G.C.: Compositional Programming Abstractions for Mobile Computing. Transactions on Software Engineering 24(2), 97–110 (1998)
14. Picco, G.P., Roman, G.C., McCann, P.J.: Reasoning about Code Mobility with Mobile UNITY. Transactions on Software Engineering and Methodology 10(3), 338–395 (2001)

The QUASIT Model and Framework for Scalable Data Stream Processing with Quality of Service

Paolo Bellavista, Antonio Corradi, and Andrea Reale

DISI - University of Bologna, Italy
{paolo.bellavista,antonio.corradi,andrea.reale}@unibo.it

Abstract. Many academic and industrial research activities have recently recognized the relevance of expressive models and effective frameworks for highly scalable data processing, such as MapReduce. This paper presents the novel Quasit programming model and runtime framework for stream processing in datacenters, with its original capabilities of i) allowing developers to choose among a large set of quality policies to associate with their processing tasks in a fine-grained way, and ii) effectively managing processing execution depending on the associated quality indications. The paper describes the Quasit programming model, via the primary design/implementation choices made in the Quasit runtime framework (available for download from the project Web site) to achieve maximum scalability, flexibility, and reusability. The first experiences with our prototype and the reported experimental results show the feasibility of our approach and its good performance in terms of both limited overhead and horizontal scalability.

Keywords: Stream Processing, Scalability, Quality of Service, Support Frameworks.

1 Introduction

In the last years we have experienced an unprecedented growth in the amount of digital information created everywhere and accumulated day by day. New data are continuously generated by very heterogeneous sources and for very different purposes: for instance, people periodically update their status on social networks and post multimedia data on the Web; industrial sensors monitor critical operational/safety parameters of production plants; most importantly, the recent mass market success of always-connected mobile and portable devices featuring rich sensing capabilities, such as smartphones or tablets, has created an unprecedented scenario where users continuously sense and share data about the physical environment in which they move and act.

A common trend to face the challenge of processing this huge amount of data is to leverage the computing power of commodity computers inside datacenters [1]: by using highly-parallel and fault-tolerant software architectures, extremely complex processing tasks can be performed while keeping costs reasonably limited. In this perspective, frameworks that help handling the complexities of parallel

C. Borcea et al. (Eds.): MobilWare 2012, LNICST 65, pp. 92–107, 2013.
© Institute for Computer Sciences, Social Informatics and Telecommunications Engineering 2013

processing on large clusters, e.g., Google MapReduce [2] and Microsoft Dryad [3], have received enormous attention and are currently widely used in production scenarios. However, while most of these frameworks make static assumptions about the input of their jobs, there is a large class of application domains that need to deal with dynamically changing datasets in form of large *data streams*.

In *data stream processing*, a possibly very large number of streams, coming from multiple and heterogeneous sources, need to be constantly monitored and processed effectively, often in (near) real-time. A very challenging and still open aspect deals with how the computational resources available for stream processing are allocated and used: differently from batch scenarios, where input-data characteristics are usually known a priori, in stream processing it is often hard to predict how the input load will dynamically change. Nonetheless, stream processing solutions are normally required to handle unexpected load peaks, especially when producing mission-critical output, e.g., when monitoring safety conditions and triggering alarms in response to constraint violations.

To properly manage the specific dynamic characteristics of load conditions in *stream processing* scenarios, we claim that there is the need for novel expressive models and effective frameworks that allow developers to describe, with the most appropriate abstraction level and detail, the application-specific requirements of their stream processing case; at the same time, there is the need of frameworks that efficiently support these models and exploit requirement descriptions to achieve the most suitable *Quality of Service* (QoS) in spite of dynamically changing runtime conditions.

The paper presents Quasit, a novel QoS-enabled stream processing model, and the framework supporting this model at runtime that is currently under implementation. Quasit is designed to run effectively on large clusters of commodity hardware and to automatically handle various types of failures. As common in many Stream Processing Engines (SPEs) (e.g., [4,5,6,7,8]), Quasit models stream processing problems as directed acyclic graphs, where nodes represent data transformation stages and edges represent information flows between them. Originally, Quasit allows every element of the *streaming information graph* to be annotated with QoS specifications, used by the runtime framework to adapt to both dynamic load conditions and user-defined quality requirements. In addition, Quasit lets developers define and reuse their custom stream processing *operators*, by supporting their easy dynamic arrangement in graphs to be automatically deployed on the infrastructure of available computational resources. The design of Quasit operators supports a functional-like programming style that clearly separates operator behavior and state, thus making it easier for our runtime framework to support different and sophisticated strategies for QoS provisioning. The source code of our Quasit prototype is freely available for download from the Quasit project Web site[1].

The paper remainder is organized as follows. Section 2 overviews the frameworks in the literature that share some common characteristics with Quasit, by clearly pointing out which are the original aspects of our proposal. In Section 3

---

[1] `http://lia.deis.unibo.it/research/quasit`

we present the Quasit stream processing model and its QoS support. A description of the Quasit framework architecture and of some central implementation insights is given in Section 4, followed by some preliminary evaluation results that show the feasibility of the approach and the effectiveness of our prototype implementation.

2   Related Work

The most popular model for processing large datasets inside datacenters is certainly MapReduce [2], which has recently received a lot of attention thanks to its ease of use and the diffusion of open source implementations, such as Apache Hadoop[2]. In MapReduce, developers have to model their processing problems only in terms of *map* and *reduce* functions. Leveraging this constraint, the MapReduce runtime takes care of efficiently running the defined functions against input data while providing fault-tolerance and horizontal scalability. This programming model makes the simplifying assumption that input consists of static datasets stored in a distributed file system such as GFS [9], and, thus, is not appropriate for dynamic streaming processing scenarios where input data cannot be statically known.

Given the industrial success of MapReduce, several authors have tried to enhance it with more dynamic and advanced stream processing capabilities. For example, [10,11,12] leverage a *map-reduce-merge* strategy (originally proposed by [13]) to run MapReduce jobs on datasets that are dynamically created as the result of *windowing* operations on data streams; partial output from these jobs is then joined through the additional *merge* step. DEDUCE [14] permits to define MapReduce operators through an extension of the SPADE language [15], and to use these operators within an IBM System S[3] stream processing graph; DEDUCE jobs can run on either static datasets or, as in the previously cited approaches, sliding windows over streaming data. In [16], instead, the authors propose HOP, a modified version of Hadoop that, by supporting intra- and inter-job pipelined communication between map and reduce tasks, permits to run continuous MapReduce jobs. All these examples show the interest in extending MapReduce to solve stream processing problems that can be modeled as a sequence of batch jobs working on "slices" of input streams. However, we claim that, by using a model that is inherently designed to work with static input, these solutions cannot offer the flexibility of a native stream-oriented programming model and are often inadequate to effectively deal with the dynamic characteristics of streaming data, such as highly variable sample rate.

Some existing solutions, similarly to Quasit, use directed graphs to model stream processing problems and to distribute processing responsibilities on available nodes. The Borealis Stream Processing Engine [4,17], for instance, allows users to create *query diagrams* to answer *continuous queries* about input data

---

[2] http://hadoop.apache.org, last accessed in June 2012.
[3] Currently commercialized under the IBM InfoSphere Streams brand.

streams. Users can choose among a set of available operators (defined in a specific query algebra [18]) to build directed graphs that model their stream processing cases. Very interestingly, Borealis allows developers to define QoS specifications for the output of their query diagrams: it is possible to estimate the output quality as a function of *response times*, *event drops*, or specific (and user-defined) *event values*. Quasit adopts these solution guidelines by improving and extending them: Quasit users can additionally define their own operators by directly programming them, and acquire a more direct control of quality-related parameters of every part of the processing graph.

Dryad [3] by Microsoft Research also models computations as directed acyclic graphs. In Dryad graphs, vertices are mapped to native programs that are executed — each in its own process — by the Dryad framework: mainly because of the overhead associated to spawning and managing full processes, the grain of Dryad computational components is coarser than Quasit operators, which, instead, are very lightweight objects confined in the Java Runtime Environment. In addition, while Quasit specifically targets continuous stream processing, Dryad, like MapReduce, seems more oriented to the execution of batch-like jobs where input datasets are fixed and known a priori.

Also SPC [5], the core of IBM System S, and S4, a recent project by Yahoo! [8], share some similarities with Quasit in terms of goals and solution guidelines. Both let developers model their continuous stream processing problems as graphs of *Processing Elements* (PEs), which, similarly to Quasit simple operators, may be user-defined. The main difference between Quasit and these two projects is that our proposal is primarily focused on the support of a rich set of QoS-related parameters to customize stream processing behavior, while SPC and S4 do not allow rich QoS specifications.

3   The Quasit Stream Processing Model

Quasit is used to process multiple input data streams concurrently, to perform arbitrary transformations on them, and to produce other data streams as output, which can be fed to other systems for storage or further processing. A Quasit data stream is modeled as a temporal sequence of data samples, whose content is a set of key-value attributes. Any stream is associated with one data type that defines the keys and types of the attributes of its samples.

The basic modeling unit in Quasit is the *Streaming Information Graph* (SIG), a weakly connected acyclic and directed graph that represents the information flow and the transformations that, applied to one or more input streams, produce an output data stream. The nodes of a SIG represent data transformation stages, while its edges model communication dependencies. Figure 1 depicts a simple example of SIG.

Three different kinds of SIG nodes are possible: *data source*, *data sink*, or *operator*. A *data source* node identifies a data stream that is conceptually out of the SIG and its role is to abstract from the actual nature of the stream

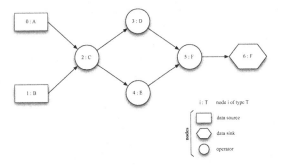

Fig. 1. Simple SIG example, with two data source nodes, one sink node, and four operator nodes. source0 and source1 respectively produce a data stream of typeA and typeB; operator2 receives them as input and produces a typeC data stream, received by operators 3 and 4, producing respectively typeD and typeE data streams. Finally, the typeF data stream generated by operator5 goes into data sink6, of the same type.

producer; it can represent either an external stream source or the output of another Quasit SIG. A *data sink* node, conversely, represents the destination of the data stream that is the output of the SIG; data sinks can be used either to redirect output streams to other systems for additional processing steps or storage, or to connect the output of a SIG with the input of another SIG. An *operator* node associates with one or more input data streams and *generates* exactly one output stream. SIG edges model communication *channels* between nodes.

Every element of a SIG (either node or edge) may be labeled with a QoS specification: QoS specifications allow users to enrich their processing graphs with additional information about non-functional quality requirements. Given the centrality of QoS specifications and their runtime support in Quasit, we will devote a specific section (Section 3.2) to them; but, before that, let us first present the basic building block of our SIG, i.e., the *operator* component, based on which developers can model their stream processing issues in terms of composition of simple transformation stages.

3.1   Operators

An *operator* performs arbitrary operations on the data samples it receives as input, and produces samples for its output stream. We designed Quasit operators having in mind three main goals. First, an operator should be *"concurrency friendly"*: whenever the application semantics allow it, the execution of different operators should be parallelized across all the available processing resources; this should require few or no effort at all for the developer defining the operator. Second, operators should be *easily manageable* in order to allow the Quasit framework to effectively control their execution at runtime, e.g., by moving them from a processing node to another, saving and restoring their processing state, or transparently recovering them from failures. Third, the operator abstraction should favor *maximum reusability* in order to let developers model their problems in terms of SIGs by writing as less new code as possible.

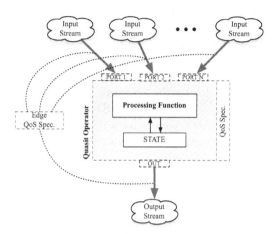

Fig. 2. Structure of a Quasit *simple operator*

Quasit operators can be *simple* or *composite*, and both types can be either *stateful* or *stateless*, depending on whether they need a processing state to be kept or not. A *simple operator* logically consists of several sub-components, as shown schematically in Figure 2. It always has one or more *input ports* and exactly one output port: input ports model the input requirements of the operator, while the output port represents its output contract. The behavior of the operator depends on the combination of its *state* and *processing function*, or solely on the *processing function* in the case of stateless operator.

The processing function is a user-defined function that the Quasit framework invokes asynchronously as data samples are available at input ports. If the operator is stateless, the function takes one parameter, which is bound at runtime to the incoming data samples; if it is stateful, a further parameter is present and is bound to the current state of the operator. The output of the processing function is a tuple made of two optional components: if present, the first is the data sample to send to the output port; the second, always absent for stateless operators, represents the new state the operator will assume. In other words, by defining an operator's processing function, developers specify the set of transformations that, applied to the input, produce its output and state transitions.

Quasit adopts an asynchronous and event-based processing approach, according to which an operator produces output and/or changes its state only in response to incoming data; this permits a large number of operators to share processing resources very efficiently, by enabling high execution *concurrency* in multi-processor and multi-core environments. Furthermore, the sharp separation between the behavior of the operator, expressed through its (stateless) processing function, and its processing/communication state gives Quasit great *flexibility* in taking transparent management decisions at runtime, in order to effectively support the execution of operator components. For instance, Quasit can offer complex and differentiated state persistence/reliability policies, which would have been much more difficult to realize if state was kept mixed with processing logic.

To achieve *maximum reusability*, Quasit introduces a mechanism that permits to use already defined operators as building blocks for creating more complex and powerful ones, i.e., *composite operators*. Developers can define composite operators by arranging existing operators (either simple or composite) into a special type of SIG that completely defines the execution characteristics of the composite operator, called *Operator Definition SIG* (OD-SIG). Operator composability permits to easily encapsulate complex behavior into composite operators, and leverage them to model many problems, with evident reusability advantages.

3.2   QoS Support in Quasit

One of the most original aspects of Quasit is its ability to let developers augment their stream processing models with very rich and differentiated QoS specifications, to be used at runtime to guide the Quasit framework in the management of system behavior and resource allocation according to the desired quality requirements. Related to the design of Quasit QoS-related features, our main goal is to support a wide spectrum of QoS policies, ranging from simple and high-level quality indications (allowing developers to express their requirements quickly and with as few effort as possible) to richer and lower-level parameters, to be used for finer performance tuning when a deeper and more QoS-aware control over processing is needed.

In particular, any SIG element can be augmented with an optional *QoS Specification*, defining a set of non-functional configuration parameters or constraints. Depending on its target, a QoS specification can consist of several *QoS Policies*, each policy influencing a different quality aspect. In this paper, because of the limited space available, we will not provide a detailed and exhaustive description of all the QoS Policies supported by the Quasit framework (some of them are currently under implementation). However, in order to provide readers at least with a high-level view of the practical aspects that can be regulated through QoS augmentation of SIGs, we report, in Table 1, a concise list of the Quasit QoS policies, also showing their applicability scope and their possible values.

As far as we know, the rich variety of QoS modeling options available in Quasit is unique in the literature about data stream processing solutions. Let us remark again that a proper tuning of the various QoS Specifications attached to SIG elements permits to flexibly adapt the Quasit runtime to different application scenarios, by deeply influencing its strategies for effectively allocating and scheduling the dynamically available processing resources; some details about how the Quasit framework effectively puts into execution the Quasit SIG elements and manages them at runtime are presented in the following part of the paper about Quasit framework design and implementation.

Table 1. Concise list of Quasit *QoS Policies*

Element	QoS Policy	Possible values
Data Sink	Output Priority	*Priority value*
Operator	Processing cap	*Time threshold*
Operator	State fault tolerance	*Replication factor*
Operator	State consistency	*Lazy, Snapshot, Strong*
Operator	Queuing Spec.	*Input queues size,*
		Scheduling policies
Operator	Input Ordering	*No order, Causal*
Channel	Delivery Semantics	*Best Effort, At most once,*
		At least once, Exactly once,
		Probabilistic
Channel	Deadline	*Time threshold*

4   The Quasit Framework Prototype

In the following, we present the results of our research work of design, implementation, experimental validation, and quantitative evaluation of a first prototype of the Quasit framework, which implements the Quasit model previously described; let us remark once again that the source code of our framework is freely available for download, evaluation, and extension at our project Web site[1].

This section is structured in three parts: in the first (Section 4.1) we present the Quasit architecture; in Section 4.2 we overview how QoS is achieved and controlled at runtime, while in Section 4.3 we provide some implementation insights about the current Quasit prototype.

4.1   Distributed Architecture

Like other systems for data management and processing in datacenters [2,3,8,9], the Quasit distributed architecture follows a simple *master-workers* model, where a logically centralized node (the *master*) implements management and coordination tasks, while a possibly large number of *worker* nodes perform data processing tasks. In particular, Quasit user-defined SIGs are deployed and executed by a set of computing nodes called *Quasit Runtime Nodes* (QRNs), which are monitored and managed by one *Quasit Domain Manager* (QDM), as shown in Figure 3. The set of QRN nodes and the QDM that manages them are collectively called *domain*. A domain runs one or more SIGs, providing advanced runtime services, such as tolerance to operator/QRN failures, and — most importantly — QoS-based management of SIG execution. New SIGs can be added to the domain dynamically at runtime. We assume that QRNs are connected through a high-speed local area network (LAN), as typically occurs in datacenter scenarios.

In order to distribute the workload and leverage all the dynamically available resources, Quasit decomposes arbitrarily complex user SIGs in smaller units, which are then assigned to individual worker nodes and executed in parallel. The granularity of work decomposition and distribution is determined by the defined *simple operators*.

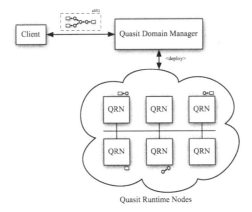

Fig. 3. A Quasit domain includes one QDM (conceptually centralized entity with monitoring and management responsibilities) and several QRNs as middleware instances performing the actual stream processing

Clients submit SIGs to the QDM, which is responsible of planning and continuously monitoring their distributed execution. As soon as a new SIG is received, the QDM must decide an initial partitioning, in order to determine its distributed execution among the available QRNs. The QDM takes this decision by running an *operator placement algorithm* that exploits information about the current status of the QRNs in the domain (e.g., the list of operators already running and their resource availability) to *optimize the execution cost* of the SIG according to the enforced QoS-aware cost function. The development of a proper cost function and placement algorithm is one of our main research challenges: in the current prototype we are exploring a greedy algorithm, called *affinity placement*, which sequentially assigns every operator to the QRN that minimizes its local execution cost, and two additional more trivial algorithms, primarily used as comparison references, i.e., *uniform* and *random* placement, which respectively distribute the operators uniformly (according to a topological ordering of graph vertices) and randomly on the QRNs. An accurate description of the algorithms is out of the scope of this paper, which aims at providing the first high-level presentation of the Quasit model and framework. Although conceptually centralized (and currently implemented in a centralized way), let us point out that the QDM does not represent a bottleneck for the Quasit architecture, because it is not directly involved either in data processing or in any data transfer; moreover, we plan to implement resilience to QDM failures through traditional replication techniques applied to the only QDM entity [21].

A QRN implements a QoS-aware execution container for Quasit operators and is responsible for offering them scheduling and communication support. Reflecting the operator model, the QRN execution model is *asynchronous and event-based*. Communication between operators is managed by the set of distributed QRNs according to a PUB/SUB interaction model: every output port of operators (or data sinks) running on a QRN associates with a named endpoint; QRNs *subscribe* to all the endpoints associated with the input ports of operators (and data sinks) that they are running, and store the samples from these subscriptions in event queues associated with the input ports. A pool of executor threads is used to pick samples from the queues, dispatch them to their destination operators, and execute the associated processing function.

4.2 QoS Management

QoS policies defined at model-level on Quasit SIGs are enforced at runtime thanks to a two level QoS-management architecture, realized through the interaction of one *domain QoS manager*, running within the QDM, and several *node QoS managers*, one for each QRN. The domain QoS manager performs global admission control and QoS-based system configuration, while node QoS managers leverage the computational resources of the QRNs on which they execute to implement and enforce the requested QoS policies on locally running operators and I/O ports.

In order to provide a better insight about this QoS management scheme, let us briefly examine its role in the process of deployment and execution of a SIG. At *deployment time*, the domain QoS manager, after having checked whether the QoS policies applied to the SIG are self-consistent, performs a translation phase, during which user-level QoS policies are transformed to implementation specific configuration parameters, which are sent to QRNs inside operator deployment commands. For example, QoS policies on channels, such as the *delivery semantics* policy, are translated into configuration parameters for the PUB/SUB protocol and for the network queues used by the ports corresponding to the channel endpoints. Node QoS managers use these data to provide an initial configuration for the instances of operator and ports they are responsible of. At *execution time*, QoS monitoring tasks are cooperatively performed by domain and node QoS managers: node managers continuously collect data about the behavior of their locally running components, and try to autonomously adjust their configuration to avoid possible QoS violations; for example, they can reallocate their local resources by giving a greater share to operators with higher priority (thus, penalizing the less important ones). At the same time, they also forward monitoring data to the domain QoS manager, which will use them to take authoritative decisions in case adaption actions of single local managers are not sufficient to avoid QoS violations; for example, it can decide to move an operator from a QRN to another in case the latter has a greater amount of resources to allocate to its execution.

4.3 Implementation Insights

Our QDM and QRN components are realized using the Scala[4] programming language. Scala has been preferred to other possible alternatives for three main reasons: first, the language runtime comes with a rich library that offers an

---

[4] http://www.scala-lang.org/, last accessed in June 2012.

excellent support for writing concurrent and multi-threaded applications; second, its elegant and concise syntax allows us to simplify the design of the user API through which developers model their stream processing problems; third, Scala code, once compiled, is executed on the solid and widely supported Java Runtime Environment.

Quasit PUB/SUB interactions are instead realized on top of the OMG Data Distribution Service (DDS) [22] middleware, which is used as the basis for both reliable group membership management and inter-QRN SIG channels. The choice of using a DDS-based communication middleware grants several benefits. First, DDS message dissemination uses an IP-multicast-based protocol that well fits the typical one-to-many communication patterns of Quasit operators and perfectly adapts to network characteristics of datacenters where nodes are commonly arranged in a hierarchy of Ethernet segments, connected by layer2 switches. Second, the DDS standard defines a rich set of QoS parameters, that can be used to configure and personalize many low-level details of the communication middleware: using DDS to implement our PUB/SUB communication layer has provided us with a solid ground on which we build our ad-hoc QoS enforcement mechanisms, especially those relative to channels. Whenever possible, in fact, we exploit mappings between high-level Quasit QoS policies and possible configurations of the various DDS QoS parameters, and set up the QRN networking layers according to them.

Finally, the scheduling of actors and the management of their queues is currently implemented using the Scala Actors framework [23]: every operator is represented by an actor instance, which perfectly suits our event-based processing model. Currently, the scheduling of these actors is taken care by a *work-stealing* pool of threads based on the Java Fork/Join framework [24]. This scheduler, in the currently available version of the Quasit prototype, does not permit any QoS-based configuration: we plan to add this feature as a future implementation step.

5   Preliminary Evaluation

In this section we present some first preliminary results collected while testing our Quasit framework prototype in a relatively small-scale deployment environment. The reported results demonstrate anyway the feasibility and the effectiveness of our approach.

The selected and simple test scenario consists of an external source producing a periodic stream of image frames. For instance, this stream could correspond to the sequence of key frames of a video produced by a security camera. These image samples are transformed through a series of manipulation steps, and then streamed again to an external destination. The samples generated from the source correspond to the repetition of a 192x128 24bpp PNG image, which is a scaled version of one of the photos from a public test set by Kodak[5]. The size of each sample is approximately 43 KB.

---

[5] kodim23.png, publicly available at http://r0k.us/graphics/kodak/, last accessed in June 2012.

We have modeled the image manipulation process as a pipeline of Quasit operators, whose processing function is implemented as stateless OpenCV[6]-based transformations. The combination of these operators forms a 30 steps pipeline-shaped SIG (as shown in Figure 4) deployed and run on top of the Quasit framework prototype. All the stages of this pipeline have approximatively the same computational complexity. Let us note that this simple scenario is anyway highly representative because i) pipeline-shaped patterns are very common in more complex SIGs and ii) the number of involved operators (30) is relatively high and close to the real size of many SIGs of practical application interest.

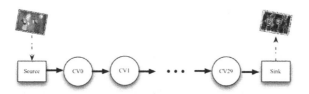

Fig. 4. The simple and pipeline-shaped SIG used in this experimental evaluation

The testbed Quasit domain consists of one machine running the QDM component, plus from one up to four different physical nodes having the role of QRNs. The QRNs are interconnected through one Ethernet segment, while the QDM, although in the same IP subnet, is separated from the QRNs by two switches. The machine hosting the QDM is also used as the external source and sink of the image frames. The hardware and software configuration of the machines is shown in Table 2.

In each experiment run, we feed the deployed SIG with 500 image samples, not counting "warm-up" and "cool-down" sets of samples processed when the SIG pipeline is not full. For each configuration, we have collected the results of 15 to 50 runs of the same experiment (depending on the variability of results).

The experimental results reported in the following aim at discussing two main performance aspects that we have measured on our testbed:

– The management overhead with respect to an ideal parallel processing scenario.
– The ability to scale horizontally, by dynamically adding QRNs to one Quasit domain.

In order to quantitatively evaluate the overhead imposed by the Quasit middleware (if compared with the maximum possible improvement of stream processing performance thanks to parallelization), we have also designed a very simple simulator that models our scenario but omits all the overhead associated with middleware-level management of operators (including operator scheduling) and inter-QRN network communication. The simulator models a group of parallel

---

[6] OpenCV, `http://opencv.willowgarage.com/wiki/`, last accessed in June 2012.

Table 2. Hardware and software configuration of QRN nodes

Host: Intel Pentium Dual-Core E2160 @ 1.80GHz w/ 2 GB RAM
RAM: 2 GB
Network Interface: Gigabit Ethernet
OS: Ubuntu 11.04 (Linux kernel 3.0.0)
DDS: OpenSplice DDS 5.4.1 Community Edition
Scala: 2.9.1-final
JVM: OpenJDK 64-bit Server VM (IcedTea7-2.0 build 147)
JVM Flags: -Xms128M -Xmx512M -Xss4M

workers arranged in a pipeline; their number reflects the number of available CPUs across all the QRNs. OpenCV transformations of the original SIG are distributed evenly among workers, and each of them executes sequentially, for each incoming sample, the transformations it is responsible for, before forwarding it to the next worker. In the simulations, we measure the average time needed to perform a complete processing of an image sample by varying the rate at which new samples are produced, and we compare the results with the performance data obtained on a real deployment environment with 4 QRNs in a Quasit domain (operators deployed according to the uniform placement strategy). In the real deployment environment, image processing time is measured as the sample *round trip time* (RTT), i.e., the time interval between the generation of a new frame and the reception of the processed version of that frame (recall that the external source/sink of the input/output streams coincide in our simple pipeline-shaped test SIG). Figure 5a shows the distribution of the measured RTTs while increasing generation rates in the real deployment and the average processing time in the "ideal" simulated scenario.

Clearly, in both cases, the processing time increases abruptly as soon as our Quasit framework is no longer able to keep up with image production rate and the input queue of the first operator (worker) starts filling up. For low sample rates, Quasit performance is very close to the ideal one, thus demonstrating a limited overhead in unloaded conditions; the difference tends to grow as the input rate increases; we experienced that this is mainly due to the overhead introduced by operator scheduling, which is completely neglected in the simplified simulated scenario.

About our second evaluation goal of verifying the ability of Quasit to scale as additional QRNs are added to a domain, we have deployed the same test pipeline-shaped SIG on four different execution environments, with respectively one, two, three, or four QRNs. In all cases we have deployed the graph using the uniform placement strategy. Figure 5b shows the results. The trend of the curves is the same in all the examined domains: as long as the production rate does not exceed the maximum processing rate in unloaded conditions, the average sample RTT is constant and low (around 450 milliseconds); as soon as Quasit is no longer able to keep up with the sample arrival rate, the average processing time starts to grow. However, the results show that by adding processing resources to one Quasit domain, it is seamlessly possible to increase the Quasit ability to

(a)   (b)

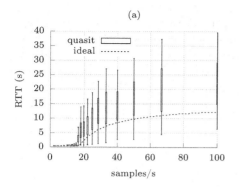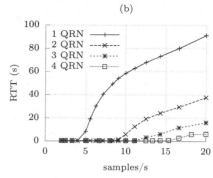

Fig. 5. (a) Distribution of sample processing with 4 QRNs and uniform operator placement. The dashed line represents the performance upper bound in ideal conditions.
(b) Comparison of average processing times using 1, 2, 3, or 4 QRNs and uniform
placement.

serve more aggressive input rates, with reasonably limited overhead. In fact, it
can be seen that by using two, three, or four QRNs Quasit case serve an input
rate respectively 1.82, 2.5, and 3.34 times faster if compared to the one QRN
configuration[7], thus showing a limited degradation. Of course, the possible speed-
up does not grow linearly with the number of QRNs because of the overhead
due to management and network communication. However, the system ability
to scale horizontally also depends strongly on the characteristics of the SIGs
being executed: for this reason, Quasit fosters a SIG design made of many fine
grained components sharing no state, giving the framework many parallelization
opportunities to be exploited according to the required QoS level and resource
availability.

6   Conclusive Remarks and Future Work

In this paper we have introduced Quasit, both a programming model and a
framework prototype for stream processing in datacenters. Compared to existing
literature and available industrial solutions, Quasit is original in its ability to
offer a large set of QoS policies to customize its processing behavior according
to user-defined application requirements. The model of data stream processing
is simple and easy to use: it is based on easy-to-define operators and events, and
it permits to model, design, and realize stream processing operations in a simple
but flexible way. Our first prototype of the Quasit runtime, although still early
and partial, represents a concrete proof-of-concept of a possible implementation
of the proposed model (available for extension and refinement to the community
of researchers/practitioners in the field), and encourages further development.

---

[7] For this comparison, we have considered the sample rate at which the system starts
to become overloaded and to accumulate data at the operator queues.

We are concentrating our future work along two main directions. On the one hand, we will extend our prototype toward the implementation of a richer set of QoS policies for SIG operators and channels, and we will experiment alternative operator placement and management strategies. On the other hand, we are performing a more significant set of experiments to verify the ability of our Quasit model and prototype to sustain challenging large-scale deployment environments, with a special focus on dynamic differentiation of stream processing services depending on QoS requirements specified at the SIG level.

References

1. Barroso, L., Dean, J., Holzle, U.: Web search for a planet: the Google cluster architecture. IEEE Micro 23(2), 22–28 (2003)
2. Dean, J., Ghemawat, S.: MapReduce: Simplified Data Processing on Large Clusters. Commun. ACM 51(1), 107–113 (2008)
3. Isard, M., Budiu, M., Yu, Y., Birrell, A., Fetterly, D.: Dryad: distributed data-parallel programs from sequential building blocks. In: 2nd ACM SIGOPS/EuroSys European Conference on Computer Systems, vol. 41(3), pp. 59–72. ACM, New York (2007)
4. Abadi, D.J., Ahmad, Y., Balazinska, M., Cetintemel, U., Cherniack, M., Hwang, J.-H., Lindner, W., Maskey, A.S., Rasin, A., Ryvkina, E., Tatbul, N., Xing, Y., Zdonik, S.: The Design of the Borealis Stream Processing Engine. In: 2nd Biennial Conference on Innovative Data Systems Research (CIDR), pp. 277–289. VLDB Endowment (2005)
5. Amini, L., Andrade, H., Bhagwan, R., Eskesen, F., King, R., Park, Y., Venkatramani, C.: SPC: A distributed, scalable platform for data mining. In: Grossman, R., Connelly, S. (eds.) 4th International workshop on Data Mining Standards, Services and Platforms (DM-SS), pp. 27–37. ACM, New York (2006)
6. Arasu, A., Babcock, B., Babu, S., Cieslewicz, J., Ito, K., Motwani, R., Srivastava, U., Widom, J.: STREAM: The Stanford Data Stream Management System, Technical report, Stanford InfoLab (2004)
7. Carney, D., Çetintemel, U., Cherniack, M., Convey, C., Lee, S., Seidman, G., Stonebraker, M., Tatbul, N., Zdonik, S.: Monitoring streams: a new class of data management applications. In: 28th International Conference on Very Large Data Bases (VLDB 2002), pp. 215–226. VLDB Endowment (2002)
8. Neumeyer, L., Robbins, B., Nair, A., Kesari, A.: S4: Distributed Stream Computing Platform. In: 2010 IEEE International Conference on Data Mining Workshops (ICDMW 2010), pp. 170–177. IEEE, Los Alamitos (2010)
9. Ghemawat, S., Gobioff, H., Leung, S.-T.: The Google File System. ACM SIGOPS Operating Systems Rev. 37(5), 29–43 (2003)
10. Alves, D., Bizarro, P., Marques, P.: Flood: elastic streaming Map-Reduce. In: 4th ACM International Conference on Distributed Event-Based Systems (DEBS 2010), pp. 113–114. ACM, New York (2010)
11. Horey, J.: A programming framework for integrating web-based spatiotemporal sensor data with MapReduce capabilities. In: ACM SIGSPATIAL International Workshop on GeoStreaming, pp. 51–58. ACM, New York (2010)
12. Logothetis, D., Yocum, K.: Ad-hoc data processing in the cloud. Proceedings of the VLDB Endowment 1(2), 1472–1475 (2008)

13. Yang, H.-C., Dasdan, A., Hsiao, R., Parker, D.: Map-reduce-merge: simplified relational data processing on large clusters. In: 2007 ACM SIGMOD International Conference on Management of Data, pp. 1029–1040. ACM, New York (2007)

14. Kumar, V., Andrade, H., Gedik, B., Wu, K.-L.: DEDUCE: at the intersection of Map-Reduce and stream processing. In: Manolescu, I., Spaccapietra, S., Teubner, J., Kitsuregawa, M., Leger, A., Naumann, F., Ailamaki, A., Ozcan, F. (eds.) 13th International Conference on Extending Database Technology (EDBT 2010), pp. 657–662. ACM, New York (2010)

15. Gedik, B., Andrade, H., Wu, K.-L., Yu, P.S., Doo, M.: SPADE: the System S declarative stream processing engine. In: 2008 ACM SIGMOD International Conference on Management of Data (SIGMOD 2008), pp. 1123–1134. ACM, New York (2008)

16. Condie, T., Conway, N., Alvaro, P., Hellerstein, J.M., Elmeleegy, K., Sears, R.: MapReduce Online. In: 7th USENIX Conference on Networked Systems Design and Implementation (NSDI 2010). USENIX Association, Berkeley (2010)

17. Ahmad, Y., Tatbul, N., Xing, W., Xing, Y., Zdonik, S., Berg, B., Cetintemel, U., Humphrey, M., Hwang, J.-H., Jhingran, A., Maskey, A., Papaemmanouil, O., Rasin, A.: Distributed operation in the Borealis stream processing engine. In: 2005 ACM SIGMOD International Conference on Management of Data (SIGMOD 2005), pp. 882–884. ACM, New York (2005)

18. Abadi, D.J., Carney, D., Çetintemel, U., Cherniack, M., Convey, C., Lee, S., Stonebraker, M., Tatbul, N., Zdonik, S.: Aurora: a new model and architecture for data stream management. The VLDB Journal The International Journal on Very Large Data Bases 12(2), 120–139 (2003)

19. Odersky, M., Altherr, P., Cremet, V., Emir, B., Maneth, S., Micheloud, S., Mihaylov, N., Schinz, M., Stenman, E., Zenger, M.: An Overview of the Scala Programming Language. Technical Report, École Polytechnique Fédérale de Lausanne, Lausanne, Switzerland (2004)

20. Emir, B., Odersky, M., Williams, J.: Matching Objects with Patterns. In: Ernst, E. (ed.) ECOOP 2007. LNCS, vol. 4609, pp. 273–298. Springer, Heidelberg (2007)

21. Guerraoui, R., Schiper, A.: Software-based replication for fault tolerance. Computer 30(4), 68–74 (1997)

22. Object Management Group: Data Distribution Service for Real-time Systems, version 1.2. Technical report, Object Management Group (2007)

23. Haller, P., Odersky, M.: Scala Actors: Unifying thread-based and event-based programming. Theoretical Computer Science 410(2-3), 202–220 (2009)

24. Lea, D.: A Java fork/join framework. In: ACM 2000 Conference on Java Grande (JAVA 2000), pp. 36–43. ACM, New York (2000)

NASDI – Naming and Service Discovery for DTNs in Internet Backbones

Sebastian Schildt, Wolf-Bastian Pöttner, Oliver Ohneiser, and Lars Wolf

Institute of Operating Systems and Computer Networks,
Technische Universität Braunschweig, Germany
{schildt,poettner,ohneiser,wolf}@ibr.cs.tu-bs.de

Abstract. Delay Tolerant Networking (DTN) approaches based on the Bundle Protocol are commonly used within mobile IP based networks. Instead of being isolated applications, the Internet is often used to provide additional services or to route through other parts of the DTN network. A major drawback is that current DTN routing and discovery protocols are not generally applicable in the Internet as there is no common protocol to resolve DTN node names to convergence layer addresses outside a local network.

We present NASDI, an approach based on Distributed Hash Tables which can support naming, routing, notifications and service discovery in a heterogeneous DTN linked by the Internet. We present the architecture and initial evaluations of a NASDI prototype system we built for the IBR-DTN software.

1 Introduction

Delay Tolerant Networking (DTN) approaches replace the end-to-end semantics of common protocols such as IP with a hop-by-hop store and forward architecture [1]. Originally devised for interplanetary networks where nodes might see each other only occasionally, this approach has also been widely applied for ad-hoc networks with high mobility such as vehicular networks [2]. The Bundle Protocol [3] is a standardized widely used DTN protocol. It supports optional end-to-end acknowledgements on top of the hop-by-hop approach. In fact, the Bundle Protocol can be seen as a superset of IP (and TCP, as it includes elements from both the networking and the transport layer): In a continuously connected network it works much like the former, while in addition it is able to deal with disruptions of the network. This leads to the use of the Bundle Protocol in networks with mobile IP devices such as smartphones, which are regularly connected to the Internet [4] [5].

However, the Bundle Protocol ecosystem has a major shortcoming when it comes to operating in large-scale fully interconnected networks such as the Internet: There is no standard mechanism to find a node or the next hop for a specific DTN nodename. Compared to the standard IP architecture there is no standardized naming system such as DNS and there is no usable routing protocol to find the next hop to a destination if that hop is located in a so far unknown

C. Borcea et al. (Eds.): MobilWare 2012, LNICST 65, pp. 108–121, 2013.

network across the Internet. The various proposed routing protocols for DTNs normally assume an ad-hoc scenario relying on different forms of flooding and network discovery, both of which are not applicable in the Internet.

In fact the "DTNBone" [6], which is a collection of DTN nodes operated in the Internet by different institutions for DTN testing purposes, consists mainly of a webpage. This page contains (often inaccurate) information about which node can be reached at which IP address using which transport protocols. A DTN administrator who wants to connect with the DTNBone takes this information in order to configure a static route within his DTN server.

Therefore, we propose NASDI, a mechanism that allows for naming, service discovery and routing between DTN nodes operated in a large backbone network such as the Internet. NASDI is able to integrate peripheral networks and nodes which are only intermittently connected to the backbone and it allows nodes which are unaware of the approach to take advantage of the benefits. As DTNs contain intermittently connected nodes that may enter or leave the network at any time, it is our goal to be notified about such events even if the node in question is not located in our direct network neighborhood. To facilitate this NASDI offers an asynchronous notification mechanism. NASDI is based on Distributed Hash Tables (DHT) and is specifically adapted to the needs of DTNs.

In Section 2 we present some related work. Section 3 describes our system architecture followed by Section 4 describing the proposed algorithms. Section 5 introduces our implementation. Finally, in section 6 we wrap up our experiences with NASDI and line out future work.

2   Related Work

For LAN or small-scale ad-hoc DTNs there exists a standard mechanism to detect neighboring nodes and services: IP Neighbor Discovery (IPND) [7]. IPND works by regularly broadcasting beacons and thus it does not scale to the Internet. In [8] Waldhorst sketches Arriba, a general architecture for routing in overlay networks spanning heterogeneous technologies based on generic node ids. That work focusses on routing, but it does not specify how to create unique node ids and assign them to device names or underlay addresses. Closely related to the problem of node discovery is the problem of routing: Most general routing protocols proposed for DTNs are designed for ad-hoc type scenarios and as such are often variants of flooding like Epidemic routing [9] or PROPHET [10]. Other approaches exploit domain specific knowledge [11] and are thus not generally applicable.

Earlier DTN specifications included the concept of "regions". DTN regions were a hierarchical naming concept for DTN nodes based on their network affiliation [12]. Current DTN specifications have abandoned this concept in favour of a more flexible flat URI based namespace. The idea is, that different networks can be identified by different URI schemes, but generally the usage of

URIs is meant to be much more open. The specification suggests things such as "expressions of interest" based URIs [1].

To allow hosts to find out the network layer address for a host name in the Internet the Domain Name System [13] is used. In addition to a number of shortcomings of traditional DNS in the Internet [14], it is also not optimal in a DTN. DNS systems are partitioned assuming a hierarchy of hostnames, which does not exist in the flat URI based namespace of DTNs. Furthermore DNS is not self-organizing but instead it involves significant organizational overhead. Also, DNS assumes that the network of servers is static and rather stable - a property, which can not necessarily be found in DTN. To overcome some of these problems, DDNS [15] has been proposed. It is based on a DHT as data storage and embeds a hierarchical namespace in the flat key space of a hash table. DDNS tries to mimic the behavior of DNS and is destined to be a DNS replacement. Although it is also based on a DHT, it has some significant differences to our approach. It just transfers DNS semantics to a distributed DHT store and thus lacks an asynchronous notification mechanism and support for groups.

As suggested in [4], DHTs might be a feasible way to tackle the naming problem in DTNs. DHTs are a robust way to store data in a distributed fashion. A DHT is a key-value store which is distributing the load evenly across participant nodes while still providing good lookup performance. Generally DHTs are resilient against node failure, have excellent scalability and support a flat name space. DHT implementations differ in the topology in which they organize participant nodes, and in the metric used to determine which key belongs to which node. One of the earliest well-known DHT is Chord introduced in the seminal paper by Stoica et al. [16]. Chord uses a ring topology. In addition to successor information, each node has a routing table which enables $O(log(n))$ communication complexity while searching for a key. Among other well known DHT variants are Pastry [17], which tries to exploit local neighborhood information and CAN [18] which organizes data in a d-dimensional grid. A more recent DHT is Kademlia [19] which is widely used in the EMule and BitTorrent P2P networks. Thus, from all DHTs Kademlia has best proven the DHT's alleged scalability and performance in real world scenarios [20]. For a more thorough DHT introduction see [21].

As lined out above, one of NASDI's goals is to provide an asynchronous event notification mechanism. Several papers about publish-subscribe solutions based on DHTs have been published, such as the SCRIBE [22] system. It is based on Pastry [17] and allows topic-based subscriptions. The XEvent [23] publish-subscribe system is based on Bamboo [24] and allows either topic-based or event-content-based subscription using XPath expressions as filter. Both approaches target networks with a large number of subscribers and events and are therefore focused on strategies to efficiently and reliably deliver these events. Our use case has only a limited number of events that does not need such sophisticated structure. In addition, neither SCRIBE nor XEvent support the notion of asynchronous, cached events that will be delivered whenever a node rejoins the network.

3   System Architecture

We propose NASDI, a distributed system that can provide naming, routing and
service discovery for Internet connected DTNs. NASDI's goal is to help connecting
to other DTN nodes from which only the name is known. As we will show,
NASDI does not necessarily find the destination itself, but possibly only a suitable
next hop that can be used to route to the destination. Due to the various,
sometimes very application specific, routing protocols available for DTNs, unlike
[8], NASDI does not try to replace former routing protocols in DTNs. It rather
augments them by bridging the gap between separate DTN networks connected
through the Internet that cannot discover each offer by the conventional link local
discovery mechanisms. For example, to reach a so far unknown node in another
network, NASDI provides the connectivity information of a suitable node. This
node can then be contacted and sent the bundle. Additionally routing packets for
a mechanism such as PRoPHET might be exchanged with the newly discovered
node to learn about the network behind it.

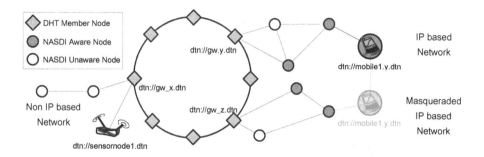

Fig. 1. Scenario Overview

An overview of a NASDI System is depicted in Figure 1. Apart from providing
naming services to well connected IP capable DTN nodes, the NASDI architecture
also allows to integrate peripheral networks that are not directly reachable or
which use a non-IP transport layer for the Bundle protocol. These networks can
be transparently proxied by gateway routers as explained in section 3.2. Additionally NASDI can also improve the connectivity of legacy nodes not supporting
NASDI.

3.1   Assumptions

The following standard DTN terminology is required to understand the information managed by NASDI: Each DTN Node has one or more EIDs (Endpoint
Identifier). EIDs identify a node or a service and have the form of URIs [1]. To
connect to an EID within a DTN it is necessary to know which convergence
layer, and which convergence layer address can be used to connect with the

node. Common convergence layers are TCP [25] and UDP [26] or the Licklider
Transport Protocol [27].

Generally, any DHT structure can be used. For the notification we do however
assume, that the location of a node in the DHT topology is deterministic, and
that this position can be determined by any DHT member. For example a node's
location within the DHT's topology can be determined by that nodes name. More
specifically, for the notification to work we assume that each DHT member is
responsible for a range in keyspace containing its own node id.

As mentioned before the EIDs used in Bundle Protocol [3] have the form
of an URI. Commonly the *dtn://* schema is used. An example EID would be
dtn://node1/echo which identifies the application "echo" on the node "node1".
For the remainder of the text we assume that we use the EID's scheme and
authority parts [28] as keys for the DHT, i.e. *dtn://node1* represents a node id
and is used as key for the DHT. Other schemes might use a different mechanism
to derive the DHT keys depending on the scheme's semantics.

3.2 DTN Node Roles

When NASDI is deployed each node can assume different roles in the NASDI
system. The different roles are depicted in figure 1. First, it is to be expected
that not all nodes will support NASDI:

- **Nasdi aware nodes:** Nodes, which implement NASDI (filled circles and
  diamonds in figure 1). These nodes can be DHT members, i.e. storing information for the DHT or query the DHT.
- **Nasdi unaware nodes:** Nodes, which do not know about the NASDI mechanism (empty circles in figure 1). Lots of unaware nodes are to be expected
  before this approach is widely adopted within the DTN community. NASDI
  unaware nodes can still be announced or proxied within the DHT by a DHT
  member. They cannot, however, query the DHT for information. They can
  benefit from NASDI by routing through a DHT member.

NASDI aware nodes can choose to become a **DHT member** (diamonds in figure
1). A DHT member is responsible for storing data which is assigned to it by
the DHT implementation. Additionally it is responsible for regularly refreshing
the DHT information of nodes it proxies or announces in the DHT. Therefore a
node with high mobility or insufficient network connection might choose not to
join the DHT. For nodes which have contact information in the DHT, two kinds
of information can be stored in the DHT:

- **Announced nodes:** Announced nodes are nodes, whose convergence layer
  information is stored within the DHT. The convergence layer information
  stored in the DHT points to the node itself, i.e. contains its current IP
  address. A node can announce itself in the DHT if it is a DHT member, or
  it can ask a DHT member to announce it.
- **Proxied node:** Nodes in networks that are not accessible via IP from the
  Internet. They need a DTN router in order to participate in the global

network. Reasons for unreachable nodes might be firewall or NAT router. Proxied nodes are nodes which have the convergence layer information of another DTN node stored in the DHT. The proxy can also be used as a gateway between different underlying network technologies such as IP and ZigBee. Another rationale behind proxying nodes is, that a node might only be intermittently available which leads to frequent DHT updates and inaccurate information. Instead, storing the convergence layer information of a node that is more likely to be online, allows other DTN members to route bundles in the correct direction while the proxy node is in a good position to relay the information to the target as soon as it is available.

Please note, that a node may be announced directly and at the same is being proxied by others.

4   DHT Information Management

This section details the information stored in the DHT and the steps needed to maintain and query the DHT. We assume that the DHT provides a method DHT_ROUTE(MSG, KEY, VALUE) which delivers a message of type msg with content $value$ to the node(s) responsible for the partition of key space containing key.

4.1   Information Stored in the DHT

The storage at DHT member nodes is assumed to be a set val_{stored} of $(key, value)$ tuples. For a given key a number of values can be concatenated, which is needed for group management and is also a way to deal with duplicate names: As the Bundle Protocol forces no structure on the EID naming space, it is valid and to be expected that for example multiple dtn://test nodes will join the network. Replacing is not an option because we do not want malicious or similarly named nodes to expunge valid entries from the DHT. Security critical applications which need to certify the identity of the other node, can use the Bundle Protocol

val_stored		
Key	ABBC2134	
Value	time_to_live	1000
	time_since_last_seen	100
	time_refresh_passive	200
	type_entry	SINGLE
	type_information_list	TCP, UDP

notify_pend		
Key	0F43014C	
Value	number_of_notifications	1
	event	reoccur
	interest	AB21

(a) val_stored single entry   (b) $notify_{pend}$ entry

Fig. 2. Data stored in the DHT

Security extension [29]. Therefore, spoofing other nodes in the DHT does not pose an additional risk.

Figures 2a shows an example entry for a stored node. The *key* is the key used as address in the DHT and it is derived from a node's id by SHA-1 hashing it. The *type_entry field* denotes whether this is a group or single node entry (the Bundle Protocol allows the same form of id to be used for either a group or a node). The *type_information_list* contains the IP address and port numbers of the TCP and/or UDP convergence layer for a single node entry, or a list of hashed node ids for a group entry.

Different timers are used to determine when to expunge an entry and to assess the freshness of the data:

– time_to_live (*ttl*): This timer determines how long this entry is considered to be valid. The initial value is determined by the node publishing the key into the DHT. The node that stores this entry decrements it. This entry is measure how long the contact information in this entry is assumed to be valid
– time_since_last_seen (*tls*): Even if the the *ttl* is very high (e.g. for announcing a stationary node), the entry should be refreshed periodically. The *tls* counts how many seconds have past since the entry was last updated.
– time_refresh_passive (*trp*): The *trp* value is constant and indicates how often the publishing nodes intends to refresh the entry. If *tls* > *trp* this means that an entry was not refreshed within the expected time. This can indicate that the publishing node has connectivity problems.

4.2   DHT RPCs

On top of the DHT the following message types have to be implemented by DHT members. We assume that a *key* (which is used for DHT routing) and a *value* is associated with each message.

– GET: Standard DHT operation. Returns all entries for *key*. The *value* parameter is ignored for this call.
– STORE: Standard DHT store. Stores *value* associated with *key*. Existing entries for *key* are extended.
– JOIN_GROUP: Allows to augment information stored for a *key* describing a group. Creates a new val_{stored} group entry if the group does not exist so far.
– LEAVE_GROUP: Deletes the node in *value* from the group entry designated by *key*. Does not touch other entries for *key*.
– NOTIFY_REQUEST: Indicates that the node id contained in *value* wants to be notified when a modification is done to key *key*. A user should be able to specify whether this should be a "one-shot" notify, i.e. whether the notification request should be cleared after the notification is fired the first time or whether this should be a permanent notification request. See also section 4.3.
– NOTIFICATION: This message contains a notification for the key *key*. If the current node's id is *key*, the notification is forwarded to the application layer. Otherwise the (*key, value*) tuple is stored.

The processing of these messages is shown in algorithm 1.

Algorithm 1. Process messages

1: **procedure** PROCESSMESSAGE($msg, key, value$)
2:     **if** $msg =$ GET **then**
3:         **return** $\{(k, v) \mid (k, v) \in val_{stored} \wedge k = key\}$
4:     **else if** $msg =$ STORE **then**
5:         $entry \leftarrow (key, v) \mid (key, v) \in val_{stored}$
6:         **if** $entry == \emptyset$ **then**
7:             $entry \leftarrow \{(key, value)\}$
8:         **else**
9:             MERGE_SINGLE($entry, value$)
10:         **end if**
11:         $val_{stored} \leftarrow val_{stored} \setminus \{(k, v) \mid k = key\}$
12:         $val_{stored} \leftarrow val_{stored} \cup entry$
13:     **else if** $msg =$ JOIN_GROUP **then**
14:         $entry \leftarrow (key, v) \mid (key, v) \in val_{stored}$
15:         **if** $entry == \emptyset$ **then**
16:             $entry \leftarrow \{(key, value)\}$
17:         **else**
18:             MERGE_GROUP($entry, value$)
19:         **end if**
20:         $val_{stored} \leftarrow val_{stored} \setminus \{(k, v) \mid k = key\}$
21:         $val_{stored} \leftarrow val_{stored} \cup entry$
22:     **else if** $msg =$ LEAVE_GROUP **then**
23:         $entry \leftarrow (key, v) \mid (key, v) \in val_{stored}$
24:         **if** $entry \neq \emptyset$ **then**
25:             $entry \leftarrow$ REMOVE_FROM_GROUP($entry, value$)
26:             $val_{stored} \leftarrow val_{stored} \setminus \{(k, v) \mid k = key\}$
27:             $val_{stored} \leftarrow val_{stored} \cup entry$
28:         **end if**
29:     **else if** $msg =$ NOTIFY_REQUEST **then**
30:         $notify_{pend} \leftarrow notify_{pend} \cup \{(key, value)\}$
31:     **else if** $msg =$ NOTIFICATION **then**
32:         **if** $key = my\_id$ **then**
33:             NOTIFY_APP($value$)
34:         **else**   ▷ Indirect notification
35:             $val_{stored} \leftarrow val_{stored} \cup \{(key, value)\}$
36:         **end if**
37:     **end if**
38:     **if** $msg \neq$ NOTIFY
39:     **and** $msg \neq$ NOTIFICATION **then**
40:         CHECK_NOTIFY(key)   ▷ See algorithm 2
41:     **end if**
42: **end procedure**

4.3   Asynchronous Notification

In a mobility enabled DTN network nodes might not be reachable at all times. This is a standard case in DTN networks and participating nodes keep bundles for an unreachable destination until a suitable next hop becomes available or the bundle expires. However, it is beneficial if the node storing the bundle is notified as soon as the destination becomes available again. This can be implemented using the DHT. To support notifications a DHT member node maintains a second set $notify_{pend}$. A $notify_{pend}$ entry is depicted in figure 2b containing the following items:

- key: This is the DHT key of the node, we want to receive notifications about
- number_of_notifications: How often this notification should fire. Typical values are 1 or ∞. For 1 the event fires once, and afterwards the $notify_{pend}$ entry will be deleted, for ∞ the event will fire every time its triggering conditions are met.
- event: Defines, which kind of event triggers this notification. Possible triggers are the reappearance of a node, the change of any value in the val_stored entry for key, or the change of a specific value.
- interest: The key of the node that wants to receive a notification when this events fires.

To demonstrate the different steps of establishing a notification request and the further processing, we will look at an example from figure 1:

Assume that in Figure 1 the node $dtn://mobile1.y.dtn$ is proxied by $dtn://gw.y.dtn$. When $mobile1.y.dtn$ becomes unavailable this will be detected by $gw.y.dtn$ and the corresponding entry will expire in the DHT. However, foreign nodes might still be sending bundles for $mobile1.y.dtn$ to $gw.y.dtn$ because they used a cached older entry with a higher ttl, or the bundles have been send before the DHT entry expired. Thus $gw.y.dtn$ stores a NOTIFICATION_REQUEST for $mobile1.y.dtn$ into the DHT, issuing the DHT command

`DHT_ROUTE(NOTIFY_REQUEST, dtn://mobile1.y.dtn, dtn://gw.y.dtn)`

This request will be routed to the same node that is responsible for the key $dtn://mobile1.y.dtn$ in the DHT keyspace. Whenever a DHT member receives a call that creates or modifies tuples in its val_{stored} it will check whether there are any notification requests pending for the modified key (see algorithm 2). In our example $mobile1.y.dtn$ joins another network and gets itself proxied by $dtn://gw\_z.dtn$. This means $dtn://gw\_z.dtn$ will issue a STORE to the DHT:

`DHT_ROUTE(STORE, dtn://mobile1.y.dtn, conv_layer(dtn://gw_z.dtn))`

The node responsible for the key $dtn://mobile1.y.dtn$ will check its pending notifications for this key and finds $gw.y.dtn$. Instead of directly trying to contact $gw.y.dtn$ it will use the DHT:

`DHT_ROUTE(NOTIFICATION, dtn://gw.y.dtn, conv_layer(dtn://gw_z.dtn))`

If $gw.y.dtn$ is online, this has the same effect as contacting $gw.y.dtn$ directly, because we assumed that we use a DHT where each node is responsible for a range in keyspace containing its own node id (see sect. 3.1). If $gw.y.dtn$ is currently not available, the notification is stored on another node currently responsible for the key $dtn://gw.y.dtn$. Once $gw.y.dtn$ becomes available again and

---

Algorithm 2. Check and transmit pending notifications

Check whether there are pending notifications for EID

```
1: procedure CHECK_NOTIFY(EID)
2:     targets ← {target | (EID, target) ∈ notify_pend}
3:     data ← {(k, v) | (k, v) ∈ val_stored ∧ k = EID}
4:     for all target in targets do
5:         DHT_ROUTE(NOTIFICATION,target,(EID,data))
6:     end for
7: end procedure
```

---

rejoins the DHT, depending on the DHT, the mechanism of the underlying DHT will hand over the data for its chunk of the keyspace, including the notification. This ensures, that receivers are notified as early as possible.

5 Implementation

While NASDI is not a routing protocol in a strict sense, it could be implemented as such using the routing module interface of DTN2 [31]. For IBR-DTN [30] a new discovery module is the best choice for integration. IBR-DTN allows different submodules to plug into its event-based core. DTN2 offers an XML based interface for external routing implementations. In our implementation we opted to use the Maidsafe library[1] which provides a Kademlia implementation including NAT traversal capabilities. The NASDI implementation is an external program using Maidsafe which communicates via TCP IP with a new IBR DTN discovery module that acts as a wrapper for the external NASDI implementation. This setup allows for great flexibility while developing NASDI and should make it relatively easy to connect NASDI to DTN2's external interfaces later.

5.1 DHT Functionality Tests

While the performance of large scale Kademlia deployments has already been examined, e.g. in [32] we performed some small scale tests, to verify that the NASDI implementation is performing as expected. We used virtual machines running instances of NASDI and IBR-DTN. The first NASDI instance is always started standalone, while the following instance get one of the running instances as booststrap partner.

Lookup Test. Figure 3 shows the time to lookup a value in the DHT. The diagram includes the min max and median values as well as the $Q_{0.25}$ and $Q_{0.75}$ quantiles. We modifed the number of NASDI nodes and the amount of tuples stored in the DHT. When the number of stored elements is increased from 1 to 1000 the average response time goes up from $\sim$ 70 ms to $\sim$ 90 ms, which shows

---

[1] http://code.google.com/p/maidsafe-dht

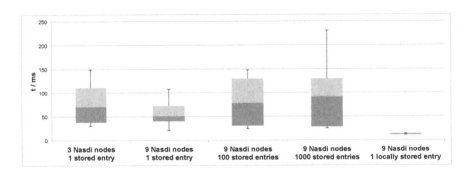

Fig. 3. Lookup times

the additional processing overhead in the NASDI instances. The variance for each measurement is due to the fact, that the DHT structure is different between runs, so that the responding Maidsafe instance might be nearer or further away. The rightmost plot shows the situation, when a node can answer the query from its local storage without the need to contact other DHT members.

Notification Delay Test. For this test we used 9 NASDI instances. The IBR-DTN node *node1* was started sending a bundle to *node2*, which was currently not available. This leads NASDI to store a notification request. Subsequently we started IBR DTN node *node2*. The NASDI instance for *node2* announces its contact information in the DHT, which leads to a notification being dispatched to *node1*, which in turn connects to *node2*, delivering the stored bundle. We measured the time between starting of *node2* and the reception of the bundle. This took around 3 seconds. A breakdown of the used time can be seen in figure 4. As can be seen in this case the notification itself is nearly instant, while the biggest amount of time is spent in the IBR-DTN daemon getting the cached bundle from storage and preparing it for transmission.

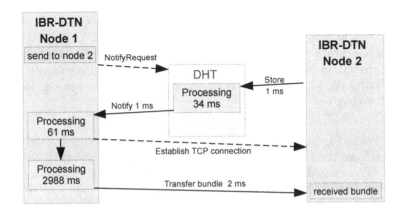

Fig. 4. Notification latencies

6   Conclusions and Future Work

We presented NASDI, an approach that allows DTN nodes connected to the Internet to efficiently store and retrieve convergence layer information of other DTN nodes in a distributed manner. NASDI supports building groups and integrates an asynchronous event notification mechanism. While NASDI's DHT member nodes should be located in the Internet and should be chosen in such a way that a long uptime can be expected, peripheral, possibly non-IP, intermittently connected networks can benefit from NASDI whenever they have a connection to the backbone. Those peripheral networks can be transparently bridged through the Internet. NASDI can be easily implemented as a routing module for widely used DTN implementations. Deploying NASDI is simple, because it can coexist with NASDI unaware nodes and still provide its benefits.

During the implementation and evaluation of NASDI we identified some areas for further improvement: We think that the services offered by NASDI can be very beneficial when they are used on a large scale in DTN implementations. To reach this goal, NASDI functionality should be shipped and enabled by default in Bundle Protocol implementations. We choose Maidsafe as basis for our DHT, which proved to be a very versatile library. However, its huge size and various dependencies may be a negative point when trying to integrate it with IBR-DTN or DTN2. This is especially a problem for IBR-DTN which is optimized for embedded devices. Therefore, we are currently looking into more lightweight DHT implementations.

We have only been able to perform tests with 9 nodes. While this shows the systems works as advertised, it makes it hard to predict how the system would perform with thousands of nodes. This also reveals a problem when the system is deployed initially: If there are only a few nodes operating in the NASDI DHT the overall resilience and reliability of the system might be less than in our controlled lab experiments. To solve this, we are currently looking into the possibility of leveraging the DHT subsystems of popular filesharing applications such as Bit-Torrent or the eMule network for NASDI. This means having less control over the DHT implementation, which could mean that some NASDI functionalities can not be implemented as efficiently or fully featured as outlined in this paper. On the other hand at any given time thousands of nodes will be online and available in the DHT, which should make the overall system very robust.

Acknowledgments. This work has been supported by the NTH School for IT Ecosystems.

References

1. Burleigh, S., Hooke, A., Torgerson, L., Durst, R., Scott, K., Fall, K., Weiss, H.: RFC4838 - Delay-Tolerant Networking Architecture. RFC (2007), http://tools.ietf.org/pdf/rfc4838.pdf

2. Lahde, S., Doering, M., Pöttner, W.-B., Lammert, G., Wolf, L.: A practical analysis of communication characteristics for mobile and distributed pollution measurements on the road. Wireless Communications and Mobile Computing 7(10), 1209–1218 (2007)

3. Scott, K., Burleigh, S.: RFC5050 - Bundle Protocol Specification. RFC (2007), http://tools.ietf.org/pdf/rfc5050.pdf

4. Ott, J.: Application protocol design considerations for a mobile internet. In: Proceedings of First ACM/IEEE International Workshop on Mobility in the Evolving Internet Architecture, MobiArch (2006)

5. Caini, C., Cornice, P., Firrincieli, R., Livini, M., Lacamera, D.: DTN meets smartphones: Future prospects and tests. In: 5th IEEE International Symposium on Wireless Pervasive Computing, ISWPC (2010)

6. Delay Tolerant Networking Research Group, DTN-Bone, http://www.dtnrg.org/wiki/DtnBone

7. Ellard, D., Brown, D.: DTN IP Neighbor Discovery (IPND). Internet-Draft (2010), http://tools.ietf.org/pdf/draft-irtf-dtnrg-ipnd-01.pdf

8. Waldhorst, O.P.: On Overlay-Based Addressing and Routing in Heterogeneous Future Networks. In: 2010 Proceedings of 19th International Conference on Computer Communications and Networks (ICCCN), pp. 1–8 (2010)

9. Vahdat, A., Becker, D.: Epidemic Routing for Partially-Connected Ad Hoc Networks. Duke University, Tech. Rep. CS-200006 (May 2000)

10. Anders, L., Avri, D., Olov, S.: Probabilistic Routing in Intermittently Connected Networks. SIGMOBILE Mobile Computing and Communication Review 7(3), 19–20 (2004)

11. Doering, M., Pögel, T., Wolf, L.C.: DTN Routing in Urban Public Transport Systems. In: ACM MobiCom 2010 Workshop on Challenged Networks (CHANTS), Chicago, USA (September 2010)

12. Fall, K.: A delay-tolerant network architecture for challenged internets. In: Proceedings of the Conference on Applications, Technologies, Architectures, and Protocols for Computer Communications (SIGCOMM) (August 2003)

13. Mockapetris, P., Dunlap, K.J.: Development of the domain name system. SIGCOMM Computer Communication Review 18(4), 123–133 (1988)

14. Balakrishnan, H., Lakshminarayanan, K., Ratnasamy, S., Shenker, S., Stoica, I., Walfish, M.: A Layered Naming Architecture for the Internet. In: Proceedings of the Conference on Applications, Technologies, Architectures, and Protocols for Computer Communications, SIGCOMM (August 2004)

15. Cox, R., Muthitacharoen, A., Morris, R.T.: Serving DNS Using a Peer-to-Peer Lookup Service. In: Druschel, P., Kaashoek, M.F., Rowstron, A. (eds.) IPTPS 2002. LNCS, vol. 2429, pp. 155–165. Springer, Heidelberg (2002)

16. Stoica, I., Morris, R., Liben-Nowell, D., Karger, D., Kaashoek, M., Dabek, F., Balakrishnan, H.: Chord: A Scalable Peer-to-peer Lookup Service for Internet Applications. IEEE/ACM Transactions on Networking (TON) 11(1), 17–32 (2003)

17. Rowstron, A., Druschel, P.: Pastry: Scalable, Decentralized Object Location, and Routing for Large-Scale Peer-to-Peer Systems. In: Guerraoui, R. (ed.) Middleware 2001. LNCS, vol. 2218, pp. 329–350. Springer, Heidelberg (2001)

18. Ratnasamy, S., Francis, P., Handley, M., Karp, R., Shenker, S.: A scalable content-addressable network. In: Proceedings of the Conference on Applications, Technologies, Architectures, and Protocols for Computer Communications (SIGCOMM) (August 2001)

19. Maymounkov, P., Mazières, D.: Kademlia: A Peer-to-Peer Information System Based on the XOR Metric. In: Druschel, P., Kaashoek, M.F., Rowstron, A. (eds.) IPTPS 2002. LNCS, vol. 2429, pp. 53–65. Springer, Heidelberg (2002)

20. Wang, C., Yang, N., Chen, H.: Improving Lookup Performance Based on Kademlia. In: Proceedings of Second International Conference on Networks Security Wireless Communications and Trusted Computing (NSWCTC), vol. 1 (2010)

21. Steinmetz, R., Wehrle, K. (eds.): Peer-to-peer systems and applications. Springer-Verlag New York, Inc., Secaucus (2005)

22. Castro, M., Druschel, P., Kermarrec, A.-M., Rowstron, A.: SCRIBE: A large-scale and decentralized application-level multicast infrastructure. IEEE Journal on Selected Areas in Communications 20(8), 1489–1499 (2002)

23. Wang, R., Rao, W., Zhang, C.: XEvent: An Event Notification System over Distributed Hash Table (DHT) Networks. IEEE Intelligent Informatics Bulletin 6(2), 19–25 (2006)

24. Rhea, S., Geels, D., Roscoe, T., Kubiatowicz, J.: Handling churn in a DHT. In: Proceedings of the USENIX Annual Technical Conference (USENIX) (June 2004)

25. Demmer, M., Berkeley, U., Ott, J.: Delay Tolerant Networking TCP Convergence Layer Protocol. IETF Draft (2008),
http://tools.ietf.org/pdf/draft-irtf-dtnrg-tcp-clayer-02.pdf

26. Kruse, H., Ostermann, S.: UDP Convergence Layers for the DTN Bundle and LTP Protocols. IETF Draft (2008),
http://tools.ietf.org/pdf/draft-irtf-dtnrg-udp-clayer-00.pdf

27. Ramadas, M., Burleigh, S., Farrell, S.: Licklider Transmission Protocol - Specification. Experimental RFC (2008), http://tools.ietf.org/pdf/rfc5326.pdf

28. Berners-Lee, T., Fielding, R., Masinter, L.: RFC3986 - Uniform Resource Identifier (URI): Generic Syntax, RFC (2005), http://tools.ietf.org/pdf/rfc3986.pdf

29. Symington, S., Farrell, S., Weiss, H., Lovell, P.: Bundle Security Protocol Specification, IETF Draft (2010),
http://tools.ietf.org/pdf/draft-irtf-dtnrg-bundle-security-17.pdf

30. Schildt, S., Morgenroth, J., Pöttner, W.-B., Wolf, L.: IBR-DTN: A lightweight, modular and highly portable Bundle Protocol implementation. Electronic Communications of the EASST 37, 1–11 (2011)

31. DTN2 implementation, http://sourceforge.net/projects/dtn/

32. Ou, Z., Harjula, E., Kassinen, O., Ylianttila, M.: Performance evaluation of a Kademlia-based communication-oriented P2P system under churn. Computer Networks 54(5), 689–705 (2010),
http://dx.doi.org/10.1016/j.comnet.2009.09.022

A Soft Handover for Service Delivery in Intermittently Connected Hybrid Networks

Nicolas Le Sommer, Ali Makke, and Yves Mahéo

IRISA Laboratory, Université de Bretagne Sud, France
{Nicolas.Le-Sommer,Ali.Makke,Yves.Maheo}@univ-ubs.fr

Abstract. Today, handheld devices equipped with Wi-Fi interfaces are used intensively by a huge number of people every day. These devices can form intermittently connected mobile ad hoc networks spontaneously. These networks appear as a relevant solution to extend a pre-existing infrastructure-based network composed of several access points in view of providing nomadic people with application services in a wide area. In such hybrid networks, intermittent connections are prevalent, and end-to-end paths between clients and providers cannot be maintained all the time. Thus, the communications must be achieved following a "store, carry and forward" principle.

In this paper, we present a new soft handover mechanism dedicated to service delivery in such hybrid networks. This handover solution exploits several pieces of information, such as the message propagation time, the path stability, and the mobility degree of intermediate nodes in order to select the most appropriate access point(s) to forward a response to a given mobile client.

1 Introduction

The recent market researches on mobile computing devices show an incredible penetration of handheld devices equipped with IEEE 802.11 interfaces (e.g., smart-phones, internet tablets) among the population, as well as a significant growth of computing devices embedded in the environment (e.g., Wi-Fi access points, wireless DSL gateways, sensors). These embedded devices are irregularly, and sometimes sparsely, distributed in the environment, and are connected to different infrastructure based networks. In order to access to the Internet or to get some services, the mobile clients must be in the communication range of an access point (see Figure 1a), thus constraining their mobility and reducing the area where a service or an Internet access can be offered. Over the last years, wireless mobile ad hoc networks have been considered in order to provide multi-hop communication between devices, and sometimes to create hybrid networks by extending fixed infrastructures in order to better satisfy the user's needs while using fewer access points to cover a given area. The access points participate in ad hoc communication and provide access to the fixed infrastructure (see Figure 1b). Nevertheless, such hybrid networks still remain rarely used today because their topology suffers from unpredictable changes and connectivity disruptions due to the mobility of the devices and the short communication range of their wireless interfaces. These changes are also the result of the volatility of the mobile terminals that are frequently switched off due

C. Borcea et al. (Eds.): MobilWare 2012, LNICST 65, pp. 122–135, 2013.

to their limited power budget. In these conditions, it is difficult, and even impossible, to maintain an end-to-end path between two devices using legacy MANET (Mobile Ad hoc NETwork) routing protocols.

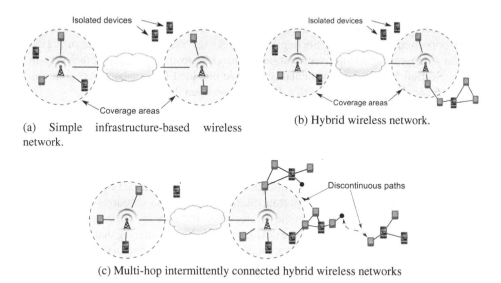

(a) Simple infrastructure-based wireless network.

(b) Hybrid wireless network.

(c) Multi-hop intermittently connected hybrid wireless networks

Fig. 1. From simple wireless networks to multi-hop intermittently connected hybrid networks

One of the most interesting evolutions of these hybrid networks is what we call intermittently connected hybrid networks (ICHN) or opportunistic hybrid networks (OHN), whose goal is to enable communications in presence of frequent and unpredictable connectivity disruptions. In such networks, communications rely on the "store, carry and forward" principle, whose basic idea is to take advantage of device contact opportunities to exchange messages, as well as of the device mobility so as to deliver messages between the different partitions of the network. In ICHN, two devices can communicate even if it does not exist an end-to-end path between them. Such hybrid networks could appear as an opportunity for service providers, such as local authorities, to provide nomadic people with new ubiquitous services, without resorting to any expensive infrastructure, such as those provided by mobile phone operators. The fixed part of these hybrid networks can obviously present various topologies. For instance, the services can be provided by dedicated servers that can be accessed by the mobile devices through the infostations, which act as gateways (see Figure 1c).

In this paper, we focus on the service delivery process in both the mobile and the infrastructure parts of an ICHN, and we present the soft horizontal handover mechanism we have designed and implemented in the infostations in order to improve the service delivery for nomadic people. Unlike the handover mechanism designed for cellular networks, the handover mechanism we propose takes the opportunistic nature of the communications into account. Indeed, the handover decisions are not taken according to the quality of the radio signal between a base station and a mobile client, but according to the quality of the multi-hop discontinuous paths between a client and an infostation. These paths, which can evolve dynamically according to the mobility and the volatility of the devices, are characterized by several properties, such as their stability or their length.

The remainder of this paper is organized as follows. Section 2 presents some related work focusing on handover mechanism as well as on communication and service delivery in opportunistic networks. Section 3 introduces service provision issues in ICHN. Section 4 presents the handover solution we propose to improve service delivery in ICHN. Section 5 shows experimental results we obtained for our handover solution. Section 6 concludes this paper with a discussion on open research directions.

2   Related Work

Communications in disconnected or intermittently connected mobile ad hoc networks have been investigated in research works dealing with delay tolerant networking, disruption tolerant networking or opportunistic networking. The solutions presented in these works are generally based on the "store, carry and forward" principle. Some of them also make assumptions about the device mobility by considering that these equipments are carried by humans that follow social mobility patterns, and that such recurrent patterns can be used to predict the future contacts between the devices and to deliver the messages efficiently with a limited number of copies of these messages. These methods traditionally use a probabilistic metric, often called delivery predictability, that reflects how a neighbor node will be able to deliver a message to its final recipient. Before forwarding (or sending) a message, a mobile host asks its neighbors to compute their own delivery probability for the considered message, and then compares these probabilities and selects the best next hop(s) among them. This estimation can require a 1-hop, and sometimes a 2-hop, network knowledge. In the Context-Aware Routing protocol (CAR) [12], the delivery probabilities are computed using both utility functions and Kalman filter prediction techniques. Propicman [13] also exploits context properties and the probability of nodes to meet the destination, and infers from that the delivery probability, but in a different way. When a node wants to send a message to another one, it sends to its neighbor nodes the pieces of information it knows about the destination. Based on these pieces of information, the neighbor nodes compute their delivery probability and return it. The node that wants to send the message will send this message only on the two-hop route(s) with the highest delivery probability (this probability must further be higher than its own one). Like CAR and Propicman, HiBOp [1] uses context properties in order to compute delivery probabilities, but it uses history information in order to improve the delivery probability instead of making predictions using Kalman filters. In Prophet (Probabilistic Routing Protocol using History of Encounters and Transitivity) [9], when a node wants to send a message to another one, it will look for the neighbor node that has the highest amount of time encountering the destination, meaning that has the highest delivery predictability. Furthermore, this property is transitive in Prophet. These protocols are designed for unicast communications. Thus, they could probably be used for service invocation, which traditionally relies on such a communication paradigm, but not for service discovery, which requires in ICHN an efficient broadcast of service discovery requests and service advertisements. Indeed, in order to avoid the broadcast storm problem and a network congestion, these messages must not be broadcast in a blindly epidemic manner, but instead using dedicated protocols such as OLFServ [8].

Software service provision with delay-tolerant, disruption-tolerant or opportunistic communications has been addressed so far in few research works [10,7,14,2]. Proposals in [10] and [2] focus on service provisioning in opportunistic networks composed solely of mobile nodes. In [10], the authors propose content-based service discovery and invocation solutions in order to exploit the redundancy of the services offered by the mobile devices that can move freely (i.e., no assumptions are made regarding the mobility of the devices). The protocol presented in [2] targets networks relying on social interactions between mobile nodes that act as both clients and providers of services. Due to the volatility and the limited resources of the mobile devices, the number of relevant services that can be offered by these devices is limited in comparison to those that could be offered in hybrid networks. Unlike in [10] and [2], the services considered in [7] are provided by fixed infostations in limited geographical areas. In [7], mobile devices and infostations are aware of their own location. Mobile devices can invoke remote infostations thanks to an opportunistic and location-aware forwarding protocol [8]. In contrast with the environments we consider in this paper, in [7], the infostations were not connected together.

The cooperation between wireless infrastructures and opportunistic networks has been investigated recently in order to enhance the content delivery to mobile clients and to relieve the infrastructure [3,4,5,16,11]. In [4], Hui et al. show that opportunistic communications can improve the content delivery ratios significantly even in infrastructures with a high access point density. Hui et al. also investigate different strategies to find the subset of mobile devices that will lead to the greatest infection ratio by the end of a message's lifetime [3]. In [5], Ioannidis et al. also focus on the delivery of dynamic content from the infrastructure to mobile subscribers that are expected to replicate it epidemically. They showed that, by supporting such epidemic exchanges and by utilizing the bandwidth of connections between mobile devices, the content providers can support more subscribers with a lower cost. [16] targets the same objective than [3,4], but it does not focus on social networks and does not assume preexisting knowledge of pairwise contact probabilities. It proposes *Push-and-Track*, a framework that exploits both wide-area wireless networks (e.g., 3G or WiMax) and local-area wireless networks (e.g., Bluetooth or Wi-Fi) in order to achieve guaranteed delivery in an opportunistic network while relieving the infrastructure. In [16], a subset of users will receive the content from the infrastructure and start propagating it epidemically; upon receiving the content, mobile nodes send acknowledgments back to the source, thus allowing it to keep track of the delivered content and assess the opportunity of sending new copies. Service invocation issues in ICHN have been addressed recently with a reactive routing protocol called TAO (Time-Aware Opportunistic Routing Protocol) [11]. In TAO, the routing decisions are taken based on the last date of contact of mobile devices with infostations. Furthermore, TAO implements several optimizations, such as source routing techniques, so as to perform an enhanced service delivery. However, in its current version TAO does not include pieces of information that could help at taking handover decisions.

Several kinds of handover mechanisms and algorithms have been proposed in the past for various types of wireless networks. Vertical handovers [6] and horizontal handovers, which can be qualified as hard or soft handovers, have been proposed. They respectively allow the switching of the ongoing network connection from one wireless interface to another (e.g., handover from an 802.11b network into a GPRS network) and the switching between two networks that use the same network technology and interface. With a hard handover mechanism, a mobile client can be connected with only one access point at the same time, while a soft handover mechanism allows to keep two or more connections with different access points. To the best of our knowledge, none of these handover solutions considers the issues inherent in the ICHNs.

3   Service Provision in ICHNs

Three main issues must be overcome in order to efficiently provide nomadic people with services in ICHNs, namely the discovery and the invocation of services using opportunistic communications and the design of a handover mechanism in order to offer a service access continuity to the mobile clients. In the first part of this section, we present different types of infrastructure of infostations, and we show how a handover mechanism should work in ICHNs. In the second part, we describe the service discovery and invocation processes in such networks.

3.1   Handover Overview and Infostation Infrastructures

The infrastructure part of an ICHN can present various topologies (mesh, bus, etc.), and the service repositories can be organized in a centralized or distributed manner. For example, the infostations can provide the services themselves and can act as service repositories (see Figure 2a), or can simply act as gateways for other providers that

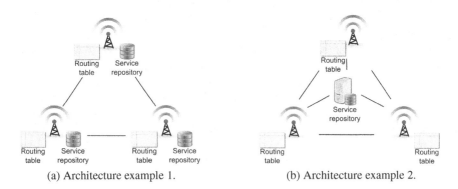

(a) Architecture example 1.   (b) Architecture example 2.

Fig. 2. Infrastuctures of infostations

register their services within a centralized repository (see Figure 2b). Other kinds of architectures can obviously be considered. In the remainder of this paper we will assume, without loss of generality, that a service is provided directly by an infostation or via another one.

In order to provide mobile clients with an enhanced service access, the infostations must estimate the "quality" of the discontinuous/disconnected paths (DPs) between themselves and the clients that require a service, must compare their estimations with those computed by the other infostations, and, if necessary, must update their routing table according to these new estimations.

In the handover solution we have devised, these estimations are obtained by the infostations by processing the pieces of information stored in the service invocation requests they receive, such as the date of emission, the lifetime, the location of the client, etc. The computation algorithm and the properties we consider are detailed in Section 4. This handover solution works as follows: When the infostations receive an invocation request from a new client, or when they compute an estimation that is better than the previous estimation they have in their routing table, they update their routing information and exchange summary vectors with the other infostations in order to allow them to update their own routing table in turn. The infostations are likely to not receive requests from a given client during a long period, because this one has moved away, has became isolated, or has been simply switched off. Thus, the information about this client must no longer be stored in the routing table of the infostations. So as to cope with this issue and to maintain only the recent connections with mobile clients in the tables, we assign a date of computation and a lifetime to each entry. All the infostations thus share the same perception of the infostation(s) that must forward the responses to a given client. In some situations, two (or more) infostations can approximately compute the same estimations for a given client. These infostations are therefore considered as equivalent for the service provision, and all of them should forward the service responses to the client, thus implementing a soft handover mechanism. In the remainder of this section, we describe how this handover solution operates with the service discovery and invocation processes.

3.2 Service Discovery

Service provision usually relies on three main operations: the discovery, the selection and the invocation. In a wired network, the service discovery process is often based on a centralized approach: the providers register the services they offer within a registry and the clients can look up available services in this registry, and can obtain a reference to the service they require. In an ICHN, the service discovery process cannot rely on a pure centralized approach since end-to-end routes between the mobile clients and the fixed infostations do not exist permanently. Therefore, each client is responsible for maintaining its own perception of the services offered in the network, and for discovering these services either reactively by processing the unsolicited service advertisements broadcast periodically by service providers and/or proactively by broadcasting service discovery requests in the network and by processing the advertisements returned by providers in response. This discovery process further helps mobile clients to select the paths they must use to forward their requests toward the infostations. Indeed, in the solution we propose the clients can process the pieces of information stored in the service advertisements they receive with an algorithm similar to that implemented in the handover mechanism so as to evaluate the quality of the DPs and to select the best(s) DP(s), and thus to avoid a blindly forwarding process. Such a discovery can be achieved efficiently with OLFServ [8], which performs a geographically-constrained epidemic dissemination of both the service advertisements and service discovery requests.

3.3 Service Invocation

A service invocation, during which a given client actually interacts with a provider, is usually performed using a unicast and destination-based communication model. Invoking a service in an ICHN basically consists in forwarding an invocation request toward a given infostation, which in turn will process the request itself if it provides the required service, or will forward the request to the infostation that provides this service. In the solution we advocate, both service invocation messages and service response messages are forwarded using source routing techniques in order to perform an efficient service delivery. Thus, while being forwarded, the messages are updated in order to include the IDs of the intermediate nodes, as well as the other properties that will allow to estimate the quality of the discontinuous path. This list of IDs will then be used to compute the reverse route.

As mentioned previously, when a client requires a service for the first time, it estimates the "quality" of the DP between itself and an infostation based on the last advertisements it receives. Then, it chooses the best reverse DP(s) that must be followed to forward an invocation. Sometimes several DPs can present approximately the same quality. When these DPs are considered as reliable enough, only one of these candidate paths is selected (the best one). Otherwise, the messages will be forwarded following each distinct candidate path (i.e. following the paths that have no intersection between their list of IDs of intermediate nodes). This DP (or these DPs) will be taken until the source routing fails. When forwarding their responses toward the clients, the infostations use the reverse route defined in the invocation message. When the source routing fails because an intermediate node is no longer reachable, the intermediate node that has detected the failure will execute the same algorithm as the initial client, thus dynamically updating the DP.

4   Handover Mechanism for Opportunistic Computing

Handover decisions and route selections rely on the estimations of the "quality" of the DPs. In the solution we propose, the DPs are characterized in terms of stability, of distance and of message propagation time. These metrics are defined below.

4.1 Message Propagation Time

The propagation time is an important metric in the service provision. It reflects the quality of service that is directly perceived by the end-users in terms of reactiveness. The propagation time is computed either by the recipient or the destination of the message (i.e., by a mobile client or an infostation). The propagation time for a message m is given by $pt(m,t) = t - m[de]$, where t is the date of reception of message m, $m[de]$ is the date of emission of message m.

4.2 Distance

We consider two different expressions of the notion of distance: a geographical distance and an estimation of the physical distance based on the number of hops between a source node and an infostation. The geographical distance between a client and an infostation is given by:

$$d'(m) = R \times \arccos(\sin(m[lat]) \times \sin(lat_I) + \cos(m[lat]) \times \cos(lat_I) \times \cos(m[lon] - lon_I))$$

Where, $R = 6378.137m$, and the latitude and the longitude of the infostation and the client are respectively defined in radians by (lat_I, lon_I) and $(m[lat], m[lon])$.

For obvious reasons of energy consumption, nomadic people activate the GPS receiver of their handheld devices only episodically. In order to cope with this issue, we use another estimation of the distance based on the number of hops between a client and an infostation. It must be noticed that, since the clients are mobiles and the links are intermittent, a minimal number of hops between a client and an infostation does not guarantee a minimal geographical distance between these two entities. The estimation we propose therefore combines this number of hops with the message propagation time in order to approximate the maximum distance between these two devices. This approximation is defined as follows:

$$d''(m) = m[nh] \times CR + s \times (pt(m,t) - m[nh] \times \Delta_{PT})$$

Where $m[nh]$ is the number of hops for message m, Δ_{PT} the delay of an immediate forwarding, CR the Wi-Fi communication range (typically 80 meters), and s the maximum speed of movement of the node (typically 2 meters/seconds for a pedestrian).

The distance $d(m)$ between a mobile client and an infostation is thus given by $d(m) = d'(m)$ if the location properties are available, and is given by $d(m) = d''(m)$ otherwise.

4.3 Path Stability

The stability of a DP is another important metric because it reflects the ability to efficiently forward a message to an infostation or to a mobile client using the source routing technique, and the ability to recover an alternative path if the source routing fails. Consequently, we consider the number of neighbors of the intermediate nodes as an element of stability since it allows to take alternative paths if the source routing fails. Furthermore, this stability depends of several factors, such as the mobility of the intermediate nodes, their power budget, etc. Indeed, the devices are carried and used by humans, and therefore can move freely or following social mobility patterns and can be switched on/off for energy consumption purposes. In the current implementation of our solution, we thus weight each estimation with the distance of a neighbor from the considered intermediate node if the locations, the speeds and the directions are known.

Otherwise, we weight these estimations with the contact times that are simply defined by : $c_i = np_i/np$, where np_i is the number of hello packets received from node i (i.e., the number of messages of presence sent by i), and where np is the number of hello packets the node i is expected to have sent since it has appeared in the vicinity of the current node. When the value of this property is equal (or close) to 1, node i is considered as a stable neighbor of the current node. At the opposite, a value close to 0 reflects the sporadic appearance of node i in the neighborhood of the current node. A lifetime is associated with this value so as to consider only the last contacts between two nodes. The path stability estimation obtained locally (i.e., for a given intermediate node) is thus:

$$\sum_{k=0}^{n} ns_k, \; ns_k = \begin{cases} d_k, & \text{if location properties are available} \\ c_k, & \text{otherwise} \end{cases}$$

$$\text{and } d_k = \begin{cases} 1, & \text{if distanceAt}(location_k, s_k, b_k k, 2 \times \Delta_t) > CR \\ 0, & \text{otherwise} \end{cases}$$

Where, $location_k$, s_k and b_k are respectively the current location and the speed of movement and the bearing of neighbor node k, Δ_t the delay to forward a message to an infostation from the local node, CR the communication range of the local node, and c_k the contact times of node k. Function $distanceAt()$ returns the distance between the local node and another node at a given time based on the location, the speed and the direction of these two nodes. The path stability value is the minimum of the estimations obtained along the path. It is thus defined as follows:

$$m[path\,statbility] = min(m[path\,stability], new\,estimation)$$

Where $m[path\,stability]$ is the stability of the path taken by message m. The function that returns the path stability is thus defined by $s(m) = m[path\,stability]$.

4.4   Handover Algorithm

The handover algorithm aims at choosing the infostations that must forward the responses to a given client based on the above presented metrics. Similarly, when they have the opportunity to forward their service invocation requests following different DPs, the mobile clients apply a quite similar algorithm than that implemented in the handover mechanism. In the remainder of this section, we focus only on the handover algorithm.

When an infostation receives an invocation request from a client, it estimates the quality of the path taken by the invocation request. Then it checks its routing table for the previous estimations it has for this client. If it has no information about this client, it stores this estimation in its own routing table and sends to the other infostations on a multicast address a summary vector including the modifications it operates on its routing table so that they can propagate these modifications on their own routing table in their turn (see Algorithm 1). If it finds some estimations for the considered client, the infostation checks if the new estimation is better than the previous ones. If so, it checks again if this estimation is greater than $\Gamma_\mathcal{E}$. If so, it removes the older estimations

---

Algorithm 1. The section of the algorithm applied upon service invocation reception

---

Data:

    $\mathscr{R}$: the routing table m: the incoming invocation request

    I: the current infostation D: the current date

    $\mathscr{F}$: the estimation function $\mathscr{V}$: the summary vector

1: $\mathscr{R} \leftarrow \mathscr{R}$ - $\{\mathscr{R}\{\text{client}=m[\text{source}] \ \& \ \text{infostation} = I\}\}$; T $\leftarrow \mathscr{R}\{\text{client}=m[\text{source}]\}$

2: $\mathscr{E} \leftarrow \mathscr{F}(m)$

3: **if** (T = Ø) **then**

4:     $\mathscr{R} \leftarrow \mathscr{R} \cup \{m[\text{source}],I,D,\mathscr{E}\}$; $\mathscr{V} \leftarrow \{\text{add},\{m[\text{source}],I,D,\mathscr{E}\}\}$; send $\mathscr{V}$

5: **else**

6:     **if** ($\mathscr{E} \geq$ max(T[estimation])) **then**

7:       **if** ($\mathscr{E} \geq \Gamma_{\mathscr{E}}$) **then**

8:         $\mathscr{R} \leftarrow \mathscr{R} \cup \{m[\text{source}],I,D,\mathscr{E}\}$ - T

9:         **for all** k $\in$ T **do**

10:           $\mathscr{V} \leftarrow \mathscr{V} \cup \{\text{remove},k\}$

11:         **end for**

12:         $\mathscr{V} \leftarrow \mathscr{V} \cup \{\text{add},\{m[\text{source}],I,D,\mathscr{E}\}\}$; send $\mathscr{V}$

13:       **else**

14:         **for all** k $\in$ T **do**

15:           **if** (k[estimation] + $\varDelta_{\mathscr{E}} < \mathscr{E}$) **then**

16:             $\mathscr{R} \leftarrow \mathscr{R}$ - $\{k\}$; $\mathscr{V} \leftarrow \mathscr{V} \cup \{\text{remove},k\}$

17:           **end if**

18:         **end for**

19:         $\mathscr{V} \leftarrow \mathscr{V} \cup \{\text{add},\{m[\text{source}],I,D,\mathscr{E}\}\}$; send $\mathscr{V}$

20:       **end if**

21:     **else**

22:       **if** ($\mathscr{E} >$ max(T[estimation]) - $\varDelta_{\mathscr{E}}$) **then**

23:         $\mathscr{R} \leftarrow \mathscr{R} \cup \{m[\text{source}],I,D,\mathscr{E}\}$; $\mathscr{V} \leftarrow \mathscr{V} \cup \{\text{add},\{m[\text{source}],I,D,\mathscr{E}\}\}$; send $\mathscr{V}$

24:       **end if**

25:     **end if**

26: **end if**

---

and only keeps the new one. $\Gamma_{\mathscr{E}}$ is a parameter of the algorithm. When an estimation is greater than $\Gamma_{\mathscr{E}}$, the path is considered as reliable and consequently it is not relevant to forward a message from two distinct infostations. If the new estimation is less than $\Gamma_{\mathscr{E}}$ and better than the previous ones, the infostation keeps only the better estimations that are considered as equivalent (i.e. the estimations whose gap with the better estimation is less than $\varDelta_{\mathscr{E}}$). A summary vector is sent to the other infostations in order to propagate the modifications.

When they receive a summary vector, the infostation execute the simple algorithm 2, which consists in adding, removing or updating lines in the routing table.

$$\mathscr{F}(m) = \alpha \times \frac{1}{pt(m,t)} \times s(m) \times \frac{1}{m[number\,of\,hops]} \times \frac{1}{d(m)}$$

The estimation of the "quality" of the discontinuous paths is computed using the function defined above. This function aims at privileging the paths that offer a good propagation time and stability, as well as the infostations closer to the client. α is a parameter of the function that allows to obtain results greater than 1 (typically α can be equal to 1000).

Algorithm 2. The section of the algorithm applied upon summary vector reception

Data:

$\mathcal{R}$: the routing table m: the incoming invocation request
I: the current infostation D: the current date
$\mathcal{F}$: the estimation function $\mathcal{V}$: the summary vector

```
1: for all k ∈ 𝒱 do
2:    if k[action] = remove then
3:       ℛ ← ℛ - {k}
4:    end if
5:    if k[action] = add then
6:       ℛ ← ℛ ∪ {k}
7:    end if
8: end for
```

5   Case Study

In this section, we present the simulation results we have obtained for the handover mechanism described in previous sections, and we analyze the impact of this mechanism on the service delivery from the client point of view. The simulations have been performed on the OMNeT++ network simulator.

5.1   Environment

The environment we consider in these simulations is a square area of 1 km^2 in which we have deployed 3 infostations. These infostations are connected together, and are separated from each other of 400 m. Each of them provides a specific service. These services are announced periodically (every 5 minutes) by all the infostations. They can be discovered and invoked by pedestrians that move in this area using their handheld devices. In these simulations, we consider two populations of pedestrians: the pedestrians that move following a random way point mobility model, and the pedestrians that move following predefined paths and that can exhibit their location. These pedestrians move at a speed between 0.5 and 2 m/s. In our simulations, 30 % of the mobile devices act as clients of the above-mentioned services, whereas the others only act as intermediate nodes. After discovering the services they are looking for, the clients invoke these services every 3 minutes. They sent a maximum of 10 requests during the simulations. In our experiments, we have assigned to all the messages a lifetime of 10 minutes and a maximum number of hops of 10. The communication range of both mobile devices and infostations varies from 60 to 80 m. In our simulations, we have considered successively 50, 100, 200 and 300 pedestrians. All these parameters are defined so as to reflect as well as possible the behavior of humans that use their mobile phone when they are strolling in a city.

5.2   Simulation Results

The objective of these experiments is to measure the impact of our handover solution on the service delivery in various configurations. For that, we focus especially on two values that reflect the quality of service that is perceived by the end-users (the ratio and delay of service delivery), as well as on a value that shows the efficiency of the solution (the number of messages that are sent by all the nodes in the network throughout the whole simulation period). The delivery ratio is the percentage of successful service invocation (i.e., the number of invocations for which a client node receives their response from an infostation), while the service delivery delay is the time needed to forward an invocation message toward the appropriate infostation, as well as to forward the response to the client. We compare the performance of our solution with the Epidemic Routing protocol [15]. In epidemic routing, messages are flooded in the network and stored by all available neighbor nodes as a result of summary vector exchanges, thus maximizing the message delivery rate and minimizing message propagation latency. The first copy of a given service invocation request received by an infostation (or the first copy a given service response received by a client) has therefore followed the path that offers the shortest delivery delay. Moreover, since the responses are disseminated by all the nodes, including the infostations, no handover mechanism is required with this protocol. In this context, the epidemic routing protocol appears as a good candidate to evaluate the efficiency of our solution, even if no precautions are taken in this protocol to limit the number of messages that are disseminated.

Figures 3a, 3b and 3c present the simulation results we have obtained. One can observe that our solution offers a better service delivery in terms of ratio and delays than the epidemic routing protocol, while reducing drastically the number of messages that are forwarded in the network, especially when the number of nodes increases. The delivery delays and service delivery ratios are often better with our proposal because the messages are forwarded using source routing techniques coupled with the handover mechanism resulting in the intervention of the infostation closest to the client, while with the epidemic routing protocol the messages are forwarded after the summary vector exchanges. Due to this short additional latency in the message forwarding, some communication disruptions can occur in certain situations, thus reducing the opportunities to forward the messages. This difference is more observable when the number of devices is low because it is more difficult to find another intermediate node. Furthermore, when the number of nodes increases in the network, the service delivery ratio increases while the service delivery delay decreases. Indeed, As we notice, when having few nodes in the network, the satisfaction ratio of both protocols is almost the same. This observation is coherent with what is expected, because more good carriers can be found among a large set of neighbors, thus reducing the number of disruptions and the disconnection times in the routes.

6   Conclusion

In this paper, we have presented a new soft handover solution suited for the service provision in intermittently connected hybrid networks. This solution provides nomadic people with an enhanced service access by selecting the most appropriate discontinuous path(s) between the clients and the infostations. The paths are characterized by three metrics, namely their stability, the propagation time they offer and their length. Furthermore, both the mobility and the number of neighbors of intermediate nodes are taken into account in the stability estimation.

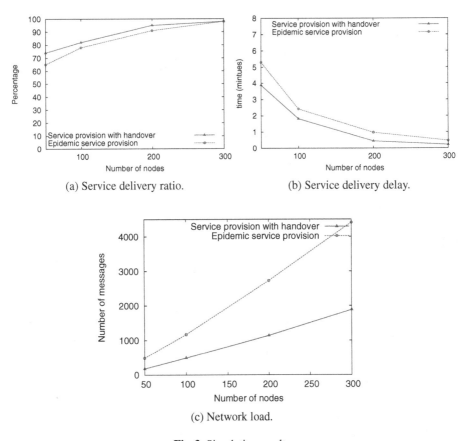

(a) Service delivery ratio.

(b) Service delivery delay.

(c) Network load.

Fig. 3. Simulation results

In the future, we plan to consider new kinds of properties such as the power budget of the mobile devices. Finally, we wish to improve our handover solution by considering the successive contacts of a mobile device with infostations, so as to predict its destination without location information and thus its next contact with an infostation. Consequently, allowing us to forward the responses in advance through this infostation.

References

1. Boldrini, C., Conti, M., Iacopini, I., Passarella, A.: Hibop: a history based routing protocol for opportunistic networks. In: Conti, M. (ed.) Proc. IEEE International Symposium on a World of Wireless, Mobile and Multimedia Networks, WoWMoM 2007, pp. 1–12 (2007)
2. Conti, M., Kumar, M.: Opportunities in Opportunistic Computing. Computer 43, 42–50 (2010)
3. Han, B., Hui, P., Anil Kumar, V.S., Marathe, M.V., Pei, G., Srinivasan, A.: Cellular traffic offloading through opportunistic communications: a case study. In: Proceedings of the 5th ACM Workshop on Challenged Networks, CHANTS 2010, pp. 31–38. ACM, New York (2010)

4. Hui, P., Lindgren, A., Crowcroft, J.: Empirical evaluation of hybrid opportunistic networks. In: First International Communication Systems and Networks and Workshops, COMSNETS 2009, Bangalore, India, pp. 1–10 (January 2009)
5. Ioannidis, S., Chaintreau, A., Massoulie, A.: Optimal and scalable distribution of content updates over a mobile social network. In: IEEE INFOCOM, Rio de Janeiro, Brazil (2009)
6. Kassar, M., Kervella, B., Pujolle, G.: An overview of vertical handover decision strategies in heterogeneous wireless networks. Computer Communication 31(10), 2607–2620 (2008)
7. Le Sommer, N., Sassi, S.B., Guidec, F., Mahéo, Y.: A Middleware Support for Location-Based Service Discovery and Invocation in Disconnected MANETs. Studia Informatica Universalis 8(3), 71–97 (2010)
8. Le Sommer, N., Mahéo, Y.: OLFServ: an Opportunistic and Location-Aware Forwarding Protocol for Service Delivery in Disconnected MANETs. In: 5th International Conference on Mobile Ubiquitous Computing, Systems, Services and Technologies (Ubicomm 2011), Lisbon, Portugal, pp. 115–122. Xpert Publishing Services (2011)
9. Lindgren, A., Doria, A., Schelén, O.: Probabilistic Routing in Intermittently Connected Networks. In: Dini, P., Lorenz, P., de Souza, J.N. (eds.) SAPIR 2004. LNCS, vol. 3126, pp. 239–254. Springer, Heidelberg (2004)
10. Mahéo, Y., Said, R.: Service Invocation over Content-Based Communication in Disconnected Mobile Ad Hoc Networks. In: 24th International Conference on Advanced Information Networking and Applications (AINA 2010), Perth, Australia, pp. 503–510. IEEE CS (April 2010)
11. Makke, A., Le Sommer, N., Mahéo, Y.: TAO: A Time-Aware Opportunistic Routing Protocol for Service Invocation in Intermittently Connected Networks. In: 8th International Conference on Wireless and Mobile Communications (ICWMC 2012), Venice, Italy, pp. 118–123. Xpert Publishing Services (June 2012)
12. Musolesi, M., Mascolo, C.: CAR: Context-Aware Adaptive Routing for Delay Tolerant Mobile Networks. IEEE Transactions on Mobile Computing 8(2), 246–260 (2009)
13. Nguyen, H.A., Giordano, S., Puiatti, A.: Probabilistic routing protocol for intermittently connected mobile ad hoc network (propicman). In: IEEE International Symposium on a World of Wireless, Mobile and Multimedia Networks (WOWMOM 2007), AOC Workshop, pp. 1–6. IEEE Explore (June 2007)
14. Pelusi, L., Passarella, A., Conti, M.: Opportunistic Networking: Data Forwarding in Disconnected Mobile Ad Hoc Networks. IEEE Communications Magazine (November 2006)
15. Vahdat, A., Becker, D.: Epidemic Routing for Partially Connected Ad Hoc Networks. Technical report, Duke University (April 2000)
16. Whitbeck, J., Lopez, Y., Leguay, J., Conan, V., de Amorim, M.D.: Relieving the Wireless Infrastructure: When Opportunistic Networks Meet Guaranteed Delays. In: 13th IEEE International Symposium on a World of Wireless Mobile and Multimedia Networks (WoWMoM 2012), San Francisco, California, USA, pp. 1–10 (June 2011)

An Adaptive Handover Decision Algorithm for Heterogenous Wireless Networks

Mario Pink, Thomas Pietsch, and Hartmut König

Brandenburg University of Technology Cottbus
Department of Computer Science
PF 10 13 44, 03013 Cottbus, Germany
{pink,piestho,koenig}@informatik.tu-cottbus.de

Abstract. The increasingly use of wireless networks and mobile technologies has raised the desire not only to have a good quality access to the network, but also to seamlessly change the network when moving. Various handover algorithmus have been proposed to handle this situation. Unfortunately, many of these algorithms have been only evaluated in simulative environments using simplified models and network assumptions. They do not take the wide range of mobile devices with varying system parameters and capabilities into account which are offered on the market. For the practical deployment, handover algorithms are required which adapt to various device parameters and network characteristics. In this paper we present a fuzzy-based vertical handover decision algorithm which adjusts itself to the given device parameters and network capabilities. Starting with a discussion on the requirements to vertical handover, we present the algorithm and describe how it is activated during the various phases of the handover process. Thereafter we present several experiments which evaluate the accuracy of the handover decision, the quality of service guarantees for the application, and the resource consumption.

1   Introduction

Mobility has become a feature for the network access. Users wish to access the Internet from different networks, such as GSM and UMTS, or WLAN and want to stay connected while changing into another network. This requires appropriate handover procedures to maintain an connection when moving from one network to another. Handover procedures are divided into horizontal and vertical ones. Horizontal or intra-technology handovers are applied for changes between different network cells of the same technology. They are mostly handled by the core network. Vertical or inter-technology handovers are required when changing between networks of different technologies. This handovers has to be performed always by the mobile devices themselves. Therefore, vertical handovers are very complex in detail because various aspects have to be taken into account, such as different network technologies, provider domains, service uses, and the kind of the connection maintenance [8]. Regarding the latter soft and hard handover are distinguished. A soft handover can be applied when the mobile device is connected with two networks simultaneously, so that the connection is moved without

C. Borcea et al. (Eds.): MobilWare 2012, LNICST 65, pp. 136–149, 2013.
© Institute for Computer Sciences, Social Informatics and Telecommunications Engineering 2013

interrupt. In a hard handover the connection is shortly interrupted and re-established when moving from the old network to the new one. Currently soft handovers are rarely supported by mobile networks. So it is not possible, for instance, to move between two networks using the same IP address. In order to support a soft handover the handover decision has to be made in time to avoid that the connection is interrupted and the application quality changes. This requires that all relevant parameters for the handover decision have to be evaluated continuously. The problem is that important parameters, such as the device speed, the network parameters, the application quality of service (QoS), or the energy consumption cannot be directly measured on the wide range of mobile devices on the market and are thus difficult to determine. This makes it complicated to estimate the time when the handover should be triggered. The parameter resolutions of the network interfaces further complicate the process. This is the reason why most existing handover algorithms are usually only evaluated in simulation environments based on simplified assumptions on the network infrastructure. It is comprehensible that these algorithms do not work efficiently in practice because they assume a generic structure that does not take the different device capabilities into account. To provide practically handover procedures algorithms are required which adapt to the varying parameter settings of the devices and network interfaces. In this paper we present an adaptive fuzzy-based handover decision algorithm which aims at supporting vertical handovers between real-life networks on off-the-shelf (DOTS) devices. The algorithm uses an adaptive parameter set, which can be reduced depending on the network- and device situation. The remainder of the paper is organized as follows. In Section 2 we give a brief overview on existing handover techniques. Section 3 formulates requirements to efficient handover algorithms. Next in Section 4, we present our adaptive handover decision algorithm. The performance and the resource consumption of the algorithm are evaluated in Section 5. Some final remarks conclude the paper.

2   Vertical Handover Algorithms

The emergence of various wireless technologies in parallel with the increasing use of multi-interface mobile devices has stimulated research on vertical handover. First work on vertical handovers was published about ten years ago [2]. Thereafter various algorithms have been proposed which apply different principles, such as *simple additive weighting* (SAW*), techniques for order preference by similarity to ideal solution* (TOPSIS), *grey relational analysis* (GRA), *analysis hierarchy process* (AHP), and *fuzzy logics* [10], which try to handle large parameter sets [7]. Over the years more and more parameters have been included in the handover decision [1][3][4][5][8][9]. To better handle the various parameters a classification of decision criteria's was proposed [7]. Such processes consume, however, a lot of resources on the mobile devices. Therefore handover decisions should be triggered only when needed to reduce resource consumption. For this, several criteria as, for instance, the round trip time (RTT) were additionally added to the decision procedure. Other approaches, in contrast, tried to reduce the set of decision criteria's. Radio signal strength (RSS)-based methods describe the expected network quality and compare the RSS of the available networks to select the best one [6]. To avoid ping-pong effects thresholds can be used. Unfortunately, the ping-pong problem still may appear if two networks have a RSS close to the threshold. To solve this problem hysteresis approaches were proposed which apply the difference to a reference signal [6]. Other approaches do not only consider the RSS. They include the estimated distance from the access points in the hysteresis derivation by comparing it with a reference cell size of a GSM/UMTS cell. Other approaches try to reduce the number of unnecessary handovers into networks with a small coverage taking the moving speed and the motion direction of the mobile device towards the network access point into account [2][6]. However, most of these approaches are only evaluated by simulations. Detailed descriptions of the algorithms are often missing. Our approach is different. It is based on parameters of off-the-shelf devices and adjusts the parameter set as well as its execution frequency at runtime depending on the resource consumption. Furthermore, it also monitors battery and temperature conditions in the environments to reduce circuit wear-out of equipment and battery aging.

3   Requirements for an Effective Vertical Handover Decision

A closer look on the numerous handover approaches reveals a wide range of different methods applied. Many of these approaches are only applicable on dedicated systems. Up to now there is no general applicable solution for handovers between heterogeneous networks which can be used on a broad range of systems. All approaches have in common that the handover process comprises the same phases. These are:

- *Pre-handover phase*: The mobile device is in a stable state. The mobility management continuously monitors the transmission quality, the application QoS, and the energy, power state of the device. When it detects a significant decrease in the connection quality it initiates the handover process.
- *Network discovery*: The mobile device scans for alternative networks preferred by the user using either physical network interfaces or dedicated web services. If alternative networks are discovered the handover decision can be started.
- *Handover decision*: The mobility management analyses the changes of network and application parameters during the movement through the current network to decide whether a real handover situation has occured. If so it starts the evaluation of the surrounding networks, otherwise it returns to the pre-handover stage.
- *Network evaluation*: The mobility management passively and actively evaluates the performance parameters of the discovered networks. When a network with a better connection quality as the current network is found it is selected.
- *Network selection*: The mobility management tries to set up new connections to the partner(s) via the selected network. If it fails, because it is behind a NAT[1]-router, it has to use an appropriate NAT traversal strategy, e.g., STUN or ICE to set up a new connection.

---

[1] NAT – Network Address Translation.

In this paper we focus on the handover decision stage. It is the most complex part of the handover process because it has to assess various networks and devices, to make the right decision. The question here is which parameters are really necessary for the decision? Therefore we first discuss in this section the requirements a vertical handover processes has to take into account. They can be grouped into network, user, application, and device requirements.

Network Requirements. The handover decision has to consider the parameters and properties of the discovered networks, such as link performance, handover latency, load balancing, device movement speed, and security policy.

- *Network link performance*: The performance of a wireless connection between a mobile device and an access point is determined by the RSS, the bit error rate (BER), the signal to noise ratio (SNR), and other parameters. For a handover decision, it is usually insufficient to only consider the first three parameters because the link quality is also influenced by network interferences. Therefore the network frequency distance should also be taken into account.
- *Handover latency*: A handover causes a certain delay to perform the necessary configurations, e.g., requesting an IP address from a DHCP server. This handover latency may affect the application quality, so that the delay should be considered.
- *Network load balancing*: Handovers usually cause a change in the application quality because variations in the network technology reduce or increase the traffic transmission capacity. Therefore it is important to identify a stepwise adjustment of the traffic load to the capacity provided by the selected network, e.g., latencies differences, to give the application the possibility to continuously adapt its data rate.
- *Network security policies*: Handovers implicate authentication with the new network to avoid unauthorized access to network resources. Differences in security policies and procedures of wireless products may create significant delays needed for negotiating the security requirements.

User Requirements. Handover decisions may include user preferences which indicate the performance the selected network should meet. User preferences may be determined by application requirements (real-time, non-real-time, background), service types (voice, data, video), network quality, and the cost of the service utilization.

Quality of Service Requirements. The handover decision has also to consider the maximal and the average network throughput, bandwidth limitations, and application latency. For example, an instant messenger may accept a new network with a low data rate and high latency, a VoIP application not.

Device Requirements. Resource consumption (battery lifetime, energy consumption, and thermal effects) is another important factor of the handover decision. It is significantly influenced by the duration and the frequency of the handover.

- *Battery management*: Mobile devices are equipped with batteries which need to be recharged. These recharge cycles exhaust the battery. To avoid continuous re- and discharging processes handovers should be avoided during recharging.
- *Energy management*: In 3.5/3.9G networks methods are needed to improve the energy efficiency because the constrained energy budget of the batteries are highly loaded by the use of different network interfaces. Hence, unused interfaces should be switched off as long as possible..
- *Thermal effects*: The mobile devices lithium-ion batteries usually show their optimal performance between 4 – 20 degree Celcius. Thus ambient heat, e.g., sun light, may reduce the battery capacity and affect the lifetime of integrated circuits. Therefore complex calculations should be avoided outside this range.
- *Device movement speed*: The mobile device have to take the movement speed into account when deciding about a handover. So an handover into a network with a small cell size is not useful when moving with great speed, since another handover will be necessary shortly later. Motion analysis helps to recognize whether the mobile device is moving or not towards the network border.
- *Handover period and decision frequency*: The handover decision estimate the time remaining to complete a handover before the connection is interupted. For it, it is waken up periodically according to the approximated trend of the network and system load. The sleeping period should be as long as possible to minimize the resource consumption.

4   A Fuzzy-Based Handover Decision Algorithm

In order to support a handover decision which can be used for a wide range of mobile devices we propose a fuzzy-based handover decision algorithm. Different methods can be applied for a handover decision algorithm, such as SAW, TOPSIS, GRA, AHP, and fuzzy logic [10]. For, it we analyzed the parameter set of several mobile devices. It showed that the parameter basis is extremely imprecise. This makes it difficult to directly correlate the parameter values. For example, the RSS is represented sometimes in dBm and sometimes in a range of 0-100%. Therefore, we have decided to use the Mamdani fuzzy theory because it allows handling of imprecise parameter sets found in practice and to model non-linear functions with an arbitrary complexity.

4.1   Handover Decision Algorithm

The Mamdani fuzzy system represents value ranges using linguistic terms. In connection with a set of rules, it allows a modeling of handover decisions. At the beginning the fuzzifier maps values onto linguistic terms using membership functions. For this, we apply triangular functions to assign each value to one of the fuzzy sets *low*, *middle*, or *high*. Thereafter these terms are correlated using fuzzy rules. Unfortunately, the rule set explodes in case of large parameter sets. Therefore we first classify the parameters using metrics. Parameters of interest are: RSS, SNR, throughput, RTT, packet loss and BER, network latency, cost of network use, energy consumption, system load, temperature, device speed, motion direction, authentication latency and the amount of surrounding networks. In the *parameter selection phase* these parameters are filtered out if they do not exceed an associated threshold and assigned to one of the four classes: connection quality, quality of service, user preferences, and device state class (see Fig. 1).

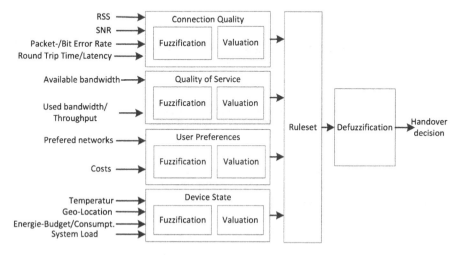

Fig. 1. Parameter classes

In the *parameter processing phase* we normalize, fuzzify these parameters, and multiply them by weights. Further, we derive additional parameters, e.g., the movement speed of the mobile device. In the following *parameter aggregation phase* we add all fuzzy values and create the fuzzy set membership function for the class metric. Table 1 shows an example of the fuzzy values for the connection quality class.

Table 1. Valuation of the parameters RSS, BER, SNR, motion direction, and trend

Level	RSS,BER,SNR	Motion Direction	Movement Speed	Signal Quality	Trend
High	3	approaching	3	good	3
Middle	2	Stationary	2	stable	2
Low	1	Leaving	1	critical	1

Function (1) gives an example for the connection quality vq of a WLAN. We estimate the parameter *trend* for each class metric using linear regression to recognize the remaining time available for network evaluation and selection. Then all four class metrics are correlated also using triangular functions and mapped onto their linguistic terms. In our example vq < 1.66 describes a low, 1.66 ≤ vq ≤ 2.33 a middle, and vq > 2.33 a good connection quality. Similar calculations have to be performed for the other three classes.

$$vq = \frac{w_1 \cdot RSS + w_2 \cdot BER + w_3 \cdot SNR + w_4 \cdot Motion + w_5 \cdot Trend}{\sum wi} \tag{1}$$

Finally we apply a handover decision rule set on these terms to decide about the handover. The rule set specifies if a handover decision should be taken. Table 2 shows an excerpt of such a handover decision rule set for a WLAN.

Table 2. Excerpt of a handover decision rule set

Rule	Signal Quality	QoS	User Acceptance	Device State	HO-Decision
1	high	High	Acceptable	Good	no
2	high	Low	not acceptable	middle	yes
3	low	High	not acceptable	good	yes

The handover decision algorithm is applied independently for each network interface. Fig. 2 summarizes the main steps of the algorithm.

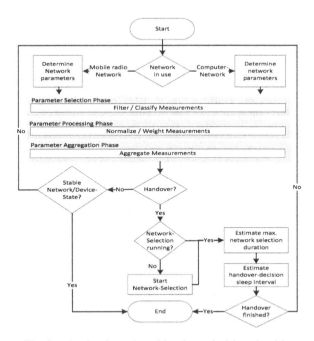

Fig. 2. Adaptive fuzzy-based handover decision algorithm

4.2   Duration of the Handover Decision

The time needed for a handover may not be sufficient in certain network situations [10]. To avoid such critical situations it is very important to determine the time t_{Init} when the algorithm should start. In addition, the maximum handover duration t_{HO} has to be determined to finish the needed handover steps before the connection aborts.

$$t_{Init} = t_{Abr} - t_{HO} \quad \text{with} \quad t_{HO} = t_{HD} - t_{NE} - t_{HS} \tag{2}$$

Hence, the handover duration t_{HO} depends on the time t_{NE} needed for the network evaluation and the time t_{HS} for selecting the network. The moment of connection abort t_{Abr} is estimated using a linear regression on a set of 10 consecutive parameter measurements. To determine it, a device dependent range adaptation of the parameters with respect to the signal characteristics and device configuration is performed. For example, the RSS range in a WLAN may have a lower limit of -90 dBm, -95 dBm, or -100 dBm on different mobile devices. For it, we developed a simple self-adaptation mechanism that adjusts the range of each parameter and threshold, e.g. using a mapping of RTT to specific RSS. Unfortunately, this adaptation takes some time. To avoid expensive configuration periods this adaptation initially starts with the average values of each parameter and threshold which are preconfigured.

4.3   Reactivation Interval

Another important parameter in this context is, as mentioned at the end of Section 4.1, is the interval in which the handover decision should be reactivated. This reactivation interval is determined by the type of the power supply, the full recharging time of the battery, and the average of the active and passive refreshing frequencies of the operating system, of the network interfaces, and of the device parameters. The active refreshing frequency considers consecutive parameter measurements, whereas the passive refresh frequency considers the refresh interval of parameters, e.g., incoming beacon in WLANs. If the device is powered without a battery the algorithm is stopped. Otherwise, at the beginning we use the RSS as the most important parameter for a handover decision and determine its active and passive refreshing frequency for every network interface. We take the lowest interval as the reference interval I_{ref}. Then we determine the refreshing interval P_{ref} of each parameter P and put it in relation to I_{ref}. Using these intervals we can poll the parameter values only when they are refreshed. Thus, the reactivation interval of the algorithm for the different network interfaces is determined using the average refreshing interval of the parameters selected for the handover decision and the last reactivation intervals. If the parameter values decreases unexpectedly during the last reactivation the next interval is adjusted according to the parameter value fluctuations during this interval. Otherwise, if no critical changes are observed the reactivation interval is increased up to a threshold $TH_{reactivate}$ to reduce power consumption. $TH_{reactivate}$ is estimated using a linear regression of the ongoing reactivation intervals.

4.4   Adaptive Handover Decision

To take the limited resources of mobile devices into account and to react on critical environmental influences on the mobile device, e.g., the battery temperature, it is necessary to apply a handover decision algorithm with a dynamic parameter selection. Our algorithm allows the handover decision to gradually adapt itself and to activate or deactivate parameters to reduce its calculation complexity. For it, the handover decision algorithm monitors itself and either adjusts its reactivation interval as described above or the parameter set used. To adjust the parameter set three mobile device states are distinguished: *idle*, *standard*, and *high load*. A mobile device is in *idle* state when the system load is below a threshold TH_{low} for several minutes, i.e., the CPU frequency is low and the network interfaces uses low power levels with a low transmission rates. It is in state *standard* when the system load and the network interface power level, as well as the transmission rate are between the thresholds TH_{low} and TH_{middle} for several minutes. The *high load* state is reached when the system load increases above TH_{middle}, the CPU works with the maximal frequency and the network interfaces use high power levels with high transmission rates. Depending on the state of the mobile device and its battery, various priorities are assigned to the parameters. In the state *high load* only parameters with the priority *high* can be applied, if the temperature does not exceed $TH_{Max-Temp}$ (40°C) or falls below $TH_{Min-Temp}$ (-5°C); In the state *standard* accordingly parameters with priorities *high* and *middle*, if the temperature does not exceed the temperature $TH_{High-Temp}$. All parameters can be used if the temperature does not exceed the temperature $TH_{Low-Temp}$ (25°C) in the state *idle*. When the temperature exceeds $TH_{Max-Temp}$ or falls below $TH_{Min-Temp}$ the algorithm stops. A reduced parameter set, however, decreases the handover decision accuracy. Therefore the parameter set need to be structured in a term-oriented function structure, as for example function (1), that always a correct handover decision can be made.

Table 3. Parameter priorities for WLAN and GSM/UMTS networks

Parameter	WLAN Priority	GSM/UMTS Priority	Substitution Parameter
RSS	high	high	RTT
BER, SNR	low	low	RTT
RTT	low	high	RSS
RSS Trend	middle	middle	RTT
Motion- Direction, Speed	middle	low	RTT, RSS
Available/Used Bandwidth	high/low	high/low	Latency
SSId , BSSId, Location Area Code, Cell-ID	high	high	-
Cost	middle	high	-
Energy Consumption/Temperatur	middle	middle	-

Table 3 gives an example for a priority assignment for WLAN and GSM/UMTS parameters. It shows that the RSS can never be ignored in any handover decision.

4.5 Substitution Parameters

Beside the adaptation of the parameter set, we also adapt the accuracy of the parameters of the handover decision using a parameter substitution approach (see Table 3). For this, we model the characteristics of a parameter using substitution parameters to increase its accuracy in time and resolution. For example, if the refreshing interval of a parameter A is too long we apply a substitution parameter B between two consecutives measurements of A. Thus parameter B is used until parameter A changes its value. Furthermore, if the parameter A is not available parameter B can be used as alternative for A. This improvement can be applied always or when the value of A falls below or exceeds a threshold. Substitution parameters are needed because several parameters cannot be determined for various mobile devices, especially for low price devices. Therefore substitution parameters can never be switched off. Even if these devices provide the parameters their refreshing interval is often too long or the parameter values provided are only average ones. For example, the *Samsung Omnia* b7610 does not supply the UMTS RSS. The *Huawei* E160 UMTS network interface is another example. It has a refreshing interval for the RSS of nearly 5 seconds. In this case the RTT has to be taken as substitution parameter to approximate the RSS.

5   Experimental Evaluation

In order to evaluate our handover decision algorithm with respect to performance and resource consumption we run three series of experiments. We used four mobile devices, a *N900* with Meego, a *Samsung* i8910 and a *Nokia* e90, both with Symbian S60, as well as a *Samsung Omnia* b7610 with Windows Mobile 6.5. The objective of the first experiment series was to prove whether our fuzzy-based decision algorithm is capable to successfully determine when to perform a handover, i.e., to investigate its ability to prevent unnecessary connection interrupts and latencies. Next we examined whether the algorithm is able to bring the available network resources in line with the quality of service demands of the application. In this case it must be also verified whether unnecessary handover decisions are avoided. Finally the resource consumption of the algorithm was measured.

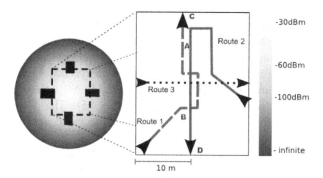

Fig. 3. Distribution of the radio signal strength of a 802.11b/g WLAN in a sub-urban area

5.1   Accuracy of Handover Decisions

To evaluate the accuracy of handover decisions we moved along different paths through a 802.11b/g WLAN in a UMTS (HSPA) covered sub-urban area with several buildings, as shown in Fig. **3**. The signal map at the left-hand side shows the distribution of the radio signal strengths among the building. The right-hand map depicts areas with good connectivity in white and worse connectivity in grey with the routes passed in the experiments.

In our experiments we moved using the mobile devices with a speed of approximately 5 km/h through the area (see Fig. 3). We passed each way ten times. At the points A and B handover decisions were initiated ($t_{Handover}$), while at the points C and D the connection was definitely interrupted ($t_{Disconnection}$).

- **Experiment 1:** In the first experiment we moved on path 1 (green line) through the WLAN network and left at point C. Every test run showed a critical network state with a positive handover decision to the UMTS network at point A. The time until connection interrupt was determined here between 4 und 7 seconds. At point C the connection with the WLAN access point was aborted. The handover decision worked optimally in this case because the RSS decreased continuously.

- **Experiment 2:** In the second experiment we moved on path 2 (solid line) and left the WLAN at point D. As in experiment 1 the RSS became critical at point A. The time till connection abort was estimated between 4 and 8 seconds, but immediately after that the RSS increased in the direction to B and the algorithm refused to handover. At point B the RSS falls down and the algorithm decided to change to the UMTS network. The estimated remaining time laid between 3 and 6 seconds.

- **Experiment 3:** In this experiment (solid dotted line) we moved along path 3 inside the WLAN without leaving it. Here the algorithm never indicated an handover.

5.2   Quality of Service Evaluation

Evaluations of handover decision algorithms mostly analyze the ability to avoid connection interrupts as a result of falling RSS. In addition, we evaluated how the decision algorithm guarantees the QoS required by the application. For this, we perform handovers at application level using two adapted SOCKSv5 proxies, one on the mobile device (*Samsung Omnia* i8910) and one on a PC with Gigabit Ethernet. These two proxy instances hide the IP address change from the application and communicate over TCP or UDP. In the first experiment we analyzed the quality of a video stream over a UDP connection using a customer 802.11g WLAN/16 MBit DSL (see Fig. 4) and a UMTS network of O2-Germany (see Fig. 5). The handover decision (HO) algorithm compared the QoS requirements of the video stream with the QoS capabilities of the network over a certain period of time ($t_{Handover}$). Due to the increasing data rate, it decided to handover from UMTS to WLAN after 170 seconds and during movement after the next 160 seconds from WLAN to UMTS.

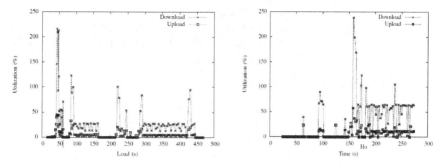

Fig. 4. *VideoStream*: HO-decision for UMTS   **Fig. 5.** *VideoStream*: HO-decision for WLAN

The second experiment analyzed the network load when requesting web pages using a relayed TCP connection. Fig. 6 and Fig. 7 show the network load for WLAN and UMTS, respectively. Here the algorithm decided against a handover because the QoS requirements increased only for a short period of time, between 10 and 20 seconds.

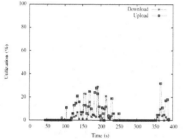   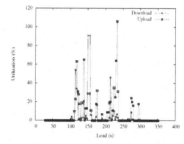

Fig. 6. *Web request*: no handover (WLAN)   **Fig. 7.** *Web request*: no handover (UMTS)

Finally we analyzed the behavior when transmitting a large file. Fig. 8 shows the relayed TCP transmission with a maximum throughput starting in a UMTS network.

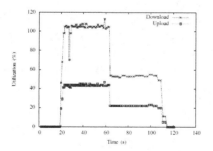   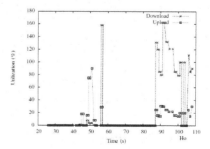

Fig. 8. *File download*: HO-decision to WLAN   **Fig. 9.** *File download*: HO-decision to UMTS

Here the algorithm decided after 60 seconds to trigger a handover into WLAN. Fig. 9 shows an opposite situation. A file download starts in the WLAN and is switched to UMTS after 90 seconds because of the better QoS capabilities of UMTS.

5.3   Algorithm Resource Consumption

The resource consumption is important for the algorithm in practice. To estimate the resource consumption we executed the algorithm 1000 times applying three different gradual levels and measured the CPU time: *high* level for high priority parameters and high accuracy, *middle* for average parameters, and *low* for low priority parameters and accuracy, (low level comprises only RSS, SNR, BER).

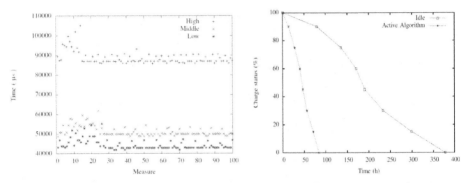

Fig. 10.   Gradual levels CPU performance   **Fig. 11.** Energy consumption

We repeated the measurement (see Fig. 10) for every level on the *Samsung* i8910. It showed the algorithm needed 89-94ms for handover decisions at high level. At middle level 48-50ms for decisions and 43-44ms at low level, respectively. It showed that the calculation efforts for high accuracy are two times higher than that for low accuracy. The difference between middle and low accuracy is about 15%. Next we analyzed the energy consumption of the algorithm. Unfortunately, it is not always possible to determine the battery current and voltage on every mobile device. The *Samsung* i8910 device distinguishes only 8 levels for the battery capacity: 100, 90, 75, 60, 45, 30, 15, and 0%. Therefore, we use an energy model to determine the energy consumption of the algorithm using the number of algorithm runs per battery level. At first, we determine the energy capacity, runtime of each battery level using the idle energy consumption with, without network interface during the whole battery runtime. At second we consider the runtime difference for each battery level when the CPU continuously executes the algorithm and create a energy consumption metric. Figure 11 show the energy consumption with a maximum accuracy in a 3 second   interval.

6   Conclusions

In this paper we presented a fuzzy-based handover decision algorithm for vertical handovers on off-the-shelf devices. The algorithm uses an adaptive parameter set, which can be reduced depending on the network and system situation. It estimates the remaining time to evaluate the discovered networks, to select the best of them, and to handover the connection to this network. We evaluated the applicability of the algorithm in various real-life experiments on mobile devices. Nevertheless, the parameter weights, the reactivation of the algorithm and the estimation of connection abort need to be further improved to forecast an upcoming handover. As next step, we improve our algorithm using Q-learning.

References

1. Marquez, J., Calafate, C.T., Cano, J.C., Manzoni, P.: An overview of vertical handover techniques: algorithms, protocols and tools. Computer Communications 34, 985–997 (2011)
2. Theodore, S.S., Antonis, S.M., Miltiadis, E.A., Michalis, E.T.: Vehicle Velocity Estimation Based on RSS Measurements. Wireless Personal Communications 40(4), 523–538 (2006)
3. Nasser, N., Hasswa, A., Hassanein, H.: Handoffs in Fourth Generation Heterogeneous Networks. IEEE Communications Magazine 10(44), 96–103 (2006)
4. Kassar, M., Kervella, B., Pujolle, G.: An overview of vertical handover decision strategies in heterogeneous wireless networks. Computer Communications 31(10), 2607–2620 (2008)
5. Nasif, E., Tara, S., Sibel, K., Kemal, F.: An Overview of Handoff Techniques in Cellular Networks. International Journal of Information Technology 2(2), 1305–2403 (2005)
6. Lee, H., Kim, D., Chung, B., Yoon, H.: Adaptive Hysteresis Using Mobility Correlation for Fast Handover. Communication Letters IEEE 12, 152–154 (2008)
7. Morales, J.D.M., et al.: Performance comparison between MADM algorithms for vertical handoff in 4G networks. In: Proceedings of the 7th Conference on Engineering, Computing Science and Automatic Control, Tuxtla Gutierrez, Mexico, pp. 309–314 (2010)
8. Yan, X., et al.: A Survey of Vertical Handover Decision Algorithms in Fourth Generation Heterogeneous Wireless Networks. Journal Computer Networks 54, 1848–1863 (2010)
9. Navarro, E.S., Wong, V.W.S.: Comparison between Vertical Handoff Decision Algorithms for Heterogeneous Wireless Networks. In: Proceedings of the Vehicular Technology Conference, Melbourne, Australia, pp. 947–951 (2006)
10. Sharma, M., Khla, R.K.: Fuzzy Logic Based Handover Decision System. Journal of Adhoc, Sensor & Ubiquitous Computing 3(4), 21–29 (2012)

Self-adaptable IP Connectivity Control in Carrier Grade Mobile Operator Networks

Marius Corici, Dragos Vingarzan, Valentin Vlad, and Thomas Magedanz

Fraunhofer FOKUS Institute
Kaiserin Augusta Allee 31, 10589, Berlin, Germany
{marius-iulian.corici,dragos.vingarzan,valentin.vlad,
thomas.magedanz}@fokus.fraunhofer.de

Abstract. The current trend in operator networks is towards the deployment of high capacity radio technologies such as LTE accommodating a high number of devices and their data traffic. However, the current network architecture was designed for a lower level of communication in which scalability was achieved through uniform operator control. Connectivity for each mobile device was handled in the same manner, no matter of its characteristics, network location or resources required resulting in a high overhead in supporting a large part of the subscribers. This paper introduces a new self-adaptation concept realized as a subscriber oriented management layer enabling the customization of the control procedures and resources reserved to the individual communication requirements for each device. The concept is exemplified for access network selection and core network path adaptation use cases, adapted for the 3GPP Evolved Packet Core architecture and evaluated through a testbed realization based on the Fraunhofer FOKUS OpenEPC toolkit.

Keywords: Self-adaptation, mobility management, Evolved Packet Core.

1   Introduction

During the last two decades, the telecommunication technologies have reached a high level of acceptance mainly due to the development of the Internet which allowed previously unimaginable levels of information exchange and due to the mobile communications which empowered users with continuous reachability. Following this trend, the mobile communication industry is currently passing into a novel massive broadband communication age through the harmonization of previously voice centered services with the Internet technologies [1]. Four factors are of significance for this evolution.

First, novel radio technologies became available and are currently rolled out by carrier grade network operators such as LTE. They come to supplement the already deployed technologies like HSPA, UMTS, CDMA and WiFi. Although heterogeneous as capacity, delay, packet loss and operational costs, the access networks altogether are offering remote wireless communication with a high level of throughput, thus being able to accommodate large levels of communication [2].

C. Borcea et al. (Eds.): MobilWare 2012, LNICST 65, pp. 150–163, 2013.
© Institute for Computer Sciences, Social Informatics and Telecommunications Engineering 2013

Secondly, the users accustomed with both Internet and mobile communication technologies are gradually adopting, as commodity, devices such as smartphones, tablets and laptops. The adoption of the heterogeneous devices corroborated with the data traffic increase enlarges the current communication subscriber based while at the same time requires an extended support from the core networks [3].

Following, due to the opportunity of delivering services anywhere and anytime and to a large set of users, novel services and applications are foreseen especially targeting mobile subscribers. Added to this, the current applications used over fixed lines access networks are adapted to the mobile networks, offering a large variety of services to the mobile subscribers [3].

Finally, due to the massive deployment of access networks offering remote communication at reduced costs, other industries such as energy, automotive and security are considering the usage of operator infrastructures for a new type of mobile communication for which the human interaction is limited, generically named Machine-2-Machine (M2M). For this, it is estimated an increase with one order of magnitude of the connected devices and a high diversification of their capabilities [4].

However, in order to be fully accepted, the massive broadband mobile communication core network infrastructure is expected to reach similar quality and reduced operational costs as the evolution to Next Generation Networks (NGN) brought to the fixed lines communication. As the wireless networks are natively cellular, the devices located at a specific moment of time at a specific location compete for the same resources, thus requiring resource mediation. Also, in order to be able to maintain the reachability of the mobile devices, the network has to be able to offer mobility support considering how the location changes for each device. These two technical limitations of the mobile technology apart from the deployment ones, such as renting of antenna sites, make the mobile technology more expensive to use and requires separate architecture design.

In fact, there is a stringent requirement for more scalable features in the core network as to be able to reduce the operational costs through the adaptation of the resources available for each subscribed device as close as possible to the resources required without deterring the communication from the perspective of the end users.

This paper proposes a novel approach for the adaptation of the communication characteristics for each mobile device. A management layer function is introduced in the core network having as main role to provide customized parameters independently for each of the subscribers according to their network profile information, current mobility pattern through the physical environment and the resources required for the communication as well as based on the network conditions e.g. available access networks at the device location or available core network entities which can support the device communication. The proposed solution enables the usage of no more resources than required for each subscriber.

The information structures and communication procedures are exemplified for the cases of customized data path selection in the access and core network as additions of the 3GPP Evolved Packet Core (EPC) ([5], [6], [7], [8]), representing the standard architecture for the future mobile communication encompassing the connectivity support for LTE and the other heterogeneous fixed and wireless access network. The practical realization of different parts of the described concept is presented as extensions of the OpenEPC toolkit and using the afferent testbed realization ([9]).

The remainder of the paper is organized as follows: Section 2 provides the background of the proposed framework, while Section 3 describes the concept, followed by the algorithm in Section 4 and the 3GPP Exemplification in Section 5. Section 6 provides an overview of the testbed and of the evaluation scenarios while in Section 7 the conclusions are provided.

2   Background

In order to be able to offer more capacity in term of connected devices and available resources, currently the network operators are deploying multiple radio technologies such as LTE, HSPA, EDGE, WiFi etc. in the same locations, highly overlapping and enabling complimentary connectivity service with different characteristics specific to the heterogeneous wireless technologies. These heterogeneous access networks are supported in a convergent manner by the functionality in the core network, including transparent mobility inside or between multiple access networks. Additionally, the network deployment sustains the allocation of resources for each subscriber based on the subscription profile and on the available resources as well as mechanisms for device authentication, data traffic accounting and charging.

With the increase in number of devices and in their data traffic supported by the radio technologies, a novel level of efficient handling of IP connectivity is reached: the network has to scale as control and as user data transport in order to enable the communication for all the mobile users. This may be reached only through the distribution of the same functionality in multiple locations through the wireless system resulting in parallel handling of the devices in different network locations geographically distributed, as depicted in Figure 1.

The radio network high overlap and the core network distribution require new algorithms for flexible selection of the access and core network control and user data plane entities. The selection ensures the optimal usage, the flexibility, the reliability and the easiness of maintenance of the carrier grade operator core network.

Currently, there are two mechanisms deployed for access network and core network path selection depending on the degree of integration of the core network functionality: one mechanism for the integrated access networks such as GPRS, HSPA and LTE ([5], [7]) and one for access networks which are separately controlled such as WiFi or WiMAX ([6]). For brevity, the second case is not further considered in this paper. However the same principles of the here proposed solution also apply.

In case of operator managed networks, the selection process which precedes a handover procedure is made by the control entities of the specific access networks i.e. the eNodeB or the Mobility Management Entity (MME) for LTE access, the Serving GPRS Support Node (SGSN) for the GPRS/EDGE and UMTS/HSPA accesses. When a handover has to be executed in order to maintain the service continuity, a target cell is selected by either the source cell for LTE or by the target control entity MME or SGSN. The target cell is selected based on the signal strength at the location of the

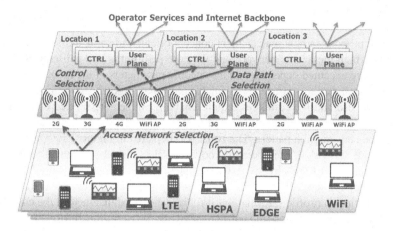

Fig. 1. High Level Operator Network Architecture

mobile device independent of its resources consumed or of the direction of its mobility through the wireless environment. Additionally, a handover to an access network of another radio technology is not possible when the service continuity over the same radio technology can be ensured from the perspective of the radio signal strength. Therefore, a device which is connected to an LTE access network will not be handed over to a HSPA access network even when the LTE is congested.

Coming to mitigate this issue the Self-Organizing Networks (SON) tries to introduce a more dynamic selection of the access network from a management perspective introducing weight-based load balancing between the distinct radio networks. This type of solution enables to steer the devices to the different accesses depending on the momentary load and on their network positioning ([10]).

A similar solution is also introduced for the selection of the core network control and user plane entities. A weighted round-robin algorithm is executed in the entity which makes the selection based on the proportions received through a DNS query. The round robin algorithm ensures that the balancing can be executed with limited errors without requiring actual monitoring of the entities.

However, the devices which are foreseen to be deployed in the future carrier grade network infrastructures have highly different capabilities. The capabilities include not only the different radio device interfaces which enable the wireless connectivity, but also the processing and storage capabilities, apart from the distinct mobility patterns through the physical environment and data path resources required such as guaranteed QoS characteristics. Due to this differentiation of devices on two dimensions: resources consumption and mobility pattern through the physical environment, the SON and the weighted-DNS solutions are not able to provide in the majority of cases the most suitable solution. For example, a device which is highly mobile would require a specific Packet Data Network Gateway (PDN GW) to be selected which reduces the number of reselections required independent of the load balancing algorithm.

3   SelfFit Concept

This article proposes a new management concept oriented towards individual connected devices in which the access network and the core path initial and subsequent selection procedures are executed depending on the specific parameters of the mobile device. The parameters include the momentary available information such as the current entities which are in use and the resources require enabling immediate service continuity and parameters acquired as knowledge related to the mobile device such as the mobility or the resource consumption pattern. The concept is depicted in Figure 2.

In the core network of the operator a novel SelfFit subscriber oriented management function is added to the already existing functionality. It contains three functional entities. First, a Subscription Profile Repository (SPR) enables the framework to access subscription profile information. It represents an extension with the customized information of the already deployed core network Subscription Information entities. Additionally, it may subscribe and receive notifications to subscription information modification events which then will require a new set of parameters to be selected for the selection decisions.

The Access Selection Management Function (ASMF) enables individual access selection parameters for each of the subscribers. When a handover is required and a cell of the same technology or another access network technology has to be selected, the selecting entity in the core network queries the ASMF on the specific target cell information. As the cell is selected on a per-subscriber basis, this query replaces the weighted-DNS query, thus not being required anymore to execute the round-robin algorithm. Based on the ASMF response, the target cell is selected. The following handover preparation and handover execution procedures require no modification. They are executed as specified in the current standards.

The Core Network Management Function (CNMF) enables the independent selection for each subscriber of the control and of the data path entities serving a specific node. The operations are triggered by either a handover of the mobile device to another access network, by the modification of the resources required from the network or by the modification of the configuration of the network through management means e.g. a control or data path entity is introduced or removed from the

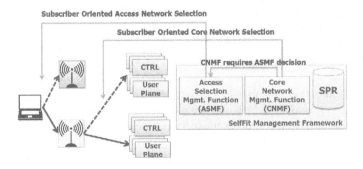

Fig. 2. Concept Architecture

network for energy efficiency reasons. Especially for the data path, a shorter data path stretch in average considering all the mobility of the device enables a lower average end-to-end delay and fewer resources consumed from the network in forwarding the data to the device. The CNMF makes such a decision either by receiving an administrative trigger or because of a request on behalf of a connected device received from the core network. The response of the decision enables the core network to select the appropriate data path for each of the devices through the core network.

In some specific cases, the core network path requires an access reselection decision. For example, a data path gateway cannot be reached unless the device is connected to a specific access network. In this case the decision of the CNMF is transmitted as trigger for the access network selection.

In order to reach the appropriate decision, in essence both the ASMF and the CNMF are executing the same algorithm in combining the subscriber related with network management information. However, the proportions in which the different parameters influence the final decision are highly distinct as the service continuity remains the main issue of the access networks, while in the core network traffic steering from a large number of subscribers between different geographically separated sites is also sustained and desirable in some situations.

In order to respond to the selection or reselection query, the ASMF and the CNMF use network management information such as a coverage map including all the access networks available at a specific location. Additionally, it uses the location information of the mobile device as well as information on which is the source cell or network entity. It is recommended that the same access technology will be used in case of a handover as not to require device driver reconfiguration. In order to make a subscriber oriented decision, the ASMF and CNMF request from the SPR information on the current resources required by the mobile device.

In addition to this, as to make an accurate decision which enables the mobile device to communicate without requiring an additional reselection procedure for a longer duration of time, the ASMF and CNMF receive from the SPR general information on the communication parameters for the mobile device. This information may include the resource consumption pattern i.e. resources consumed in specific time intervals etc. It is assumed that an access selection with a high capacity will be selected for a device which requires a high level of resources. A similar assumption is made also for the core network entities.

4   Algorithm Description

The selection algorithm is based on the computation of a selection utility for all the possible choices based on the following formula:

$$U_{x,MS} = L_x * MP_{MS} * RP_{MS} \tag{1}$$

where X is one of the possible choices to be selected for mobile station MS, U_x is the computed utility, L_x is the proportion of the capacity, MP_{MS} and RP_{MS} represent the probability that MS moves respectively uses resources in the area best covered by X.

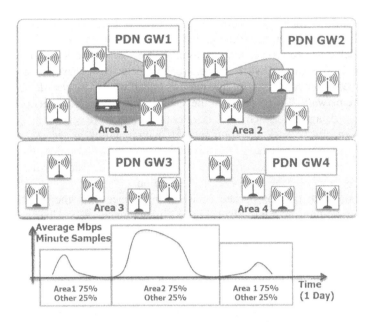

Fig. 3. Simplified Network Model

In order to grasp the concept presented in the previous section and its implications on the selection procedure, a simple network model was realized as depicted in Figure 3. A network system containing a single access network, separated into four distinct areas was considered. Each of the areas is served by a local PDN GW. It is assumed that any PDN GW can support the mobile device in any of the areas, however the local one is considered better due to the shortest data path stretch for the signaling and the data traffic i.e. similar to local break-out scenarios.

The selection scenario presumes that a Mobile Station (MS) is establishing an initial data path for the communication, procedure in which the most appropriate PDN GW has to be selected. The steps of the algorithm as well as the probabilities and the coefficient are exemplified in Figure 4.

The weight representing the capacity proportions of the PDN GWs assumed presumes that PDN GW 1 is able to receive 30% of the system data traffic, PDN GW 3 50% while PDN GW2 and PDN GW4 10% each.

It is assumed that the MS is active for a day and that its mobility pattern is presuming that the user is located in Area 1 and in Area 2 in the same measure while not passing through the Area 3 and Area 4. The assumptions on the accurate prediction of the mobility pattern are based on the results presented in [11] where human mobility predictability was extensively analyzed. We assume in the model a potential predictability of 75% which is highly conservative compared to the results from [12] where a potential predictability of 93% was obtained. Thus the probability that the MS will move out of the mobility pattern is considered of 25% and split equally between Area 3 and Area 4.

Additionally we assume the depicted data traffic pattern which correlated with the mobility pattern information assumes that 20% of the data traffic will be executed while the device is in Area 1 and 80% while it is located in Area 2. The same potential predictability of 75% is assumed also for the data traffic. Similarly to the mobility pattern, the probability that the data traffic will be exchanged in the Area 3 and Area 4 is considered of 25% and split equally. The algorithm here presented assumes that all the data traffic receives the same QoS classification and thus is handled in the same manner in the core network.

When the reselection trigger is received (Step 1), the subscription profile including the subscription and the data traffic pattern are retrieved from the SPR (Step 2). Then the candidate PDN GWs are retrieved including their weighted parameters. For each of the PDN GWs a coefficient is generated based on these probabilities. This coefficient will evolve through the execution of the steps of the algorithm into a final one representing the opportunity of selecting one of the gateways. In case of the current deployed algorithm, due to the deliberately and arbitrary selected proportions in which PDN GW3 can handle 50% of the data traffic, for the given MS there is ½ chance that the PDN GW3 will be selected and that the data path for none of the data traffic is optimal.

Based on the assumed mobility pattern, a set of probabilities are generated. The previously designed coefficient is multiplied with these probabilities resulting in a new coefficient representing the probability that the device is located in the specific network area combined with the capacity proportion of the specific PDN GWs. The resulting coefficient makes the PDN GW1 as the best selection as it can hold a larger proportion of the overall system data traffic. As it was assumed that the MS is roaming in the Area 1 for 50% of the time this result is acceptable, especially in the case when the data traffic pattern of the MS is uniform.

However, the mobile devices communication over the network is highly non-uniform. We assume in this paper a distribution of the data traffic in time as depicted in Figure 3. This information correlated with the area location information, as derived from the mobility pattern results in a new set of probabilities in which of the areas the data traffic will be exchanged. A large simplification was considered here through the

Algorithm	Assumed Parameters	PDN GW1	PDN GW2	PDN GW3	PDN GW4
1. Trigger of reselection decision					
2. Retrieve Subscriber Structure					
3. Possible Candidates Match	30% PDN GW1 10% PDN GW2 50% PDN GW3 10% PDN GW4	30	10	50	10
4. Mobility Pattern Fit	50% Area 1 50% Area 2 75% Trust	P=50%*75% 11.25	P=50%*75% 3.75	P=25%/2 6.25	P=25%/2 1.25
5. Resource Pattern Fit	20% Area 1 80% Area 2 75% Trust	P=20%*75% 1.6875	P=80%*75% 2.25	P=25%/2 0.78	P=25%/2 0.15625
6. Make Policy Decision			PDN GW2		

Fig. 4. Example Algorithm Coefficient Computation

consideration of a mobility pattern in which the MS is moving between Area 1 and Area 2 at specific moments in time. As it is assumed that a large proportion of the data traffic will be executed in Area 2 (80%), the resulting coefficient from the multiplication of the previous one with the obtained probabilities is giving a large proportion selection to PDN GW2 followed by PDN GW1 representing the areas in which the MS is connected.

However, if the proportions of the data traffic would have been selected in a different proportion between the Area 1 and Area 2 (40%-60%), the PDN GW1 would have gained a larger final coefficient. Therefore, even though for the specific MS, PDN GW2 would have been the best selection as the most of the data traffic is exchanged in the specific area, PDN GW1 would have been selected as considered better by the system due to the handling of a larger proportion of the overall data traffic.

The algorithm here presented represents a first tentative in introducing subscriber oriented wireless system components selection. It is assumed that the proposed method requires further probability adjustments depending on the deployments. Additionally, parts of the information may not be gathered in a specific operator networks, therefore simplifications as number of steps have to be also considered.

In case of an access network selection, it may not be any more assumed that all the base stations are visible at all the locations or that all can in a specific measure support the data traffic of the subscriber. In this case, the algorithm should become stricter in its probabilities as local parameters specific to the area where the device is can be better determined. Additional, to the selection of a next cell in order to ensure the service continuity, the algorithm offers a simplified solution to the access network selection enabling the balancing of subscribers between the different radio networks controlled by the same operator.

5   EPC Exemplifications

The 3GPP Evolved Packet Core (EPC) was selected as the exemplification core network architecture due to its capability to enable connectivity for LTE and for the other heterogeneous access networks including all-IP connectivity features such as authentication and authorization, mobility support, resource reservations and charging.

A minimal architecture for LTE access is depicted in Figure 5. The connection to the other access networks is not depicted for brevity. The LTE base stations (eNodeBs) are handling the radio connectivity for the User Equipment (UE). A Mobility Management Entity (MME) controls the connectivity to the LTE access network including the data path components selection and the intra-LTE handovers. For its decisions, the MME is able to retrieve subscription profile information from a Home Subscriber Server (HSS). The data traffic is anchored in a Serving GW (S-GW) for the 3GPP accesses and in the Packet Data Network GW (PDN GW) for the complete system. In the example, a single MME is deployed with multiple eNodeBs and co-located S-GW + PDN GW.

The EPC can be extended with the SelfFit framework functionality in all the selection processes including the selection of the MME, S-GW and PDN GW in case

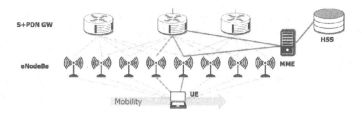

Fig. 5. Simplified EPC Architecture

of an initial attachment and of the target eNodeB, MME and S-GW in case of an intra-LTE handover.

For the attachment procedure, as a single MME is included in the system and as the S-GW is co-located with the PDN GW, the single selection required is the one for the PDN GW. The data flow of the procedure is depicted in Figure 6. When the Attachment Request is received by the eNodeB from the UE, it is forwarded to the MME (Step 1). Based on this request authentication and location procedures are executed including the subscription profile retrieval from the HSS (Step 2).

In order to establish a data path, the MME has to select an appropriate PDN GW. For this, it queries the SelfFit framework (Step 3). As to bring a minimal modification of the system, the MME is querying the SelfFit framework with a Diameter communication interface, similar to the interface between the MME and the HSS used for the retrieval of the subscription profile. Based on this one of the SelfFit a framework deployment alternative includes its integration as a front-end to the HSS.

The SelfFit framework retrieves the weighted PDN GWs identities from the DNS server as in the current network solution (Step 4). The lists of PDN GWs as well as the weights are used as parameters in making a selection decision along with the mobility and data traffic pattern which may be stored locally or retrieved from the HSS. The decision is made based on the previously described algorithm (Step 5).

The response in the form of a single PDN GW or of multiple weighted PDN GW identities are send back by the SelfFit to the MME (Step 6). In case of multiple PDN

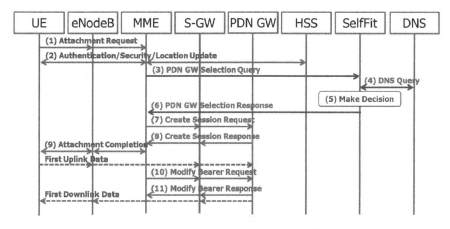

Fig. 6. Simplified LTE Attachment Procedure

GWs, the MME executes the weighted round robin algorithm and selects one of the PDN GW. Then, the MME controls the establishment of a data path to the selected PDN GW through a session establishment procedure (Step 7 and Step 8).

The rest of the LTE attachment procedure is executed including the notification on attachment complete to the UE over the radio link (Step 9) and the modification of the session to include the IP address allocated to the UE by the core network (Step 10 and Step 11).

Through this procedure, the PDN GW which will be maintained for the full attachment duration of the UE to the core network considering the mobility of the device through the wireless environment and the resources consumed as predicted based on previous knowledge of the operator network. Through this means, the appropriate PDN GW is selected not only based on the current location or on the network capacity, but also on the subscription profile information. For the intra-LTE handover, an S1-based procedure was chosen in which the decision to which target cell to execute the handover is taken by the MME. Similarly with the previous case, as the example system proposed has a single MME and that the S-GW are co-located with the PDN GW, there is no need for an MME or S-GW selection procedure. It is assumed that the UE is connected through a Source eNodeB to the EPC core and exchanging data with correspondent nodes through a previously selected PDN GW. The data flow is depicted in Figure 7.

Due to modifications in the physical communication with the UE, a handover is requested by the Source eNodeB (Step 1). It is assumed in this scenario that the source eNodeB is not aware of the eNodeBs in its vicinity and can not execute direct X2 procedures. This is also the case when the eNodeB is at the border of an LTE deployment and the handover has to be executed to other 3GPP access networks such as HSPA or GPRS.

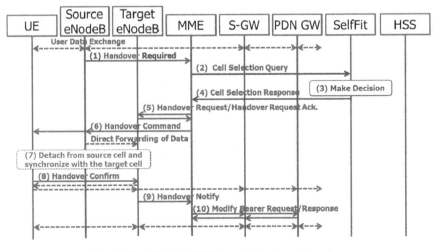

Fig. 7. Simplified LTE S1-based Handover Procedure

When receiving the request, the MME makes a "Cell Selection Query" to the SelfFit framework, including the identity of the UE, its momentary location and the handover requirement (Step 2). The SelfFit function makes a handover decision following the algorithm previously described adapted for cell selection (Step 3). The selected cell along with the specific handover parameters are forwarded to the MME (Step 4).

The rest of the procedure follows the standard operations for S1-based handovers. The MME transmits a Handover Request which is acknowledged to the Target eNodeB (Step 5) and a Handover Command to the Source eNodeB (Step 6), command which is forwarded to the UE. An indirection tunnel is established between the Source and the Target eNodeB enabling zero-packet loss handovers even for downlink data. The UE detaches from the source eNodeB and attaches to the Target eNodeB (Step 7) and then transmits a handover Confirmation (Step 8) which is transformed into a Handover Notification send from the Target eNodeB to the MME (Step 9) which at its turn issues a request for the modification of the communication to the new path in the S-GW and PDN GW (Step 10).

Through this procedure, the Target eNodeB cell is selected based on the subscriber's requirements for sustaining the future communication. This is especially important in the case when the communication may be established through multiple eNodeBs at the same location for example in case the macro-network is augmented with femto-cells of the same network provider and in the case a network provider is deploying multiple cells in different frequency bands.

The same procedure is to be used in case of handovers from LTE to other 3GPP access networks. However, in this case the selection decision is first transmitted to the SGSN which makes a new selection decision which is the most appropriate 2G or 3G cell to be used.

With several extensions which are not considered in this article, the procedure can be adapted for handovers to other non-3GPP accesses. However, the handover command including the target network cannot be transmitted directly over the LTE wireless link, thus requiring another communication mechanism.

The handover duration is time critical and as the respective subscriber oriented decisions may affect also other handover parameters such as the LTE Radio Time-To-Trigger (TTT) parameter which defines the duration in which the UE is maintaining the connectivity to the Source eNodeB in order to avoid rollbacks and other exception cases. In order to reduce the duration of the newly introduced procedure steps, it is expected that the MME will executed this steps immediately when the UE is attached to the Source eNodeB and will cache the information until requested as part of the state information maintained on the UE. Further investigations on the specific procedure have to be considered especially for the case when the selection is made by the Source eNodeB.

6   OpenEPC Testbed

For evaluating the opportunity of the previous proposed SelfFit concept as well as for enabling demonstrations and proof-of concept of novel R&D features related to the core networks and to the delivery of applications in the future mobile wireless environments, Fraunhofer FOKUS developed the OpenEPC toolkit as depicted in Figure 8 ([9]).

OpenEPC Rel. 3 enables the docking of off-the-shelf base stations for a large set of access networks such as LTE, HSPA, EDGE and WiFi and enabling the realization of complete operator testbeds including the radio and the core network features while using commercial available smartphones and modems.

Currently, OpenEPC features all the 3GPP standard components including the procedures for the attachment and the detachment for the various radio technologies and transparent mobility management between the access networks. It also enables convergent resource reservations and charging based on the requirements from the applications and on the device subscription profile.

Regarding the concept here presented, OpenEPC was deployed with two distinct PDN GWs which may be selected while attaching to the different base stations of the same or of different access technologies with different priorities. Through this testbed the initial attachment scenario was implemented and demonstrated.

The SelfFit framework was implemented as a separate component using a proprietary interface of the OpenEPC which enables fast development of a simple communication protocol between two distinct entities. The SelfFit was capable of making a simple decision on which PDN GW to select. Currently, no information on the mobility or data traffic pattern was included as this presumes further network modeling. It was observed that for the PDN GW selection a delay less than 50ms was introduced on the network side which in a real operator environment will be compensated by the parallel execution of the attachment procedures over the radio link.

From the perspective of the OpenEPC practical implementation, the duration and the computation required for the PDN GW selection is acceptable, due to the single execution of the procedure per attachment. However, the delay is considered too large for the eNodeB selection, thus a different mechanism for the transmission of the selection parameters should be considered, such as the caching here proposed.

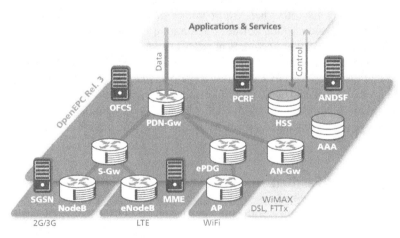

Fig. 8. OpenEPC Rel. 3 Testbed Architecture

7   Conclusions and Further Work

In this article we have described a novel concept for the customized selection of network entities by using a subscriber oriented management framework which makes decisions considering the specific characteristics of the communication of the mobile device based on the subscription profile, momentary network topology and status and based on predictions of the mobility and data traffic patterns.

The presented concept addresses carrier grade operators enabling connectivity to large number of devices using highly overlapping heterogeneous access networks and geographically distributed core networks. For this environment, the concept presented reduces the number of required reselections by customizing the selection process for each mobile device independently.

The practical implementation of the LTE attachment procedure using the Fraunhofer FOKUS OpenEPC proves the feasibility of the presented concept for selecting core network entities. A further optimization of the proposed signaling has to be considered for the cell selection as the potential duration may be too large.

Further work will include the optimization related to the cell selection in LTE environments as well as the integration with the X2 intra-eNodeB interface and with other SON related functionality. Also a special attention with be given to the integration of OpenEPC with off-the-shelf LTE eNodeBs enabling the evaluation of the procedures through friendly trials.

References

1. Cisco Visual Network Index, Visual Networking Index: Forecast and Methodology 2011-2016 (February 2012), http://www.cisco.com
2. Global Mobile Suppliers Association (GSA), GSM/3G and LTE Market Update (March 2011), http://gsacom.com
3. Meeker, M., et al.: The Mobile Internet Report. Morgan Stanley Research (December 2009), http://www.morganstanley.com/institutional/techresearch/
4. GSMA, Machina Research Overview, Connected Intelligence Database: 2020 connected devices overview (October 2011), http://www.gsma.com/documents/
5. 3GPP TS 23.401, General Packet Radio Service (GPRS) enhancements for Evolved Universal Terrestrial Radio Access Network (E-UTRAN) access, http://www.3gpp.org
6. 3GPP TS 23.402, Architecture enhancements for non-3GPP accesses, http://www.3gpp.org
7. 3GPP TS 36.300, Evolved Universal Terrestrial Radio Access (E-UTRA) and Evolved Universal Terrestrial Radio Access Network (E-UTRAN) Overall Description, http://www.3gpp.org
8. 3GPP TS 24.301, Non-Access Stratum (NAS) protocol for Evolved Packet System, http://www.3gpp.org
9. Fraunhofer FOKUS OpenEPC toolkit, http://www.openepc.net/
10. 3GPP TR 36.902, Self-configuring and self-optimizing network (SON) use cases and solutions, http://www.3gpp.org
11. Song, C., Qu, Z., Blumm, N., Barabasi, A.-L.: Limits of Predictability in Human Mobility. Science Maganzie 327 (February 2010), http://www.sciencemag.org
12. González, M.C., Hidalgo, C.A., Barabasi, A.-L.: Understanding individual human mobility patterns. Nature Journal 435 (June 2008), http://www.nature.com

A Common Platform API for Android

Arno Puder

San Francisco State University
Computer Science Department
1600 Holloway Avenue
San Francisco, CA 94132
`arno@sfsu.edu`

Abstract. Cross-platform frameworks for mobile devices promise to facilitate the porting effort of applications between different smartphones. Our approach is to cross-compile Android applications to other platforms such as iOS or Windows Phone 7. Doing so requires to refactor the Android source code base in a platform-dependent and platform-independent part separated by a *Common Platform API*. This paper discusses the cross-compiling of Java-based Android applications and the design and implementation of the Common Platform API.

1 Introduction

Smartphones have become the major driving force in the mobile market. Currently iOS and Android dominate the scene with Microsoft's Windows Phone 7 (WP7) and HTML5-based platforms such as Tizen or Firefox OS vying for market share. From a developers perspective it is desirable to be present in as many app stores as possible to increase dissemination and thereby revenue. However, making an application available on different platforms requires significant efforts. This has to do with the fact that smartphone platforms have developed into technology silos where cross-platform approaches are made difficult through technical and legal means. Apple in particular has tried in the past to ban other execution platforms other than its own on iOS. Making an application available on different platforms necessitates to reimplement it in a different programming languages. Android uses Java, iOS uses Objective-C while WP7 requires either C# or VisualBasic [6,5,2] (see Figure 1).

To some extend Android is the most liberal smartphone platform, not only because its core code base is released under an Open Source license [1]. Android was designed to run on a variety of devices with different hardware capabilities. An Android developer is expected to write applications in such a way that they adapt to specific capabilities (such as different screen resolutions). For this reason we have chosen Android as the canonical platform for our cross-platform framework, called XMLVM [9]. Android applications can be cross-compiled to other platforms with the help of our byte-code level cross-compiler. The cross-compiled application should have the look-and-feel of the target platform. E.g., an Android button should be mapped to the native button of the respective platform.

C. Borcea et al. (Eds.): MobilWare 2012, LNICST 65, pp. 164–177, 2013.
© Institute for Computer Sciences, Social Informatics and Telecommunications Engineering 2013

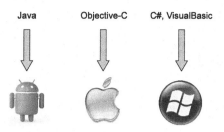

Java   Objective-C   C#, VisualBasic

Fig. 1. Technology silos

In previous work we have shown how to cross-compile from Android to iOS [7]. However, the necessary changes to the Android code base were tightly linked to iOS. Targeting another platform such as WP7 would have required to redo this work leading to two independent variations of the Android library that need to be maintained separately. Instead, we decided to refactor the Android code base in such a way that platform-dependent parts are clearly separated from the platform-independent parts by what we call the *Common Platform API* (CP-API). Ultimately, the refactored code base increases reusability and maintainability of our Android compatibility library.

This paper is organized as follows: Section 2 discusses the limits to cross-platform approaches and Section 3 presents various cross-platform frameworks. Section 4 introduces our cross-platform approach and more specifically the design of the CP-API. In Section 5 we briefly discuss our prototype implementation before providing conclusions and an outlook in Section 6.

2   Limits to Cross-Platform Frameworks

Cross-platform frameworks are hampered by legal and technical hurdles. Legal limitations are often tied to UI style guidelines. E.g., Apple will reject applications that have an "Exit" button to terminate the application. In iOS the only permitted way to exit an application is via the device's home button. Apple also permits the use of dynamic execution technology such as virtual machines for the purpose of loading additional code from a server.

In this section we focus on the limits of cross-platform approaches from a technical perspective. Table 1 gives an overview of some key differences between Android, iOS, and WP7 both from the hardware and software perspective. Developers for Android and WP7 devices can expect the presence of certain hardware buttons such as menu or search buttons. If the application is to be ported to a platform without those buttons (e.g., iOS), the same functionality needs to be incorporated into the UI in a different way. Likewise there exist differences in the physical screen resolutions between the platforms. Android makes no assumption on the screen resolution while iOS and WP7 being closed systems prescribe a limited number of resolutions.

Table 1. Comparison between Android, iOS, and WP7

	Android	**iOS**	**WP7**
Buttons	Back, Menu	None	Back, Search
Screen Res	Flexible	Limited	Limited
Language	Java	Objective-C	C#, VisualBasic
Memory Mgt	Garbage Collection	Reference Counting	Garbage Collection
Layout	Declarative	Absolute	Declarative
Intents	Yes	No	No

From the software side, each platform uses a different programming language. Cross-compiling between Turing complete languages is possible, so this does not present an obstacle [3]. However, iOS uses reference counting for memory management, so any cross-platform framework would need to address this. When it comes to layouting a UI, Android and WP7 support declarative UI descriptions while iOS expects the programmer to place every widget in terms of absolute coordinates. Android introduced a powerful late binding mechanism called intents that has even been adopted in other frameworks (e.g., W3C's WebIntents [10]). However, iOS and WP7 do not offer a comparable feature. Here again the question arises how missing functionality of one platform can be compensated on another.

The list presented in Table 1 is by no means exhaustive. There are numerous other differences between platforms. E.g., in Android, the label inside a button can be placed anywhere within the borders of the button. iOS and WP only allow the label to centered. The implication of these differences is that cross-platform frameworks will need to make compromises. Either an application will need to settle for a lowest common denominator in terms of functionality, or extra efforts must be made to overcome platform differences.

While it would be possible to provide a custom widget under iOS that looks like a button and that can place its label in the top-right corner, doing so is not advisable since it would break that platforms UI idioms. The challenge of cross-platform frameworks is to provide some best practices that make it easier to port an application. While certain features should not be used, as will be shown in a subsequent section, it is possible to mimic other features without compromising the UI idiom of a platform. The following section discusses various cross-platform frameworks.

3   Related Work

Several frameworks promise to facilitate the development of cross-platform applications. In the following we briefly discuss the approach taken by Cordova, Adobe AIR, and In-the-Box. Each framework will be classified with regards to the mobile platforms it supports, the programming languages it offers, the API it uses, the IDE it can be used with and finally the license under which it is released.

Apache Cordova (formally called PhoneGAP) is an Open Source project that addresses web developers who wish to write mobile applications. It is available for iOS, Android, WP7 and other platforms. Applications need to be written in JavaScript/HTML/CSS. But instead of downloading the application from a remote web server, the JavaScript is bundled inside a native application. E.g., for iOS devices a generic startup code written in Objective-C will instantiate a full-screen web widget via class `UIWebView`. Next the JavaScript that is embedded as data in the native application is injected into this web widget at runtime. Special protocol handlers allow the communication between JavaScript and the native layer. All iOS widgets are rendered using HTML/CSS mimicking the look-and-feel of their native counterparts. Cordova supports a common API for sensors such as the accelerometer. Platform-specific widgets have their own API. Cordova is available under the MIT Open Source license at `http://incubator.apache.org/cordova/`.

Table 2. Comparison of Cross-Platform Frameworks

	Cordova	**In-the-Box**	**Adobe AIR**	**XMLVM**
Platforms	iOS, Android, WP7, others	iOS	iOS	iOS, Android, WP7
Language	JavaScript	Java	ActionScript	Java
API	Common Sensor API	Android	Graphics-only	Android API mapped to iOS, WP7
IDE	Xcode	Eclipse	N/A	Eclipse
License	Open Source	Open Source	Commercial	Open Source

Another cross-platform framework is the Adobe Integrated Runtime (AIR) for iOS development. Adobe AIR includes an (Ahead of Time) AOT compiler based on the LLVM compiler suite that translates ActionScript 3 to ARM instructions. This facilitates porting of existing Flash applications while not relying on an installation of a Flash player on the iOS device. AIR offers API based on ActionScript to the device's sensors, but does not provide access to the native iOS widgets which limits AIR applications to games. AIR is available under a commercial license at `http://www.adobe.com/products/air/`.

A project called In-the-Box takes yet another approach: Android's virtual machine, called Dalvik [4], is ported to iOS to execute original Android applications under iOS. From iOS perspective, Dalvik and the class files comprising the Android app are bundled into one native binary. Back in 2009 Apple relaxed the terms and conditions of their SDK to allow such deployments. The benefit of this approach is complete Android compatibility. However, one major downside is that In-the-Box creates iOS apps that have the look and feel of Android applications. It can also not solve the problem of Android's hardware button that do not exist under iOS. In-the-Box is released under the Apache Software License and is available at `http://www.in-the-box.org/`.

Table 2 summarizes the distinguishing factors of the various cross-platform frameworks. Our framework XMLVM is similar in the respect that it offers one programming language (Java) for different mobile devices. It also includes an AOT compiler to translate Java to native applications in order to avoid the installation of a Java virtual machine on the target platform. Similar to In-the-Box, XMLVM also relies on the Android API for application development. However, one major difference to In-the-Box is that the Android API is mapped to the native API of the respective platform. E.g., an Android button is mapped to a native `UIButton` when cross-compiled to iOS.

4   Cross-Compiling Android Applications

This section provides some details of our cross-compilation framework. First, we discuss the its design principles. Next we describe how to expose non-Java API of the target platform in Java followed by the introduction of the Common Platform API.

4.1   Design Principles

Our approach is to cross-compile Android applications to other platforms such as iOS or WP7. Considering the unique features of every platform, it is not possible to cross-compile arbitrary applications. Certain best practices must be followed such as not making use of the Android menu button. It is important that the cross-compiled application uses the UI idioms of the target platform. It is not acceptable to have and iOS or WP7 application that looks and feels like an Android application as is the case of the aforementioned In-the-Box framework. The implication is that certain features in Android will not be mimicked on the target platform. E.g., if an Android application does not place the label in the center of a button, the cross-compiled version would still do so.

In order to accomplish this, the Android code base needs to be refactored in such a way that Android widgets can easily be mapped to their native counterpart of the target platform. The goal of the refactoring is to distinguish between platform-dependent and platform-independent parts of Android. Significant portions of Android are platform-independent and can be cross-compiled as-is to the target platform. Most importantly, Android's layout manager, activity lifecycle and the intent system have little dependence to the native layer. E.g., the layout manager reads declarative layout descriptions from the file system to compute a layout. The implementation of the various layout managers such as `LinearLayout`, `RelativeLayout`, or `GridLayout` have no other external dependencies.

The refactoring yields a Common Platform API (CP-API) that isolates the platform-dependent parts of Android. Adding a new platform will only require to implement the CP-API. Designing the CP-API is the contribution of this paper and will need to balance re-use of the existing Android code base vs. the ability to do a deep integration to achieve the native look-and-feel of the target platform. The following section first discusses the adding of a Java layer over a non-C platform followed by a description of the CP-API.

4.2 JNI for Non-C Platforms

The first step is to expose the native API of the target platform in Java. That is to say, an API expressed in a language L needs to be accessible in Java. Given a solution to this problem, it is possible to write apps for this platform in Java using the native API of that platform. The challenge consists in the fact that the native programming language may follow different paradigms than Java. E.g., Objective-C used for iOS development supports dynamic typing and the memory management mechanism is based on reference counting. While creating a Java API from a platform's native API is mostly a mechanical process, one has to decide how to generate strongly typed interfaces common to Java programming based on an API that exploits dynamic typing. We have studied this problem in earlier work [8].

Once a Java API has been generated, the question remains how an invocation of a Java method results in a call to the corresponding native method. The Java Native Interface (JNI) [6] specification introduced a mechanism by which a Java application can break out from the VM sandbox to access the native layer. JNI describes how data structures are passed between the VM and C-based applications. Since the JNI is limited to the C programming language, it cannot be used for platforms that do no provide access to the C layer.

For that reason we have extended the JNI model by keeping the Java interface (via the **native** method modifier) and allowing arbitrary programming languages on the native side. In the following we give an example how the API of class **Button** in WP7 can be exposed in Java. Class **Button** extends from base class **ButtonBase** in WP7 and has amongst others a method **setContent()** to set the label of the button. This method is marked as native and consequently has no implementation:

```
─────────────────────── Java: WP7 Button Wrapper ───────────────────
1 public class Button extends ButtonBase {
2   native public void setContent(String content);
3
4   //...
5 }
```

As can be seen in the listing above, the implementation of the class is left empty since its only purpose is to provide a Java API against which the developer can implement an application. Properties in C#, such as **Button.Content**, are represented by appropriate getter/setter methods. Our cross-compiler translates the wrapper class to the target language; C# in this case. For methods marked as native the cross-compiler inserts special comment markers into the generated code. The programmer can inject manually written code between these comment markers. This code is tying the wrapper class together with the native class it wraps. The following code excerpt demonstrates this concept for the Button class.

```
───────────────── C#: Cross-compiled WP7 Button Wrapper ─────────────────
1 public class Button : ButtonBase {
2
3   public virtual void setContent(java.lang.String n1) {
4     //XMLVM_BEGIN_WRAPPER
5     wrapped.Content = Util.toNative(n1);
6     //XMLVM_END_WRAPPER
7   }
8
9   //...
10 }
```

Note that the wrapper class above is not implementing the widget itself, but only wraps the WP7 API Button class. Code between XMLVM_BEGIN_WRAPPER and XMLVM_END_WRAPPER comments is manually written C# code which gets injected on either method- or class-level during cross-compilation. The comment markers allow the manually written code to be automatically migrated if it should become necessary to regenerate the wrappers. Method setContent() converts a java.lang.String instance to a native C# string via a helper function and sets the Content property of the wrapped button to the converted string. Once the native API of the target platform has been exposed in Java, it is possible to implement the platform-specific portions of the refactored Android code base.

4.3   Common Platform API

The Common Platform API, CP-API for short, isolates the platform-specific parts of Android. The platform-independent parts can be reused while the CP-API needs to be implemented for each target. In the following we discuss the CP-API for the view hierarchy. Every UI framework features a view hierarchy featuring a variety of widgets. The view hierarchy typically has a common base class from which the various widget classes are derived. Android's base class of the view hierarchy is class View, the base class for iOS is UIView and for WP7 the class is called Panel. The base class combines various capabilities that are inherited to all derived classes. The following code excerpt shows the API for setting a background color/image:

```
───────────────────── Java: View hierarchy ─────────────────────
1 // Android
2 public class View {
3   native public void setBackgroundDrawable(Drawable d);
4   // ...
5 }
6
```

```
 7 // iOS
 8 public class UIView {
 9   native public void setBackgroundColor(UIColor c);
10   // ...
11 }
12
13 // WP7
14 public class Panel {
15   native public void setBackground(Brush b);
16   // ...
17 }
```

In Android the background of a widget can be an arbitrary `Drawable`. A `Drawable` can be static color, a gradient, an image, or a custom drawable where the application can manually draw the background. iOS is more restrictive and only allows a background to be a static color (represented via class `UIColor`). More complex backgrounds in iOS require to place a separate `UIView` that serves as the background. WP7 is more flexible by allowing the background to be a `Brush`. A `Brush` can be a static color, a gradient, or an image. But unlike Android it is not possible to provide an application-specific custom `Brush`.

Considering the differences in functionality, the CP-API introduces a Java interface that serves as an abstraction for the common base class of the view hierarchy:

```
———————————————— Java: CommonView interface ————————————————
 1 public interface CommonView {
 2   public void setBackgroundDrawable(Drawable d);
 3   // ...
 4 }
```

Given this interface, the question arises how to implement it under iOS and WP7. In case a specific `Drawable` is supported by the respective platform, it can be mapped directly to the native API. E.g., a solid color `Drawable` can be directly mapped to an appropriate `UIColor` under iOS and a `Brush` under WP7. The more interesting case is when the `Drawable` is not supported by the native platform. In this case we rearrange the view hierarchy by adding an extra view that represents the background as shown in Figure 2. If the application sets the background on view V_3, a new view B_3 is inserted into the view hierarchy. View V_3 is the child of B_3 and its size and position are changed such that V_3 completely overlaps with B_3. It is then possible to render the `Drawable` in B_3. Since the Z-order of B_3 is such that it is below V_3 it effectively serves as the background.

Interface `CommonView` therefore serves as an abstraction of the platform-specific portions of an Android `View`. A platform-specific implementation has to be provided based on the native API. The device-independent portions of Android need to be refactored to make use of the interface. Instantiating platform-specific views is done via a factory. The main entry point to the CP-API is a singleton

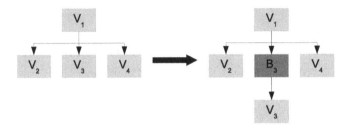

Fig. 2. Adding a background to a view

implementing the `CommonPlatformAPI` interface that provides access to the various subsystems:

```
──────────────────── Java: CP-API and Widget Factory ────────────────────
1 public interface CommonPlatformAPI {
2   CommonFileSystem getFileSystem();
3   CommonAccelerometer getAccelerometer(SensorManager sensorManager);
4   CommonWidgetFactory getWidgetFactory();
5   CommonFontFactory getFontFactory();
6   CommonPowerManager getPowerManager();
7   CommonMediaPlayer getMediaPlayer(MediaPlayer mediaPlayer);
8   // ...
9 }
10
11 public interface CommonWidgetFactory {
12   CommonView createCommonView();
13   ButtonAdapter createButton();
14   ImageViewAdapter createImageView();
15   TextViewAdapter createTextView();
16   RadioGroupAdapter createRadioGroup();
17   // ...
18 }
```

The `CommonWidgetFactory` interface can be obtained via the top-level `CommonPlatformAPI` interface and it allows the creation of the various Android widget adapters. The adapter interfaces declare the platform-specific API of the corresponding Android widgets ensuring reduced overhead for the refactoring of the platform-independent portions. The following code excerpt shows the declaration of the `ButtonAdapter` interface:

```
──────────────────── Java: ButtonAdapter interface ────────────────────
1 public interface ButtonAdapter extends CommonView {
2   void setText(CharSequence text);
3   void setOnClickListener(OnClickListener listener);
4   // ...
5 }
```

The interface features a subset of the methods declared in the Android class `Button`. In the following we show how the two featured methods of `ButtonAdapter` are implemented for iOS and WP7:

──────────── Java: Implementation of ButtonAdapter for iOS ────────────
```
1 public class IOSButtonAdapter implements ButtonAdapter {
2
3   private UIButton nativeButton;
4
5   public IOSButtonAdapter() {
6     nativeButton = UIButton.buttonWithType(UIButtonType.RoundedRect);
7   }
8
9   @Override
10  public void setText(CharSequence text) {
11    nativeButton.setTitle(text, UIControlState.Normal);
12  }
13
14  @Override
15  public void setOnClickListener(final OnClickListener listener) {
16    nativeButton.addTarget(new UIControlDelegate() {
17
18      @Override
19      public void raiseEvent(UIControl sender, int eventType) {
20        listener.onClick(IOSButtonAdapter.this);
21      }
22    }, UIControlEvent.TouchUpInside);
23  }
24 }
```

Class `IOSButtonAdapter` is a wrapper of a native iOS `UIButton`. The methods declared in interface `ButtonAdapter` are implemented based on the `UIButton` API, e.g., the `setText()` method is mapped to the corresponding `setTitle()` method of the `UIButton`. Another example is method `setOnClickListener()` that defines a delegate in the application to be called when the user taps on the button. The iOS `UIButton` features a method `addTarget()` that serves the same purpose. The iOS delegate has to implement a callback method called `raiseEvent()` that simply delegates the click event to the Android application. This example shows that for upcalls done by Android to the application it is possible to use the original Android interfaces (`OnClickListener`) and it is not necessary to create special wrapper interfaces in the CP-API.

Analogous to the iOS implementation, the following code excerpt shows the same implementation of the `ButtonAdapter`, this time for WP7:

──────────── Java: Implementation of ButtonAdapter for WP7 ────────────
```
1 public class WP7ButtonAdapter implements ButtonAdapter {
2   private OnClickListener listener;
3   private System.Windows.Controls.Button nativeButton;
4
```

```
5   public WP7ButtonAdapter() {
6     nativeButton = new System.Windows.Controls.Button();
7   }
8
9   @Override
10  public void setText(CharSequence text) {
11    nativeButton.setContent(text);
12  }
13
14  @Override
15  public void setOnClickListener(OnClickListener listener) {
16    this.listener = listener;
17    nativeButton.Click.__add(new RoutedEventHandler(this,
18                                         "button_onClick"));
19  }
20
21  public void button_onClick(Object sender, RoutedEventArgs e) {
22    listener.onClick(this);
23  }
24 }
```

In this case `WP7ButtonAdapter` is a wrapper for a native WP7 `Button`. The `setText()` method here is mapped to the equivalent `setContent()` method. The previous section showed how the Java version of this method is routed to the native C# method via code injection. The Android click listener is installed via WP7's event and delegate model. Method `__add` is the Java version of C#'s overloaded + = operator with which a delegate can be added to the `Click` event. Method `button_onClick()` will be called whenever the user pressed the WP7 button. Its implementation delegates the call to the Android application via the usual `OnClickListener`.

Figure 3 visualizes the structure of the refactored Android code base. The platform-independent portions are common to all supported platforms and contain modules such as layout management or activity lifecycle. Classes such as `android.widget.Button` are refactored into platform-independent parts that access platform-dependent implementations via interfaces of the Common Platform API. Adapter classes implement the CP-API based on features of the respective target platform.

5   Prototype Implementation

The concepts presented in this paper have been implemented as part of the XMLVM project. Android 2.3 served as a starting point for the refactoring effort. The platform-independent portions include the Activity lifecycle management, Intents, and layout management. The CP-API covers the majority of the Android widgets as well as the complete sensor API (accelerometer, gyroscope, GPS, camera, etc). Platform-specific implementations exist for iOS and WP7. Android applications complying to the best practices mentioned earlier

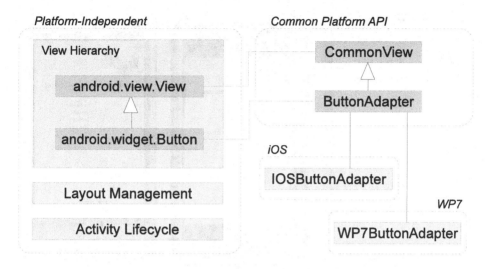

Fig. 3. Refactored Android code base

can be cross-compiled to Objective-C and C#. The refactored Android library is cross-compiled to those languages as well, yielding in native applications for the respective platform.

To demonstrate the feasibility of our approach we have cross-compiled an existing Android monitoring application. We have used the same application to show the cross-compilation from Android to iOS [7]. Based on the CP-API we have added a platform-specific version that allows the same application to be cross-compiler to WP7. The application issues HTTP requests to a network appliance and displays usage statistics in a custom widget that draws a graph. The original Android version uses a `RadioButton` group (see Figure 4). The corresponding `RadioGroupAdapter` of the CP-API maps this Android widget to a `UISegmentedControl` under iOS and a `RadioButton` under WP7. Since a `UISegmentedControl` is wider than high, Android's layout manager automatically stretches the custom graph-drawing widget, resulting in a native look-and-feel of the application on all platforms.

6   Conclusions and Outlook

Porting smartphone applications to various mobile platforms requires significant efforts. Various cross-platform frameworks seek to facilitate this process. The approach taken in this paper is to cross-compile Android applications to other platforms. It is important to keep the UI idioms of the target platform and not make the cross-compiled application look and feel like an Android application. To accomplish this the Android code base needs to be refactored in order to introduce a Common Platform API that isolates the platform-specific portions of Android.

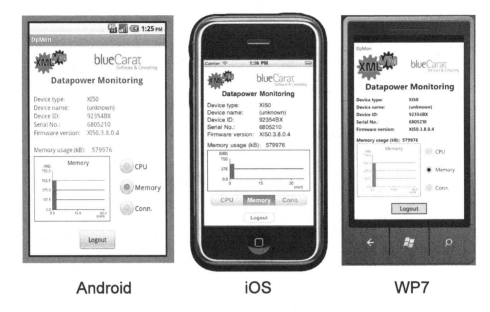

Fig. 4. Example

This approach works well for Android applications that follow certain best practices, such as avoiding the use of the menu button. In some cases the best practices require unnatural workarounds in order to cross-compile an application. In the future we plan to investigate a partial cross-compilation approach where only certain portions of the Android application are cross-compiled. For those parts of the application that are not cross-compiled the developer would have to provide a customized implementation for the target platform that can exploit its capabilities that may not be present in Android.

Acknowledgements. Markus Neubrand and Oren Antebi have implemented the concepts described in this paper as part of their master thesis work at the San Francisco State University.

References

1. The Android Open Source Project. Dalvik eXchange (DX),
   http://www.git://android.git.kernel.org/platform/dalvik.git
2. ECMA. C# Language Specification, 4th edn. (June 2006)
3. El-Ramly, M., Eltayeb, R., Alla, H.A.: An Experiment in Automatic Conversion of Legacy Java Programs to C#. In: ACS/IEEE International Conference on Computer Systems and Applications, pp. 1037–1045 (2006)
4. Google, Inc. The Dalvik virtual machine,
   http://en.wikipedia.org/wiki/Dalvik_virtual_machine

5. Kochan, S.: Programming in Objective-C, 4th edn. Addison-Wesley Professional (December 2011)
6. Lindholm, T., Yellin, F.: The Java Virtual Machine Specification, 2nd edn. Addison-Wesley Pub. Co. (April 1999)
7. Puder, A.: Running Android Applications without a Virtual Machine. In: Venkata-subramanian, N., Getov, V., Steglich, S. (eds.) Mobilware 2011. LNICST, vol. 93, pp. 121–134. Springer, Heidelberg (2012)
8. Puder, A., D'Silva, S.: Mapping Objective-C API to Java. In: MobiCASE, Mobile Networks and Applications, Seattle. Springer (2012)
9. Puder, A., Lee, J.: Towards an XML-based Byte Code Level Transformation Framework. In: 4th International Workshop on Bytecode Semantics, Verification, Analysis and Transformation. Elsevier, York (2009)
10. W3C. WebIntents (2012), `http://www.w3.org/wiki/WebIntents`

Adaptive Application Configuration and Distribution in Mobile Cloudlet Middleware

Tim Verbelen[1], Pieter Simoens[1,2], Filip De Turck[1], and Bart Dhoedt[1]

[1] Ghent University - IBBT, Department of Information Technology
[2] Ghent University College, Department INWE

Abstract. Despite recent advances in mobile device capabilities in terms of CPU power, memory, connectivity, etc, these devices still fall short to execute complex media rich and data analysis applications. Therefore, the concept of cloudlets was introduced, where nearby infrastructure is used by the mobile user for code offloading. However, the way this infrastructure is used is often left to the application developer, leading to a best effort approach in utilizing remote resources. In this paper we present a middleware approach for such cloudlet environments, that manages mobile applications on a component level. The middleware monitors application components in the cloudlet, and optimizes both the configuration and the deployment of all components in the cloudlet for the current execution context. We present a prototype implementation of the middleware platform, and show the effectiveness of our adaptation strategy using an augmented reality use case.

1 Introduction

Nowadays, mobile computing devices are becoming widespread given the increasing popularity of smartphones. Gartner reports that although worldwide sales of mobile phones declined by 2% during the first quarter of 2012, smartphone sales increased by 44.7% [4]. People no longer only use their mobile device for telephony, but also for a myriad of other mobile applications offered, such as location based services, multimedia applications, games and many more.

Despite many advances in technology, mobile devices will always be resource poor, as restrictions on weight, size, battery life, and heat dissipation impose limitations on computational resources and make mobile devices more resource constrained than their non-mobile counterparts [13]. Therefore, mobile devices still fall short to execute many media rich and data analysis applications that require heavy computation, and often also have (near) real-time constraints such as augmented reality (AR).

To address the resource limitations of mobile devices, cloud computing can be leveraged to offload tasks to the infrastructure of public cloud providers [5]. However, Hassan et al. [7] show that cloud computing is not a silver bullet, and is outperformed by outsourcing to nearby residential computers. Depending on the use case, outsourcing to the cloud can even be slower than local execution on the mobile device due to limited bandwidth and high WAN latencies. Therefore,

C. Borcea et al. (Eds.): MobilWare 2012, LNICST 65, pp. 178–191, 2013.
© Institute for Computer Sciences, Social Informatics and Telecommunications Engineering 2013

Satyanarayanan [13] introduced the concept of VM based cloudlets: trusted, resource rich computers in the near vicinity of the mobile user (e.g. near or co-located with the wireless access point), on which virtual machines (VMs) are instantiated for remote execution.

Instead of adopting virtual machines as the unit of deployment, we choose a more fine grained approach where applications are managed on a component level [16]. This approach offers a number of advantages. First, the component management middleware allows for a more fine grained optimization than an "all or nothing" approach using VMs. Second, starting and migrating a component is an order of magnitude faster than starting and provisioning a virtual machine. Third, resources are managed by the middleware, which allows for dynamic discovery of resources in the network, that can join or leave the cloudlet at runtime. Finally, the middleware can optimize the component distribution and configuration for all users involved in the cloudlet, and optimally coordinate the allocation of resources that should be shared by multiple end users.

Adopting a fine-grained, component level approach however poses a number of issues. In addition to deciding on where to deploy, components should also be configured to run optimally on the available resources. This typically involves setting configuration parameters of components, such that the application is perceived to run at good quality. To achieve this, components can be specified to gracefully degrade when executed on low-end hardware and to perform better when they can exploit additional resources. When aiming for optimal application quality, constraints concerning total CPU- and network load should be satisfied, as well as timing constraints defined by the application developer. The problem at hand is therefore to solve the deployment and configuration problem, subject to both infrastructure and application constraints.

In this paper we present a component based middleware architecture, that configures and distributes application components at runtime. We propose a model driven middleware decision algorithm that optimizes both the application configuration and distribution, taking into account the network connectivity, the available resources and application constraints imposed by the application developer. To show the effectiveness of our approach, we use a mobile augmented reality application.

The remainder of this paper is structured as follows. In the next section, we discuss related work in the domain of code offloading. Section 3 describes in detail our cloudlet middleware architecture. In Section 4 a mathematical model is presented for the infrastructure, the application behavior and the application constraints. A heuristic algorithm is proposed to search for the global optimum. The algorithm is then evaluated in Section 5 using a mobile augmented reality application. Finally we conclude this paper in Section 6 and discuss future work.

2   Related Work

Offloading computation from mobile devices to remote resources has been a research topic for over a decade [1]. Several systems exist, offloading either at class, method, component or virtual machine level.

Ou et al. [12] present an adaptive offloading framework for offloading Java classes, in combination with a (k+1) partitioning algorithm. The fine granularity of class offloading however requires extensive monitoring and causes significant overhead.

Other systems use methods as units to outsource, such as the Scavenger cyber foraging system [10], which outsources Python methods. A dual-profile scheduler is used, weighting tasks according to their parameter input sizes and run time. MAUI [3] outsources method calls on the Microsoft .Net runtime environment. This platform generates a program partitioning by formulating and solving an integer linear programming problem to maximize energy savings.

A more coarse grained approach is to outsource software components. Zhang et al. [17] offloads platform independent software components – called weblets – to the cloud using a Bayesian learning scheduler. Giurgiu et al. [5] and Verbelen et al. [15] use OSGi components as units to outsource. To distribute these components, a graph model of the software is built and graph cutting algorithms are used to calculate the most appropriate deployment.

Goyal et al. [6] propose the use of virtualization on the infrastructure for remote execution. Here a client can request a virtual machine (VM) with specific resource guarantees to offload services to. Su et al. present Slingshot [14], where the VMs are co-located with the wireless access point to overcome the WAN latency. Chun et al. present CloneCloud [2], where virtualized clones of the mobile device are executed in the cloud. Different binaries of the application are generated in an off-line profiling stage, with special VM instructions added at migration points for selected methods. At runtime a clone VM is instantiated at the server side, and the application transparently switches between execution at the device or at the clone.

Satyanarayanan et al. [13] propose the concept a of cloudlet: a trusted, resource-rich computer or a cluster of computers well connected to the Internet and available for use by nearby mobile devices. Cloudlets offer their resources to mobile devices by dynamic VM synthesis, where small VM overlays are sent to the cloudlet from which a complete VM is created.

All these systems aim to optimize application execution solely by offloading. In this paper we combine the offloading problem with dynamic configuration adaptation, which allows the application to gracefully degrade when no or insufficient remote resources are available. All these systems also tackle the case of one mobile device offloading to one or more remote devices. In this contribution, we state a general optimization problem that also takes into account multiple mobile users sharing the same network and CPU resources.

3   Cloudlet Middleware

We envision the cloudlet architecture as shown in Figure 1, with three layers: the component level, the node level and the cloudlet level.

A component is the unit of deployment and is specified by its providing and required interfaces. Components are managed by an *Execution Environment (EE)*,

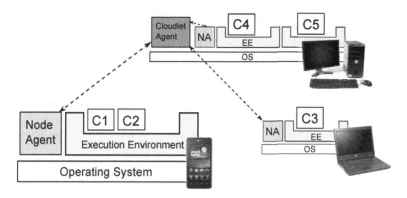

Fig. 1. The application components are distributed among nodes in the cloudlet, consisting of a mobile phone, a laptop and a desktop computer. All components are managed and monitored by an Execution Environment (EE). Different EEs on a node are managed by a Node Agent (NA), that in turn communicate with the Cloudlet Agent (CA).

that can start and stop components, resolve component dependencies, expose provided interfaces etc. To support distributed execution, dependencies can be resolved with other (remote) Execution Environments. In that case, proxies and stubs are generated and the components can communicate by remote procedure calls (RPCs). Components can also define performance constraints (e.g. the maximum execution time of a method), and expose configuration parameters to the EE. By monitoring the resource usage of each component, the EE can assess the behavior and the performance of the application, and detect violations of the imposed performance constraints.

Multiple EEs can run on top of an operating system (OS), which in turn can run on both virtualized or real hardware. The (possibly virtualized) hardware together with the installed OS is called a node, and is managed by a *Node Agent (NA)*. The Node Agent manages all the EEs running on the OS, and can also start or stop new Execution Environments, for example for sandboxing components. The NA also monitors the resource usage of the node as a whole, and has info about the (maybe virtualized) hardware it runs on (e.g. the number of processing cores, processing speed, etc.).

Multiple nodes that are in the physical proximity of each other (i.e. low latency) form a cloudlet. The cloudlet is managed by a *Cloudlet Agent (CA)*, that communicates with all underlying Node Agents. Nodes can dynamically join or leave the cloudlet, and are discovered using a service discovery protocol. Within one cloudlet, the node with the most resources is chosen to host the Cloudlet Agent.

The Cloudlet Agent has a global overview of all application components running on the different EEs, and contains the decision algorithm to optimize the deployment and configuration of all components in the cloudlet. This decision algorithm is triggered when an event occurs in the cloudlet, e.g. when a new device joins the cloudlet, when an EE detects a constraint violation, etc.

4   Decision Algorithm

We first present mathematical application and infrastructure models that capture all monitor information and are used to define constraints and an objective function to optimize. Because the solution space is too large to calculate the absolute optimum in a timely manner, we also present a heuristic to calculate a local optimum fast.

4.1   Application Model

An application consists of a number of components, that can offer a number of methods as service interface. An example application consisting of five components is shown in Figure 2. The arrows denote call dependencies, for example component C1 calls method m1 from component C2, which on its turn calls method m3 and method m4 of component C3. However, to take a decision on how to deploy the components, more information is needed on the actual control flow of the application.

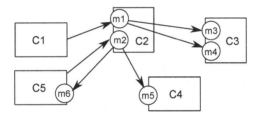

Fig. 2. An example component based application. Each component offers a number of methods in a service interface. Components communicate with each other by calling these service methods.

To capture the actual control flow of the application, we use sequence diagrams for all the scenarios of the application. For example, the sequence diagrams of the application presented in Figure 2 are shown on Figure 3.

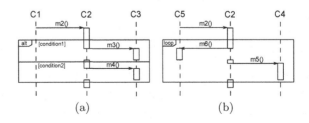

Fig. 3. The actual behavior of the application is captured in UML sequence diagrams

However, the sequence diagrams depicted in Figure 3 still fall short to describe the application behavior in sufficient detail. For example, in Figure 3(a) the total execution time before the call of method m2 by component C5 returns, depends on the number of times the loop is executed, and in Figure 3(b) the execution depends on the conditional path taken.

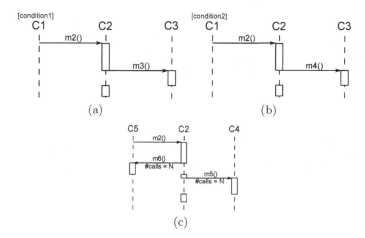

Fig. 4. The two UML sequence diagrams shown in Figure 3 are split up in 3 sequences. The loop is replaced by an annotation how many times each method is called within the sequence, and conditional sequences are split up in a separate sequence for each condition.

Therefore, sequences are represented as shown in Figure 4. To model the loop, the method calls in a sequence are annotated with the number of times they are called within the sequence as shown in Figure 4(a). The conditional sequence in Figure 3(b) is split up in multiple sequences (Fig. 4(b) and Fig. 4(c)), each representing one conditional path. To capture the overall application behavior, we also keep track of the number of times each sequence is called per time unit.

More formally, let C and M represent the set of application components and the set of public methods offered by all components. A sequence $s \in S(C, M)$ represents a sequence of calls of methods $m \in M$ between application components $c_i, c_j \in C$. $m_{sc_ic_j}$ denotes a call to method m of component c_j in sequence s by component c_i. To further define the application behavior $\#calls_s$ is the number of times sequence s is executed per time unit, and $\#calls_{m_{sc_ic_j}}$ is the number of times method call $m_{sc_ic_j}$ is executed in sequence s.

Finally, for each call $m_{sc_ic_j}$ we also track the size of the arguments of the method $A_{m_{sc_ic_j}}$, as well as the size of the return value $R_{m_{sc_ic_j}}$ and the relative CPU load $Load_{m_{sc_ic_j}}$ of the method call. The argument size, return size and CPU load of a method call $m_{sc_ic_j}$ are to be expressed as a function of the configuration parameters, which can be given by the developer, or can be estimated from monitoring information.

4.2   Infrastructure Model

The cloudlet consists of a number of interconnected devices $d \in D$. Each device processor has a rate at which load can be processed $CPUspeed_d$ and a number of cores $\#CPUcores_d$.

The devices are connected by a (wireless) network, that is characterized by its bandwidth BW and latency Lat. The bandwidth denotes both the capacity (maximum number of bytes that can be sent per time unit) as the speed (the rate at which bytes are sent) of the network. The latency is the round trip delay of the network.

4.3   Constraints

A number of constraints are defined that restrict the number of allowed deployments and configurations. The network is limited in capacity by the maximum number of bytes that can be sent per time unit, and also the devices have a maximum load that can be processed per time unit. In addition to the constraints imposed by the infrastructure capabilities, the application developer can also define constraints on the execution time of methods, for example restricting the maximum execution time of a method.

Let X_{id} be defined as

$$X_{id} = \begin{cases} 1 & \text{if component } c_i \text{ is deployed on device } d \\ 0 & \text{otherwise} \end{cases}$$

and $h_{ij} = 1 - \sum_d X_{id} \times X_{jd}$, meaning that h_{ij} equals 1 when c_i and c_j are deployed on a different device.

The bandwidth used (the number of bytes sent over the network per time unit) should be less than BW or

$$bandwidth = \sum_s \sum_m \sum_i \sum_j h_{ij} \times (A_{m_{sc_ic_j}} + R_{m_{sc_ic_j}}) \times \#calls_{m_{sc_ic_j}} \times \#calls_s$$
$$\leq BW$$

We assume that all methods called in the same sequence run on the same thread, and thus the load generated by a sequence on one device $load_{sd}$ should not exceed the maximum load that can be processed per time unit by one core or thus $\forall d$:

$$load_{sd} = \sum_m \sum_i \sum_j X_{jd} \times Load_{m_{sc_ic_j}} \times \#calls_{m_{sc_ic_j}} \times \#calls_s$$
$$\leq CPUspeed_d$$

Also, for each device the maximum load should not exceed the maximum load that can be processed per time unit on the whole device or $\forall d$:

$$load_d = \sum_s load_{sd}$$

$$\leq CPUspeed_d \times \#CPUcores_d$$

Note that this is only an approximation of the maximum load of the device, as this also depends on the internal thread scheduling. However, we employ this constraint for simplicity, and because this already gives sufficient results.

Finally for each constrained method m the execution time of a method call $T_{m_{sc_ic_j}}$ should be lower than the imposed threshold or $\forall s, c_i$:

$$T_{m_{sc_ic_j}} = (\sum_d X_{jd} \times Load_{m_{sc_ic_j}} \times \frac{1}{CPUspeed_d})$$

$$+ h_{ij} \times ((A_{m_{sc_ic_j}} + R_{m_{sc_ic_j}}) \times \frac{1}{BW} + Lat)$$

$$+ \sum_{m \in children(m_{sc_ic_j})} T_{m_c}$$

$$\leq threshold_m$$

4.4 Optimization Objective

The optimization objective is to maximize the utility of all components, where the utility function denotes the quality of the end user as a function of the configuration parameters:

$$max \sum_j utility_{c_j}(config\,params)$$

This utility function can be provided by the application developer. In this paper, we use the load generated by all methods of the component as utility measure, assuming that more work done by the component results in a better quality or $\forall c_j$:

$$utility_{c_j}(config\,params) = \sum_s \sum_m \sum_i Load_{m_{sc_ic_j}}$$

However, also another utility function could be used, for example one could define an utility function for minimizing the energy usage, when the devices energy characteristics are known (i.e. energy usage per CPU load, energy usage per byte received/sent, etc.).

4.5   Optimization Algorithm

To find the optimal configuration and deployment, the goal is to find an assignment of each component to a device, and a value for each configuration parameter that optimizes the utility function, while adhering to all imposed constraints. In the situation of d devices, c components, p parameters and v_p possible values for parameter p, the number of possible solutions is $d^c \times \prod_p v_p$. Therefore, a brute force search for the optimum is inappropriate for use at runtime due to the long calculation time. To find a valid (although possibly suboptimal) solution in acceptable time, we use the heuristic explained in pseudocode in algorithm 1.

The algorithm is inspired by the KL graph partitioning algorithm [8], and consists of two loops. The outer loop continues until no better solution is found. The inner loop calculates a number of possible "moves" in solution space. A possible move is an increase or decrease of a configuration parameter value, or a migration of a component to another device. For all possible moves, an objective function is evaluated, and the gain is calculated as the difference with the objective of the current best solution. Subsequently, the move with the highest gain is performed and a new solution is found. The performed move is kept in an *ExploredMoves* list, that ensures that this move is not repeated later on in the loop.

Algorithm 1. Configuration and deployment decision algorithm

$CurrentSolution \leftarrow StartSolution$
$BestSolution \leftarrow StartSolution$
repeat
    $ExploredMoves \leftarrow InitialMoves$
    repeat
        Calculate possible moves K such that $\forall k \in K : k \notin ExploredMoves$
        Calculate objective gain $g, \forall k \in K$
        Perform move k_{best} with maximum gain g to get $NewSolution$
        $CurrentSolution \leftarrow NewSolution$
        Add k_{best} to $ExploredMoves$
        if $objective(BestSolution) < objective(CurrentSolution)$ **then**
            $BestSolution \leftarrow CurrentSolution$
        end if
    until no more moves possible
until no better solution found
return $BestSolution$

The objective function to calculate the gain is the following:

$$objective = W_1(\sum_j utility_{c_j}(config\,params)) + W_2(\frac{bandwidth - BW}{BW})$$

$$+W_3(\sum_d \frac{load_{sd} - CPU\,speed_d}{CPU\,speed_d}) + \sum_{constrainted\,m} W_4(\frac{T_{m_{sc_ic_j}} - threshold_m}{threshold_m})$$

where the functions $W_i(x)$ are defined as:

$$W_i(x) = \begin{cases} w_i \times x & \text{if } x < 0 \\ 0 & \text{otherwise} \end{cases}$$

Thus, the objective function maximizes the utility, but adds in penalty factors weighted by w_i when the constraints are not met.

Note that also moves with a negative gain are performed when no better moves are found. This enables the heuristic to escape from local maxima. At the start of the inner loop, the *ExploredMoves* list is also initialized with all moves that lead to the current solution (*InitialMoves*), in order to prevent the algorithm to get stuck in the current solution when a local optimum is found.

5   Experimental Results

5.1   AR Use Case

As a use case, we present an augmented reality application featuring markerless tracking as described by Klein et al. [9], combined with an object recognition algorithm presented in [11]. The application is shown in Figure 5. In the middle a greyscale video frame is shown with the tracked feature points, from which the camera position is estimated. The left part shows the resulting overlay with a 3D object, and a white border around the recognized book. On the right two mobile devices running the application are shown, forming a cloudlet with a laptop connected via WiFi.

Fig. 5. The augmented reality application tracks feature points in the video frames (middle) to enable the overlay of 3D objects (left). Multiple mobile devices can run the same application while offloading components to a laptop in the cloudlet (right).

A component based implementation of this application was realized, and the three sequences shown in Figure 6 were identified. The first sequence (Fig. 6(a)) shows the tracking and rendering thread: the Video component periodically fetches a camera frame from the hardware, which is processed by the Tracker component. The tracker estimates the current camera position from tracked feature points, which is used by the Renderer to render the correct overlay. From time to time the Tracker sends a video frame to the Mapper for map generation and refinement, which is shown in the second sequence (Fig. 6(b)) By matching 2D features in a sparse set of so called keyframes, the Mapper can estimate their 3D location in the scene and generate a 3D map of feature points. Finally, the keyframes are also analyzed for SIFT features, which are more complex to calculate, but can be used for object recognition by matching them against a database of SIFT features of known objects. This way objects can be recognized and localized in the map, which process is shown in third sequence (Fig. 6(c)).

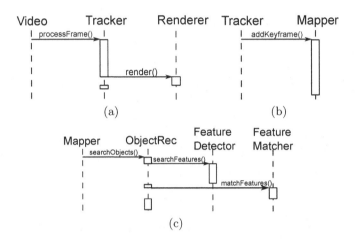

Fig. 6. The augmented reality application consists of three sequences. In (a) the tracking and rendering sequence is shown, which processes the video frames. The map refinement sequence is shown in (b), and (c) depicts the object recognition sequence.

5.2   Results

We evaluated the AR use case on two mobile devices, forming a cloudlet together with a laptop connected via WiFi. The laptop is equipped with an Intel Core 2 Duo CPU clocked at 2.26GHz. As mobile devices we use a HTC Desire, with a single core Qualcomm 1 GHz Scorpion CPU, and an LG Optimus 2x powered by a dual core Nvidia Tegra 2 CPU, also clocked at 1GHz.

Two crucial configuration parameters affecting the application quality were identified: the camera resolution and the number of tracked features. Both devices support two resolutions: 800x480 and 400x240. The number of features to track affects the processing time of a frame by the Tracker (which is crucial to achieve an acceptable frame rate). Typical values for this parameter are 1000, 950, ..., 200. The more features tracked, the more robust the tracking, but the longer the processing time.

The monitored execution times of the tracker and object recognition sequences for different configurations are shown in Figure 7. Figure 7(a) shows that the time to process a frame increases linearly with the number of feature points tracked. It also shows that the LG Optimus is 2 to 2.5 times faster than the HTC Desire. Figure 7(b) shows the processing times for object recognition, and again the Optimus is 2 to 3 times faster than the Desire, but the only acceptable processing times are achieved with the laptop, which is about 10 times faster than the Optimus. Therefore we set the relative $CPUspeed$ parameter as 0.4, 1 and 10 for the Desire, Optimus and laptop respectively.

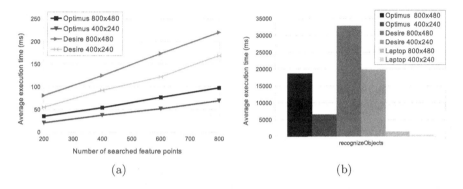

(a)   (b)

Fig. 7. Monitored execution times of the tracker (a) and object recognition (b) sequences, for different configurations

From the monitoring information we can set values for $Load_{m_{sc_ic_j}}$, $A_{m_{sc_ic_j}}$, $R_{m_{sc_ic_j}}$ for each method call. In this case each method call is executed only once in the sequence ($\#calls_{m_{sc_ic_j}} = 1$). Every five seconds one frame is added to the map and searched for objects ($\#calls_s = 0.2$). For the tracker sequence, the developer wants a minimal frame rate of 15 frames per second ($\#calls_s = 15$), meaning that a frame should be processed within 60ms, and objects should be recognized within 3 seconds. The devices are connected using a WiFi network of 10 Mbps and a latency of 1 ms.

Using this information, we can now calculate the optimal deployment and configuration. The Mapper, ObjectRecognizer, FeatureDetector and Feature-Matcher components are offloaded to the laptop. The Tracker components run on the mobile device, because of the limited bandwidth. Depending on the CPU capacity, the configuration is adapted to achieve the required frame rate. For the HTC Desire images are captured in 400x240 resolution and only 250 feature points are tracked, the Optimus captures frames in 800x480 resolution and tracks 500 points, as could be expected from Figure 7(a). The heuristic finds this result in 400ms, while a brute force implementation takes 16 minutes on the same hardware.

Figure 8 shows how the maximum achieved utility of the best solution varies as a function of the relative $CPUspeed$ of the device. The sudden increase around

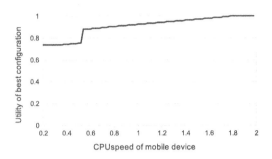

Fig. 8. The utility of the best possible configuration and deployment as a function of the devices $CPUspeed$

0.5 indicates the minimal $CPUspeed$ needed to process higher resolution frames. The small increments represent increases in the number of feature points tracked.

6 Conclusion

In this paper we present a cloudlet middleware architecture, that manages application on a component level. The middleware can both adapt the deployment and the configuration of the components at runtime, in order to optimize the offered quality of experience to the end user. We propose a decision algorithm that optimizes the application configuration and distribution, taking into account the network connectivity, the available resources and application constraints imposed by the application developer. Experimental results for a mobile augmented reality application show that the algorithm is indeed able to calculate the optimal solution, at a fraction of the time of a brute force implementation. Future work consists of further evaluating the quality of the heuristic, as well as integrating the algorithm in a full implementation of the cloudlet middleware.

Acknowledgment. Tim Verbelen is funded by Ph.D grant of the Fund for Scientific Research, Flanders (FWO-V).

References

1. Balan, R., Flinn, J., Satyanarayanan, M., Sinnamohideen, S., Yang, H.: The case for cyber foraging. In: EW 10: Proc. of the 10th Workshop on ACM SIGOPS European Workshop, pp. 87–92 (2002)
2. Chun, B., Ihm, S., Maniatis, P., Naik, M., Patti, A.: Clonecloud: elastic execution between mobile device and cloud. In: Proc. of the Sixth Conference on Computer Systems, EuroSys 2011, pp. 301–314 (2011)
3. Cuervo, E., Balasubramanian, A., Cho, D., Wolman, A., Saroiu, S., Chandra, R., Bahl, P.: Maui: making smartphones last longer with code offload. In: Proc. of the 8th International Conference on Mobile Systems, Applications, and Services, MobiSys 2010, pp. 49–62 (2010)

4. Gartner Group. 2012 press releases,
   http://www.gartner.com/it/page.jsp?id=2017015
5. Giurgiu, I., Riva, O., Juric, D., Krivulev, I., Alonso, G.: Calling the Cloud: Enabling Mobile Phones as Interfaces to Cloud Applications. In: Bacon, J.M., Cooper, B.F. (eds.) Middleware 2009. LNCS, vol. 5896, pp. 83–102. Springer, Heidelberg (2009)
6. Goyal, S., Carter, J.: A lightweight secure cyber foraging infrastructure for resource-constrained devices. In: WMCSA 2004: Proc. of the Sixth IEEE Workshop on Mobile Computing Systems and Applications, pp. 186–195 (2004)
7. Hassan, M.A., Chen, S.: An Investigation of Different Computing Sources for Mobile Application Outsourcing on the Road. In: Venkatasubramanian, N., Getov, V., Steglich, S. (eds.) Mobilware 2011. LNICST, vol. 93, pp. 153–166. Springer, Heidelberg (2012)
8. Kernighan, B.W., Lin, S.: An efficient heuristic procedure for partitioning graphs. Bell System Technical Journal 49(2), 291–307 (1970)
9. Klein, G., Murray, D.: Parallel tracking and mapping for small ar workspaces. In: Proc. of the 6th IEEE and ACM International Symposium on Mixed and Augmented Reality, ISMAR 2007, pp. 1–10 (2007)
10. Kristensen, M.D.: Scavenger: Transparent development of efficient cyber foraging applications. In: 2010 IEEE International Conference on Pervasive Computing and Communications (PerCom), pp. 217–226 (2010)
11. Lowe, D.G.: Distinctive image features from scale-invariant keypoints. Int. J. Comput. Vision 60(2), 91–110 (2004)
12. Ou, S., Yang, K., Zhang, J.: An effective offloading middleware for pervasive services on mobile devices. Pervasive and Mobile Computing 3(4), 362–385 (2007)
13. Satyanarayanan, M., Bahl, P., Caceres, R., Davies, N.: The case for vm-based cloudlets in mobile computing. IEEE Pervasive Computing 8(4), 14–23 (2009)
14. Su, Y., Flinn, J.: Slingshot: deploying stateful services in wireless hotspots. In: MobiSys 2005: Proc. of the 3rd International Conference on Mobile Systems, Applications, and Services, pp. 79–92 (2005)
15. Verbelen, T., Hens, R., Stevens, T., De Turck, F., Dhoedt, B.: Adaptive Online Deployment for Resource Constrained Mobile Smart Clients. In: Cai, Y., Magedanz, T., Li, M., Xia, J., Giannelli, C. (eds.) Mobilware 2010. LNICST, vol. 48, pp. 115–128. Springer, Heidelberg (2010)
16. Verbelen, T., Simoens, P., De Turck, F., Dhoedt, B.: Cloudlets: Bringing the cloud to the mobile user. In: Proc. of the 3rd ACM Workshop on Mobile Cloud Computing & Services, MCS 2012 (2012)
17. Zhang, X., Jeong, S., Kunjithapatham, A., Gibbs, S.: Towards an Elastic Application Model for Augmenting Computing Capabilities of Mobile Platforms. In: Cai, Y., Magedanz, T., Li, M., Xia, J., Giannelli, C. (eds.) Mobilware 2010. LNICST, vol. 48, pp. 161–174. Springer, Heidelberg (2010)

Determining Trustworthiness and Quality of Mobile Applications

Ilung Pranata, Rukshan Athauda, and Geoff Skinner

School of Design, Communication and IT
University of Newcastle, Australia
University Drive, Callaghan, NSW 2300, Australia
{Ilung.Pranata,Rukshan.Athauda,Geoff.Skinner}@newcastle.edu.au

Abstract. The growth of "smart" mobile devices, such as smartphones and tablets, has been exponential over the past few years. Such growth was mainly attributed to the development of mobile applications. To date, mobile applications have been increasingly used to improve our productivity and also to provide the entertainment contents. However, with a huge number of mobile applications that appear in the application stores; in particular those that provide similar functionalities, users are often confused with the selection of trustworthy and high quality mobile applications. At the current state, there is a limited research embarked to provide solutions for measuring the trustworthiness of mobile applications prior to download. Thus, the aims of this paper are to review the current research in this area and to discuss several issues in measuring the trustworthiness of mobile applications. In addition, this paper also proposes MobilTrust, a similarity trust measurement method to solve the identified issues.

Keywords: trust, reputation, mobile application.

1   Introduction

The proliferation of mobile computing technology has gained a significant momentum since its first introduction in the 70s. This can be seen from its growth rate that has rocketed over the years. According to the International Telecommunication Union (ITU), the subscribers of mobile devices have surpassed 5.3 billion in 2010 [1] while the total world population in the same year was just about 6.8 billion [2]. Such figures show that in 2010 alone, the percentage of mobile device subscribers is accounted for more than 75% of the world population. In the past few years, "smart" mobile devices such as smartphones and tablets have dominated the growth of mobile devices. An independent research firm IDC [3] published a study that shows the growth of "smart" mobile devices will reach 659.8 million in 2012, up to 33% from the previous year. Furthermore, IDC also forecasted that such growth will remain double digit in the years to come. This is mainly due to the strong user demand and also the production shift from the traditional mobile devices to the new era of "smart"

C. Borcea et al. (Eds.): MobilWare 2012, LNICST 65, pp. 192–206, 2013.

mobile devices. Therefore, it is evident that "smart" mobile devices such as smartphones and tablets have and will continue to become part of our everyday life.

The growth of "smart" mobile devices over the past few years has been predominantly caused by the exponential growth of mobile applications (termed as Mobile Apps). Such cause is mainly due to several benefits that Mobile Apps offer to improve their users' quality of life, such as functionalities, productivity improvements, entertainments, etc. For many years, the development of Mobile Apps was centered and managed by the device manufacturers, network operators and content providers. However, the introduction of application stores (i.e. Apple apps store [4] and Android Google Play [5]) has opened up application businesses to the hand of freelance developers and start-up companies. Since then, the number of mobile applications has increased exponentially. For example, Apple application store that started with only 500 apps in 2007 has reached 350k apps by March 2011. Similarly, Android Google Play reached 250k apps in the same time period [6].

Although mobile devices and its applications provide great benefits, it also produces significant threats for both individuals and organizations. Threats on the confidentiality of critical information and data privacy are just a few. Thus, in order to reduce such threats, there is a need for the users to trust Mobile Apps prior to downloading and consuming them. However, with a huge number of Mobile Apps appears in the application stores, many individuals and organizations are unsure on how to determine their trustworthiness. Nevertheless, determining the trustworthiness and quality of a mobile application is crucial. Thus, in this paper, we put our focus on discussing several issues pertaining to Mobile Apps trust measurement, and we also review several existing works in trust management. Additionally, we propose MobilTrust, a similarity method for determining the trustworthiness value of Mobile Apps.

The remainder of this paper is organized as follow: section 2 provides several reasons as to why initial trust of mobile applications is important to be determined, section 3 reviews several existing works in online trust, section 4 provides several issues in determining the initial trust of mobile applications, section 5 details our solution (termed as MobilTrust) to solve the identified trust issues, section 6 presents the implementation strategy for MobilTrust, section 7 provides the experimental simulations of MobilTrust, and section 8 provides the conclusion of this paper.

2   Why Initial Trust in Mobile Applications

Trust in electronic forefront, according to Grandison et al. [7], is defined as the competency belief that an agent would act reliably, dependably and securely within a given context. Further, authors in [7, 8] stress the importance of trust for the success implementation of any online environment. That is, trust significantly affects the decision of an entity to transact with other entity. The authors argue that both consumers and providers in an electronic market must trust each other before decisions to consume or to provide the services are made. If trust is not established between them, entities will not fully share their resources and fraudulent transactions may occur regularly. Such situation would disadvantage the honest consumers and providers, and it further refrain them from taking the advantage of the online environment.

Similar to the online environment, trust also plays a pivotal role in the mobile applications environment. With hundreds of thousands Mobile Apps that appear in the application stores, customers are always faced to make a decision whether to download and/or to consume the Mobile Apps. Such decision is even harder to make when there are several Mobile Apps that have similar functionalities appear in the application stores as customers need to decide the most trustworthy mobile application. From customers' point of view, they always prefer to download and consume a Mobile App that is functional, reliable and also with a good quality. However, selecting such functional, reliable and high quality Mobile App is challenging. This can be seen from several customers' comments that are found in the application stores in which customers downloaded the bad quality Mobile Apps, and they are frustrated with such buggy and low performance Mobile Apps. Therefore, there is a critical need to build the initial trust of Mobile Apps prior to downloading and consuming them.

From the security and privacy view point, the emergence of Mobile Apps further produces a number of threats to the confidentiality of information and data. A number of incidents occurred where Mobile Apps mined and harvested customer's confidential data, such as address books, photos, etc. [9, 10]. Such incidents clearly show the violation towards customer privacy and further disadvantage the customers. However, sadly to say, research in [11, 12] shows that more than half of popular Mobile Apps in Android and IOS under the study are transmitting customer data to the external servers. Besides the individual privacy concern, a growing number of organisations and businesses are also critical on the use of mobile devices by their employees [13]. They are extremely concerned about the capability of Mobile Apps to access and harvest the critical and confidential business documents (e.g. through business emails in the mobile devices). To address this concern, some businesses and organisations have prevented employees for using their devices for business related activites while most of them have implemented security measure and BYOD (Bring Your Own Devices) policies.

While implementing security measures and policies may reduce the risk of confidential business documents being released to the public, such measures and policies must also be supplemented and strengthened through the use of trust measurement. Most security practitioners would say that the best way to reduce the risk of documents leakage in Mobile Apps is by not installing the applications in the first place. However, such approach may not be favorable for the employees and businesses, particularly when Mobile Apps improve employee's productivity and bring benefits for businesses. Therefore, the efforts to safeguard the critical business information are left with two methods: (i.) educating employees for selecting the valid Mobile Apps, and (ii.) providing means to measure the trustworthiness of Mobile Apps prior to downloading and consuming them. Measuring trust of Mobile Apps is crucial as it provides the first and additional layer to security and privacy protection. This is also supported by authors in [14, 15] who argue that trust supplements security such that it improves the security protection of information and resources.

3   Related Work

At the current state, to the best of authors' knowledge, there is none research embarked in measuring the trustworthiness and quality of Mobile Apps. There are, however, several research that focus at protecting the security and privacy of user information from Mobile Apps, such as TaintDroid [11], PrimAndroid [17], etc. Although such research is important to reduce privacy violation and data leakage, the protection that they provide is functioning only after the user has downloaded or consumed the Mobile Apps, not prior to downloading or consuming them. This is where trust, as discussed in previous section, provides an extra layer and also serves as the first layer of protection.

Several prominent application stores, such as Apple application store and Android Google Play use a rating system to measure the trustworthiness and quality of the listed Mobile Apps. The recommender (or rater) is someone that has downloaded and consumed a Mobile App, and therefore he/she could provide the rating (in scale of 1 to 5 stars) and comment for others. The total rating of a Mobile App is the average of all raters' comments. Other users, particularly those who have not downloaded the Mobile App, tend to view the rating before making a decision as to whether to download the Mobile App. While the rating system is popular in use by several application stores, Authors in [18] show that such traditional rating system is prone to several misuses and unfair computation. Additionally, such rating system is also prone to several threat strategies as they do not measure the honesty of raters in providing their reviews. Moreover, our review on the jailbreak community (i.e. iPhone users that do not want to use the restrictive Apple Application Store but instead, they look for alternative markets, such as Cydia Market [19]) shows that there is no rating mechanism in presence to measure the trustworthiness of Mobile Apps.

Due to the limited research focuses at measuring the trustworthiness of Mobile Apps, we extend the literature review to the current internet environments, such as peer-to-peer, e-commerce and mobile agent. Literature review classifies trust mechanisms into two main categories: centralized mechanism and decentralized mechanism. The centralized mechanism relies on single point of collection and computation of trust value. PathTrust [20], peer-to-peer multi-dimensional trust model [21], DEco Arch [22], and the e-commerce trust models such as Certificate Authority (CA) and Credential Provider (CP) belong to this category. On the other hand, the decentralized approach allows each entity to request feedback values from other entities in the environment. A consumer entity aggregates all feedback values and further uses these values to derive the total trust value of its provider entity. Some decentralized approaches have been proposed in internet environment such as TrustMe [23], PeerTrust [24], P2PRep [25], and EigenTrust [26]. One major issue with TrustMe, PeerTrust and P2PRep is they broadcast trust request to all peers in the environment for obtaining reputation feedbacks. Thus, it slows down the performance of the entire network.

EigenTrust incorporates both local trust (belief) and global trust (reputation) in its trustworthiness calculations. It uses a normalized principal eigenvector for computing trust. However, EigenTrust suffers major drawback as it assumes that the honesty of the peers in providing the recommendations are based on the trustworthiness value of these peers in providing the services. Subjective Logic/TNA-SL [27] is another distributed trust mechanism that encompasses 3 degrees (belief, disbelief, and uncertainty) to derive the trustworthiness value of an entity. Its trust model focuses on the operators that represent logic for managing the feedbacks from referrals. REGRET [28] is a reputation system which analyzes the individual, social and ontological dimensions of entities. Several trust models have been proposed in multi-agents system environment, such as Travos [29] and BRS [30]. BRS measures trustworthiness of a provider using bayesian approach. Travos measures the trustworthiness of a provider by probabilistic and beta distribution approach that observe others' opinions and adjust these opinions with buyer's opinions.

4   Issues in Determining the Initial Trust of Mobile Applications

Trust in an electronic network can be divided into two types: direct (personal) trust and third party trust [31]. Direct (personal) trust is a situation where a trusting relationship is nurtured by two entities. This type of trust is formed after these entities have performed transactions with each other. For example, a user inherently trusts a Mobile App after he/she has consumed this Mobile App. On the contrary, third-party trust is a trust relationship of an entity that is formed from the third party recommendations. This means no previous transaction ever occurred between the two interacting entities, i.e. user trusts a Mobile App because this Mobile App is trusted and recommended by other users. We further termed direct trust as *belief* while third-party trust as *reputation* for the rest of this paper.

Belief can be straightforwardly determined due the availability of one's own past experience. However, trust value that is derived from the reputations, which is critical for measuring the trustworthiness of mobile applications, is often harder to compute. This is due to many factors as follows:

1. *Difficulty in finding other users that have consumed the Mobile Apps*: As trust through reputations is heavily relied on third-party (termed as raters) recommendations, there is a need for a user to identify other users (raters) that have downloaded and consumed the Mobile Apps for the purpose of requesting the recommendations. However, finding raters is a challenging task as raters are mostly unknown to the users.

2. *Relativeness perception of different users on the satisfaction levels of Mobile Apps*: The perception of each user on the satisfaction (i.e. quality, security, privacy level, etc.) of a Mobile App varies. For example, a user may rate a Mobile App as good although it has fair performance and it collects user's information. However, other users may rate the same Mobile App as bad.

3. *Dishonest raters in providing rating feedbacks*: It is highly possible that raters are malicious or dishonest in providing rating feedbacks. For example, the seller or developer of a Mobile App may get his friends and families to

give good rating to his application although it has low quality and violates privacy. In this case, the legitimate users may be tricked to believe that such application is good and therefore, they download and consume it.

4. *Several threat strategies subverting rating system*: Literature has presented a number of threat strategies that are used to subvert trust system [24, 26]. One of the most severe threat strategies is providers (i.e. sellers and developers of Mobile Apps) engage in a collaborative agreement to provide good ratings to each other Mobile Apps while give other Mobile Apps bad ratings.

5. *Incentives to rate*: Another challenge in building a successful reputation trust system is in providing the incentives for users to give their rating feedbacks.

Several prominent application stores such as Apple Apps store and Android Google Play suffer from the above issues, in particular issue no. 2-5. From the issues discussed above, it is evident that, in the absence of user own belief, the initial trustworthiness value of a Mobile App that is solely relied on the perceived reputations of others is harder to determine. Nevertheless, such initial trustworthiness is critical to be measured as consumers always tend to select the Mobile Apps that have good level of quality, privacy and security. Further, as discussed in previous section, trust provides the first and extra layer of protection. Thus, in the next section, we attempt to solve the identified issues by proposing our trust solution.

5   The Proposed Trust Model

Considering all issues that were discussed in the previous section, in this section, we present our proposed trust model for measuring the trustworthiness of Mobile Apps. We termed our proposed trust model as **MobilTrust**, a personalized binary trust model with a centralized approach. This personalized trust model takes into account the similarity measurement between the reported reputation values and the perception of the buyer. A thorough discussion on the similarity measurement and trust architecture will be provided later in this section.

For the rest of this paper, we termed the following:

- Mobile App is the mobile application that is available for download and/or consumption from the application stores.
- Buyer is someone that considers whether to download and/or to consume a Mobile App. Buyer will attempt to measure the trustworthiness of a Mobile App prior to download and consumption.
- Rater(s) is other user(s) that provides rating feedback(s) about a Mobile App. Raters are usually the previous buyers and consumers of a Mobile App.
- Rating feedback(s) is the reputation/trustworthiness value(s) of a particular Mobile App that is provided by the rater(s) and buyer. the rating feedback is in a scale of 0 (not trustworthy/not satisfied) – 1 (very trustworthy/very satisfied)

5.1   Classification of the Raters

In MobilTrust, we classify raters into two categories based on buyer's previous interactions with the raters. These categories are further defined as follow:

- *Known Raters*

  When computing the trustworthiness of a Mobile App, a buyer classifies a rater as a known rater under two conditions: (i.) if buyer has previously obtained and used rater's rating feedbacks on other Mobile Apps and (ii.) if buyer has provided his rating feedback on other Mobile Apps which he/she obtained the rater's rating feedbacks from. For example, a buyer previously consumed and provided his rating to a Mobile App x, in which prior to consuming x, he/she obtained the rating feedbacks from rater A, B. When the same buyer considers the trustworthiness of another Mobile App y and he/she found that rater A and B have provided their rating feedbacks to y, rater A and B will be considered as the known raters due to their feedbacks on Mobile App x.

  As buyer has previously obtained the rating feedbacks from the known raters, buyer would be able to derive the similarity measure of the known raters. The similarity measurement will be discussed in the next section.

- *Unknown Raters*

  A rater is classified as unknown rater if the buyer has not obtained any previous rating feedback from this rater. Therefore, the buyer is not able to measure the similarity with this rater.

The classification of the raters plays a pivotal role in measuring the trustworthiness of a Mobile App in our proposed trust model. Such classification allows more precise trustworthiness measurement as it takes into account the differentiation between the raters with whom buyer has the experience and the new raters with whom buyer has no experience at all.

5.2   Introducing Similarity Measurement on the Rating Feedbacks

In order to measure the honesty and the perception similarity of each rater's rating feedback, we introduce the measurement of *similarity*. Fundamentally, similarity is the combination between honesty and perception of the rater's rating feedback, as depicted in (1). Honesty is about measuring the credibility of rater's rating feedback in telling truth opinion, while perception is about measuring the relativeness of opinions between rater's rating feedback and buyer's perception. Both honesty and perception of rater's rating feedback, or known as similarity value, are measured from previous rater's feedbacks on other Mobil Apps. Similarity value is important to be measured as it is possible that a rater acts malicious by providing dishonest feedbacks about the trustworthiness of a mobile application. It is important to note that various raters may have different similarity values that reflect their honesty and relativeness perception in providing the rating feedback.

$$SIMILIARITY = HONESTY + PERCEPTION \qquad (1)$$

How does the similarity value of raters' rating feedbacks is assigned or measured? MobilTrust assigns the similarity value to each rater after buyer downloads and consumes a Mobile App. This is done by reviewing each rater's rating feedback with the validity of transaction and perception rating that is experienced by the buyer. Essentially, after buyer downloads and consumes a Mobile App, he/she will give his rating feedback about the trustworthiness of this Mobile App. MobilTrust then measures the compatibility between each rater's rating feedback and buyer's rating feedback. We further introduce the *SimilarityRange* to assign the similarity value for each rater's rating feedback. Any rater's rating feedback that is between the *SimilarityRange* is considered as compatible with buyer's rating feedback while the rater's rating feedback that is not between the *SimilarityRange* is considered as not compatible. MobilTrust assigns 1 (similar) as the similarity value for those rater's rating feedbacks that are within the *SimilarityRange*, and it assigns 0 (dissimilar) as the similarity value for those rater's rating feedbacks that are outside of *SimilarityRange*. Each similarity value will be added to the *TotalSimilarity* field in the central database and the number of past feedback (*TotalPastFeedback* field) will be increased. Algorithm 2 in sub-section 5.4 further details this process and section 6 provides detail on the implementation.

From all similarity values that a buyer assigned to each rater in the past, MobilTrust derives the average similarity value of each rater that will be used for the initial trust computation of new Mobile App. We derive the average similarity value by dividing the *TotalSimilarity* field and *TotalPastFeedback* field of each rater that are obtained from the database as shown in (2).

$$Sim(i) = \frac{TotalSimilarity(i)}{TotalPastFeedback(i)} \qquad (2)$$

Let i denote the rater who provides the rating feedback on a new Mobile App, $Sim(i)$ denote the average similarity value of rater i. *TotalSimilarity(i)* denote the total similarity value of past rating feedbacks given by rater i on other Mobile Apps. *TotalPastFeedback(i)* denote total number of past rating feedbacks given by rater i.

Note that, the average similarity value can only be computed for the known raters as buyer has previously obtained their rating feedbacks from other Mobile Apps. For the unknown raters, due to non-availability of previous rating feedbacks, MobilTrust assigns 0.5 (neither similar nor dissimilar) as their average similarity values.

5.3   Computing Mobile Apps Trustworthiness

Once the average similarity value of each rater is computed, the trustworthiness of a Mobile App from buyer's perspective will be derived. MobilTrust computes the trustworthiness of a Mobile App based on (3).

$$Trust(x) = \sum_{1}^{i} \left(\frac{Sim(i)}{\sum_{1}^{i} Sim(i)} * RF(i) \right) \qquad (3)$$

Let *Trust(x)* is the trustworthiness value of a Mobile App *x* that is computed from buyer's perspective. *Sim(i)* is the average similarity value of rater *i*. *RF(i)* is the rating feedback that is given by rater *i* on Mobile App *x*.

In order to increase the accuracy of trustworthiness computation, we utilize the exogenous approach [32] in MobilTrust. That is, the rating feedbacks which average similarity value does not meet a particular threshold (*SimilarityThreshold*) will not be counted in the trustworthiness computation. We further set the *SimilarityThreshold* value to 0.5 (neither similar nor dissimilar) such that the rating feedback which average similarity value is below such threshold is discarded. Algorithm 1 further shows the procedures in computing the trustworthiness of a Mobile App.

Algorithm 1. Computing Trustworthiness of a Mobile App

Input:
R = a set of all raters that provided rating feedbacks.
Sim = a set of average similarity values of the raters.
Temp = temporary variable array to hold all raters that will be included in trust computation.
TotalAvgSim = total average similarity values that are included in computation.
Output: *Trust(x)*.
Algorithm:
```
TotalAvgSim = Null;
for i = 1 to Length(R) do
   Retrieve Sim(i) from database;
   if Sim(i) ≥ SimilarityThreshold  then
        Temp ← i;
        TotalAvgSim += Sim(i);
   end if
end for
if Length(Temp) > 0 then
   for j=1 to Length(Temp) do
        Retrieve Sim(j) and RF(j) from database;
        Compute (3) using Sim(j), RF(j) and TotalAvgSim;
   end for
end if
```

The computed trustworthiness value of a Mobile App (*Trust(x)*) ranges from 0 (not trustworthy) to 1 (very trustworthy). The range of MobilTrust trustworthiness value can be easily adapted to the 5-star rating that is commonly used in the application stores. For example, using the step of 0.2, the results could be: 0 trust value means no star, 0.2 trust value means 1 star, 0.4 trust value means 2 stars, and so on.

5.4   The Learning Algorithm for Assigning Similarity Value

Once a buyer provides his rating feedback on a Mobile App, MobilTrust will automatically assign the similarity value to the raters. As discussed in previous sub-section 5.2, MobilTrust assigns the similarity value to the raters by evaluating whether their rating feedbacks are within the *SimilarityRange* of buyer's rating feedback. It assigns either 0 (similar) or 1 (dissimilar) based on the inclusivity.

Algorithm 2. Learning Algorithm for Assigning Similarity Value

Input:
R = a set of all raters that provided rating feedbacks.
RF = the rating feedback obtained from R.
$RF(buyer)$ = the rating feedback obtained from the buyer.
$TotalSim$ = a set of total similarity value of R.
$TotalPastFeedback$ = a set of total number of R past feedbacks.
Algorithm:
Retrieve $RF(buyer)$ from database;
for i = 1 to Length(R) **do**
  Retrieve RF_i from the database;
  if RF_i ≤ ($RF(buyer)$ + $SimilarityRange$) **and** RF_i ≥ ($RF(buyer)$ –
  $SimilarityRange$) **then**
    $TotalSim_i$ += 1;
    $TotalPastFeedback_i$ += 1;
  else
    $TotalSim_i$ += 0;
    $TotalPastFeedback_i$ += 1;
  end if
end for

Note that both *TotalSim* and *TotalPastFeedback* from Algorithm 2 are subjective for each buyer and they are stored in the central database (will be detailed in next section).

This learning algorithm is crucial for determining the similarity value of each rater based on buyer's perspective. Further, this learning algorithm also serves as incentives for buyers to keep providing their rating feedbacks on the Mobile Apps that they have downloaded and consumed. Buyers that do not provide the rating feedbacks will be disadvantaged as they are not able to derive the similarity value of the raters for the subsequent Mobile Apps download.

6   Implementation Strategies

As discussed briefly in the section 5, we propose the use of centralized mechanism in MobilTrust for both trust computation and rating databases. The centralized approach is selected due to its simplicity and also its appropriateness to the current mobile applications architecture, in which mobile applications are hosted and distributed by the central application stores. The centralized trust architecture is composed of two main components: the rating database and the centralized trust engine, as depicted in figure 1a. The rating database stores the rating feedbacks for all listed Mobile Apps in the application stores as well as the similarity values of all raters and buyers. Raters (or buyers after they downloaded the Mobile Apps) provide their rating feedbacks to the rating database. The centralized trust engine consists of (i.) computation engine for computing the trustworthiness value of a Mobile App (sub-section 5.3) and (ii.) similarity engine for assigning the similarity value (sub-section 5.4).

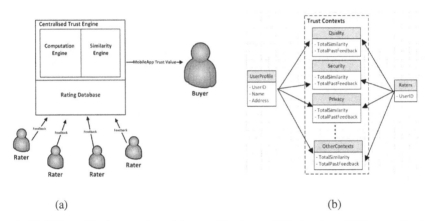

(a)   (b)

Fig. 1. MobilTrust Implementation: (a) centralized trust infrastructure (b) buyer-rater trust context relationships

In order to identify each user in MobilTrust, we leverage the use of user ID which has been used in several application stores, such as Apple ID [33] and Google Account [34]. In MobilTrust, each user is given a unique user ID (in UserProfile database table) for downloading and/or rating Mobile Apps. Such user ID becomes an identifier for each user in MobilTrust. Note that, in future implementation, this user ID can be in form of user accounts in the respective application stores.

The relationships of buyers and raters in the rating database are depicted in figure 1b. For facilitating the personalized trust computation, each buyer has a list of the raters with whom he/she has obtained the rating feedbacks from. For each rater that is associated with the buyer, buyer has the *TotalSimilarity* and *TotalPastFeedback* for computing the average similarity of rater based on a number of pre-defined trust contexts. Trust contexts (e.g. quality, security, privacy, etc.) allow more expressiveness in measuring the trustworthiness of a Mobile App.

7   Simulation Results

We performed two preliminary simulations in RM simulator [16] to measure the effectiveness of MobilTrust. In such simulations, we considered a typical Mobile Apps environment in which user can consume and produce Mobile Apps. Our simulation environment consisted of 100 users and run over 1000 downloads for each test cycle. There are 50 Mobile Apps simulated in the environment, and each Mobile App can be offered by more than one user. This is to simulate the real Mobile Apps environment in which several providers may offer similar mobile apps. For the purpose of collecting the statistics, we modified the *SimilarityRange* in algorithm 2 such that rater whose similarity rating (*RF*) is higher than 0.5 while buyer's similarity rating (RF_{buyer}) is positive was considered as similar (Thus, similarity rating of 1 will be given), and vice versa. In each simulation, we collected statistics from 5 test cycles and averaged the results. We were particularly concern on the valid downloads performed by the "good" users. The collected statistics are assessed in the following evaluation metric:

$$Metric: \frac{\#\ of\ valid\ Mobile\ Apps\ downloaded\ by\ "good"\ entities}{\#\ of\ transactons\ performed\ by\ "good"\ entities}$$

In the first simulation, we filled our simulation environment with a number of malicious providers (i.e. provide invalid Mobile Apps but always provide credible feedbacks). For each step of 15%, we ran the simulation and obtained the statistics as shown in figure 2a. The results show that MobilTrust has effectively reduced the number of invalid download performed by "good" users when compared with no trust model in the environment. This further demonstrates the success of MobilTrust algorithms to reduce the invalid downloads.

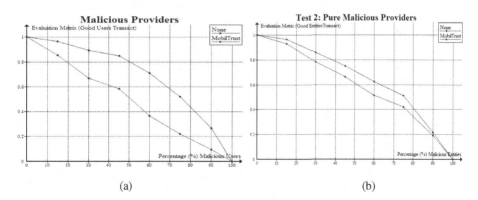

Fig. 2. MobilTrust Evaluation: (a) malicious users (b) purely malicious users

In the second simulation, we filled our simulation environment with purely malicious users (i.e. consistently provide invalid Mobile Apps and non-credible feedbacks). The purely malicious users give a significant threat to the Mobile Apps environment. The non-credible feedbacks that they provide may reduce the credibility of "good" Mobile Apps while improving the credibility of "bad" Mobile Apps. For each step of 15%, we ran the simulation and obtained the statistics as shown in figure 2b. The results show that MobilTrust has successfully increased the number of valid Mobil Apps download for the "good" users.

8   Conclusion

This paper has reviewed the current state of art in mobile applications trustworthiness measurement. Further, it shows the importance of trust as the first and extra layer of protection in mobile applications environment. Determining the initial trustworthiness of mobile applications is challenging due to several issues such as finding the raters, different perceptions, dishonest rating feedbacks, several threat strategies and also the unavailability of incentives. This paper further provides a unique trust model, termed as MobilTrust, for solving the identified trust measurement issues. An important feature of MobilTrust is the similarity value that measures the honesty of raters in providing feedbacks and the similarity perceptions between raters and buyer. The trustworthiness of a mobile application is computed based on the average similarity value of the raters and also the raters' rating feedbacks. Several trust formulas and algorithms have been introduced to measure the trustworthiness of mobile applications and also to learn and update the average similarity value of the raters. These trust formulas and algorithms also measure the credibility of each rater and are used to mitigate the treat strategies. In addition, the learning algorithm provides incentives for buyers to provide their rating feedbacks. This paper also introduces the centralized implementation strategy for MobilTrust. Future work will be focusing on the evaluation of trust formulas and algorithms in reducing the invalid transactions and also its effectiveness against other threat strategies.

References

1. International Telecommunication Union (ITU), ITU estimates two billion people online by end 2010, Access to mobile networks available to over 90% of world population 143 countries offer 3G services, Press Release Report (2010), viewed at
   `http://www.itu.int/net/pressoffice/press_releases/`
   `2010/39.aspx`
2. PRB, 2010 World Popilation Data Sheet (2010),
   `http://www.prb.org/publications/datasheets/2010/`
   `2010wpds.aspx`
3. IDC Research, Worldwide Smartphone 2012-2016 Forecast and Analysis, Research report (2012), `http://marketresearch.com`.
4. Apple, Apple Application Store (2012),
   `http://itunes.apple.com/us/genre/ios/id36?mt=8`
5. Google Play, Android Google Play (2012),
   `https://play.google.com/store?hl=en`

6. BusinessInsider, Number of Apps Available at Smartphones' Apps Stores (2011), viewed at
   `http://articles.businessinsider.com/2011-03-09/tech/30011803_1_app-store-google-s-android-market-twitter`
7. Grandison, T., Sloman, M.: A Survey of Trust in Internet Applications [IEEE Communications Surveys and Tutorials, Fourth Quarter] (2000), `http://www.comsoc.org/pubs/surveys/`
8. Josang, A., Ismail, R., Boyd, C.: A survey of trust and reputation systems for online service provisioning. Decision Support System 43, 618–644 (2007)
9. Osborne, C.: IOS Apps: Massive invasion of user privacy, ZDNet news (2012), `http://www.zdnet.com/blog/igeneration/ios-apps-massive-invasion-of-user-privacy/15138`
10. Lowenshon, J.: Congress probing iOS developers on user privacy, address books, CNet news (2012), `http://news.cnet.com/8301-27076_3-57402957-248/congress-probing-ios-developers-on-user-privacy-address-books/`
11. Enck, W., Gilbert, P., Chun, B.-G.: Taintdroid: An information-flow tracking system for realtime privacy monitoring on smartphones (2010)
12. Smith, E.: iPhone applications & privacy issues: An analysis of application transmission of iPhone unique device identifiers (UDIDs), `http://www.kompatscher.biz/phocadownload/iPhone-Applications-Privacy-Issues.pdf`
13. Ferro, G.: BYOD Policies vs. the Realities of Corporate IT, NetworkComputing.com, `http://www.networkcomputing.com/wireless/240000916`
14. CoreGrid, D.IA.03 Survey Material on Trust and Security, European Research Network on Foundations, Software Infrastructures and Applications for large scale distributed, GRID and Peer-to-Peer Technologies, Technical Paper (2004)
15. Rasmusson, L., Janssen, S.: Simulated Social Control for Secure Internet Commerce. In: Proceedings of the 1996 New Security Paradigms Workshop, Lake Arrowhead, CA, USA (1996)
16. University of Pennsylvania, TM/RM Simulator (March 2012), `http://rtg.cis.upenn.edu/qtm/p2psim.php3`
17. Benats, G., Bandara, A., Yu, Y., Colin, J., Nuseibeh, B.: PrimAndroid: Privacy Policy Modelling and Analysis for Android Applications. Presented at 2011 IEEE International Symposium on Policies for Distributed Systems and Networks, Pisa, Italy (2011)
18. Dellarocas, C.: Immunizing Online Reputation Reporting Systems against Unfair Ratings and Discriminatory Behavior. In: The Proceedings of Second ACM Conf. Electronic Commerce (2000)
19. Cydia Market, `http://cydia.saurik.com/`
20. Kerschbaum, F., Haller, J., Karabulut, Y., Robinson, P.: PathTrust: A Trust-Based Reputation Service for Virtual Organization Formation. In: Stølen, K., Winsborough, W.H., Martinelli, F., Massacci, F. (eds.) iTrust 2006. LNCS, vol. 3986, pp. 193–205. Springer, Heidelberg (2006)
21. Ion, M., Danzi, A., Koshutanski, H., Telesca, L.: A Peer-to-Peer Multidimensional Trust Model for Digital Ecosystems. Presented at the Second IEEE International Conference on Digital Ecosystems and Technologies (IEEE DEST 2008), Phitsanulok, Thailand (2008)
22. Schmidt, S., Steele, R., Dillon, T.: DEco Arch: Trust and Reputation Aware Service Brokering Architecture in Digital Ecosystems. Presented at the Inaugural IEEE International Conference on Digital Ecosystems and Technologies (IEEE DEST), Cairns, Australia (2007)

23. Singh, A., Liu, L.: TrustMe: Anonymous Management of Trust Relationships in Decentralized P2P Systems. Presented at the Third International Conference on Peer-to-Peer Computing, Sweden (2003)

24. Xiong, L., Liu, L.: Peertrust: Supporting reputation-based trust for peer-to-peer electronic communities. IEEE Transactions on Knowledge and Data Engineering 16, 843–857 (2004)

25. Damiani, E., Vimercati, S.: Managing and Sharing Servents' Reputations in P2P Systems. IEEE Transactions on Knowledge and Data Engineering 15, 840–854 (2003)

26. Kamvar, S., Schlosser, M., Garcia-Molina, H.: The EigenTrust Algorithm for Reputation Management in P2P Networks. Presented at the 12th ACM International Conference on World Wide Web, USA (2003)

27. Jøsang, A., Hayward, R., Pope, S.: Trust Network Analysis with Subjective Logic. In: Proceedings of the 29th Australasian Computer Science Conference (2006)

28. Sabater, J., Sierra, C.: REGRET: A reputation model for gregarious societies. In: Proceedings of the Fifth International Conference on Autonomous Agents, Montreal, Canada (2001)

29. Teacy, W.T.L., Patel, J., Jennings, N.R., Luck, M.: Travos: Trust and reputation in the context of inaccurate information sources. Journal of Autonomous Agents and Multi-Agent Systems 12 (2006)

30. Josang, A., Ismail, R.: The Beta Reputation System. In: Proceedings of the 15th Bled Electronic Commerce Conference (2002)

31. Entrust: The concept of trust in network security, Version 1.2 [White Paper] (2000, April 2011), http://www.entrust.com/resources/pdf/trust.pdf

32. Jøsang, A., Ismail, R., Boyd, C.: A survey of trust and reputation systems for online service provision. Decision Support Systems (2005) (to appear)

33. Apple, What's an Apple ID?, https://appleid.apple.com/cgi-bin/WebObjects/MyAppleId.woa/

34. Google, Google Accounts, http://www.google.com/intl/en/landing/accounts/index.html#utm_campaign=en&utm_medium=et&utm_source=gaia

Seamless Context Adaptation on a Service-Oriented Framework

Dana Popovici, Mikael Desertot, and Sylvain Lecomte

UVHC, LAMIH UMR 8201 CNRS,
University Lille North of France
59313 Valenciennes, France
`firstname.surname@univ-valenciennes.fr`

Abstract. This article describes an easy, efficient way to manage context-aware applications with the help of metadata. We rely on CATS, our proposition for an application framework embedded on mobile devices. It is designed to host applications conforming to the SOA principles for achieving a flexible and dynamic architecture. Our framework provides non-functional capabilities for context management and for the adaptations required at context changes. In this article we focus on the use of iPOJO handlers and the advantages they bring to the OSGi technology.

1 Introduction

Mobile devices such as smartphones and tablets are becoming more and more part of our daily lives. In the past years they have known a great success and also a great evolution. These devices are meant for personal and frequent use, with a multitude of interesting and helpful applications (notes, maps and navigation, weather, email, etc.). The mobile devices follow users on their trips, assisting them along the way. We wish to improve the functioning of the devices through context-awareness and flexible applications.

Users move from one place to another, causing their applications to run in different contexts. Moreover, some places can have specific applications, like shops, museums, car parks, etc. Our goal is to provide a simple way for users to benefit from these specific applications and in the same time have their own applications adapt to the context changes. For better understanding, let us take as an example the Vespa [3] application for information sharing between drivers. On one hand, it shares all kinds of information: accidents, emergency brakings, emergency vehicles passing by, etc. On the other hand, it is also concerned with parking places, a different type of information, as it can cause competition between the drivers. This is a good example for the importance of context: if only a few users are in the same vicinity, a free parking place can be announced to all cars; if a greater number of users are present, the free place should be reserved for a single driver to avoid competition (see [4]); if the user is next to an indoor car park, he should request a parking place from the server of the car park. Thus, a single application has multiple ways of functioning, depending on the context.

C. Borcea et al. (Eds.): MobilWare 2012, LNICST 65, pp. 207–220, 2013.
© Institute for Computer Sciences, Social Informatics and Telecommunications Engineering 2013

In our previous work [16,15], we have proposed an application framework called CATS, hosting transportation applications that accompany users on the move. CATS is the execution environment for service based applications, offering management capabilities on top, for context-awareness and adaptation. Thanks to this framework, applications can be designed by dividing their functionalities into modules. For a same functionality, we can provide multiple implementations, each suited for a different context situation. As such, Vespa has been adapted for the CATS framework, with multiple implementations for the parking service.

This article describes our approach for achieving context-awareness and dynamic adaptation through the use of iPOJO Handlers. It is an efficient and non intrusive solution that allows applications to be developed in a clean manner while keeping the framework light. We evaluate our proposition through a series of tests on several Android devices.

2   Related Work

There are two important issues related to our work: the context and the architectures that allow for flexible and adaptable applications. First of all, what is context and how should it be used? If we start from the rather general definition given by Dey and Abowd [6] we should include "everything" that could influence the behavior of the applications as context information. We can cite some surveys on modeling and processing context information, [10,17] who show the different strategies used in research. From our point of view, the context should be modeled and used once for all transportation applications, as they run on the same device, for the same user. We have described the context elements that affect applications in the transportation domain in our previous work [5].

Identifying what context is and how it influences our applications resolves only half of the problem. The second half concerns the reaction to changes. How do our applications modify their behavior? It seems clear that their architecture should be as modular as possible, providing an easy way of changing parts of an application when the context imposes it. In a related work, [14] proposes a Dynamic Software Product Line to create applications using the most suited components, taking context into consideration. They describe a context-aware framework using sensors [2]. In this solution, applications have predefined configurations that are chosen with respect to the execution context. Solutions for context adaptation are also available with Composite Capability/Preference Profiles (like [13]), but they relate rather to the adaptation of content and not that of the functionalities. Finally, works like [1] introduce middleware to consider context adaptation for applications. This framework in particular targets the assembly of distributed applications whereas we consider the assembly of standalone context-aware applications embedded on a mobile device.

We would like to go a step further, by allowing to download and install new services while the application is still running. This provides more flexibility and adaptability to the applications. To the best of our knowledge, there is no literature concerning the download and installation of application components (services) "on the fly" for mobile devices involved in transportation applications.

The service-based approach has also been employed by [12] in their work for an autonomic management system. Our work too nears the concepts of autonomic computing through the desire to provide a framework with self-management capabilities. The concept of autonomic computing has been stated for the first time almost 10 years ago, one of the first works to mention it being [11]. For now the vision is not fully attained, as indicated in [7].

3   Context and Context-Awareness

The context is one of the main concerns when building applications nowadays, especially for mobile users. From the developers point of view, it is important to define all context elements and situations that influence the one application he is writing. From our viewpoint, our framework CATS must be able to support all context elements for a multitude of applications. This is why we propose a simple generic structure to represent any Context Element (CE) (Table 1).

Table 1. Representation of a Context Element (CE)

CE	
Name	- *the unique name of the context element*
Type	- *the type of information it contains*
Value	- *the value of this element at a time being*
[Unit]	- *(optional) the unit of measurement*
[Category]	- *(optional) a category from a classification*

A Context Element is represented by a unique name. It could be of great help to have one or more ontologies describing the Context Elements, to avoid giving different names for the same element or the same name for different elements. There could be an ontology for the transportation domain, another for the CE related to the device, and so on. However, it is not the scope of this paper to discuss ontologies, we only retain that a unique name is required for each CE.

We have judged necessary three types of Context Elements: *boolean, discrete* and *continuous*. A "boolean" element will only have two possible values, true or false. This type of Context Element describes mostly a resource that is available or not, like the Wifi or the GPS signal. An unavailable resource represents an important context situation that probably needs an adaptation, so it should be represented in our framework. A "discrete" Context Element is related to a context situation represented through discrete values. For example, if we would like to represent the type of road for a driver, we could differentiate between "city", "highway", "car park" and others. At last, a "continuous" element is one that can be characterized through a numeric value, like the speed at which the user is moving. Two optional pieces of information can be added to the description of a Context Element. The Unit, representing the unit of measurement for elements of type "continuous". A Category can also be specified, based on some classification of the elements. For instance, some Context Elements are related to the *device/hardware*, like the GPS module or the Wifi module, while others are related to the *environment*, like the number of neighbors.

Context-awareness implies that applications react to the changes in their context. Because the user is on the move, the environment changes frequently, and so do many important elements like the communication networks, the number of neighbors, the type of road, etc. The context should be evaluated repeatedly during the functioning of the context-aware applications. We propose to use some lightweight modules called Context Monitors, to evaluate the state of the context. Each Monitor should handle a single Context Element and either have a configurable evaluation frequency or expose a method to force the evaluation. Context-awareness can be achieved thanks to the Monitors which detect changes when they occur (or sufficiently fast after) and notify the interested applications.

4   Application Composition

Applications are composed of multiple functionalities, which can be divided into independent modules. First, we can identify the functionalities that are common to most applications, like for example positioning. When possible, it is more interesting to have a single piece of code handling the localization, rather than having multiple applications implement similar code. Second, each part of an application providing a certain functionality can be implemented in multiple ways. For each computation we can choose the most appropriate way to do it.

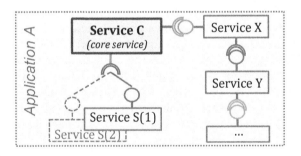

Fig. 1. Application example for the CATS Framework

In order to achieve the separation of functionalities, we chose to follow the principles of Service-Oriented Architecture (SOA). We use applications built out of services: a "core service" representing the business logic (the central part) of the application and several other services implementing different functionalities, which are used by the "core service", as represented in Fig. 1. An application is the assembly of multiple services. Like explained in [9], a service is an interface representing the contract between the service providers and clients. The service providers are objects accessed via direct method invocation. This way, we can have the same functionality with different implementations, each one adapted to a certain context situation. We call "equivalent services" the different implementations of the same interface, *Service S*(1) and *Service S*(2) in our example.

We say that *Service S* is a Context Dependent Service, as it depends on the context of execution. As such, if the user is in one context situation, *Application A* should use *Service S*(1), the first implementation of *S*. If the user is in another context situation, *A* should use *S*(2), the second implementation. To make this possible, each of the implementations must define its dependencies on Context Elements, with a representation similar to that given in Section 3. For each CE that *S*(1) or *S*(2) depends on, the services must provide the corresponding informations. There is a difference with respect to the representation of the CE, notably in what concerns the value of the Element. A Context Dependent Service must thus describe for which value of the CE it is supposed to work best. If it depends on a CE of the type "boolean", then the service depends on a resource and will work only if the resource is available. For example a positioning service might depend on the GPS signal and not work if it is not available. If the CE is of type "discrete", the service must specify the value for which it works. In the case of a "continuous" CE, the service can specify an interval of values for which it works. For example a service might have an implementation adapted for a low average speed, 0-50 km/h, and a second implementation for an average speed of over 50 km/h. With the help of the Context Monitors, the CATS framework detects when the values of the Context Elements change, and can thus bind the suitable implementation of each service dynamically.

5   CATS Framework and VESPA

The CATS Framework, introduced in our previous work [16], is the execution environment for multiple service based applications, as well as the management modules that allow for context-awareness. There are several advantages to the use of our framework. First, it allows to share services between applications. The positioning service is one of the best examples, as most transportation applications will use it. A second advantage is that the context is managed by the framework, allowing applications to be lighter and to concentrate on the functional parts. Moreover, a context change can concern more than one application, so when it is handled is to the benefit of several applications. For example, when the GPS signal becomes unavailable, the management modules will find an equivalent service as a replacement. Fig. 2 shows an overview of the CATS Framework with two applications that share the "Position" service. On the right side we represent the management modules: the Context manager, handling the context-related information; the Execution manager, dealing with the execution of the services; the Trader, handling the download of new services.

Vespa consists of a core and several other services, from which only a few are represented here. As explained in the introduction, on of the functionalities proposed by Vespa concerns the ad-hoc management of parking places. A first

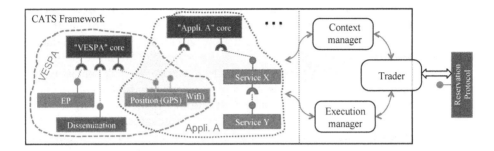

Fig. 2. VESPA and other applications on the CATS Framework

protocol consists in disseminating the information of a free place (using a special protocol that avoids flooding the network). If there are many interested neighbors, this solution can prove to be inefficient, as there would be a high number of cars trying to get the same place. The "Dissemination" service must be stopped and replaced with the "Reservation Protocol", in order to reserve the place for a single driver among the interested ones. Fig. 2 shows the "Dissemination" service being stopped, and the "Reservation Protocol" service being downloaded by the Trader to be installed and started on the CATS Framework. We note that the two services mentioned here are both implementations of the "Parking" service, and their alternative use is based on the number of neighbors.

6   Prototype with iPOJO

We have developed our prototype as an Android Activity which embeds the Felix Framework and iPOJO [1] [8]. The CATS Framework has been constructed on top of **Felix** 3.2.2, an OSGi implementation by Apache released in May 2011. It is a certified platform[2], conforming to the OSGi specification, Release 4 Version 4.2 from March 2010. We used the implementation of iPOJO version 1.8.0 from January 2011. The CATS Framework is an execution environment for multiple applications compatible with both Android and OSGi. The applications are built of modules, which are bound at the execution. Each application must have its own component handling the display (GUI), and may use the services available on the framework. The management modules are implemented as services running on the platform and oversee the non-functional capabilities of our framework. Besides the management modules that were already described in our previous work [16] (Context manager, Execution manager and Trader) we introduce in this paper a set of iPOJO Handlers for the CATS framework.

The Execution Manager oversees the execution of the services. It must know all the Context Dependent Services that are available on the CATS framework and can decide to start or stop services based on notifications from the Context

---

[1] http://felix.apache.org/site/apache-felix-ipojo.html
[2] http://www.osgi.org/Specifications/Certified

Manager on context changes. If there is no suitable version of a service, i.e. one that is adapted to the current context situation, the Execution Manager must call the Trader to search for a replacement.

The Context Manager can evaluate the state of the context on demand, but also on a continuous basis, when certain elements need to be monitored. It keeps track of all Context Elements, being informed by the Monitors when changes occur or requesting the Monitors to reevaluate the context. It then informs the Execution Manager of the changes.

The Handlers

There are several advantages to the iPOJO component model. One of them is the use of handlers to manage non-functional concerns like the binding of components by injecting the needed code inside the services. Moreover, iPOJO is extensible, it allows developers to create their own handlers for specific functionalities for their framework. Another advantage is the development of simple components as plain old Java objects. The component's metadata can all be set in an XML file, having thus a complete separation of the functional code (shown in Fig. 3(b)). Furthermore, it allows us to reuse code that has been written for other purposes. For example, we can adapt a piece of code measuring the state of a resource periodically, and use it as a Context Monitor. The modifications imply simply adding metadata for the iPOJO information and for the handler to be plugged. In the following we present shortly the handlers we use for CATS.

The Context Monitor Handler is used to link the Monitors to the Context Manager. It reads the information about the Context Element that is monitored: name, type, value field, [unit, category]. The handler intercepts all modifications of the value field and updates the Context Manager. This way, the Context Manager is updated with the most recent context state and can detect changes.

The Context Dependency Handler is plugged to the Context Dependent Services in order to register them with the Execution Manager. It relies on the description of the CE that each service implementation must provide, as seen in Section 4. The Execution Manager has knowledge about all implementations of a certain service and about the context conditions in which to use each of them.

The Statistic Handler is used for measurement purposes, as it detects the state changes of client components. It then registers the time when a component has been invalid because of a missing dependency, allowing us to measure the impact of switching between components at runtime.

In Fig. 3 we present an example with a set of components and their associated handlers. The component C is a client requiring as a provider the Context Dependent Service S. The two implementations of S, S1 and S2, have the Context Dependency Handler plugged, in order to inform the framework of the execution conditions that they need. Based on the values read by the Context Monitors, the Execution Manager will decide which of these services can execute. If none of them is suited with the current context, C will not be able to function, as its dependency will be unsolved. The Statistic Handler is plugged on C and registers

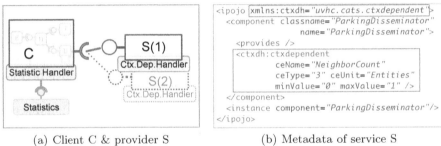

(a) Client C & provider S   (b) Metadata of service S

Fig. 3. Test configuration with a component C and a Context Dependent Service S

the unavailability periods, when C's dependency is not satisfied. Fig. 3(b) shows the metadata needed by Service S to declare the Context Dependency Handler. The service specifies which handler is plugged and the metadata related to the Context Element that it depends on (inside the red square). Other metadata includes the "<provides />" tag, showing that S is a provider, the name of the service ("ParkingDisseminator") and the creation of an instance.

7 Evaluations

We have evaluated the execution of our framework and the adaptation of applications at context changes with the configurations described above. We have used two types of phones and a tablet: Sony Ericsson Xperia ray - running on Android 2.3.4, Samsung Galaxy 551 - running on Android 2.3.6 and the HTC Flyer tablet - running on Android 3.2.1.

The goal of the evaluations is to asses the adaptation time when the context changes. For this reason, we consider the moment when the change has been detected by the Context Manager and wish to see how long it takes until the suited service is ready for use, as well as the impact this action has on the application. We considered the Vespa application, which uses a parking service to advertise free parking places to other vehicles and get information about free places from the other entities. The parking service is context dependent and has several ways of negotiating the parking places between vehicles, based on the number of neighbors. Here are the elements used in the evaluation:

- **Context Element** {*Name* = NeighborCount; *Type* = Continuous *(coded as the integer "3" in Fig. 3(b))*; [*Unit* = Entities; *Category* = Environment;]}. In this case, the value is an integer greater than or equal to 0, representing the number of neighboring devices.
- **Context Monitor for "NeighborCount"** is a service that evaluates the number of one-hop neighbors every 15 seconds. For testing purpose, the service has been modified to return the same series of numbers repeatedly, to force the same service exchanges.

- **Vespa**, an application that uses inter-vehicles communication to share information about the traffic. It requires a Parking Service.
- **Parking Service**, a Context Dependent Service with the following implementations, depending on the CE NeighborCount
    - ○ **DPS** *Dissemination Parking Service*: a vehicle liberating a parking place broadcasts the information to the surrounding vehicles. This version should be used if NeighborCount $\in \{0, 1\}$.
    - ○ **RPS** *Reservation Parking Service*: the vehicle liberating a place advertises it and reserves the place for one of the interested vehicles. This version of the Parking Service works when NeighborCount $= 2$.
    - ○ **DPSv and RPSv** *versions of the two previous services*: work similarly to the DPS or RPS services, for NeighborCount $\in \{3, 4, 5, 6, 7\}$.

We note that the context conditions for each Parking Service here have been chosen for experimentation purposes only. For the final implementations of DPS and RPS a careful study should be carried out considering the NeighborCount (number of neighbors) that represents the switching point. Up to a certain limit, the information of a free parking place can be disseminated without causing competition. After this limit, the place should be subjected to reservation.

The experimentations have been carried out with either two or six equivalent services present on the devices. The same set of tests have been executed for DPS and its versions, then for RPS and its versions, allowing us to compare the impact of a "heavier" service. The DPS versions have a size of around 5 kB and don't launch any threads, so they can be considered as "light" versions of the Parking Service. The RPS versions are around 15 kB and launch a thread, so we consider them as a "heavier" version of the Parking Service. The goal of our experimentations is to measure the reaction time from the detection of a context change until the application is adapted, i.e. the current Parking Service, which is now inappropriate with respect to the new context, is stopped and a new one is bound, complying to the new context conditions. All the services used for testing are registered in a given order in the Execution Manager and processed one at a time when started or stopped. As a consequence, it matters when the services are switched on and off: for short periods of time, we can either have two equivalent services working or none working. The Vespa application can thus stop working due to the missing dependency.

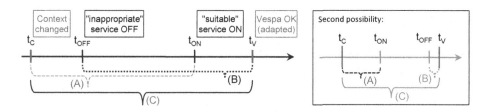

Fig. 4. Experimental measurements

Fig. 4 shows the events taking place during the execution of the Vespa application, when the context changes. We consider t_C, the moment when the context change is detected, t_{OFF} when the current service is switched off, t_{ON} when the most suitable service is switched on (and ready to use) and t_V, when the Vespa application is adapted by having the new service bound. Based on the order in which the actions take place, t_{OFF} and t_{ON} can be in any order. In the experiments, we have measured the different time periods: Time (A) - from the detection of the context change to when the suitable service is started and ready to use; Time (B) - the period in which Vespa has been unavailable because of the missing dependency; Time (C) - from the detection of the context change until Vespa is adapted and operational again. Depending on the order in which the services are handled, Vespa might not become unavailable, making it impossible to measure Time (B) and Time (C). This behavior is due to the iPOJO framework, which manages the bindings of services when there is more then one available. We can thus optimize the behavior of our framework by ensuring that the suitable service is switched on before switching off the other one. Nevertheless, our goal here was to measure the time from the detection of the change until the adaptation was achieved, represented by the Time (C), so no optimization has been done.

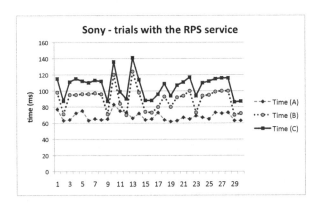

Fig. 5. Times (A), (B) and (C) when switching between versions of the RPS service

The first type of experimentation is intended to study the three times presented above over a set of 30 trials. Fig. 5 shows the times (A), (B) and (C) on the Sony phone in the case when the inappropriate service is stopped before switching the new one on, causing Vespa to stop functioning. We can notice that $t_V > t_{ON}$: the time that iPOJO requires from the detection of the new service until it is bound is always superior to 0. Therefore, we can say for sure that Time (C) is greater than the other two times, as it can be seen also in Fig. 5. For Time (A) and Time (B) there is no rule of which is greater than the other, but several of our simulations have shown Time (B) to be slightly greater than (A). We can notice from the figure that Time (C) follows the same path as

Time (B), which can be explained when looking at the significance of the two:
$Time(C) = t_V - t_C$; $Time(B) = t_V - t_{OFF}$; $Time(C) - Time(B) = t_{OFF} - t_C$
The fact that the difference between these two time spans is almost constant
implies that the time needed to switch off the inappropriate service varies very
little. The averages and the standard deviations of these measurements are presented in Table 2 and show that the complete adaptation of the application in
case of a context change takes about 106 ms.

Table 2. Average and standard deviation for Times A, B and C, with the RPS

	Time (A)	Time (B)	Time (C)
Average (ms)	68,16	90	106,26
Standard deviation	5,34 ms (7,83%)	14,09 ms (15,65%)	14,17 ms (13,33%)

A second type of experimentation has been performed with a twofold goal:
first to estimate the influence of having more than one alternative service, and
second to estimate the impact of services with different complexities. For this
purpose, we have used six equivalent services, either versions of DPS (the "light"
implementations) or versions of RPS (the "heavier" implementations). In the
results that we present, the services are called $S1, S2, ..., S6$ and represent either
the six versions of DPS, or the six versions of RPS. The indexes indicate the
position of the service in the list of the Execution Manager, allowing us to deduce
the overhead introduced by the number of equivalent services. We have imposed
the context conditions such that the services were switched either from $S1$ to
$S6$ or the other way around. A switch indicated as $S_{i+1} \rightarrow S_i$ implies that S_i is
started to replace S_{i+1} (which is stopped right after that). This is the case were
Vespa continues to function without noticing the service switching. The results
for this case are presented in Fig. 6(a). A switch indicated as $S_i \rightarrow S_{i+1}$ implies
that S_i is stopped before starting S_{i+1}, causing Vespa to be interrupted while its
dependency is unresolved. The results of this case can be seen in Fig. 6(b). We
note that the transitions $S_1 \rightarrow S_6$ and $S_6 \rightarrow S_1$ are different, because they cause
the opposite behavior as the other ones. For a more clear view of the results,
these two transitions are not presented, but their values are consistent with the
rest of the experimentations. In the first case, when S_1 is stopped, S_6 is started
in 68,4 ms and 71,63 ms for DPS and RPS respectively. In the second case, S_1
is started in 4,3 ms and 4,46 ms respectively.

In Fig. 6 we examined the time it takes from the detection of a context change,
until the suitable service is started (i.e. the service that works best for the new
context situation). Two different aspects were taken into consideration here: the
number of equivalent services and the complexity of the services. In 6(a) we
notice a clear influence of the position of the service in the list of equivalent
services. The further it is in the list, the longer it takes until it is completely
switched on. This value increases steadily from 3,1 ms to 5,9 ms and from 3,8
ms to 7,5 ms for the DPS and RPS respectively. We can also observe a difference
between the lighter DPS and the slightly heavier RPS which is a little longer to

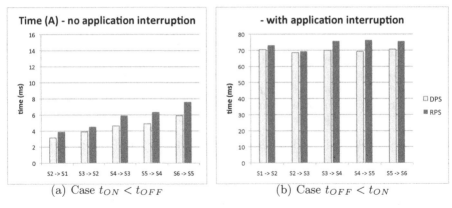

(a) Case $t_{ON} < t_{OFF}$ (b) Case $t_{OFF} < t_{ON}$

Fig. 6. Time (A) on the Sony phone - "light" vs. "heavier" service

start. The tests have been carried out on the other two testing devices, the HTC tablet and the Samsung phone. They have shown similar results with respect to the increasing tendency based on the number of services and their complexity. In Fig. 6(b) we present the case where the inappropriate service is switched off before starting the new one. Because it is the same thread that stops and starts the services, an overhead is induced and it takes around 70 ms until the suitable service is ready to use. In this case, the influence of the number of services and their order in the list isn't obvious any more. Nevertheless, the services have a rather uniform behavior, with the average values varying between 68,5 ms and 70,7 ms for DPS and between 69,3 ms and 76,2 ms for RPS. For each transition, the "heavier" RPS is still slightly longer to start than DPS. These results allow us to conclude that service number and complexity do influence the adaptation time, but within reasonable bounds. They are also an indication of an easy way to optimize our framework, by simply fixing the order of events: first the suitable service is switched on, and only after that the inappropriate one is switched off.

In order to have an overview of the times (A), (B) and (C), as well as the differences between the testing devices, we present the average results of these experimentations in Fig. 7. It is important to prove that our solution is efficient on different phones running the Android operating system, and that the CATS framework behaves in a similar way on all of them. Of course, the Android version and the supporting architecture have an important influence on the execution time, but the results rest consistent.

From the results presented in Fig. 7, Time (C) is the most important one, showing the total time of adaptation. As expected, the best performance is achieved with the HTC Flyer tablet, which is able to switch the services and adapt an application in little over 90 ms. The difference between the Time (A) and Time (C) is given by the time needed by iPOJO to bind the new service to the application. The Samsung phone, the oldest of the devices, is the least performant, while still providing an acceptable result: 145 ms in average for a complete adaptation of the application. The results that have been described here represent the average results of 30 trials for each test.

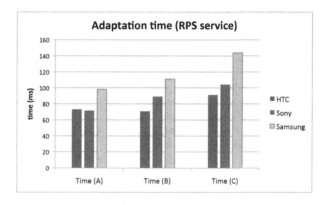

Fig. 7. From context change to an adapted application

8   Conclusion

In this paper, we propose an approach based on iPOJO handlers for our embedded application framework called CATS. This framework is dedicated to mobile devices such as smartphones, offering an execution environment for transportation-oriented applications which conform to the SOA principles. We provide adaptation by switching between equivalent services, based on context criteria. As such, an application will use the service that is adapted to the situation it is in. In this paper we have evaluated the time necessary from the detection of a context change until an adapted service is ready to use. An important part of the non-functional operations are carried out by the iPOJO handlers.

We have introduced a series of handlers to help manage the framework during the process of context detection and application adaptation. A first type of handler works with the Context Monitors, who update regularly the value of a certain element. The use of a handler has the great advantage of being able to reuse code with almost no modifications. Indeed, suppose that an existing piece of code is used to read a certain value (battery level, speed, etc.). In order to transform this into a Monitor, we must only describe the metadata of the Context Element and plug the appropriate handler to it. A second type of handler is used to cope with context dependency while keeping the service development as clean as possible. A service describes the non functional elements with the help of metadata, leaving the rest to the handler. At last, a handler was used for testing measurements, as it detects the invalidation and validation of the applications when dependencies are not resolved.

In this paper, the adaptation of applications was examined from various points of view and with different scenarios. Based on the order in which the stopping and starting actions are performed, on the number and on the complexity of the services, the adaptation time can vary, but remains reasonably fast. In order to optimize the performance of our framework, we can ensure that a context change is handled by first switching a new service on and only then switching the inappropriate one off.

References

1. Capra, L., Emmerich, W., Mascolo, C.: Carisma: Context-aware reflective middleware system for mobile applications. IEEE Trans. Softw. Eng. 29(10), 929–945 (2003)
2. Conan, D., Rouvoy, R., Seinturier, L.: Scalable Processing of Context Information with COSMOS. In: Indulska, J., Raymond, K. (eds.) DAIS 2007. LNCS, vol. 4531, pp. 210–224. Springer, Heidelberg (2007)
3. Delot, T., Cenerario, N., Ilarri, S.: Vehicular event sharing with a mobile peer-to-peer architecture. Transportation Research Part C: Emerging Technologies 18(4), 584–598 (2010)
4. Delot, T., Cenerario, N., Ilarri, S., Lecomte, S.: A cooperative reservation protocol for parking spaces in vehicular ad hoc networks. In: 6th International Conference on Mobile Technology, Applications and Systems (Mobility Conference 2009), pp. 1–8. ACM Digital Library (September 2009)
5. Desertot, M., Lecomte, S., Popovici, D., Thilliez, M., Delot, T.: A context aware framework for services management in the transportation domain. In: 2010 10th Annual International Conference on New Technologies of Distributed Systems, Tozeur, Tunisia, pp. 157–164 (2010)
6. Abowd, G.D., Dey, A.K.: Towards a Better Understanding of Context and Context-Awareness. In: Gellersen, H.-W. (ed.) HUC 1999. LNCS, vol. 1707, pp. 304–307. Springer, Heidelberg (1999)
7. Dobson, S., Sterritt, R., Nixon, P., Hinchey, M.: Fulfilling the vision of autonomic computing. Computer 43, 35–41 (2010)
8. Escoffier, C., Hall, R.S., Lalanda, P.: ipojo an extensible service-oriented component framework. In: IEEE International Conference on Service Computing (SCC 2007), Salt Lake City, USA, pp. 474–481 (2007)
9. Hall, R.S., Pauls, K., McCulloch, S., Savage, D.: Osgi in Action: Creating Modular Applications in Java. Manning Publications (2010)
10. Hoareau, C., Satoh, I.: Modeling and processing information for context-aware computing: A survey. New Gen. Computing 27(3), 177–196 (2009)
11. Kephart, J.O., Chess, D.M.: The vision of autonomic computing. Computer 36(1), 41–50 (2003)
12. Maurel, Y., Diaconescu, A., Lalanda, P.: Ceylon: A service-oriented framework for building autonomic managers. In: IEEE International Workshop on Engineering of Autonomic and Autonomous Systems, pp. 3–11 (2010)
13. Mukhtar, H., Belaid, D., Bernard, G.: User preferences-based automatic device selection for multimedia user tasks in pervasive environments. In: 5th Internat. Conf. on Networking and Services, p. 43. IEEE Computer Soc. (2009)
14. Parra, C., Blanc, X., Duchien, L.: Context awareness for dynamic service-oriented product lines. In: 13th International Software Product Line Conference SPLC 2009, vol. 1, pp. 131–140 (August 2009)
15. Popovici, D., Desertot, M., Lecomte, S., Delot, T.: A framework for mobile and context-aware applications applied to vehicular social networks. In: Social Network Analysis and Mining, pp. 1–12, 10.1007/s13278-012-0073-9
16. Popovici, D., Desertot, M., Lecomte, S., Peon, N.: Context-aware transportation services (cats) framework for mobile environments. International Journal of Next-Generation Computing 2(1) (2011)
17. Strang, T., Linnhoff-Popien, C.: A context modeling survey. In: Workshop on Advanced Context Modelling, Reasoning and Management, UbiComp 2004 - The Sixth International Conference on Ubiquitous Computing (2004)

Selecting Access Network for BYOD Enterprises with Business Context (eBC) and Enterprise-Centric ANDSF

Rebecca Copeland and Noel Crespi

Rebecca.copeland@coreviewpoint.com, noel.crespi@it-sudparis.eu

Abstract. enterprises that adopt BYOD (Bring Your Own Device) need to optimize network selection for refundable employees' business usage. They can 'force-on-net' business sessions when employees are on-site and seek 'best connection' when employees are off-site, perhaps via hospitality partners that provide WiFi connectivity. For non-fundable, unproductive personal usage, service requests should be 'forced-off-net' and deferred back to the personal carriers. To achieve this, we propose that the Enterprise decides whether to accept or change the originating access network, having established the funding status via the eBC (enterprise Business Context) model. For each service request, the Enterprise evaluates QoE and Affordability vectors that are derived from prioritized STANDS and CART factors respectively and the results are used to select the optimal access network. An enterprise Access Discovery and Selection Function (eANDSF) is proposed to enable recommending preferred corporate hospitality partners to employees, instead of the carrier's list.

Keywords: ANDSF, BYOD, Always-Best-Connected, ABC, QoS, QoE, Context, MVNO, Hospitality, MOS, WiFi, WLAN.

1 Introduction

Selecting an access network for Mobile Broadband Data is the first frontier in establishing what services are selected for both Data services and Voice. Enterprises have long tried to persuade employees when they are on-site to use internal network resources instead of Mobile carrier's expensive services. The need to select affordable best connection is even more urgent for enterprises adopting consumerization, or BYOD (Bring Your Own Device), which is a trend sweeping the developed world [1]. BYOD means that personal devices are used for both business and private purposes and business usage is mixed with personal, yet legitimate business communication expenses still need to be refunded. Therefore, these enterprises need to optimize access selection to save costs of those sessions that are deemed refundable, whether on-site or off-site. They will save considerable costs when using spare capacity on their eWLAN for business usage. Enterprises also need to protect their own network from excessive personal use by employees and defer such service requests to the user's own carrier network, to be served and charged by the carrier. By doing so, enterprises will make better resources use and avoid unnecessary network upgrades.

C. Borcea et al. (Eds.): MobilWare 2012, LNICST 65, pp. 221–235, 2012.
© Institute for Computer Sciences, Social Informatics and Telecommunications Engineering 2013

Defining the best network connection is different when seen from the point of view of the carrier or that of the Enterprise. In most cases, carriers optimize across technologies (WLAN, UMTS, LTE) within their own network. The Enterprise's need of optimization is driven by the desire to minimize communications expenditure while providing QoE (Quality of Experience), reliability and security.

Researching cost models and charging levels is hard as information is not easily available and is often deemed private. The difficulty of defining what is 'best connection' was highlighted in [7], listing issues with the range of different technologies, compatibilities of terminals and radio networks, range of applications with different selection criteria and the many ways of measuring user satisfaction.

Beyond network optimization, most research papers looking at 'best connection' address the open WiFi access market. Hospitality establishments, such as café and hotel chains, are becoming aware that offering good connectivity attracts high-spending consumers to their premises. They may offer bulk discounts to enterprises that direct their employees to use preferred partner lists, where secure WiFi is offered, perhaps as part of the corporate rates of hotel rooms or business lunches.

In this paper we examine access selection for the Enterprise market. We suggest that the Enterprise uses the output from the previously proposed eBC function to determine what access network should be used. We also propose that the Enterprise maintains an enterprise-centric ANDSF and conveys its preferred lists to the devices. The paper includes related work and research in part II; in part III analysis of stakeholders motives and selection criteria; in part IV a description of the proposed enterprise ANDSF-eBC solution; in part V the decision process logic and call flows for handover between access networks; in part VI computing QoE and Affordability vectors from the STANDS and CART factors; in part VII illustrating cost savings and in part VIII – the conclusions.

2   Related Work

The proposed solution in this paper is based on the previously proposed enterprise Business Context (eBC) policy and the 3GPP ANDSF standards. The eBC has been developed particularly for enterprises that embrace BYOD. It enables differentiating business usage service requests from personal, so that business requests can be funded by the Enterprise, while personal requests are handles under the user's own subscription. In this paper we propose a new application utilizing the same eBC model – enterprise-centric access network selection, directing on-site business sessions to the eWLAN (enterprise WLAN) and personal sessions to the mobile carrier. The eBC policy concept has been introduced in [16]; requests detection and mapping to PCC (Policy & Charging Control) rules are proposed in [17]; the eBC platform and logic in [18]; and the computational model in [19].

ANDSF is the 3GPP standard mechanism of informing user devices of available access networks within range (see [11] and [15]). It allows carriers to convey access selection preferences to the device. ANDSF information is relayed between the network and the device over the 3GPP standard S14 interface. The protocol is based on the OMA (Open Mobile Alliance) Device Management (DM) function for a special ANDSF Management Object, using a SyncML- a sub-set of XML that is defined for it. The device communication with the provisioning server is secured by authentication with a 'stateful' dialogue, to prevent tampering.

In [12], a Prototype is described which simulates ANDSF in EPC (Evolved Packet Core). It demonstrates the use of ANDSF mobility rules, transferring from a trusted non-3GPP access gateway to an untrusted non-3GPP ePDG (evolved Packet Data Gateway) when connecting to 3rd party hotspots. In [6] and [7], Issues are raised regarding access discovery via broadcasting WiFi beacons, including high power consumption of always-on searching, user price privacy, price-QoS variations etc.

There is extensive research into Always Best Connect (ABC) methods. ABC has captured researchers' imagination, but implementations are hampered by both technical and business difficulties. The concept is often limited to network optimization, where carriers look for the most efficient transport of large volumes of data, as in the example of [3], with the proposed 'LessDamage' algorithm that needs no a priori traffic data. In [2], still from the carrier's perspective, the ABC algorithm combines network-context and user-device context, where 'user utility' is achieved via resource allocation through the mathematical 'knapsack' (or 'bin packing') problem. Addressing the consumer needs in [4], a discovery method of local access networks is proposed via a client that captures advertised service data (in this case, for video broadcast carriers) and filters it to present 'always best connected and best served' (ABC&S) recommendations. In [22], the complexity of defining ABC is discussed, where calculating user-centric options from price packages is declared as a 'combinatorial optimization problem' that is 'NP-hard' and cannot be computed within a reasonable time. We have to concur with these findings.

While selecting best connection for network traffic optimization can be evaluated by objective, computational means, it is harder to assess the best connection by user satisfaction or QoE. Achieving high QoE is not just a function of the access network performance, but also all transport networks that are involved in the delivery. Measuring QoE relies on human perception of the delivered service, often captured by MOS (Mean Opinion Score). Various research papers attempted to quantify QoE, as in [14], which found a non-linear relationship with increasing network bandwidth, i.e. just adding capacity will not automatically increase user satisfaction. More recently in [21], an 'exponential relationship' by logarithmic computation of QoE values (in contrast with achieved QoS measurements) is proposed, where the QoE is presented as a distribution of logged MOS. This is still based only on generic QoS problems (loss, delay, jitter, reordering or throughput limitations) that appear to users as QoE problems (glitches, artifacts, pixilation or excessive waiting times).

There is little or no research on optimizing costs, yet user decisions are often swayed by affordability more than by quality. In [5], a user-centric approach is confused with device based approach, which is still under the carrier's control. Dealing with pricing issues is summarily dismissed 'because of flat rates'. In fact, subscription fees bundle usage costs up to a threshold, with additional costs levied when exceeded, and this occurs more frequently with the advent of video services.

Context based decision-making methods have been researched by many disciplines, not just Telecom. In [20], context quality is aided by modified WPM (Weighted Product Method), where context attribute values are processed by MADM (Multi Attribute Decision Making) that employs fuzzy logic to achieve deterministic values. For mobile operators seeking best connectivity for roaming subscribers, several computed methods are described in [10], comparing mathematic models such as SAW (Simple Additive Weighting) as well as WPM. Other popular computational methods are based on TOPSIS (Technique for Order Preference by Similarity to Ideal Solution) and AHP (Analytic Hierarchy Process), as described in [8].

3   Access Selection Criteria

The issue of access selection is not merely having enough resources, but also having the right resources for the particular service, i.e. achieving QoE, not just improved QoS. In fact, users are far more influenced by pricing than QoE. The subjective view of the level of charges defines an 'Affordability' vector. It can be said that Affordability is to charging as QoE is to QoS - adding the human perception perspective. Neither Affordability nor QoE are absolute determinants without context, e.g. attitudes to a high price may be changed if the expense is refundable or the communication service is especially urgent.

Affordability and QoE present a conundrum: satisfaction is raised with better quality - this requires more resources and higher infrastructure cost - so charges are raised - but this leads to lower satisfaction - and raising satisfaction needs higher resources, and so on. In reality, this is solved by adding the dimension of context. This problem may be resolved by using the TOPSIS method [8] that identifies the option that has the shortest distance from the positive ideal solution and the farthest distance from the negative worst solution. However, using the TOPSIS method still needs separate handling of the QoE and the Affordability vectors, as we propose here.

The enterprise acts as an access provider when its employees are on the premises and as an access consumer ('buying' network resources from carriers and hospitality agents) when the employees are out of range. As an access provider, the Enterprise must curb excessive use, especially for unproductive personal usage, which could be charged to users' personal accounts, perhaps under their flat rate regime. As an access consumer, the enterprise needs to minimize refundable expenses by connecting to the lowest cost service with acceptable QoE and Affordability, and also ensure that business services are delivered at appropriate level of security. This means that the Enterprise should 'force' on-site business service requests onto the eWLAN and force unproductive personal usage out of the eWLAN. For personal usage, this means that the Enterprise policy may reject eWLAN requests and re-route to the user's own carrier, who will then decide whether to serve it on its 3G/4G network or to offload it to WiFi. When employees are off the premises, the Enterprise can select best partnering hospitality services, if they are better options than the carrier's offer.

To execute this enterprise-centric access selection, the enterprise first needs to obtain the context for the service request via the eBC Model [19]. In this paper, we propose to use the same eBC model (with prioritized STANDS factors) to determine the QoE vector and to use the CART factors, which are derived from employees' profile data, to generate the Affordability vector. Using both vectors, decisions can be made for business requests to be 'forced-on-net' and personal requests 'forced-off-net' when on-site, and use carrier's 3G/4G or hospitality WiFi when off-site. Additionally, enterprise-centric preferred lists of hospitality agents can be forwarded to the device when off-site. By optimizing session costs and maximizing utilization of existing internal capacity, considerable savings can be made.

4   Proposing eBC - eANDSF Solution

For best effect, BYOD enterprises should become MVNOs [17]. This allows the Enterprise to determine session policies and convey them to carriers, using the S9 standard interfaces, as defined in 3GPP [11]. Enterprises can also use eBC Policy when they have no MVNO status, but a Sponsor agreement instead. The Sponsor's particulars and the authorized service details are transferred via the Rx interface, which allows some, but not all, session parameters to be set by the Enterprise.

As an MVNO, the Enterprise acts like a 'home' network for the BYOD user's access via 3G/4G and can select access network. Service requests that are deemed as 'sponsored' will also reach the enterprise. However, not all WiFi/Internet sessions will be forwarded. Detecting and intercepting such requests are discussed in [17]. Figure 1 shows service request flows between the Enterprise and the access network providers. Business service requests (1, 2, 3) and personal requests (4, 5) can reach the Enterprise from its own eWLAN, from hospitality access or from the user's chosen carrier. The initial requesting access networks may or may not be the best choice for the Enterprise, in which case the Enterprise can instruct the employee's device to change it.

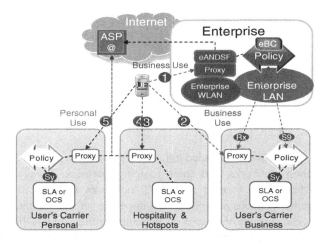

Fig. 1. Access for BYOD users in Business/Personal mode

The general access discovery process by beacon broadcasting is successful because no prior data needs to be provided, but it involves many issues, including excessive power consumption (due to constantly polling), pricing privacy and complex QoS/Policy packages. Hence, downloading coverage lists as a discovery method is deemed superior by [6], which proposes both terminal-based method (pull information continuously) and network-based method (server push, using location-based services). WiFi beacons enable local connectivity without a formal association with the device, a feature that can be exploited by local businesses for distributing coupons and promotions, as proposed by [13]. This can be a nuisance, and has inspired a contra proposal in [4] to discard such unsolicited broadcast data while collating local intelligence into more useful recommended lists.

3GPP defines ANDSF as an advisory service only, allowing configuration by local setting (device/user), home networks (MVNO/enterprise) or visiting networks (the user's carrier). Usually, device clients contain three WLAN lists: discovered un-prioritized advertised list, user/device preferred list and Carrier's (user's network) list. The enterprise can use the second list type and the device will be configured to prefer the Enterprise ANDSF as first choice. As shown in Figure 2, the mobile handset may connect to hotspots, carriers' WiMAX, UMTS, LTE and WLAN, and to Enterprise WLAN, and more than one ANDSF may be available for the device to download.

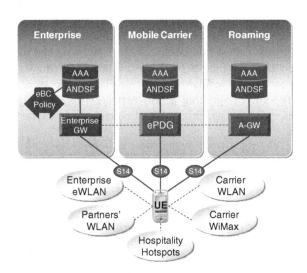

Fig. 2. Enterprise ANDSF as well as Carrier ANDSF

The ANDSF procedure is intended for carriers to assist devices in finding and connecting to their networks and their roaming partners. However, the 3GPP specifications [15], which support non-3GPP networks as well, are designed to support 'open', heterogeneous network environment, rather than dictate carriers' own selection. Hence, the concept of enterprises maintaining their own ANDSF should not be considered controversial. In providing an enterprise-centric ANDSF, the Enterprise can enforce its own access selection policies, direct employees to partners who provide discounted connectivity but also the required business quality and security.

Unlike WiFi beacons that anyone can tune to, the ANDSF information is confidential and specific. The information includes rules of selection, prioritized list of preferred networks in the vicinity and pricing details. This can be extended in the eANDSF to include enterprise-negotiated rates and historical evaluations of past QoE and affordability, thus providing meaningful selection information.

Using ANDSF is also safer – information is exchanged only when a secure connection is established, protecting devices from potential fraud and phishing. Another advantage is the unintended benefit of providing geo-location to the ANDSF server. In [12], this is highlighted as means of obtaining accurate geo-location for applications. This location data can also be used to determine the Spatial Factor for the eBC status, where the user's location is an important consideration.

5   The Access Selection Decision Process

The eBC evaluation score is the main input into the access selection process that determines a 'business' or a 'personal' service request. Another input is the request's original access – mobile carrier, enterprise internal network or hospitality WiFi. These aspects are analyzed in the logic flow as shown in Figure 3, which considers the two main scenarios - eWLAN generated and 3G/4G generated requests.

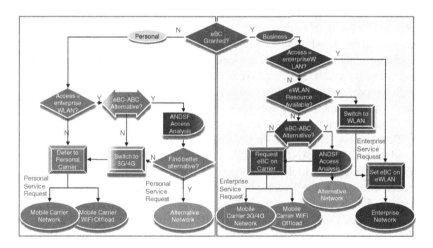

Fig. 3. ANDSF in BYOD usage

If a funded business request arrives on the eWLAN, it goes ahead, but if it arrives from the carrier's network, the device is instructed to switch to the eWLAN, i.e. perform 'force-on-net'. When there are no sufficient eWLAN resources, the Enterprise can still look for an alternative among the hospitality partners nearby. The UE device contacts the eANDSF and downloads the corporate preferred partner list in the vicinity. If, as a result of the eBC computation, the carrier's QoE and

Affordability are superior to the hospitality partners, the carrier's network will be chosen and the access network will be switched over, if necessary.

Alternatively, the device re-launches the service request towards the carrier and it is up to the carrier to serve it or offload it, using its own ANDSF partners with its own policies. In Figure 4, switching from the carrier's 3G access to eWLAN is shown.

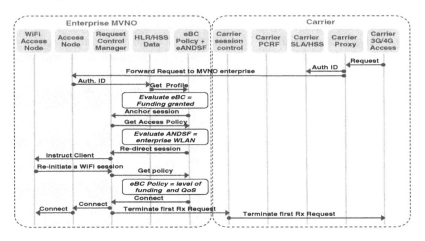

Fig. 4. Switching Access from 3G/4G to WLAN – Forced-on-Net

Requests that are not granted eBC status are deferred back to the carrier's network, to be charged to the user's personal account. If the unfunded request comes over the eWLAN, it will be transferred. However, the Enterprise can still support employees' access selection and protect BYOD devices by providing secure preferred partner, and by using the safer eANDSF. Employees can still benefit from enterprise negotiated deals with the preferred hospitality businesses.

In this example, the carrier forwards the request to the Enterprise as the Home network. The Enterprise authenticates the user and authorizes the service via the eBC Policy. The request is managed in a proxy function which interacts with the eBC policy and the proposed eANDSF. In this scenario, the eANDSF policy decides to use the eWLAN. It may still look for alternatives during peak hours or for a non-urgent session, according to its QoE vector that is received from the eBC Policy server.

In Figure 5, the scenario of switching from eWLAN to carrier's 3G or 4G is shown. The eWLAN session is assessed by internal proxy and eBC server.

In this scenario, a request on the eWLAN is not granted funding and is deemed 'Personal'. The user is notified that an enterprise service is not available and is given the choice of alternative access network prioritized by the Enterprise or the carrier's normal service. In this scenario, the eANDSF analysis shows that the carrier's network is still best value and the user selects it manually. Performing this automatically could be configured, as it is today, on the device. The request is re-launched towards the carrier access network, where the user is authenticated against the personal account, with the personal quota and charging band. The session is connected according to the carrier's policy and will be charged to the user directly.

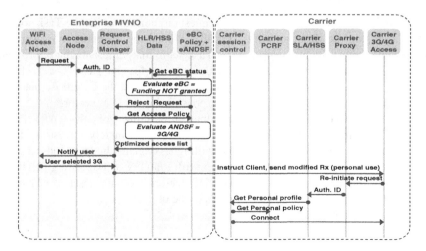

Fig. 5. Switching Access from WLAN to 3G/4G – Forced-off-Net

6   The Context Factors (STANDS and CART)

The network selection decision needs to consider both QoE and Affordability and keep the cost in proportion to required QoE. The QoE requirements are defined by a set of factors - the STANDS (Spatial, Temporal, Activity, Network-type, Destination and Service-type) on the eBC policy server ([19]). Affordability level is not just ability to pay, but also 'cost tolerance', the willingness to pay in a particular circumstance. Affordability is derived from the CART (Cost band, Available quota, Role uplift, Time limits) factors. In selecting which access network to use, the required QoE level needs to be compared with the quality level of the offered service and the Affordability needs to be compared with the perceived service cost, as far as it is known. Other human factors may also influence the decision. For example, the lack of available alternatives in the vicinity, in which case both QoE and Affordability are immaterial for a crucial service delivery. Another such factor is the ability to postpone the requested service until a better or cheaper connection is available.

To evaluate QoE, the Enterprise determines the eBC status by evaluating the dynamic STANDS factors, which are computed from sources of data that are available to the Enterprise (email, calendar, server logins, work-schedules etc.). An important source is the service request with details of user ID, destination and service media - see [19]. The STANDS Factors include:

– Spatial aspect (roaming, regional, at-home, at-work);
– Temporal aspect (calendar, hour, date, lunch-hour);
– Activity engagement (holiday, sick, booked activity e.g. customer visits);
– Network type (mobile/fixed, enterprise, hotspots);
– Destination type (human/machine, approved/banned);
– Service type (media, conversational).

The STANDS factors describe the service request circumstances i.e. the Task context. Such Tasks can be Routine-work, Travel, Abroad or Essential-job. Applying customizable factor weightings produces a Task score that represents the priority and desirability that the Enterprise assigns to this service for the Task. The Tasks are prioritized further, to reflect the urgency and importance that the Enterprise places on a quality delivery of this service, i.e. an enterprise-generated QoE vector.

While the STANDS factors are instrumental in defining QoE, the CART factors are crucial to establishing Affordability. Affordability is not merely a question of cost, but also comparative spending power and willingness against budgets and perceived session priority. The CART factors represent affordability and spending privileges. Unlike the dynamic environmental STANDS factors that are session-related, the CART factors are pre-determined and related to the user.

The CART factors include:

- Cost band (approved level of spending) which is a level of charging that may be approved for users according to their role and grade within the organization. In a flat rate charging regime, this is the quota status, which entails higher prices when the threshold is exceeded, especially when roaming.
- Available credit, quotas and budgets, indicate remaining spending power. If there is no credit left, the Enterprise may revert back to personal use.
- Role/grade uplift represents privileges within the Enterprise that may be granted per seniority or particular job requirements. For example, higher budget may be granted if the user's role entails time-critical activities.
- Time limits (duration limits and re-validation periods) are imposed on long sessions but may be relaxed for a particular activity, e.g. monitoring security cameras. Duration limits can achieve 'fair usage', letting in other users in congested networks.

The scalar values of the CART factors are 'normalized' to enable comparison regardless of different measure units. Like the STANDS, the CART factors are assigned weights that reflect their importance within the Task. The CART prioritization values are assigned within each type of Task.

The QoE and Affordability vectors are derived from the STANDS and the CART by applying prioritization. These vectors are computed, using SAW (Simple Additive Weighting) techniques that inject enterprise objectives and priorities in the form of weighting. The STANDS factors prioritization discovers the 'prevailing' Task (Local Travel, for example) that the user is engaged in while requesting the service. This prevailing Task identifies the weighting ratios to apply to the CART factors. Computing a QoE Vector (QV) requires first to apply the Task prioritization to the Task score margin. Highest Task scores are the best fit to the Enterprise objectives.

For Threshold THn, Task TTn, Task weighting ratio TTWn and QoE vector QV:
If TH= {TH1,TH2,...THn}   and   TTW = {TTW1, TTW2...TTWn}
Then, Threshold Margin THMn = TTn -THn   and   QV = THMn · TTWn.   (1)

The second step assesses the CART factors. CART parameters (measured as 1-5, representing very-high/high/mid/low/very-low ratios) are taken from employees' profile data and their prioritization per Task is applied. Priorities must add up to 1. The Affordability vector is calculated from the weighted CART factors:

If CART factors are: CU:= CiUj and their weighting ratios within each Task are in CT:= CiTn, then → Affordability Vector AV = CiUj · CiTn.   (2)

The third step compares QoE Vector (QV) and the Affordability Vector (AV) with measurement of user satisfaction from previous services deliveries by the various access providers. MOS (Mean Opinion Score) is used to measure subjective assessments, having gathered feedback via after-session messaging. Keeping QoE and Affordability as two separate criteria helps users to respond sensibly and provides more flexibility. Figure 6 shows a worked example of the three steps in the evaluation of a session request, in order to find the 'Affordable Best Connection'.

Computing Affordable Best Connection

1. Establish eBC Task and prioritize it

Threshold = 45.00

eBC Task	eBC scores	eBC margins per scenario	Importance % within Task	computed STANDS Scalar
Routine	36.00	-9.00	0.10	-0.90
@Home	42.50	-2.50	0.05	-0.13
Local travel	58.00	13.00	0.20	2.60 QoE vector
Essential job	24.31	-20.69	0.40	-8.28
Abroad	38.33	-6.67	0.25	-1.67
			1.00	

2. Establish user's affordability and privilege uplifts per eBC Task

CART	User profile data current level 1-5	Importance % within Task	computed CART scalar
Cost band	5.00	0.25	1.25
Available budget	4.00	0.40	1.60
Role/grade uplift	2.00	0.25	0.50
Time allowance	1.00	0.10	0.10
		1.00	3.45 = Affordability

3. Compare with MOS values per Access Provider

MOS (1-5)	Required Level	User's Carrier	Hospitality	Ad-hoc WiFi
QoE	2.60	3.00	4.00	2.00
Affordability	3.45	2.00	1.00	1.00
	6.05	5.00	5.00	3.00

Fig. 6. Example of computed Affordable Best Connection

As shown in this example, the results may favor one vector or or both. Here the 3G carrier is more affordable (e.g. the user is travelling locally - no roaming charges), but the hospitality partner provides higher quality service, e.g. WiFi for video conference. Comparing the totals of both vectors with MOS for both criteria may provide a 'tie', as shown in this example (both carrier and hospitality =5.0), so further decision is needed. As a rule, higher affordability vector wins (carrier = 2.0), rather than the higher QoE, but precedence can be configured per Task context e.g. QoE may dominate the decision for 'Essential Job', while 'Routine' remains Affordability led.

7   Quantifying Cost Savings

A cost saving model can be a useful tool for enterprises to assess the potential benefits from selecting access networks for their employees. Such a model has to assess cost per session, not per megabyte, because the cost improvements are achieved for each session. Unfortunately, most access providers charge for bandwidth usage, not for sessions. Therefore, to quantify cost saving, the model must compute the Average Cost per Session (ACpS) first, taking account of average consumed bandwidth per session, multiplied by the bandwidth charges. This needs to be done for each of the delivering network types: eWLAN, 3G/4G, Hospitality.

Calculating ACpS per network depends on a great many scenarios, a wide range of bandwidth usage patterns and just as many charging regimes. Even if average bandwidth per session is obtained, its costs cannot be generalized. For example, the bandwidth in 'flat rate' is part of the average cost, but also a portion of the higher rate when the limit is exceeded. Roaming charges as well as local charges should be factored in, the proportion of which varies between business and personal. Cost-per-megabyte has already been declared as 'NP Hard' in [22], i.e. too complex to calculate, and we have to concur that ACpS cannot be reliably modeled.

However, each enterprise can still estimate its own costs and bandwidth usage. These estimates are based on obtained usage statistics from the internal network, and the cost of providing eWLAN/LAN capacity from equipment and maintenance prices, allowing for the write-off period for infrastructure investment. It is important to factor in the value of using up spare capacity, when the investment cost is not incremental per session, i.e. increasing benefits of sunk costs.

Specific usage /cost information must also be obtained from the mobile carriers and hospitality agents for comparison. Carrier usage/charging data is derived from historical accounts, carrier agreements and business expenses processing. Hospitality agents have simpler charging models (per hour/day) but the number of sessions needs to be estimated, if not available.

For such a specific case of cost saving assessment, we provide a model that indicates the cost sensitivity to shifting access networks, as shown in the cost saving sensitivity model in Figure 7.

To test sensitivity, the calculated example shows the change when 10 %, 20% and 30% of sessions are shifted from one access network to another, to optimize service delivery costs. This model includes three scenarios: On-site business sessions (shifting sessions from 3G/4G to eWLAN), Off-site business sessions (shifting sessions from 3G/4G to hospitality) and On-site personal (shifting sessions from eWLAN to 3G/4G). The scenario of off-site personal session on hospitality access is not needed since it is not charged to the Enterprise but is paid directly by the user.

The estimated ACpS per network type in this example are merely for illustration. Note that it is assumed that Personal ACpS is higher than Business ACpS, not just due to higher consumer prices, but also due to higher bandwidth consumption average – personal usage is more likely to include pictures and video streaming while most business sessions involve email, text and browsing. We also assumed a discounted rate for hospitality WiFi that is on the Enterprise preferred list.

Quantify Savings p.a.	Business Calls			Personal Calls		Costs	Savings
Average Cost per Session:	€0.35	€2.55	€8.00 €6.50	€1.50	€3.80	per user	per user
Current	eWLAN	3G/4G	Hospitality	eWLAN	Personal 3G/4G		
On-site no. Sessions per annum	450.0	350.0		320.0	100.0		
On-site Cost per annum	€157.5	€892.5		€480.0	€380.0		
Off-site no. Sessions per annum		500.0	120.0				
Off-site Cost per annum		€1,275.0	€960.0				
Total Cost per user p.a.	€157.5	€2,167.5	€960.0	€480.0	user's cost	€3,765.0	
10% change	eWLAN+10%	3G/4G-10%	Hospitality+10%	eWLAN-10%	Personal 3G/4G	0.10	
On-site no. Sessions per annum	485.0	315.0		288.0	132.0		
On-site Cost per annum	€169.8	€803.3		€432.0	€501.6		
Off-site no. Sessions per annum		450.0	132.0				
Off-site Cost per annum		€1,147.5	€858.0				
Total Cost per user p.a.	€169.8	€1,950.8	€858.0	€432.0	user's cost	€3,410.5	€355
20% change	eWLAN+20%	3G/4G-20%	Hospitality+20%	eWLAN-20%	Personal 3G/4G	0.20	
On-site no. Sessions per annum	548.0	252.0		230.4	189.6		
On-site Cost per annum	€191.8	€642.6		€345.6	€720.5		
Off-site no. Sessions per annum		360.0	158.4				
Off-site Cost per annum		€918.0	€1,029.6				
Total Cost per user p.a.	€191.8	€1,560.6	€1,029.6	€345.6	user's cost	€3,127.6	€637
30% change	eWLAN+30%	3G/4G-30%	Hospitality+30%	eWLAN-30%	Personal 3G/4G	0.30	
On-site no. Sessions per annum	623.6	176.4		161.3	258.7		
On-site Cost per annum	€218.3	€449.8		€241.9	€983.1		
Off-site no. Sessions per annum		252.0	205.9				
Off-site Cost per annum		€642.6	€1,338.5				
Total Cost per user p.a.	€218.3	€1,092.4	€1,338.5	€241.9	user's cost	€2,891.1	€874

Fig. 7. Cost Saving Sensitivity Model – Case Study

In this example, a 1000 strong enterprise can save 355,000 Euros per year with just 10% session shifting, and 874,000 Euros with 30% changes of access per year. We acknowledge that these results entirely hinge on the relative differences between the ACpS rates in each network, which could not be accurately ascertained in a generalized model, however, this example shows that there is remarkable cost elasticity for relatively small number of access shifts, indicating that the eBC/eANDSF access selection solution is well worthwhile.

8 Conclusions

In this paper we focus on satisfying the enterprise needs for best access selection. An enterprise adopting BYOD has a particular issue with protecting its own network resources from a surge of unproductive personal traffic. The enterprise seeks to optimize usage of spare capacity on its internal network resources rather than paying mobile carrier prices for sessions initiated on-site. It also seeks to select hospitality partners who not only offer discounts but can also be relied on to provide secure, quality connectivity. This means that the enterprise should 'force-on-net' business traffic and 'force-off-net' personal traffic, and should indicate to off-site employees which WiFi partner to choose.

This paper proposes that enterprises use the eBC techniques to establish users' context and execute access selection according to the resulting business status. The decision process needs to consider the STANDS factors for the requested level of QoE, and the CART factors for the Affordability aspect. For personal service requests that are not allowed on-net, the Enterprise will suggest an alternative, either the carrier's

3G/4G or local non-3GPP partner. For business usage, when employees are out-of-range or when the Enterprise WLAN is overloaded, alternative access networks will be selected. To do this, an enterprise-centric 3GPP-compatible ANDSF is proposed. This eANDSF maintains corporate access selection policies and corporate preferred partner list, with their negotiated corporate discounts.

By selecting the most cost-effective access network and optimizing utilization of internal network resources, enterprises can realize considerable savings. Although the potential savings can be computed case by case, it is not possible to produce a generalized model, however an illustrative specific case calculation shows that there is considerable cost sensitivity to shifting access network of service requests, hence there are considerable benefits for the Enterprise.

References

1. Decisive Analytics: Mobile Consumerization Trends & Perceptions IT Executive and CEO Survey (2012)
2. Gazis, V., Alonistioti, N., Merakos, L.: Toward a generic Always Best Connected capability in integrated WLAN/UMTS Cellular mobile networks (and beyond). IEEE Wireless Communications 12(3) (2005)
3. Cananéa, I., Mariz, D., Kelner, J., Sadok, D.: An On-line Access Selection Algorithm for ABC Networks Supporting Elastic Services. In: IEEE WCNC Proceedings (2008)
4. Ji, Z., Ganchev, I., O'Droma, M.: An iWBC Consumer Application for 'Always Best Connected and Best Served': Design and Implementation. IEEE Transactions on Consumer Electronics 57(2) (2011)
5. Kellokoski, J., Hamalainen, T.: User-Centric Approach to Always-Best-Connected Networks. In: IEEE ICUMT (2011)
6. Yiping, C., Yuhang, Y.: A new 4G architecture providing multimode terminals always best connected services. IEEE Wireless Communications (2007)
7. Chen, Y., Deng, C., Yang, Y.: Access Discovery in Always Best Connected Networks. IEEE (2008)
8. Lahby, M., Leghris, C., Adib, A.: A hybrid Approach for Network Selection in Heterogeneous Multi-Access Environments. IEEE (2011)
9. Vodafone user guide: Enterprise Install Guide: Vodafone Mobile Broadband (2011)
10. Savitha, K., Chandrasekar, C.: Vertical Handover decision schemes using SAW and WPM for Network selection in Heterogeneous Wireless Networks. In: GJCST (2011)
11. 3GPP TS 23.402: Architecture enhancements for non-3GPP accesses (Release 11)
12. Corici, M., Fiedler, J., Magedanz, T., Vingarzan, D.: Access Network Discovery and Selection in the Future Wireless Communication. ACM, Springer (2011)
13. Chandra, R., Padhye, J., Ravindranath, L., Wolman, A.: Beacon-Stuffing: Wi-Fi Without Associations. Microsoft Research (2007)
14. Khirman, S., Henriksen, P.: Relationship between Quality-of-Service and Quality-of-Experience for Public Internet Service. In: PAM (2001)
15. 3GPP TS 24.302: Access to the 3GPP Evolved Packet Core (EPC) via non-3GPP access networks Stage 3 (Release 11)
16. Copeland, R., Crespi, N.: Analyzing consumerization - should enterprise Business Context determine session policy decisions? In: IEEE ICIN (2012)

17. Copeland, R., Crespi, N.: Controlling enterprise context-based session policy and mapping it to mobile broadband policy rules. In: IEEE ICIN (2012)
18. Copeland, R., Crespi, N.: Establishing enterprise Business Context (eBC) for service policy decision in mobile broadband networks. In: ICCCN ContextQoS (2012)
19. Copeland, R., Crespi, N.: Implementing an enterprise Business Context model for defining Mobile Broadband Policy. In: IEEE CSNM (2012)
20. TalebiFard, V., Leung, C.M.: A Dynamic Context-Aware Access Network Selection for Handover in Heterogeneous Network Environments. In: IEEE Infocom MobiWorld (2011)
21. Fiedler, M., Hossfeld, T., Tran-Gia, P.: A Generic Quantitative Relationship between Quality of Experience and Quality of Service. In: IEEE Network (2010)
22. Gazis, V., Houssos, N., Alonistioti, N., Merakos, L.: On the Complexity of "Always Best Connected" in 4G Mobile Networks. In: VTC (2003)

Context-Aware, QoE-Driven Adaptation of Multimedia Services

Karthik Srinivasan[1], Poorva Agrawal[1], Rajat Arya[1], Nadeem Akhtar[2],
Deepak Pengoria[2], and Timothy A. Gonsalves[3]

[1] Infosys Limited, Bangalore, India
{s_karthik,poorva_agrawal,rajat_arya}@infosys.com
[2] Centre of Excellence in Wireless Technology, Chennai, India
{nadeem,deepak}@cewit.org.in
[3] Indian Institute of Technology Mandi, Himachal, India
tag@iitmandi.ac.in

Abstract. Delivery of multimedia services over heterogeneous wireless
networks is a challenging proposition because of the diverse characteristics of the underlying wireless technologies. The problem is compounded
further by the availability of a wide range of end user devices such as
desktops, notebooks, tablets and smartphones. To provide a consistent
and uniform Quality of Experience to the end user, we propose a context-
aware service adaptation framework in this paper. The basic idea is to
monitor the user and network context and leverage this information for
adapting services to match the device and network characteristics.

Keywords: Multimedia services, service delivery, service adaptation,
QoE, context-awareness, heterogeneous network.

1   Introduction

The fast-changing telecommunications market is characterized by increasing
heterogeneity of access technologies and devices. On the access side, we see a
plethora of wireless technologies like 3G, 4G and WiFi etc. Despite increasing
convergence between these networks, there exist differences in terms of network
architecture, QoS mechanisms, supported data rates and so on. On the end-user
side, there is great diversity in the hardware and software capabilities of these devices. The challenge is to provide access to multimedia services to heterogeneous
devices over heterogeneous access networks, with consistent and uniform Quality of Experience (QoE) to the end user, while utilising the available network
resources efficiently.

QoE is generally considered as a subjective measure of a customer's perception
of the performance of a network and the services it offers (web browsing, phone
call, TV broadcast etc.). While QoS refers to the performance in terms of metrics
such as packet loss, delay and jitter etc, QoE relates to the overall user experience
while accessing and using the provided services. For instance, a user with a low-
bandwidth connection may be satisfied by a low/moderate quality video stream

C. Borcea et al. (Eds.): MobilWare 2012, LNICST 65, pp. 236–249, 2013.
© Institute for Computer Sciences, Social Informatics and Telecommunications Engineering 2013

whereas someone who is paying a premium for a high-bandwidth connection will be satisfied only if the video is of a high quality. In other words, QoE is influenced greatly by the context.

1.1   Background

We first present a set of use cases, using video as an example, to show the need for context aware adaptation to improve QoE.

- Case 1: Consider a user with a subscription for 3G data connection, with volume-based charging. Assume that the user has multiple 3G-capable devices with different screen sizes and resolutions. When the user accesses YouTube videos over a low-resolution device, to push a high-resolution video wastes valuable billable bandwidth.
- Case 2: Consider a user with a device that has a high-res display and that is capable of using both 3G and WiFi. Typically, while streaming a video, the user will choose the access technology that provides a higher data rate. However, if the residual battery power is low, the user may switch to a lower-bandwidth connection and opt for a low-res version of the video.
- Case 3: Consider an example where a user has a 3G subscription that costs more while roaming. To reduce the cost of streaming a video, the user may choose a low-res stream even though sufficient bandwidth is available and the device is capable of displaying high-res videos.

In all the three examples mentioned above, the choice of video quality was determined by multiple factors such as cost, screen resolution, available bandwidth and battery power. For the end user, the acceptable QoE also varies in consonance with these factors. Bearing this in mind, we propose a framework for service adaptation that takes into account several types of context, to provide the best possible QoE to the user.

1.2   Related Work

There are two aspects to service adaptation: i) feedback and trigger(s) for adaptation and ii) the actual modification of one or more characteristics of the multimedia stream. To achieve consistent QoE for video services, adaptive streaming techniques are used such that variations in resource availability can be matched by appropriate adaptation of the video stream. Such adaptation is realized using techniques such as caching [1] [2] [3], rate-adaptation, and buffer tuning. Rate adaptation techniques mainly employ three methods: 1) transcoding; 2) scalable encoding and 3) stream-switching. Transcoding [4] uses on-the-fly encoding of the raw content for varying the bit-rate of the stream to match the resource constraints. Scalable encoding relies upon scalable codecs for manipulating the streaming rate without re-encoding [5]. Stream-switching requires that multiple copies of the content is encoded at different rates and stored at the source [6]. The streaming server chooses the appropriately encoded stream depending on network quality and/or user feedback. There are many commercial implementations of adaptive streaming such as Adobe Dynamic HTTP Streaming, Apple HTTP Adaptive Streaming, and Microsoft Smooth Streaming.

Research in rate-adaptation has focused on quality feedback, determining resource availability and the adaptation logic. The adaptation approaches described in [7] [8] [9] focus primarily on matching the rate to available bandwidth. In [10], context-aware content adaptation for mobile devices is proposed. Context here refers to profile repositories, user preferences and real-time information such as network speed, connection protocol etc. The emphasis here is on one-time adaptation of content. In [11], the authors present an approach for content adaptation procedure for web-based mobile services by utilizing device capability databases and generic page transformation. Here, the focus is on web browsers and only device characteristics are considered. [12] takes a more holistic view of context and proposes a multi-dimensional adaptation framework. However, the approach is somewhat static since the decision on adaptation is taken at the beginning. Context-aware adaptation for ubiquitous web access is described in [13]. This uses a middleware for context-awareness along with an intermediary based architecture for content adaptation. The focus here is on device-centric adaptation of Web content. [14] proposes a context aware and resources aware dynamic service adaptation approach for a pervasive computing system device. The adaptation is applied to computing services in this case.

As the preceding discussion indicates, significant research efforts have been undertaken on service adaptation. However, the proposed methods are restrictive in terms of the type of context used, the type of service for adaptation that is supported and the type of adaptation. Furthermore, the notion of QoE is rarely mentioned in the context of service adaptation.

1.3 Our Contribution

We propose an elaborate context-aware framework for dynamic adaptation of services (particularly multimedia services). In particular, we focus on three aspects: a) multi-dimensional contexts b) model driven adaptation and c) operation under constraints to optimize end user QoE.

The rest of this paper is organized as follows. In Section 2, we present a model for analyzing services and evolving guidelines for context aware adaptations. Section 3 describes our framework to enable effective implementation of the model and Section 4 applies the same for multimedia services. In Section 5, we present details of a Proof-of-Concept implementation of the proposed framework. We conclude in Section 6, with pointers to future work.

2   A Model for Analyzing Context Aware Service Adaptation

Our key objective is to deliver optimal QoE to users under varying runtime conditions. As discussed in section 1, this can be achieved by dynamic adaptation of the service based on the current context. Towards this, we propose a model driven approach to analyze a service and evolve comprehensive guidelines for service adaptation under different constraints. We first present the key components of the model and then describe the approach for analyzing the service using the same.

The model comprises of two key components entities and functions. Entities describe the environment associated with the delivery of a service, along with the constraints under which service needs to be delivered. Functions define how the different entities can be combined for effective adaptation. Entities associated with a service are as follows:

a. *Domains:* Represent the participants/actors involved in the delivery of a service.
b. *Contexts:* Collection of information that together provides a comprehensive view of a domain. Information can be static and/or dynamic (varying during the course of service delivery).
c. *Actions:* Activities that can be executed by a domain that leads to appropriate adaptation of the service.

Figure 1 depicts the relation between the above defined entities as well as a sample representation for multimedia content delivery.

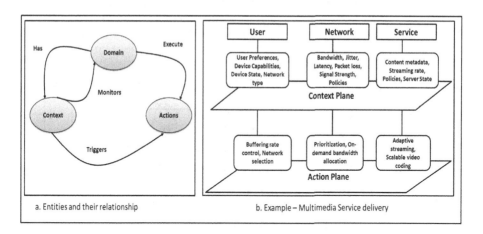

Fig. 1. Entities: Relationships and Example

Functions can be classified into those that provide information and those that process the same for effecting adaptation decisions.

a. Monitoring functions are responsible for continuously gathering information associated with the different contexts. A single function can monitor one or more contexts and provide specialized features like aggregation and selective notification.

b. Decision functions are responsible for detecting when a service needs to be adapted and recommending the appropriate action(s). Decision functions embed within themselves, the mapping between contexts and their impact on QoE as well as the possible sets of actions that can help in delivering the best possible end-user experience. They can also act as constraint enforcers, limiting the set of adaptations that are possible in a given instance based on current context.

We propose a 2-step approach, to arrive at the guidelines for adaptation. This is depicted in Figure 2 and the activities to be performed at each step are described below.

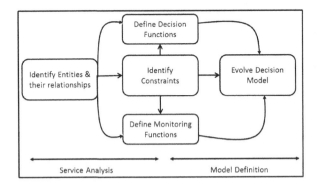

Fig. 2. Service analysis and model definition

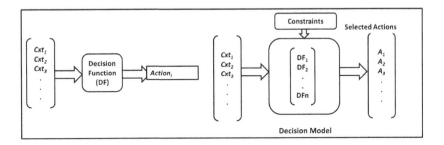

Fig. 3. Decision functions

a. *Service Analysis:* This involves identification of relevant entities and their relationships. These include domains participating in the service delivery, their associated contexts and actions. Also, for each action, the contexts whose variations can trigger the execution of the action are identified.

b. *Model Definition:* We propose representation of adaptation guidelines as decision models. A decision model incorporates within itself, a multitude of decision functions and intelligence about the triggers for execution of different decision function sequences. Figure 3 depicts the operation of a decision model. Triggers to the model are typically changes in context. The model specifies the decision function sequences to be executed for a given trigger. Decision models offer the flexibility of dynamic addition/removal of contexts from the model based on runtime constraints. The exact decision model depends on the monitoring and decision functions available for a given set of constraints.

3   An Implementation Framework for Context Aware Service Adaptation

In Section 2, we described a model for analyzing services and arriving at guidelines for service adaptation. Real world implementation of such a model would need to take into account different types of constraints including those related to contexts to be monitored (what and how) and the adaptation actions to be performed (what and who). Constraints can also include restrictions around domains accessible at runtime.As an example, we list below a few constraints or opportunities related to delivering multimedia content across different networks and devices.

- Service provider not having information about the state of mobile device and the last mile network through which the device is accessing the content.
- End users should be able to specify their preferences for the network(s) to be used while viewing specific type(s) of multimedia content.
- Where the end user device and the service provider infrastructure can collaborate, it should be possible to exploit the same to improve QoE.

From the above, it is clear that an effective adaptation solution should provide a high degree of flexibility when it comes to executing the different aspects of the model. We propose a framework with the following properties to address the requirements and constraints discussed so far.

- The framework consists of a set of loosely coupled components, each of them highly configurable and capable of independent operation.
- Interactions between components are event driven.
- End-to-end service adaptation is achieved by deploying instances of the framework across one or more participating domains.
- Each instance of the framework can be configured to a high level of granularity.

Figure 4 depicts our service adaptation framework. The different framework components are described below.

a. *Control Unit:* This is the brain of the framework. It is responsible for setting up and managing a framework instance. Key functions include, activation/deactivation of components, configuration of different components tuned to a specific implementation, monitoring the state of different components and enabling run-time control/re-configuration of individual components. It has direct access to all components in the framework via services published by each of the components.

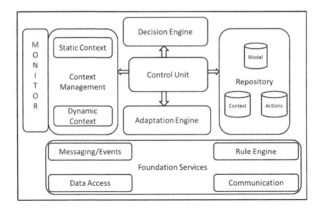

Fig. 4. Service Adaptation Framework

b. *Foundation Services:* The framework includes a set of common services that is required for effective functioning of the different components. These include a messaging service to enable exchange of information across components, a rule engine to support execution of decision functions, a uniform data access service to retrieve persistent information related to different components and a communication service to support information exchange between different framework instances running across domains.

c. *Context Manager & Monitor:* Contexts can be static (values are fixed) or dynamic (values can change at run-time). The context manager provides services for accessing static context and generates events notifying changes in the values of dynamic contexts. It supports switching on/off monitoring of specific contexts, selection of monitoring function for a specific context as well as controlling how monitored context needs to be reported. Reporting options include support for selective (based on pre-set conditions) reporting of context values.

d. *Decision Engine:* This component is responsible for loading and executing decision models. Decision models and their associated functions are represented as rule sets that can be dynamically executed based on received context change triggers.When an adaptation trigger is detected, this component will generate an event specifying the list of actions to be executed. Actions can include any of the following.
   - Adaptations that can be performed in the current domain.
   - Adaptations that need to be performed in a different domain.
   - Information that needs to be sent to another domain (where the decision model is being executed in a distributed fashion).

e. *Adaptation Engine:* The execution of actions selected by the decision engine is managed by this component. Implementation of actions will typically be platform specific. The adaptation engine interfaces with platform specific components to execute the selected action(s). For actions that are not associated with the current domain, it will send details of the adaptation trigger and recommended action(s) to the target domain (where it can be executed) using the communication services.

f. *Repository:* All persistent information associated with the service is managed through the repository. These include information pertaining to contexts, actions as well as the decision model.

Figure 5 depicts the flow of information between different components during initialization and processing of a change in context values. For clarity we have separated the monitor component from that of context manager.

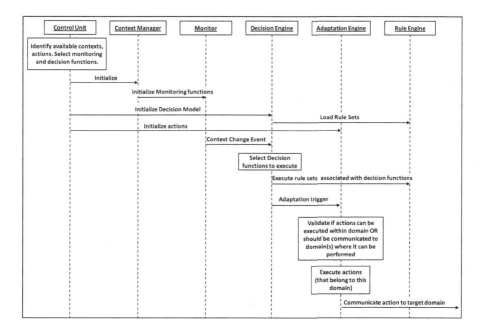

Fig. 5. Framework Message flow

4   Delivering Context Aware Multimedia Services

We now proceed to show how the model described in section 2 and the framework described in section 3 can be used to deliver multimedia streaming services over heterogeneous devices and networks with optimal QoE. We apply the 2-step approach presented in Figure 2 to arrive at the decision model that can be used for service adaptation.

a. *Service Analysis:* Figure 1 identifies the participating domains (User, Network and Service) as well as an indicative list of associated contexts and actions for multimedia delivery services. An analysis of the different contexts show that some of them (e.g. network state), can be monitored with different levels of granularity at all participating domains. Also, it is possible to exchange information about static context (e.g. device capabilities, content metadata) between the different domains.

b. *Model definition:* Here, we first identify the monitoring and decisions functions and then evolve the decision model based on the same. The decision model can be further refined based on constraints related to specific deployment scenarios.

The monitoring functions associated with the service include those related to device (CPU, Memory, Battery levels), network (Current connection type, Signal strength, session state (Jitter, Latency, Packet Loss), Available bandwidth) and server (CPU, Memory, Energy utilization, Server load (number of simultaneous streaming sessions))).

Decision functions are derived using a 3-step process:

a. Identifying the cause-effect relationship between the different contexts and the estimated as well as acceptable QoE.
b. Identifying the set of actions that can lead to best possible QoE in a given situation.
c. Using the above to identify trigger points for adaptation and the recommended actions.

The above process is iterative, beginning with individual contexts and their relationship to the QoE. Subsequently multiple related contexts are combined and their impact on QoE evaluated. For example, both network congestion and weak signal strength manifests as playout delays in the case of HTTP streaming. However the adaptation actions to be triggered in each of the cases are different. The decision function evaluates both signal strength and packet latency to decide on the required adaptation. Signal strength variations are handled by controlling the buffering rate at the user side. Congestion can be eased by switching to a lower bit rate video.

As discussed in section 3, in the real-world, context aware adaptation has to happen under different kinds of constraints. For example, in the case of multimedia services, based on how the service is delivered, the service provider may be able to control one or more of the participating domains. Constraints are handled in the following manner.

- Deriving the decision model that can operate within the stated constraints by adding/removing contexts, decision functions and associated actions.
- Leveraging the flexibility offered by the framework defined in section 3 to effectively implement the above across participating domains. This is depicted in Figure 6.

Figure 6a depicts how the framework components are distributed across domains when the adaptation decisions can be made only in the client.

Figure 6b describes the scenario where the user and service domains collaborate to deliver optimal QoE. Here both the monitoring and decision functions are distributed across the user and service domains. Also, the server can now use additional context information (e.g. policies, SLAs, server state information) to control how and where adaptations need to be done. In both the scenarios, the device can receive information about the content being streamed as application data. Information such as supported bit rates helps the decision model to limit the set of adaptations that can be performed.

Component	Features	Deployment Domain	Component	Features	Deployment Domain
Context Manager	User, Device, Content, Network	Client	Context Manager	User, Device, Network (Connection type, signal strength)	Client
Monitor	Device State Monitor, Network Connection Monitor, Network State Monitor	Client		Content, Network (jitter, latency, available bandwidth), Policy	Server
			Monitor	Device State Monitor, Network Connection Monitor	Client
Decision Engine	Decision model based on the selected context and available actions	Client		Network State Monitor	Server
			Decision Engine	Decision model split across client and server to enable localized decision making (e.g. control buffering rate based on signal strength)	Client and Server
Adaptation Engine	Vary Buffering Rate, Select Network	Client	Adaptation Engine	Vary Buffering Rate, Select Network	Client
	Vary streaming rate	Server		Vary streaming rate	Server
a. Client side adaptation			b. Client and Server side adaptation		

Fig. 6. Sample Framework configurations

5   Proof of Concept Implementation

We now describe a proof of concept (PoC) application developed using the framework described in Section 3. The PoC demonstrates a sample multimedia service operating in a constrained environment. It enables users to search and access video content over web using mobile devices with the following constraints.

- The service should support mobile devices running android version 2.2 or higher.
- Video content is hosted on a third party hosting infrastructure that supports APIs to dynamically switch the video bit rate of the served content through APIs.
- Metadata about the content is available in a locally hosted web server.
- The service should be accessible over a range of devices (with different resolutions) and access networks (WiFi/3G/4G).

The need to deliver content over web restricts the possible adaptation to that of varying the video bit rate using APIs provided by the video hosting infrastructure. Also, Android OS restricts network state monitoring to only detection of network type change and transmit/receive statistics.

Applying the steps described in section 2, we evolved a decision model subject to constraints specified above. The associated decision functions can be categorized as those triggered during startup and continuously at runtime.

a. Startup functions determine the initial video quality (and hence the corresponding bit-rate) using the static context associated with device (e.g. form factor, resolution) and current network type (WiFi/3G/4G).
b. Run-time functions are selected based on corresponding context change triggers. These include decision functions to handle changes in network type and available bandwidth, variations in traffic arrival patterns and video playout state changes (e.g. Seek, Pause, Resume).

The model is implemented using the framework presented in section 3. Given the above described constraints, the framework is largely implemented on the client side. However, the actual adaptation function is distributed across client and server, with the client invoking the requests to change video bit rate and the server performing the actual switch. A logical view of the implemented system is presented in Figure 7.

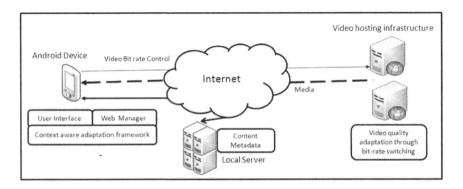

Fig. 7. System Description

The local server holds information about the content (metadata) that is being served. The PoC has three major client side components:

a. User Interface interacts with the local server to enable end-users to search and select video to view.
b. Web Manager interacts with the video hosting infrastructure to fetch and render the video. It also sends video bit rate change requests to the server based on triggers from the adaptation engine.
c. Framework components responsible for monitoring context and triggering appropriate adaptations.
   - *Monitoring:* Static context information is fetched at the beginning of the session. These include device capabilities as well as content metadata. We register receivers with the Android operating system to detect network change events (e.g. switching from 3G to WiFi). Available bandwidth is estimated by continuously monitoring application specific network traffic statistics. Arrival traffic patterns are deduced based on the variance in traffic statistics.

- *Decision engine:* Decision model is represented as rule sets and executed using a rule engine.
- *Adaptation engine:* Triggers appropriate events in the web manager which in turn triggers video bit rate changes by the server.

The User Interface and Web Manager components are implemented as native Android activities. The framework is implemented as a service invoked when the user selects a video to view.

The effectiveness of adaptation was verified using the following tests. The tests were started after the user selects the content to view.

a. Changing the network from WiFi to 3G and vice-versa.
b. Continuously varying the available bandwidth (e.g. throttle bandwidth to 256kbps, increase the same to 512kbps and then to 1Mbps and so on).
c. Use devices with different form factors and resolutions (e.g. HTC Desire S (480x800) and HTC Explorer (320x480)).

For each test, we observed the variations in QoE when compared to a system without adaptation. This is measured as a function of variation in number of times the player moved between buffering and playing. Larger the number, lower the QoE as user experience is impacted by frequent buffering. The expected adaptation triggers were verified with actual adaptations.

Figure 8 and Figure 9 depict the QoE as a function of variation in buffering in 2 different scenarios. Figure 8 depicts the scenario where bandwidth is varied as per the following sequence (Normal 300kbps 512 kbps 300kbps 512kbps). Bandwidth was maintained at each level in the sequence for a period of 5 minutes. Figure 9 depicts the performance under consistently low bandwidth (256kbps). As we can see, in both cases, introducing adaptation smoothens out the playout leading to an improved QoE.

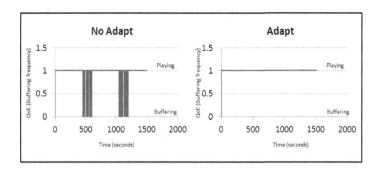

Fig. 8. Buffering under varying bandwidth

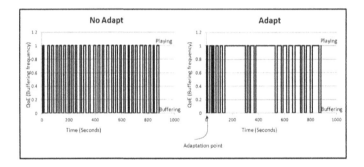

Fig. 9. Buffering under low bandwidth

6   Conclusions

This paper presents an approach to analyze services and evolve guidelines for adaptation to optimize end user QoE. We also described a generic framework to enable effective implementation of the adaptation model. As a specific case, we presented a context-aware service adaptation framework for multimedia service delivery over heterogeneous wireless networks and devices. The objective of such adaptation is to provide a consistent QoE to the end user while making the most efficient use of resources in heterogeneous networking environment characterized by wide diversity in access network characteristics and device capabilities.

To demonstrate the framework, we have implemented a PoC which shows how the key characteristics (bitrate, resolution etc) of a video stream can be modified on the fly in response to change in network bandwidth and/or device handover. This is realized with the help of a context monitor which provides feedback to the adaptation engine located at the server side.

This work is currently being applied in a pilot project for the National Program on Technology Enhanced Learning (NPTEL) [15], an initiative of the Indian government to promote e-learning using videos of lectures by faculty at different IITs (Indian Institute of Technology). Work is also underway to enhance the model to enable multi-modal communications and information delivery in disaster management systems.

Acknowledgments. This research is funded by the Indo-UK Advanced Technology Centre (IU-ATC), a research initiative funded jointly by the Department of Science and Technology (DST) in India and the Engineering and Physical Sciences Research Council (EPSRC) in UK. We would also like to acknowledge Ms. Naga Jyothi for her efforts in implementing parts of the PoC.

References

1. Goebbels, S.: Smart Caching for Supporting Video Streaming in Heterogeneous Wireless Networks. In: Proceedings of the 11th International Symposium on Wireless Personal Multimedia Communications (2008)

2. Gomaa, H., Messier, G., Davies, R., Williamson, C.: Media Caching Support for Mobile Transit Clients. In: Proceedings of the IEEE International Conference on Wireless and Mobile Computing, Networking and Communications (2009)
3. Lee, S.J., Ma, W.-Y., Shen, B.: An interactive video delivery and caching system using video summarization. Elsevier Computer Communication Journal (2002)
4. Xin, J., Lin, C.-W., Sun, M.-T.: Digital Video Transcoding. Proceedings of the IEEE 93(1) (January 2005)
5. Schwarz, H., Marpe, D., Wiegand, T.: Overview of the Scalable Video Coding Extension of the H.264/AVC Standard. IEEE Transactions on Circuits and Systems for Video Technology 17(9) (September 2007)
6. Zambelli, A.: IIS smooth streaming technical overview. Microsoft Corporation (2009)
7. De Cicco, L., Mascolo, S., Palmisano, V.: Feedback Control for Adaptive Live Video Streaming. In: Proceedings of the Second Annual ACM Conference on Multimedia Systems (2011)
8. Tappayuthpijarn, K., Liebl, G., Stockhammer, T., Steinbach, E.: Adaptive video streaming over a mobile network with TCP-friendly rate control. In: Proceedings of the 2009 International Conference on Wireless Communications and Mobile Computing: Connecting the World Wirelessly (2009)
9. Balk, A., Gerla, M., Maggiorini, D., Sanadidi, M.Y.: Adaptive video streaming: pre-encoded MPEG-4 with bandwidth scaling. Computer Networks 44(4) (2004)
10. Lemlouma, T., Layada, N.: Context-Aware Adaptation for Mobile Devices. In: Proc. IEEE Int. Conf. on Mobile Data Management (2004)
11. Schmohl, R., Baumgarten, U., Kothner, L.: Content Adaptation for Heterogeneous Mobile Devices using web-based Mobile Services. In: Proceedings of MoMM (2007)
12. Attou, A., Moessner, K.: Context-Aware Service Adaptation Management. In: Proceedings of the IEEE International Symposium on Personal, Indoor and Mobile Radio Communications (2007)
13. Malandrino, D., Mazzoni, F., Riboni, D., Bettini, C., Colajanni, M., Scarano, V.: MIMOSA: context-aware adaptation for ubiquitous web access. Journal of Personal and Ubiquitous Computing 14(4), 301–320
14. Miraoui, M., Tadj, C., Fattahi, J., Ben Amar, C.: Dynamic Context-Aware and Limited Resources-Aware Service Adaptation for Pervasive Computing. Advances in Software Engineering (2011)
15. National Programme on Technology Enhanced Learning, http://www.nptel.iitm.ac.in

Tracommender – Exploiting Continuous Background Tracking Information on Smartphones for Location-Based Recommendations

Yang Wang, Abdulbaki Uzun, Ulrich Bareth, and Axel Küpper

Telekom Innovation Laboratories, TU Berlin, Service-centric Networking
wangyang.tub@gmail.com, abdulbaki.uzun@telekom.de,
ulrich.bareth|axel.kuepper@tu-berlin.de
http://www.snet.tu-berlin.de/

Abstract. In this paper, we propose *Tracommender*, a context-aware recommender system, which uses background tracking information from smartphones to generate location-based recommendations. Based on the automatically collected data that consist of locations with timestamps, the dwell time at certain locations can be derived in order to use it as an implicit rating for a location-based collaborative filtering. We further introduce two alternative path matching algorithms that utilize continuous location sequences (paths) to compute path patterns between similar users. In addition, in order to overcome the cold-start problem of recommender systems, clustering algorithms are used to calculate so-called *Activity Zones* - locations taken from an existing database of categorized points of interest. Synthesized movement data has been applied to perform evaluations on performance, scalability and precision of an implemented prototype of the proposed recommendation algorithms.

Keywords: location-based services, background tracking, recommendations, path matching.

1 Introduction

With the increasing number of location-based services, context-aware recommender systems become more and more relevant when recommending content items, such as products, restaurants or shops. Contextual data (e.g., location, time of day or weather) is a promising information source to exploit in order to generate more precise recommendations that do not only fit to a user's profile and ratings given to those content items by a community, but also on the contextual situation the user is in.

However, not all kinds of content items are suitable for context-based recommendations. Moreover, the automatic detection of some context parameters (e.g., the mood of a user or companions) turns out to be very difficult (or sometimes impossible) and can only be integrated in the form of manual input, such as a

C. Borcea et al. (Eds.): MobilWare 2012, LNICST 65, pp. 250–263, 2013.

scrollbar where users can adjust the "mood" of a song [1]. Due to the possibility of users providing false information, these types of manual input are no reliable information sources and the scenarios in which those context data is used, seem not very applicable in real business services. Another aspect is that context is often treated as a single and static piece of information, it is not considered as a continuous sequence. However, the former and latter pieces of information in a context sequence may also be useful in order to determine a user's intention.

The location information, on the other hand, is the most important context that fulfills the requirements mentioned above and is therefore very suitable when creating context-aware location-based recommendations. It can be determined in an accurate manner utilizing smartphones and positioning methods like Cell ID, WiFi and GPS [2] making it trustworthy and automatically detectable. Using background tracking data generated by mobile devices as a reliable, relevant and constant information source, a history of user paths (location sequences) can be calculated and used in the recommendation process, which might give a hint on which locations a user might be interested when taking a certain path. Each location on a path can also be enriched by context information that is directly derived by the location information like the location dwell time or weather, in order to provide much more precise recommendations.

In this paper, we propose *Tracommender*, a novel context-aware location-based recommender system that utilizes background tracking information collected by mobile devices via a crowd-sourcing approach in order to provide location recommendations. The system incorporates a hybrid approach including a location-based collaborative filtering algorithm, two alternative path matching methods and an innovative concept of *Activity Zones* to overcome the cold-start problem [3].

The remainder of the paper is organized as follows: First, an overview about related work in the area of context-aware and location-based recommender systems is presented. Section 3 describes the concept of *Tracommender*, including the location-based collaborative filtering method based on location dwell time frequencies, the two alternative path matching approaches, the innovative concept of *Activity Zones* for tackling the cold-start problem and the system architecture. A performance evaluation is done in Section 4, whereas the last section concludes the paper.

2   Related Work

In a world of information overload, recommender systems filter relevant information and provide personalized content item recommendations to users based on their personal background, preferences and interests. Numerous recommendation methods were designed over the years to enhance the preciseness of recommendations. Besides the content-based algorithm, collaborative filtering is one of the most well-known and established recommendation methods [4].

Collaborative filtering uses the previously rated items of a user community as a basis in order to predict content items to the active user. The user-based collaborative filtering approach utilizes the ratings of the active user and the ratings of other users in order to compute similarities between them. The items of the similar users are then recommended to the active user. In order to increase the performance and quality of user-based collaborative recommendations, Sarwar et al. [5] introduced an item-based collaborative filtering approach. The main idea of this method is that instead of detecting similar users, the similarity of items is calculated based on the ratings given by different users. Two items are considered more similar the more users have rated both of them. After identifying the most similar items, the weighted average of the active user's ratings on these items is used to calculate predictions. Similarities between users or items are measured by using two alternative equations, the *Pearson Correlation Coefficient* and the *Cosine Similarity* measure, which are adopted in Section 3.1.

Traditional recommendation approaches solely focus on recommending items to users without considering the context the user is in. However, thinking of mobile applications and especially location-based services, the contextual situation of a user is an essential factor for providing relevant recommendations. Contextual information can support recommender systems in three possible phases: During the preparation phase, the contextual situation serves as conditions for information filtering, such as in the works of Baltrunas et al., who propose a context-aware item splitting approach for collaborative filtering [6] and the "best context" for music recommendations [1]. In the second phase, context is regarded as a special item processed and filtered by recommendation approaches, such as in the paper of Domingues et al., who use contextual information as virtual items on recommender systems [7]. Finally, during the phase of presenting results, context works as a post-filter to correct inappropriate recommendation results, as proposed by De Carolis et al. [8].

The location information as the most important context is utilized in many previous works like *CityVoyager* [9], *TouristGuide* [10], *Shopper's Eye* [11] or `foursquare.com` in order to provide location-based recommendations. But location is only regarded as a static piece of information independent from other context. None of these approaches recognize the spatial and chronological continuity of the whole context or uses the whole sequence of historical location and other contextual information to derive habits and dependencies. Here, background tracking could be of immense use by continuously recording location information and other context data over time to improve the overall quality of recommendations.

3   Concept of the Tracommender

In this section, we propose our concept called *Tracommender*, which is a portmanteau out of the two words *tracker* and *recommender*. The first word *tracker* describes that background information, such as location and context data is continuously being collected and used for *recommendations*, which is the second word with a rather obvious meaning.

Tracommender uses a hybrid recommendation process including a location-based collaborative filtering algorithm that determines the similarity of users in terms of the locations they have visited. In addition, the system provides two alternative path matching approaches, the *adjacency matrix* and *minimum distance matching* algorithms, which identify path patterns out of historical paths of the nearest neighbours computed by the location-based collaborative filtering method and the current path of the user in order to predict future locations on his current path. The third component of the hybrid approach comprises the concept of *Activity Zones* that define areas clustered by geographic regions offering similar places in high density. The *Activity Zones* tackle the cold-start problem of *Tracommender* when lacking a critical number of path information in the initial phase in order to be able to generate precise recommendations. Last but not least, the system architecture used for the implementation is presented.

3.1   Location-Based Collaborative Filtering

Tracommender uses path similarities calculated out of historical paths in order to predict locations that might be of interest for a user on his current path. Those historical paths can either be generated by the user himself or by other people. Taking only the paths of the active user as a basis for recommendations might produce results that fit to the user's personal movement patterns. However, the amount of candidate paths considered in the recommendation process will be limited. Extending the data basis for recommendation calculation by all paths of all users available will provide more paths, but will weaken the correlation between the user's current path and the historical paths of others.

In order to combine both approaches and determine only paths of those users relevant to the active user, collaborative filtering is utilized as a preperation for the path matching algorithms. Generally, in collaborative filtering, users who rate items similarly are considered as being nearest neighbours. We adopted this paradigm, so that we can collect all users in a set of neareast neighbours that share the same location preferences as the active user. The paths of those neighbours are then used when generating path patterns via the path matching algorithms.

Collaborative filtering usually works with numerical rating values when calculating recommendations. A high numerical rating value represents a user's strong interest towards a certain content item. Locations can also be seen as content items that can be rated. Therefore, we exploited the users' dwell time on specific locations (being a context parameter that is directly derived by the location information) as implicit and automatic feedback to indicate their personal interests and preferences for certain locations. If we consider a user's dwell time on a single location as an implicit rating given by this user to this location, we can construct a *user-location-dwell-time-frequency matrix* similar to a *user-item-rating matrix*, which is used within the collaborative filtering algorithm.

Based on the definition of *term frequency (TF)* [4], which is defined as the result of dividing the occurrence count of a term in a document by the total number of terms in the document, we can define the dwell time frequency $f_{u,l}$ of user u on location l as the result of dividing the sum of dwell times on location l by the sum of dwell times on all locations belonging to the location set $L(l \in L)$, i.e.,

$$f_{u,l} = \frac{S_l}{\sum_{k \in L} S_k} = \frac{\sum_{t=T_1}^{T_2} n_{t,l}}{\sum_{k \in L} \sum_{t=T_1}^{T_2} n_{t,k}} \tag{1}$$

where S_k is the sum of dwell times on location k. T_1 and T_2 denote the starting and ending time of a given time period; $t = \{T_1, \ldots, T_2\}$, on the other hand, denotes a specified point of time during the given time period. The interval and unit of the time period can range from seconds to minutes, which depends on the accuracy of the tracking unit of the system. $n_{t,l}$ is a binary value: $n_{t,l} = 1$ if and only if user u was at location l at moment t, otherwise $n_{t,l} = 0$. Equation (1) indicates that the longer a user has accumulatively stayed at a location than other locations during a time period, the higher rating the user gives to the location. Assume a set of users $U = \{1, \ldots, m\}$ and a location set $L = \{1, \ldots, n\}$ existing in the database, the *user-location-dwell-time-frequency matrix* M can be expressed as:

$$M = \{f_{u,l} | u = \{1, \ldots, m\} \text{ and } l = \{1, \ldots, n\}\} \tag{2}$$

The similarity of two users a and b can be calculated with the *Pearson Correlation Coefficient Similarity* or *Cosine Similarity* measure [4]. In the case of dwell time frequency, the two similarity equations are adapted and expressed as

$$sim(a, b) = \frac{\sum_{l \in L} (f_{a,l} - \overline{f_a})(f_{b,l} - \overline{f_b})}{\sqrt{\sum_{l \in L} (f_{a,l} - \overline{f_a})^2} \sqrt{\sum_{l \in L} (f_{b,l} - \overline{f_b})^2}} \tag{3}$$

$$sim(a, b) = cos(\boldsymbol{a}, \boldsymbol{b}) = \frac{\boldsymbol{a} \cdot \boldsymbol{b}}{\|\boldsymbol{a}\| \times \|\boldsymbol{b}\|} = \frac{\sum_{l \in L} f_{a,l} f_{b,l}}{\sqrt{\sum_{l \in L} f_{a,l}^2} \sqrt{\sum_{l \in L} f_{b,l}^2}} \tag{4}$$

where $\overline{f_a}$ and $\overline{f_b}$ denote the average dwell time frequency of users a and b on all locations. Having the similarities computed between each user, the historical paths of the nearest neighbours can be used in the path matching process.

In comparison to explicit ratings given by users, the dwell time frequency has several advantages in terms of credibility and density. First, the dwell time frequency is automatically derived from background tracking information making it a very reliable information source. Secondly, users are not required to rate locations manually. This also ensures reliability due to the fact that it is not guaranteed that users will provide true rating values. Furthermore, it supports the user experience, because users are not asked to give ratings all the time at each location on their path. In addition, it tackles the sparsity problem [4] of collaborative filtering, since the automatically calculated dwell time frequency guarantees a high number of ratings (in comparison to the number of manually given ratings), which is essential for a recommendation algorithm to work accurately. Finally, the implicitly given feedback reflects factual interests of the users rather than a subjective opinion in the form of explicit feedback (user a and b may like a location equally, but rate it differently). Depending on the time spent on a location, the frequency of favourite places will have a higher rating than places temporarily visited by them. However, one drawback of this approach is that it is not distinguished between places that are really favoured by users and places where they are "forced" to spend much time like workplaces. This problem will be addressed in the near future by integrating semantic information (e.g., ontologies about location classification) and a mixture of explicit/implicit feedback into the recommendation process.

The location-based collaborative filtering algorithm enables *Tracommender* to provide location recommendations to a user based on the opinions of like-minded users in the community. Theoretically, this recommendation method can work as a stand-alone service in the system. Having a database with users, locations and the ratings given to those locations computed by the dwell time frequency, the system can provide location recommendations to a user independent from the current path he is on. However, since *Tracommender* does not only care about single locations, but also about sequences of locations, the results provided by the collaborative filtering algorithm are integrated into the path matching process, which is described in Subsection 3.2.

3.2   Path Matching Algorithms

The nearest neighbours computed using the location-based collaborative filtering algorithm build the basis for the path matching approaches described in this section. The *adjacency matrix matching* and *minimum distance matching* algorithms are utilized to find path patterns between the paths of the nearest neighbours and the current path of the active user. These path patterns help to predict the movement of the user in order to recommend him locations that he might like to visit on his path.

Depending on the data model, two different methods can be used. If the location sequences are modeled in a list fashion, their similarity can be expressed as the distance between those two, which is calculated with our minumum distance implementation. Another way to compute the similarity of location sequences is by expressing them as paths in adjacency matrices as explained below.

Adjacency Matrix Matching. Given a finite directed graph, an adjacency matrix is a boolean square matrix that represents the directed edges between vertices of the graph. The edges $E_{i,j}$ of a path P can be expressed as 1 when there is an existing (directed) connection between the vertix i and vertix j and 0 otherwise.

$$E_{i,j} = \begin{cases} 1, (V_i, V_j) \\ 0, (V_i, V_j) \end{cases} \tag{5}$$

The directed graphs of the two paths $P = \{p_1, \ldots, p_m\}$ and $Q = \{q_1, \ldots, q_n\}$ are modeled as G_p and G_q. The adjacency matrix of graph G_p can be expressed as:

$$A = \{a_{i,j}|i,j \in P;\ a_{i,j} = E_{i,j}\} \tag{6}$$

where $a_{i,j} = 1$ when a directed edge (i,j) exists in graph G_p, which is the case when location i can be reached from location j within path P; and $a_{i,j} = 0$ if the directed edge (i,j) does not exist. The adjacency matrix of graph G_q is defined the same way. If the two paths contain different locations, they have to be modeled and matched in a collective set of locations $S = P \cup Q$. Equation 6 can be rewritten as follows:

$$A = \{a_{i,j}|i,j \in S;\ a_{i,j} = E_{i,j}\} \tag{7}$$

where A is a square matrix of dimension k-by-k and $k = |S|$ is the cardinality of set S. The exclusive-or matrix D out of adjacency matrix A of path P and adjacency matrix B of path Q is generated with the logical operation exclusive disjunction on each pair of counterpart entries of the two adjacency matrices, i.e.,

$$D = A \oplus B = \{d_{i,j}|d_{i,j} = a_{i,j} \oplus b_{i,j}\} \tag{8}$$

which represents how many exclusive-or relations the two matrices have in common. Thus, the similarity between the two paths through adjacency matrix matching is defined as:

$$sim(P,Q) = sim(A,B) = 1 - \frac{\sum_{d \in D} d}{\sum_{a \in A} a + \sum_{b \in B} b} \tag{9}$$

The two paths share all their path segments with each other if the similarity equals one, thus they are said to be structurally the same. The two paths are independent if the similarity equals zero.

Example: Two paths $P:\ a \to b \to c \to b$ and $Q:\ b \to a \to c \to b$ are shown in Figure 1a, where a, b, c describe locations or vertices on the path with the grey node as starting point. The adjacency matrices of P and Q and their exclusive-or matrix are expressed as:

$$\mathbf{A} = \begin{pmatrix} 0\ 1\ 0 \\ 0\ 0\ 1 \\ 0\ 1\ 0 \end{pmatrix} \quad \mathbf{B} = \begin{pmatrix} 0\ 0\ 1 \\ 1\ 0\ 0 \\ 0\ 1\ 0 \end{pmatrix} \quad \mathbf{D} = \mathbf{A} \oplus \mathbf{B} = \begin{pmatrix} 0\ 1\ 1 \\ 1\ 0\ 1 \\ 0\ 0\ 0 \end{pmatrix} \tag{10}$$

Acording to equation 9, the similarity of the adjacency matrices is

$$sim(A,B) = 1 - 4/6 = 1/3 \tag{11}$$

Since an adjacency matrix can represent the relations of vertices, it also holds for a mathematical expression of directed graphs. By comparing two adjacency matrices, their similarity can be calculated, which expresses how many numbers of locations two paths have in common in relation to the total number of their locations. Although sometimes, even if two paths do not have any location in common, their locations might be geographically close to each other. An example are the two paths in Figure 1b, which would have a similarity result of 0 when computed with adjacency matrix matching, because they share no common location. But the two paths seem to be quite similar. Therefore, another path matching method capable of measuring the geographical distance between paths of different locations is presented in the following.

Minimum Distance Matching. To also express the similarity of nearby paths that have no locations in common, minimum distance matching selects the nearest paths from a set of known candidates for an object path by calculating the sum of the minimum distances. The distance of a point to a candidate path is defined as the minimal euclidean distance from the point to every point on the path. In Figure 1b, for example, the points a, b, c, d, e on the object path have the best similarity to f, g, h, i, j on the candidate path, when the sum of their minimal euclidean distances is smaller than the sum of other candidate paths. If the sum of these distances from each point on the object path to the candidate path is shorter than to other paths, then the candidate path is regarded as the nearest path to the object path.

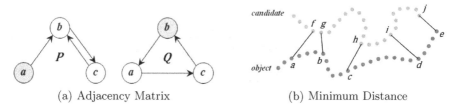

(a) Adjacency Matrix   (b) Minimum Distance

Fig. 1. Path Matching Algorithm Examples

Two locations $p = (x_1, y_1)$ and $q = (x_2, y_2)$, with x_1 and x_2 as longitude, y_1 and y_2 as latitude, when neglecting height and the spherical equation of the earth's surface for simplicity and scalability reasons, the distance between the two locations can be described by the Euclidean distance:

$$d(p, q) = \sqrt{(x_1 - x_2)^2 + (y_1 - y_2)^2} \tag{12}$$

Given an object path $P = \{p_1, \ldots, p_m\}$ and a candidate path $Q = \{q_1, \ldots, q_n\}$, for each $p_i \in P$ there is a set $\{d(p_i, q)| \ q \in Q\}$ resembling the collection of distances from p_i to every point on the path Q. The sum of the minimum distances from P to Q is defined as

$$MD(P, Q) = \sum_{i=1}^{m} min\{d(p_i, q)| \ q \in Q\}$$

$$= \sum_{i=1}^{m} min\{d(p_i, q_1), \ldots, d(p_i, q_n)\} \tag{13}$$

where $p_i \in P$ and min is a function returning the minimum value in a set.

The sum of the minimum distances is inverse to their similarity meaning that the smaller the sum of minimum distances of two paths are, the more similar they are. The algorithm can be repeated for several candidate paths to find the nearest or most similar paths.

While *adjacency matrix* is stronger related to the structural similarity of two location paths or sequences, the *minimum distance* expresses geographical similarity or proximity of two graphs.

3.3   Activity Zones

Recommender systems inherently suffer from the cold-start problem [3], which basically means that no recommendations can be calculated as long as no relevant data exists yet. Therefore, *Activity Zones* can be created to overcome the cold-start problem for location-based recommendations by clustering existing locations for certain categories of interest.

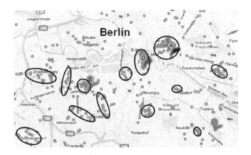

Fig. 2. Shopping Activity Zones in Berlin

Activity Zones are created by applying clustering methods to databases of locations with the same categories like restaurants, shops or theaters. For this purpose, several clustering methods have been analyzed. Nonhierarchical methods are not effective due to the fact that the number of clusters is not known beforehand. Furthermore, a maximum distance and cluster density has to be specified to not generate clusters, which are too big or incoherent. Therefore, the complete linkage or average linkage method has been chosen to create the desired *Activity Zones* of *Tracommender*.

In this way, users' locations are classified to certain categories and recommendations for other locations of the same category can be made. Figure 2 shows the resulting clusters of shopping locations in Berlin on *Google Maps*. Note that not circles but ellipses are used to more accurately describe the clusters.

3.4   System Architecture

Tracommender's system architecture contains several primary components as described in the previous sections working in an offline and an online phase. The three different blocks (see Figure 3) reflect the major steps in the recommendation process. During the *Crowd-Sourcing Phase*, mainly location data is collected continuously in a background process on the users' mobile terminals. Based on a certain time interval, it is aggregated and sent to the *Tracking Sequence Database* where additional context like dwell time at certain locations are extracted during the *Offline Phase*. The *Location-based Collaborative Filtering* algorithm detects nearest neighbours based on the dwell time frequency of locations, which is then used in the *Path Matching* process. In addition, clustering is being performed in order to create *Activity Zones*. In the *Online Phase*, locations of an *Activity Zone* are recommended if the system detects that the user is in or near to such a cluster. Otherwise, locations are recommended based on the *Path Matching* algorithms.

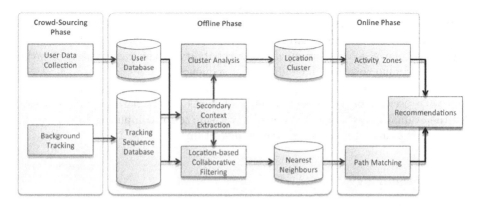

Fig. 3. Tracommender - System Architecture

4 Evaluation

The recommendation approach proposed in this paper is evaluated against precision and performance of the recommendation results computed by the path matching algorithms based on a critical mass of user, location and path information obtained by mobile devices and background tracking information. Since we were currently not able to run a real field test with a big number of mobile devices in a crowd-sourcing approach, we created a simulated crowd-sourcing database including user, location and path information for evaluation and demonstration of our proof-of-concept.

4.1 Simulated Crowd-Sourcing Data

The simulated crowd-sourcing database that is created in order to evaluate the recommendation approaches and algorithms proposed in this paper, consists of 50 users, 240 factual locations obtained from *Google Maps*, and 3837 pieces of background tracking information generated with our *Crowd-sourced Path Simulation Algorithm*. This algorithm is designed to create personalized path records.

For this purpose, a number of locations are marked as publicly favourite places of all users in the user community simulating common location preferences of a group of users. In another step, other locations are appointed as privately favourite places of each single user representing personal preferences. The simulated paths for each user are composed by selecting random locations where the favourite places (private and public) have a higher probability to occur in those paths. These randomly created paths are then rearranged according to their distance to the former point in order to avoid having "senseless" paths. By doing so, each point is followed by a relatively close point on the path, which refers to the *nearest destination first* scheduling policy.

Using the simulated personalized path patterns created by the *Crowd-sourced Path Simulation Algorithm*, the quantity and quality of the nearest neighbours computed by the location-based collaborative filtering algorithm is increased. A high number of similar users are measured due to the fact that a lot of users share publicly favourite places on their path and also several privately favourite places. Furthermore, through the *nearest destination first* scheduling policy, paths are formed regularly, which minimizes the probability of the case that two paths including similar locations have dissimilar sequences.

There are approximately 1000 paths in the database with different lengths and with users having different number of paths. These paths build the basis for the evaluation, which is done by a server-side script computing the precision and running time of the path matching algorithms.

4.2 Methodology

The following methodology is applied for the evaluation:

1. Perform location-based collaborative filtering, build a nearest neighbour list for each user.
2. Select a user and let him be the current user.
3. Create a set of candidate paths from the historical paths of the user and his neighbours.
4. Select one path from the user's historical path records in the database.
5. Assume the length of this path is n. Take its first $n - 1$ points and build a new path with these points. Appoint the new path as the object path.
6. Perform path matching approaches with the object path and the set of candidate paths.
7. Compare the recommendation result produced in step 6 with the nth point on the path processed in step 5. If the result indicates the same functional category of locations, the recommendation is correct, otherwise it is wrong.
8. Accumulate the number of correct recommendations and the total number.
9. Return to step 4 until all paths have been selected once.
10. Return to step 2 until all users have been selected once.
11. Report the final precision and running time.

The precision is defined as the result of dividing the number of correct recommendations by the total number of recommendations, i.e.,

$$precision = \frac{|correct\ recommendations|}{|recommendations|} \qquad (14)$$

The hardware and software configuration used during the evaluation is: AMD Phenom II X2 560 3.20 GHz CPU, 3GB RAM, Microsoft Windows XP Professional with Service Pack 3, Apache HTTP Server 2.2.17, PHP 5.3.6 and MySQL 5.5.10.

The evaluation function is performed with each path matching approach alternately in five groups of work load including the quantity of 135, 288, 431, 581 and 696 recommendation tasks. The precision and running time of each group of work load is recorded and illustrated in the form of line charts.

4.3   Results

Figure 4 illustrates the precision of the path matching approaches. *AM* denotes *adjacency matrix matching* algorithm, whereas *MD* stands for *minimum distance matching*. *HA* is the hybrid approach through which recommendations are the logical conjunction of the results produced by the two path matching approaches.

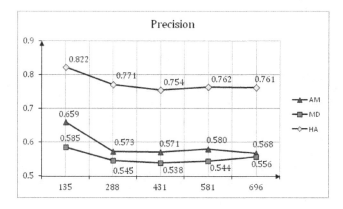

Fig. 4. Path Matching Algorithms - Precision Comparison

The chart shows that *AM* exceeds *MD* in precision. The reason is that *AM* is applied among the paths, which share a majority of path segments (connections between locations) with each other, whereas *MD* is performed even among the paths, which have no shared location. Therefore, the correlation between the paths of *AM* is stronger than that of *MD*. Nevertheless, the performance of the two approaches is not satisfactory enough when being applied individually. In addition, it is also found that when the current path is too short, e.g., containing one or two locations, the *AM* cannot work, because it needs at least two points on a path to build matrices and an extra point to make a prediction. *MD*, on the other hand, works as usual in that case. Combining both approaches in one recommendation procedure in a hybrid approach, the precision can be significantly enhanced and the drawbacks can be overcome, which indicates that the two approaches complement each other very well. In other words, when *AM* does not perform acceptably caused by lacking shared path segments between two paths, *MD* could replace it for continuous services, and vice versa.

In Figure 5, the running time of the path matching approaches are presented.

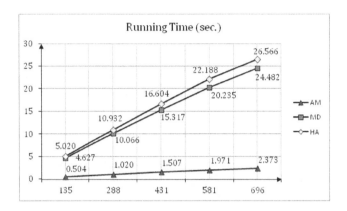

Fig. 5. Path Matching Algorithms - Running Time Comparison

The *AM* approach also performs better than *MD* in efficiency, due to the fact that the *AM* algorithm has lower time complexity of $O(n)$, while the *MD* algorithm with two nested loops has higher time complexity of $O(n^2)$, where n denotes the length of paths. Furthermore, *AM* measures similarity with logical operations, whereas *MD* computes geographical distance with latitudes, longitudes, and trigonometric functions. The running time of the hybrid approach appears to be lesser than the sum of the time of the two single approaches. Considering its precision, the hybrid approach can be regarded as an efficient solution.

The results of testing the recommendation approaches showed that the personalized path patterns produced by the *Crowd-sourced Path Simulation Algorithm* have enhanced the performance of *Tracommender*. The precision of the recommendation approaches computed with personalized path patterns expressed a little superiority over the one computed with random path patterns. Even though the personalized simulating algorithm can be more optimized, we will focus on utilizing personal path information from real users in a future evaluation.

5   Conclusion

In this paper, we proposed a location-based recommender system called *Tracommender* that exploits background tracking data in order to generate location recommendations. The evaluation shows the feasibility of the concept and very promising results regarding precision and performance. However, more evaluation needs to be performed, especially on real world background tracking data from actual smartphones. In addition, more contextual information can be considered and classified in order to recognize more complex dependencies for improved recommendations.

References

1. Baltrunas, L., Kaminskas, M., Ricci, F., Rokach, L., Shapira, B., Luke, K.-H.: Best Usage Context Prediction for Music Tracks. In: Proceedings of the 2nd Workshop on Context-Aware Recommender Systems, Barcelona, Spain (2010)
2. Bareth, U., Küpper, A.: Energy-Efficient Position Tracking in Proactive Location-based Services for Smartphone Environments. In: Proceedings of the IEEE 35th Annual Computer Software and Applications Conference, Munich, Germany, pp. 516–521. IEEE (2011)
3. Lam, X.N., Vu, T., Le, T.D., Duong, A.D.: Addressing Cold-Start Problem in Recommendation Systems. In: Proceedings of the 2nd International Conference on Ubiquitous Information Management and Communication, pp. 208–211. ACM, New York (2008)
4. Jannach, D., Zanker, M., Felfernig, A., Friedrich, G.: Recommender Systems - An Introduction. Cambridge University Press (2010)
5. Sarwar, B., Karypis, G., Konstan, J., Riedl, J.: Item-Based Collaborative Filtering Recommendation Algorithms. In: Proceedings of the 10th International Conference on World Wide Web, pp. 285–295. ACM (2001)
6. Baltrunas, L., Ricci, F.: Context-Dependent Items Generation in Collaborative Filtering. In: Proceedings of the Workshop on Context-Aware Recommender Systems, New York, USA (2009)
7. Domingues, M.A., Jorge, A.M., Soares, C.: Using Contextual Information as Virtual Items on Top-N Recommender Systems. In: Proceedings of the Workshop on Context-Aware Recommender Systems, New York, USA (2009)
8. De Carolis, B., Mazzotta, I., Novielli, N., Silvestri, V.: Using Common Sense in Providing Personalized Recommendations in the Tourism Domain. In: Proceedings of the Workshop on Context-Aware Recommender Systems, New York, USA (2009)
9. Takeuchi, Y., Sugimoto, M.: CityVoyager: An Outdoor Recommendation System Based on User Location History. In: Ma, J., Jin, H., Yang, L.T., Tsai, J.J.-P. (eds.) UIC 2006. LNCS, vol. 4159, pp. 625–636. Springer, Heidelberg (2006)
10. Simcock, T., Hillenbrand, S.P., Thomas, B.H.: Developing a Location Based Tourist Guide Application. In: Proceedings of the Australasian Information Security Workshop Conference on ACSW Frontiers 2003, Darlinghurst, Australia, vol. 21, pp. 177–183. Australian Computer Society, Inc. (2003)
11. Fano, A.E.: Shopper's Eye: Using Location-based Filtering for a Shopping Agent in the Physical World. In: Proceedings of the 2nd International Conference on Autonomous Agents, pp. 416–421. ACM, New York (1998)

Author Index